My Three
Grey Mistresses

Memoirs of a lad from Leigh

A new home for "CAMPION" - low water on her drying mooring off Chalkwell, Michael Beaumont standing by port quarter.

My Three
Grey Mistresses

Memoirs of a lad from Leigh

Stewart Platt

Atlantic
NAUTICAL PRESS

Published 2002
by Atlantic Nautical Press
Trevithic House,
West End,
Penryn,
Cornwall
TR10 8HE
www.AtlanticPublishers.com

ISBN 1-902 827-06-6

A CIP catalogue record for this book is available
from the British Library.

Typeset in 10pt Palatino
Printed in England by
The Cromwell Press Ltd

Book production: Designed and project managed by
Fred Barter ARCA

Contents

Illustrations

*To Beryl, who has cheerfully
and stalwartly tolerated these mistresses
for over fifty years.*

Acknowledgements

Firstly, I would like to thank my good friend, neighbour, and crew member Michael S Rose for laboriously reading through the first draft of the text and making useful suggestions.

To The Editor "Yachting Monthly" for permission to reproduce extracts from early articles on cruises made in the early 40s and 50s, first published in "Yachting Monthly".

To Janet Harber, Editor of "East Coast Rivers" for permission to use a photograph taken by her late father, and extracts from the very first edition of that publication.

"Essex County Standards" group for the use of their photograph showing my mother about to launch "CELANDINE".

To Fred Barter, Editor of the Cruising Association's quarterly magazine, "Cruising" for his immense help in bringing this all about. Although professionally involved with the publishing, his advice and suggestions have gone far beyond the call of duty.

A NOSTALGIC REFLECTION

ONCE the scene of bustling commercial activity with fishing and cargo vessels discharging alongside, the Quai Ste Catherine in Honfleur is now a central tourist attraction; where cargoes were formerly unloaded, there are now the tables and brightly coloured umbrellas of cafes and restaurants, whilst yachts are berthed in the Vieux Bassin where the commercial vessels once lay. As a backdrop to the scene stand the ancient tall and narrow timber framed houses overlooking the quay, some rising to seven storeys and all seeming to depend on each other for support. Brooding over the scene was the Vieux Lieutenance, once the Governor's house and part of the old fortified ramparts, under whose walls I had berthed many times, in this boat and her predecessor, "CELANDINE". It was on this quay, on a sunny day in June 1998, that the crew of "CORYDALIS" were enjoying an al fresco lunch beneath the umbrellas of a quayside cafe; although there was a breeze blowing, little of it disturbed the air here, with the tall buildings behind us. On the opposite side of the dock lay the more substantial stone and brick buildings on the Quai St Etienne, even older than those behind us, and historically forming the old centre of Honfleur.

The voyage bringing us to this pleasant and historic port had not been an easy one; 1998 will be remembered by many as a wet and boisterous summer with only brief intervals of calm and sunny weather. We had pushed into head seas all the way from Levington in Suffolk, and the only really calm day was the passage from Dover to Le Treport on the Normandy coast, when the sea was smooth and windless - and blanketed in dense fog. Crossing the busiest shipping lanes in the world in dense fog, maintaining a constant watch on the radar screen, is hardly relaxing, but a few relaxing days in Dieppe, when Beryl came over for a few days, compensated. During those days it blew hard most of the time, and as with most of the French Channel ports in such conditions, the boat is always fidgeting about and straining at her moorings. There were crew changes when Beryl returned home, and it was this crew that were now enjoying a hedonistic break in such a historic setting. We were good company, all having sailed together many times before, and our pleasure was completed when strolling musicians came to serenade us. The leader used his position in the group to bow his violin close to Mary's ear - she was the only woman member of the crew. I hope both enjoyed the experience.

Our strolling musicians then played "*La Vie en Rose*", which from before Beryl and I married has been our theme tune, and suddenly I was overwhelmed with a wave of emotion - as old age advances, so one becomes more prone to emotional feelings, and I knew that this might be the last voyage I would be taking down Channel. There had been many years of voyaging down the English Channel from my native Essex waters; often a struggle against the prevailing winds, but sometimes a delightful experience. Good or bad, there was always a long haul to get down Channel. Much as I might want to go on doing it, I knew that in sailing terms the time was coming to shorten horizons and restrict activities to the area closer to home where my boating activities started all those years ago. Hopefully, nobody else noticed that my eyes were moist - captains are not supposed to do this kind of thing. My mood soon changed, but during those few moments I stretched my mind back to the boat-mad boy who once had ever widening experiences all to come, and then to the old man who now saw it retracting into decline. There is no purpose in dwelling on the fact, because we must all bow to the inevitable and accept what God has decreed for us; the moment passed and my mind returned to the enjoyment of lunch in the sun on a French quayside in the company of good friends.

MUD AND COCKLES

ARLIEST memories of a fascination for the sea come from a childhood spent in my native Leigh, in Essex, where, during school holidays I would walk with my father to Old Leigh Station, where he caught the train to London and I would walk home alone. Our route lay first on top of the cliffs, overlooking the Thames Estuary with its never ending procession of ships ploughing their way towards London on the flood tide, followed by another armada heading seawards on the ebb. There was the excitement of a large passenger liner from time to time - the P & O liners, rather severe with black hulls and funnels and buff superstructure, heading for India and the East (later they introduced the great "white sisters", all white, topped with yellow funnels, which did seem more appropriate). There were large passenger carrying cargo vessels Ellerman, Union Castle - the smaller but smart cargo steamers of the General Steam Navigation Company trading to continental ports, those of the Dundee Perth & London Company, and small steam coasters bearing the rust and grime of toil. Coal for the London electricity stations and gas works was carried by "flatirons" - vessels with long low profiles and a funnel aft that could be lowered for passing under the bridges. Even lower in the social scale were the powered hopper barges, towing yet another hopper barge full of soil from the great Northern and Southern sewage works at the terminals of Bazalgette's great Victorian London sewage system. Sailing barges were ten a penny - patched sails and rough hulls with their cargoes of bricks, cement, and hay ("stackies"). Higher in the barge hierarchy were the superior large coasting barges, carrying grain and coal, sporting bowsprits and deeper bulwarks.

Sleeping on their moorings out there were also the laid -up ships - grim reminders that times were hard - the post 1914-8 war boom was over, and the depression had set in. Some were hastily constructed war-time cargo carriers, and there was one smart two funnelled liner off Southend pier, the "METAGAMA"; even at the age of six I was disturbed by the sight of these unemployed vessels, once pulsing with power across the seas, now rusting hulks. From our high vantage point, we crossed the coastal railway line by a foot-bridge and descended to a sea wall path, the "cinderpath", passing a sea water swimming pool, towards what looked to me like a very large ship - in fact a former Tilbury passenger ferry boat serving as head quarters of the Essex Yacht club. All the while my father would tell me about the ships we saw, including vesels lying at rest on the silver grey mud awaiting the return of the tide. The shapes of the hulls, particularly of the sailing bawleys lying ("lusting" the locals would call it) over on one bilge fascinated me. Sometimes there would be a small powered coaster, flat bottomed and sitting upright, waiting with a cargo of coal to deliver on the next tide to the gas works which were just downstream from the famous cocklesheds of Leigh. From an early age I loved watching working boats going about their business; early impressions go deep, and I think it could be a reason why my boats have always had a hint of the working boat about them, and never looked like the traditional concept of a yacht. Then there were the busy rail sidings on the landward side of our route, and on the other side the exciting bustle of Bell Wharf with its puffing steam cranes loading and unloading from Thames sailing Barges, all overlooked by Turnidge's weatherboarded sail loft, where their grimy and patched sails were repaired and re-tanned. Thus to the station, with a level crossing separating up and down platforms, and a signal box within which the keeper laboriously controlled the opening and closing of the gates by turning a great handwheel. There was always so much going on, and if the timing was right and the tide up, there would be the cocklers and shrimpers coming and going (even then they were nearly all powered, but still carrying some well furled sails), and perhaps the thrill of watching a barge leave under sail - few of these had any engines

A childhood friend of the 1930's - the magnificent "Royal Eagle" coming alongside Southend Pier (Aerofilms Ltd)

in those days, and great skill was required for such manouevres.

During the summer months, there were the pleasure steamers calling at Southend pier, and I was taken aboard these for regular trips, when for me, the great fascination was to watch the engine driving the thrashing paddle wheels. Great connecting rods of polished steel drove an enormous crankshaft which went right across the vessel, giving a very obvious display of great power, accompanied by that wonderful aroma associated with steam engines - a mixture of steam, hot oil and paint. In the early thirties came the last one to be built for the Thames, the ultimate in paddle steamers, "THE ROYAL EAGLE". This ship, bigger than all her predecessors, was built by warship builders Cammell Laird; in my young eyes, she was magnificent, a young liner. Later in the thirties, not long before the outbreak of the second World War, a new breed of excursion vessels appeared on the Estuary; white hulled twin screw vessels propelled by Sulzer diesels which were already beginning to drive out steam as a source of power for ships, and we transferred our custom to this new breed, the first of which was the "QUEEN OF THE CHANNEL". My mother did not like excursion steamers and so did not usually come on these ventures. So, with a father who loved the sea and ships, and on my mother's side seafaring folk going back some generations in Southwold, Suffolk , is it any surprise that I grew up likewise?

Suddenly, at the age of 11, there was a great upheaval in this pleasant and settled routine when it was announced we were moving; the seaside walks to the station would be no more - the station had closed and two new ones built in its stead. At the same time, I enrolled into the 3rd Chalkwell Bay Sea Scouts, and passed the entrance exam to the local grammar school (Westcliff High School) - this latter rather surprising because it was already obvious I was never going to star as an academic. The new house was in a superb position on the cliff top at the West end of New Leigh, which was being extended by development on the last area of level agricultural land on the town's Western boundary. I protested about the house which I thought ugly and unattractive - but it had superb uninterrupted views across the Estuary to the North Kent downs. I would have liked an old red brick Georgian house, but my father pointed out that you lived on the inside of a house and looked out; with that superb outlook, and being given the bedroom with a balcony from which I could survey the daily armadas going to and fro, I could hardly complain.

The first formal sailing tuition I received was with the Scouts, who also gave rowing tuition, and taught us to scull a boat with one oar over the stern - this was regarded as essential, so that you could still make progress even if you lost or broke an oar. We also worked on maintaining our motley collection of boats - often on bitter March days with scraper, sandpaper and paintbrush. A wonderful group of people, under a genial and slightly portly skipper - Peter Dawes - were dedicated to the encouragement of youngsters with nautical leanings. At first we met in a hall at the back of the town, rather far removed from the sea, but later they were able to rent the "down" platform at the now disused Old

The after part of "Implacable", showing the stern gallery, now replicated in the National Maritime Museum.

Leigh Station; a wire fence near the platform edge prevented any of our troop ending up on the line. All trace of this part of Old Leigh Station went long ago in a new road layout - no one could complain that it was a great architectural loss. With the Sea Scouts I spent a fortnight aboard the old wooden three decker "IMPLACABLE" - the only remaining ship that fought at Trafalgar still afloat, in a backwater of Portsmouth harbour (by this time Nelson's "VICTORY" was preserved in a graving dock). At the time of Trafalgar she had been the French "DUGAY TROUIN", escaping after the battle but later captured. Perhaps at that time, I was too young to appreciate the historic vessel I was aboard, but I loved every minute of it - we worked hard, scrubbing decks, keeping our mess tables and traps clean - and played hard, rowing heavy naval cutters, sailing and rowing whalers, as well as sailing smaller dinghies. There were excursions, inluding a visit to some of the ocean racers that were assembling for that year's Fastnet race. We fed well aboard her, but I returned home looking like a well bronzed skeleton (so I was told). After the end of the second World War, this historic ship was suffering from neglect, and in spite of the efforts of many nautical historians , she was towed out into the Channel and sunk by gunfire - with difficulty, as the Navy by that time had no idea how difficult it was to despatch a wooden ship. Some recompense for that act of vandalism has now been made by the creation of an accurate replica of her stern gallery in the National Maritime Museum.

It was inevitable that before long I started to hint that I would like a boat of my own, and my father bought me a rather boxy 12 foot sailing dinghy - heavy and safe, a far cry from the sleek racing dinghies of more recent times. My trusting parents let me take this dinghy out, usually in the company of school friends who had similar boats, out into the shipping channels of the busy Estuary - in those days there were no such things as lifejackets or buoyancy aids, and it was a miracle that we all survived. One memorable incident which cut my ego down to size was an encounter with a Thames sailing barge. I had learnt my rule of road at sea thoroughly and was master of my own ship, sailing close-hauled on the starboard tack, which point of sailing at that time gave you right of way over all else. The barge had come away from one of the wharves at Leigh, heavily laden so that her side decks were almost awash (this was quite normal) and was closehauled on the port tack. Platt stood on, expecting the great lumbering mass to give way as per the book. When it was too late to avoid a collision somewhere about half way down the barge's side decks, the skipper left the wheel without saying a word, neatly fielded my forestay and spun my tiny dinghy around so that I was sailing away on the opposite tack, causing great damage to my ego.

With my school friends we seemed to manage a great many expeditions between us, usually sailing in company. Everything we did was governed by the tide - the coast at this point is famous for the twice daily retreat of the sea, exposing vast areas of mud - sticky mud close to the shore, which rapidly becomes firm sand as you walk further out. Once, on a hot and misty calm summer's day when I was awaiting the return of the waters to float off my boat, I was astonished to see a square rigger coming upriver, towed by a steam tug, but still with one or two sails limply hanging from her yards. It was a historic moment, for that ship was the famous tea clipper "CUTTY SARK" - I had read that she was due to come upriver, but counted myself lucky to actually see her nearing the end of her very last voyage. She was moored further upstream at Greenhithe as part of the Thames Nautical Training college; years later, after the second World War, she was in a poor condition and a great movement started to ensure her preservation. The result was to put her on permanent display in a graving dock at Greenwich, where she is maintained as a memorial to the great days of commercial sail.

All too soon, summers seemed to end and I laid up my dinghy in a small yard adjoining a fishmonger's shop in old Leigh, where I paid three shillings and sixpence for a winter's sojurn. I was vaguely aware that the shop, with living accomodation over, was rather special, but it was only later in adult life, after a Philistine Council had ordered its demolition, that I realised it was a very ancient timber framed lath and plaster house, with a jetted upper storey. Nearby was another fishmonger, Juniper's, in a similar ancient cottage; I was always told that John Constable stayed there when he produced his famous painting of Hadleigh Castle. That historic cottage went as well; much of Old Leigh's character and history were ruined in this way. Our dinghy sailing gang each had their own laying up methods; Peter was the proud possessor of a boat trolley with rather wobbly iron wheels, and thus able to take his boat home for the winter. A group of us would help him get it up Leigh Hill to the more modern Leigh Broadway, where the going was level but had the challenge posed by having to cross the tram tracks near the end of the line from Southend. Here, by the ancient clifftop church of St Clements, the two lines merged into a single track spur and the long trailing pole collecting electricity from over-head lines was reversed by means of a boathook on a long bamboo pole. Unfortunately, one autumn, a wheel of Peter's trolley caught in a large space in the points which switched trams on to the other track for their return journey. We struggled to clear it, embarassed by a growing audience, and knowing that we had managed to trap no less than two of these clanging monsters in the spur. It was not long before a uniformed official, the peak

Some of the 12ft sailing dinghy gang anchored in the entrance to Leigh Creek off Crowstone Hard in 1938. At the right hand end of the line is Peter van den Brul (seated), whose boat nearly brought Southend's trams to a standstill.

of his cap smothered in gold scrambled eggs, came along and ordered us to remove this obstruction; at least one of his trams was already due to leave for Southend. Although clearly such a high official could not help, one or two burly bystanders came to our rescue and forced the jammed wheel out so that both we and the trapped trams could resume our journeys. The hazards of sailing are not just capsizing, dismasting, or sinking.

A DARK CLOUD ON THE HORIZON

OUR family rented a tent on a private beach not far from where the dinghy was moored; sometimes my sister Lorna would come with me; she had learnt to swim from this beach by hanging on to the stern of a departing boat, and when everybody shouted "hang on" as the water became deeper, let go. She swam. The whole of the foreshore westwards from Chalkwell Bay to Bell Wharf at Leigh was owned by the London Midland & Scottish Railway Company, and the small private beach leased to an operator who rented out the tents and ran it almost like an exclusive club (Joscelyne's Beach). It goes without saying that in the wave of egalitarianism that swept through post-war Britain, it came to an end and became part of the public beach, but as children we enjoyed it and swam, rowed and sailed from it. Through all this pleasure was the dark cloud of approaching war with Hitler's Germany, casting a shadow across our minds. Our young minds were obsessed with the feeling that if it came, we would all be obliterated by waves of bombers coming up the Thames Estuary. Although not an economist, I remain convinced that it was preparation for war that revived the depressed economy of the early thirties, so that there was a plus side to the feeling of apprehension. A diversion from these gloomy thoughts was made by my father's purchase of an eight ton shallow draught centreboard cruising boat - Bermudian rigged and with roller foresail. Many years later such foresails became almost standard fittings for yachts, but this was unusual in those days and copied from the beach boats which carried passengers out on short sailing trips from the Chalkwell beaches ("arf an hour out - do yer a world o' good"). Roller foresails in those days did not have the aluminium roller used today, but a wooden roller as used for shop blinds, and such a device enabled the beach boats to reduce sail quickly just before running on to the beach.

"EUONYM" was a beamy 25 foot long clinker built sloop, built by Parsons of Leigh, who also built many of the local fishing boats. She drew only 2 foot six inches of water with the centreplate raised; it lowered through a slot in the heavy cast iron keel to give her just over 5 foot draught. There was an auxiliary engine - a high speed American Kermath petrol engine, which for those days was quite a sophisticated piece of machinery - it certainly pushed her along quite impressively. With this vessel, life entered a new but all too brief phase of exploring the Essex and Kent coasts en famille. My mother was not a good sailor and did not really enjoy it, but like generations of long suffering women she endured it for the sake of the family. There was an extremely heavy dinghy which had to be towed astern, but my sister and I enjoyed rowing it - it was well equipped with 2 pairs of good oars, and we could get it up to a fair speed with both of us rowing; we rather enjoyed upsetting people motoring with outboards on their dinghies by keeping pace with them, or just occasionally, actually overtaking them. She was seven years younger than me, but developed into a powerful oarswoman; in a boat we made a good team.

Our last cruise in "EUONYM" was in August 1939; the war clouds were gathering and we listened anxiously to the radio news. The weather was superb, and with our shallow draught we were able to leave Leigh and cut across the sands and the Whitaker Spit on the end of Foulness to take another short cut inside the Buxey Sand, where a yacht followed our tall rig about a quarter of a mile astern. By then we had our centreboard almost right up to cross the shallow water, and it was not long before they came to a grinding halt and were left behind, fading into the mist astern. An early lesson learnt, at someone else's expense - never assume the boat ahead either draws as much water as you do, or that he knows what he is doing.

We sailed up the broad Blackwater Estuary, where we anchored near the disused Tollesbury pier (still at that time carrying two red lights on the pierhead), from which there had once been a scheme to run a cross-channel service, linked to the main Great Eastern Railway line by a branch line through Tiptree and Tollesbury and crossing the main Colchester road with a level crossing at Feering. We walked ashore up the overgrown old track bed where the sleepers and chairs were still in place, but from which the rails had already been removed. Then we anchored off Osea Island, to go ashore where, in the middle of the Island, the post box announced "next collection according to state of tide". My father always found a local to chat up wherever we went, and here we were told tales of the Island. The big house overlooking the river was built by a member of the Charrington brewing family as a temperance home where inebriates might dry out. The local fishermen quickly found a useful boost to their income by smuggling booze across from the mainland.

During the first World War it became a coastal motor boat base, complete with engineering workshops, and additional accommodation was built for Naval personnel, as well as a pier and slipway. Our informant then told us of the sudden post war evacuation and closure of the base. It was still fully manned a year or so after the war, when an opposition MP put down a written question about the annual cost of the base and numbers of men still on the strength. It was an embarassing question, and immediate orders were given to abandon it, so that vast quantities of stores were left behind, supplying nearby villagers with mattresses, lightbulbs and many other useful domestic articles for some years to come. When the day came to reply to the question, the Minister was able to assure the questioner that there was no naval base at Osea Island.

Our next port of call was West Mersea, where we anchored in a muddy cut, taking advantage of our shallow draught. Here we took our two gallon metal fresh water cans ashore (no plastic then!) where, again, my father got into conversation with a local. He (and many others) told us the tapwater supply was foul and tasted of bad eggs. He directed us to St Peter's well in the low cliff below the coast road, where we found cool clear spring water issuing out of a spout from which we could easily fill our water cans. I have visited the same well in more recent times to find notices warning that the water is unfit for drinking! We survived.

Then on to Brightlingsea, whence we sailed up the coast past Clacton and Walton, with the occasional paddle steamer thump-thumping her way past us, and so into Harwich harbour and up the river Orwell - it was all a great and thrilling adventure as far as I was concerned - the Orinoco would have been no more exciting. In 1939 few people posessed a car or boat; neither the cars or roads encouraged long journeys, so that people's horizons were much closer in those days. We anchored a short distance below the hard at Pin Mill, clear of the

Pin Mill, 1939. Up to 20 boats on moorings made it difficult to anchor near the hard.

moored boats and spent a few days in this delightful spot. As usual, my father was soon chatting to the locals, who said there were too many moorings there so that one could no longer anchor near the hard. There must have been a good score of boats swinging to moorings there; if only the old boy could see it now, when moorings stretch all up and down the river! At the top of the tide there was a small sandy beach beneath the densely wooded hill, where we could draw up the dinghy for a swim or exploration. We went ashore for supplies and walked up to the village of Chelmondiston; the butcher's was an open fronted shop in which great pieces of meat hung, and when we returned aboard (after lunch at a pub called "The Riga" - long since gone) with a large piece of steak, my father removed the oak tiller from the rudder stock and proceeded to beat the meat into tenderness on the stern deck. While we were in the Orwell, the onshore sea breeze blew hard from the East, and we went out for one or two sails in the sheltered river waters. There were working barges to be seen under weigh - many of them proud coastal barges - a very superior breed compared with the rougher barges I was used to at Leigh. One day a magnificent barge, the "WILLIAM CLEVERLY" came tacking down river under full sail, taking the ebb tide from Ipswich. There were no more than three men aboard controlling this proud spread of canvas which thundered and cracked as she tacked near us in Long Reach, off Levington village. Many years later, on the stern of a hulk drawn up against the sea wall at Heybridge Basin, Maldon, I sadly detected the name "WILLIAM CLEVERLY". By nightfall, the fresh East wind died away and across the glassy water came the strains of singing from the "The Butt and Oyster" - favourite at that time was *"South of the Border"*. The news from our portable radio became more serious by the hour, and it was decided we must make for home; fortunately the East wind moderated and helped us to speed home. We reached the vicinity of Southend Pier at about dusk, and were overtaken by several of the pleasure steamers we knew so well, speeding for London - they were to evacuate hundreds of children to coastal towns and beyond - everyone was convinced that

"Euonym" sailing in Long Reach on the River Orwell - author at the helm - a trusting father was in dinghy with camera!

London would be bombed as soon as war was declared. Later in the war, some of these places to which they were taken were going to be right in the forefront of the danger area, but that could not be foreseen then. It was almost dark by the time we picked up our mooring off the foreshore and rowed ashore. It was to be the end of cruising for another seven years; the sense of gloom and foreboding dominated all other thoughts. Within a few days of our return home at the end of August 1939, war was declared. "EUONYM" was hauled out and stored under cover at Bundock's yard in Old Leigh.

THE STORM BREAKS

A STRANGE state of limbo prevailed whilst we awaited the predicted waves of bombers. Why Germany did not strike then, when we were so unprepared, I cannot think, but it gave the country more breathing space to prepare for the inevitable onslaught, whilst at the same time causing a certain atmosphere of complacency. We filtered back to the beach to enjoy the late autumn sunshine; school term began again and I think we were surprised to be still there. One day on the beach, the air raid sirens sounded - we were not sure what to do. It later turned out that a worm or maggot infiltrated the switch gear and short circuited the sirens over the whole area.

The Leigh cockle bawley "Renown" lost due to enemy action when returning from Dunkirk, from a water colour by the author.

It was not until May of the following year, 1940, that the storm broke as the German army, with fast moving tactics, swept through Holland and Belgium into Northern France, helped by spreading panic and confusion among both civilians and the military. A letter was received from the Admiralty asking how quickly our boat could be made operational; it had become obvious we were going to evacuate our Army from France over the beaches as they were by then hemmed in a pocket between Calais and Dunkirk. My father ordered the yard to have "EUONYM" ready for launching, but she was hemmed in by several other boats at the back of the yard; events moved swiftly and by then the Dunkirk evacuation was already in what proved to be its closing stages so she never went. Had she done so, almost certainly she would never have returned from the shambles of those beaches. Shallow draft boats and ships of every description were hastily rounded up to take part in this extraordinary operation in which the enemy had almost complete mastery of the skies, causing havoc among all the vessels engaged in the evacuation. Miraculously, the weather was calm. Many of the ships associated with my childhood were lost. The "CRESTED EAGLE" was abandoned, a blazing wreck in the shallows off the port; the "QUEEN OF THE CHANNEL" broke in two and sank following enemy action - the losses were very heavy. The biggest impact on my adolescent mind was the loss of the flagship of the Leigh cockle bawley fleet, the "RENOWN", together with two members of the Osborne family and one from the Noakes, both fishing families still to be found in Leigh. Many other ships limped back to Dover and Ramsgate badly damaged; it was remarkable that ships built for summer pleasure trips survived terrible battering, and in many cases were repaired and went on to distinguish themselves in other roles for which they were never intended.

Whilst the outbreak of war did not greatly alter our lives, the evacuation of Dunkirk and subsequent occupation of the whole of the Western Coast of Europe by hostile forces certainly did. They were the times when it was difficult to know how we could ever survive as a nation; we were the only part of Europe not in the federated state enforced by the supreme dictator Adolf Hitler. Winston Churchill's inspiring rhetoric boosted our morale at a time when everyone was very depressed, and thought that the invasion of our country could not be far away. Coastal areas in the South and East were compulsorily evacuated with the exception of essential workers to keep services running; there was no nanny state to help you - you just had to go. My school, Westcliff High School for Boys was evacuated to Belper in Derbyshire, travelling by specially chartered trains that went from Southend LMS station straight through. My parents found a furnished house in the village of Bray, near Maidenhead, having locked up our house at Leigh as it stood, with all the furniture in it. On and near the coast frantic efforts were made to erect "dragon's teeth" and other obstacles in concrete to halt the progress of tanks, and strange scaffolding obstacles appeared on beaches and mud flats to wreck gliders, whilst concrete pillboxes sprang up at strategic points on the coast and inland to create further lines of defence. The atmosphere was grim, but we certainly put everything into turning our island into a fortress. I returned to Leigh (with a special permit) some time later, and my footsteps echoed in the ghost of Leigh Broadway - the shops had nearly all closed, the road was devoid of people and traffic, and those tram lines which once trapped a dinghy were silent. My stay in Belper was short; leaving as soon as I had taken my matric - which I obtained, to my amazement. In those days you had to pass the lot in one go, and could not go down in any of the essential subjects without failing the whole exam.

During the fine late summer weather of 1940 the desperate "Battle of Britain" was fought out in the clear skies over the South East; Hitler knew that control of the English Channel was essential for an invasion to take place and that the Royal Air Force must be eliminated; without air cover our Navy could not operate. The German losses were heavy, and by September a different tactic was employed - saturation bombing of London. On the night of Saturday, September the 7th 1940, the East End of London, with its docks, warehouses and factories, was devastated. The fires that raged could be seen lighting the sky as far away as Maidenhead. The factory housing our family textile business was totally destroyed, along with the machinery. I was up in West Ham on the Monday morning helping to salvage what we could. I will never forget the rapidity with which the business was re-established, along with others who had suffered in that cruel blow. In a very short time we had rented garage workshops at Gallows Corner on the A12 London to Colchester Road - petrol rationing had virtually brought private motoring to a standstill, so they were pleased to find a source of income. Other premises were rented for storage, including the stables of nearby Harold Hall. Workshop premises were found in which the less badly damaged machinery could be repaired: I was recruited into the business in an extremely lowly position, earning a pound a week.

Early in 1941, by which time the night bombing raids on London were damaging and destroying so many buildings - many historic but not really vital to the war effort, a bomb fell not too far from the boatyard in which "Euonym" was stored - it landed in the mud, I believe, which must have made a spectacular mess without causing damage or injury. Permission was obtained from the Admiralty, which by now controlled all shipping movements on the Thames, to take her upriver to the non-tidal Thames, where we planned to put her on a mooring at Bray. The voyage was made in February, with three of us aboard - my father, myself and cousin Bob Crowe who by then was awaiting call up papers into the Navy. The mast and boom had to be left at Leigh, so we set off as a motor boat, and reached Greenwich Pier for the first night, where we moored alongside a steam tug. At that time no one stayed in London at night unless on essential duty, and the inhabitants took to their shelters or Underground stations which served as nightly shelters. We decided to keep watches overnight, and sheltered from the chill drizzle in the lee of the tug's warm funnel. Fortunately the Luftwaffe seemed to be having a night off, and apart from one air raid warning and signs of distant flak, it was quiet. The next day we reached Teddington - "Tide-end-Town", where Thames Conservancy inspectors came aboard. They wanted to seal the WC outlet, but we had the simplest and most effective type of yacht WC yet invented - the "bucket and chuck it" system (pretty usual in those days) and they had to admit defeat.

THE NAVY

L IKE many others of my age, we were really marking time until we joined up in one of the services. I was determined it was to be the Navy, and in the summer of 1941 I signed on for the Royal Naval Patrol Service - the yachts-men's and fishermen's navy - at a merchant Navy office in Dock Street , London E.1. I had not reached my 18th birthday, and therefore was not yet eligible, so a mistake was made which went all through my naval career. In fact, I need not have done this, because by the time my calling up papers arrived I was past my 18th birthday anyway. The base for the Patrol Service was Lowestoft (HMS "Europa") which town they succeeded in turning into a vast Naval Barracks. We matelots were billeted on Lowestoft landladies, and as they were no doubt paid by the numbers housed, they were pretty skilful at fitting in as many as possible in their small yellow brick terrace houses. The centre of activity was the "Sparrows Nest", a large seaside concert hall in the attractively wooded low cliffs near the lighthouse, and a playing field known as the Oval was the parade ground, where every vestige of grass had been eliminated by the tramping of naval issue boots. It was to this place I arrived early in 1942 and quickly realised by the bitter wind blowing that I was in the most Easterly point in the British Isles. Civilian clothes were replaced with matelot's uniform, and I learnt the intricacies of wearing a sailor's collar, the black silk scarf (said by some to be mourning for Nelson) and how to fold a pair of bell bottom trousers with their inward vertical side creases, and seven horizontal ones. A heavy overcoat was issued (and necessary in that harsh climate), and shown how to master the problem of putting it on without creasing up the sailor's collar. In fact, I soon found the best (and most pleasant) solution was to ask a pretty girl to put her arms under yours and round your back to hold it down - unfortunately, in Lowestoft itself at that time, there did seem to be a shortage of these important items of Naval equipment. While I was there, I found time to take a bus to Southwold, my mother's home town. Her family, the Magubs, were seafarers going back over many years, but her father did not follow the family tradition - he owned ships trading from that port, bringing in coal and building materials, and also was a founder shareholder in the Southwold light railway. This collapsed in 1929, and I remember as a boy being shown the two silent steam engines that had worked the line. The track bed was still clearly visible, and the old station building still stood; today there is little trace of the line.

From Lowestoft, I was sent to Port Edgar, South Queensferry, hard by the famous Forth Bridge, for a minesweeping course aboard an ancient wheezing paddle steamer, "THE DUCHESS OF FIFE". Then I had a spell ashore after they discovered I was reasonably literate and numerate, collecting stores and cold weather clothing from depots in Edinburgh and delivering them to newly commissioned minesweepers calling at Port Edgar. This was a wonderful cushy job, complete with van and Wren driver. I don't know how our predecessors did it, but as a team we polished off the work very fast, allowing me time to take her to enjoy morning coffee in Mackies on Princes Street - it was a civilised interlude. I developed a great liking for Edinburgh - in the Missions to Seamen, I met a lovely girl, Jean, with whom I would sometimes go to the theatre in the evenings; an oasis of civilization in a life otherwise devoid of any kind of cultural activity. I had considerable pangs of homesickness, and the one event in which I found comfort was the Sunday Church parade and service (which was compulsory), singing the hymns I knew - the familiarity seemed to create a link with home. Probably not the best reasons for a strengthening of faith, but the padre prepared me for confirmation. I don't think I appreciated it at the time, but it was an honour to be confirmed by the Bishop, in the Cathedral, at a confirmation service specially for me. Soon after, I was on my way back to Lowestoft, to another billet - I discovered that my previous one had been bombed in one of the "hit and run" raids from which Lowestoft suffered throughout most of the war.

CAMPBELTOWN and HMS "TUSCARORA"

FOLLOWING the minesweeping course, the Navy, in their wisdom, sent me to a ship equipped with Anti-Submarine Detection gear ("ASDIC"). In the spring of 1942, I joined the former steam yacht "TUSCARORA", based at Campbeltown, near the Mull of Kintyre. She had been purchased outright from her peacetime owner for conversion into an anti-submarine ship, and there were still one or two members of her peacetime crew aboard - known as "T124" personnel. Although my knowledge of ships was still scant at the age of 18, I realised that the ship was something of a classic in spite of all the naval alterations and additions which did their best to mask her beauty. As an "ordinary seaman" - not yet an "AB" (able bodied), I joined a mess deck whose members were nearly all Scottish trawler hands. The cultural shock for a youngster brought up in a genteel middle class English family was great, and I also learnt that my Scottish messmates regarded Englishmen as a different breed; I was a "Sassenach". Our family had friends who were Scottish,

HMS "Tuscarora" at Cambeltown. The false bow wave was no doubt painted on to deceive the enemy about her speed.

HMS "Tuscarora" in Kilbrannan Sound, 1942 -
sketch by the author.

there was Scottish blood in my mother's family (Magub) and an Aunt belonged to a large family of Scottish farmers who came from Ayrshire to Essex in late Victorian times - indeed Essex is full of Scottish farmers who came, "lock, stock and barrel" to take the tenancies of Essex farms on very advantageous terms following crop disasters which bankrupted many farming families, leaving empty farms all over the county. It had naturally never occurred to me before this episode in my life that many Scots still living in Scotland take this view of the English; it seemed to me (and still does) that this is a kind of insularity which makes about as much sense as if East Anglians were to regard all others as foreigners.

HMS "TUSCARORA" was 200 feet long overall, and equipped with a 4" quick firing gun of First World War vintage on her foredeck, under the weight of which she staggered through the seas. Her peacetime open bridge had been closed in and enlarged to accommodate two sets of instruments for submarine detection. Her funnel had received an outer casing and a typical naval style funnel top; the mainmast had been removed from aft of the funnel (she had been schooner rigged) and a wireless cabin put in its place on the boat deck. Aft, over her long graceful yacht's counter stern, were two rails of depth charges - enough to blow her, and the whole of Campbeltown, into the next world. Concrete had been poured into her bottom to compensate for loss of stability caused by all this extra weight, and the net result of this was that she floated about 18" deeper than her designed draught of 14 feet:- all the portholes on the lower deck had been welded over. Forward she had graceful clipper bows,but unfortunately, the combination of fine clipper bows and the 4" gun mounted on them gave the foc'sle in which we seamen lived an unbelievable motion - rather like going up and down in an express lift. At the top of the upward journey, the whole unsupported bow section shuddered violently before descending deep into the sea which gave it support again. The effect of all this on my stomach was disastrous; I had never known seasickness before, but in bad weather (of which we had plenty) I suffered. Again, it was, in its way, good for me, because one had to continue carrying out duties such as gunnery practice and steering (I was quickly made a "Quartermaster" whose duties included steering). The wheelhouse was far enough aft in the ship to have an easier motion and was a cure for my seasickness.

Her triple expansion steam engine was a joy to observe, quietly pushing her along with engine revs that seem strange to the modern diesel orientated mind. In order to go astern, the engine had to be stopped and re-started by injecting the steam the opposite way round; I am not a steam buff and do not understand it, but to do this it was important to have a thing called "the vacuum". One day we were going alongside the quay at Campbeltown, and the engine room telegraph rang down for "astern" to check her way. Nothing happened, and a plaintive voice came up the copper voice pipe from the engine room "I've lost the vacuum sir". Our fine bows rode up on the stern of a coaster lying in the berth ahead, and her magnificent figurehead of a Tuscarora chieftain clattered down on the coaster's steel deck. Later, muggins was sent with another rating, a wheelbarrow, and very red faces, to go to the coaster and reclaim our fallen figure head, which was put in a large locker below the focs'le. It was still there when I left the ship months later.

Leave (apart from local shore leave) was rare; to reach home from Campbeltown was a major journey, and today, you could almost reach Australia in the time it took. You either took a bus all the way to Glasgow to join the London train, or you would take a much shorter bus trip to East Loch Tarbert, where you joined the smart fast MacBrayne ship "LOCH FYNE" which took you to Wemyss Bay on the Ayrshire coast, where a short train journey took you into Glasgow. It was infinitely preferable, and you could dine on the ship, using your issued meal vouchers and supplementing them with cash. The ship was propelled by diesel electric power - the diesel engines generated electricity to large electric motors which turned the twin screws. During the war, this ship was a vital means of travel between isolated communities on Loch Fyne and the Kyles of Bute and Glasgow. The beauty of the Kyles of Bute impressed me; many houses had beautiful grounds which swept down to the shore, contrasting with the wilder parts of rugged mountain scenery. I promised myself that one day I would return to these magic waters in my own boat; a promise that in fact was to take thirty years in fulfilment. During my time aboard her, "TUSCARORA" had a fairly major refit at Ardrossan, where she was drydocked, and I volunteered to remain aboard as part of a skeleton crew - this suited me, as I was able to roam about the ship more and also admire her graceful underwater lines. At the end of the refit, the boiler fires had to be relit; the only stoker aboard who would have undertaken this broke his arm a day or so earlier, and a volunteer was called for. This was yet another experience, and I was a ready volunteer. There were three furnaces, and the fires were started by using diesel oil soaked in cotton waste - we carried diesel oil aboard to fuel a diesel generating set that was a back up to the original steam generator, as well as fuel for her diesel powered launch. Coal was placed on top of the mound of cotton waste, and a piece of burning paraffin soaked rag thrown in each one. They all drew up beautifully, but I received a mild scolding for letting them draw up too quickly - it was all supposed to warm up from cold very gradually. I was privately rather pleased with the success of my fire raising effort; there was something satisfying about the smoke issuing from her funnel top.

My turn for home leave came after she went back into service, so I rejoined her back at Campbeltown, using my favoured route aboard the "LOCH FYNE" from Wemyss Bay. The weather up on the West Coast of Scotland can change very rapidly, and certainly during the winter months the strong winds came in quick succession, but in mid summer I do remember some wonderful calm nights when dusk and dawn almost seemed to merge because we were so far North. When I first joined her, the background news of the war was not encouraging - there was a portable radio on the messdeck with which we could hear the news from time to time. Disasters in the far East were followed by bad news from North Africa, where we were driven back from previous gains to the Egyptian border and all too close to the vital Suez canal, but late in October of that year (1942), came the great news of Montgomery's victory at El Alamein which marked the beginning of a series of successes. When the time came to leave "TUSCARORA", my messmates wished me good luck - the whole experience had been a cultural shock, but I found some good friends aboard her, and there is no doubt it was part of my education in that I learnt about the values and customs of people with a very different background from my own. At the same time, I realised

"Tuscarora" - a gouache painting C1898 by Antonio de Simone of the "Neapolitan School".

that I had been aboard a classic piece of late Victorian steam yacht design; I was too young to appreciate it properly and wish now I had been able to note more details. The one thing I did remember well was the big brass plate in the engine room, and clearly visible through the teak skylight (completely covered in Admiralty grey paint - "Pusser's crabfat"), on which was engraved "Scott & Co, Greenock, 1897" This was the year of my mother's birth, and, of course, Queen Victoria's diamond jubilee. Years later, through a chance find by my friend George Jones, who dabbled in marine art, I acquired an original gouache painting of "TUSCARORA" painted in the bay of Naples by the Italian artist Antonio de Simone. The Simones, father and son, together with others of the "Neapolitan School" used to paint a stock of backgrounds featuring Vesuvius, on which they could superimpose the Englishman's new yacht - this painting was probably executed in 1898. Using this method, they would guarantee to return with the completed picture within 24 hours.

The acquisition of this painting, over thirty years after my service in her, made me research her history through old copies of Lloyd's Register of Yachts in the library of the Cruising Association. Designed by the famous firm of G L Watson, designers of King George Vth's racing cutter "BRITANNIA", she was built for Mrs E B Laidlaw of Largs, Ayrshire, and the design was innovative in that her main deck was plated in to the topsides, giving a dining saloon the full width of the ship and enclosing alleyways on either side of the engine room trunking, galley and pantries. Up to her time nearly all ships had the superstructure built as an island on the main deck, usually of teak in a yacht. By painting this plating in a teak effect scumble, a traditional appearance was retained. Another innovation was the provision of electric light from a steam powered generator, which also powered fans to give a forced draught to the furnaces - this removed the necessity for her tall thin "Woodbine" funnel to promote natural draught, but such was the fashion and ship design is very much prone to fashion. Anyway, the height did help to ensure that ladies in their fine clothes on the top deck did not get showered with smuts. The quality and strength of her construction were superb, - an example of Scottish shipbuilding and engineering skills at their very best. In 1902, she crossed the Atlantic to an American owner, Walter Jennings of New York, and in 1910, went to a Spanish owner, Ramon de Sota, and thus spent the First World War in a neutral country. She returned to British ownership in 1923, and had a series of owners until her outright sale to the Admiralty at the outbreak of war.

Her most notable owner in that period was the Lord Queenborough who took her round the world during his ownership between 1925 and 1929, in the days when there were still enough coaling stations spaced out on the world trade routes to satisfy her voracious appetite for coal . None of her owners kept her for very long; by then she was becoming a costly vessel to run, requiring a large crew and heavy upkeep; the crash of 1929 bit very deeply, causing world wide unemployment, and reducing the numbers of those wealthy enough to run such an expensive means of enjoying exclusive leisure. On the messdeck we used to joke about what would happen to this 45 year old veteran at the end of the war - "turn her into razor blades" was the usual answer. However, she was surveyed at Alexandria in May 1947, when she was owned by the Bienvenido Shipping Co of Panama, and renamed "ANATOLI". Lloyd's archivist, Barbara Jones, was kind enough to give me more details of this remarkable ship that would not die. The survey was rather grudging in its report, and she was later removed from the register of yachts and classified as a commercial ship. She was then sold to a Greek company and laid up at Piraeus; her activities therefrom are unknown, but she was not finally broken up until 1967.

OFF TO BRIGHTON & LOCHAILORT

EARLY in 1943 I was sent back to Lowestoft as a candidate for a commission; but first I had to be shaped up as a proper sailor, and was sent to HMS "GANGES" at Shotley, on the peninsular that divides the rivers Stour and Orwell. Here we received some pretty tough training, all exactly as per the Admiralty manuals, and including a lot of "squarebashing" armed with ancient Lee Enfield rifles whose loose magazines rattled smartly when you "presented arms". I doubt whether you could have shot anything with them. The most daunting part of the course was climbing the mast. We only had to go to the first platform, but this was a long way up by my standards; going up the ratlines wasn't so bad, but you finally reached the platform by going outwards on the "futtock shrouds" which meant you were climbing like a spider with your back facing down towards the tarmac parade ground. I don't remember how high it was - the mast is still there to this day for all to see, but it was enough to scare me out of my wits. Once up there, the view was dramatic. The Stour up to Parkeston Quay and beyond was full of Naval ships; Felixstowe dock (quite a small affair in those days) had smaller vessels, and just downstream from that was the RAF seaplane base with its giant crane. The mud flats of Shotley point were covered in wrecked craft dragged there to keep the main channels free of war casualties; mixed with the scaffolding put there to deter airborne landings, the area looked a dreadful sight. There was not much time to take all this in as the tricky descent had to be made - all you can say was that with every step down those ratlines life got better and fear began to fade. There were one or two brief periods of local leave which usually meant going to the pictures in Ipswich; one very civil interlude was a visit with a chum to tea with some friends of his family at a charming house at Melton, just outside Woodbridge.

After briefly returning to Lowestoft, I journeyed to Brighton, where the Navy had set up HMS "KING ALFRED", whose parade ground was an underground car park on the seafront. The Navy was remarkably adaptable at putting its own stamp on shore bases that were created out of towns, holiday camps and other unlikely venues. At Brighton, once again, seaside landladies again provided billets, but they were distinctly more up-market than those at Lowestoft. A catering company, Cliffords, had the contract for feeding us comunally with the kind of fare you would be expected to eat as an officer and gentleman. Everywhere you were being watched to ensure you had "officer like qualities" and it gave the feeling that incorrect handling of a knife and fork would count against you.

During the time at "KING ALFRED", there was a fortnight at Lancing College, beautifully sited in the South Downs overlooking the Channel. Here we were given intensive navigation courses, using traditional methods. One of the regular features was "action plotting" sessions. In these, our tutor would simulate a sortie, giving us navigator's information from the bridge to enable us to plot the ship's movements. He would seducingly indulge in some small talk about the big picture this week at the Odeon, and then suddenly say "Oh, I forgot - we altered course to 210 degrees and increased speed to 15 knots five minutes ago. Various alterations of course had to be put on the chart, but then suddenly he would give a report on a sighting of the enemy, steaming such and such speed on a course of 045 degrees. What is the course to intercept at our top speed of 18 knots? Just as you were completing your calculations and getting them on the chart, there would be a loud explosion as he let off a thunderflash in the classroom, and ran like a madman along the desks, tipping them and projecting parallel rule, pencils and all the instruments to the floor, saying "That was a close one". I'm sure he enjoyed doing this. You picked them up and got on with the plot again as fast as you could. We were taught that in such circumstances a certain amount of accuracy had to be sacrificed for speed in keeping the ship's position. It was good training for the years to come, when plotting the erratic movements of a pitching and heeling sailing boat on passage.

At the end of my time there, I was told I had not been accepted, but I had already volunteered for combined operations because I had heard on the grapevine that they were looking for officers to run the new landing craft being built to carry the invading armies into Europe. It seemed the most likely possibility of my ever getting a command of my own. For the last time I returned to Lowestoft; travel by train during those times was a dreary business with blacked out windows and low lighting - through small apertures in the blackout on the windows you could with difficulty identify the minute name signs of stations - all the larger signs were removed to avoid helping an invading army or low flying aircraft. Inevitably most of my journeys to Lowestoft took me to Liverpool Street Station, which at that time must surely have been the dreariest of all the London termini. In those days, the route through Ipswich and Woodbridge was still a main line; the splendid corridor trains were painted in the wood grain finish beloved by the London & North Eastern Railway, usually included a restaurant car and were hauled by a powerful main line steam engine. I always tried to get a window seat on the East side of the train, because that gave glimpses of the River Deben with the attractive waterfront and Ferry Quay at Woodbridge, where there were interesting boats and many laid-up yachts to remind me of happier times.

Leaving Lowestoft for the last time, I was despatched to Lochailort, on the West Coast of Scotland North of Oban, by way of a long since closed railway line. Going through Oban, a nostalgic reminder of more peaceful childhood days lay out in the anchorage - the unmistakable profile of the paddle steamer "ROYAL EAGLE" in her drab Admiralty grey paint. Lochailort was set up by Lord Louis Mountbatten specifically for training combined operations officers - he is reputed to have said that the purpose was to train officers, not gentlemen. The course was tough, and included running up the side of a mountain before breakfast, as well as assault courses tacked on to more general training in boat handling, navigation and types of landing craft. One was taught fighting at close quarters - how to creep up behind a sentry and cut his throat silently, and other such delights, which, I am happy to say, I never had to put into practice. One member of our class could not cope with all this, and did not last more than two weeks before being sent back to his depot. At the end of a relatively short course, those of us who made it were commissioned as sub-lieutenants RNVR ("the wavy Navy"). A welcome spell of leave at our war time home in Bray, near Maidenhead followed, during which time I was kitted out with my Sub-Lieutenant's uniform; my father (who had served as a Sub-Lieutenant RNVR in the First World War) insisted it should come from Gieves.

A new shore base became my "Mecca" from now on - another of the Navy's "stone frigates" - HMS "DINOSAUR" at Troon, whence I was despatched to Instow on the Torridge Estuary in North Devon where there was a fleet of tank landing craft being used in various experiments to improve their usefulness in a landing. I became first Lieutenant on an American built craft which had an extra midships section bolted in. The American tank landing craft were very poor things compared with the British, and had less capacity - hence the experiment with the extra section; our task was to take it out across the bar in rough weather to observe the effect on the bolts. During my time in her, she stayed in one piece, but I don't think the idea went any further. The one good thing about her was the anchor, which in tank landing craft was always dropped over the stern to haul off the beach.

It was a new design called a "Danforth", and its holding power was vastly superior to those in the British craft, whether used for beaching purposes or as an anchor for lying to. One of the other experiments carried out at Instow consisted of hinged ramps fitted to the outer end of the bow door which were folded outboard shortly before beaching; they were known as "Mulocks", named after their inventor, a Commander of that name. They reduced the steepness of the bow door, which was particularly important on a flat beach. We cursed these heavy pieces of equipment, but they became standard equipment on all tank landing craft and greatly facilitated disembarkation of vehicles on the beaches we were destined to use.

A frightening episode occurred whilst at Instow; there was not a lot of entertainment ashore, and one day I went to the cinema at Bideford on my own. It was not a very good film and the cinema not very full. In the darkness, I suddenly became aware of a movement further along the row in which I was sitting. A woman was removing her wedding ring from her finger and then proceeded to move nearer to my seat; I did not stay for the end of the film and fled. I firmly believe that the male does the chasing, although I am not so naive as to think that a woman may not have lures and charms with which to ensnare a male.

Early in 1944, I was sent back to Troon for a commanding officer's course. where we were accommodated in the "Dormy House" on the famous golf course at Barassie. More instruction in navigation followed, but for me the best part was being taught the design and construction details of the Mark 3 & 4 landing craft which were by then the standard vessels in use. We were given practical tuition in handling these somewhat unwieldy vessels, and went across to undertake practice beachings at Brodick Bay on the Isle of Aran. The vessels we used had not been fitted with the much cursed "Mulocks", nor were they necessary as the beach was perfect - steep and easy. Berthing back in Troon was tricky - there were the usual apocryphal stories of the dreadful accidents that had befallen some of the candidates, but as far as I was concerned, I loved it all - it was food and drink to me. At last I was doing something that motivated me, and passed every test and exam with flying colours, whereas at school I had consistently poor exam marks (except in French, which I enjoyed - was this a throwback to the Huguenot ancestry on my father's side?). At the end of all this, I was sent to a Mark 4 tank landing craft, but still as first lieutenant. They considered I was still too immature and needed further experience - of course, they were probably right, but I was disappointed. Intensive exercises in preparation for the invasion of mainland Europe were in full swing - they were busy times and there was a growing sense of awareness that it could not be far away. Strange inexplicable devices were appearing everywhere, ashore and afloat. However, my opportunity came - a commanding officer was invalided ashore with a nervous breakdown and I was catapulted into promotion. Looking back on those days, it was incredible that a youngster of 20 (of course, they thought I was 21 due to the earlier mistake I had made about my age) should be given command of 186 feet of steel ship with two 500 horse power diesel engines, but I could not see anything wrong with it and certainly suffered from excess of confidence. Nelson got his first command, a bomb ketch, at the same age, so perhaps there had been a precedent!

During the Spring there was a very big exercise - I can't recall how long before the real thing, but with information now freely available from the many books subsequently written, my feelings at the time that this was a serious deceptive ploy have been confirmed. Organisation by then was superb, and no one was told more than they needed to know, but the courses we were to take during the night took us towards the Pas de Calais, so a number of us felt that it was part of an elaborate series of feints. Our capacious tank hold had been covered in camouflage netting; we spent some hours on a loading hard at Southampton waiting for tanks or vehicles to arrive, but eventually our flotilla (12 tank landing craft) was ordered to proceed as part of "G" force, in accordance with instructions. At the end of this exercise, which involved the long sweep towards the

Exercises off the - Dorset coast - gun's crew closed up with first lieutenant supervising. Our only armament was 2 Oelikon guns.

French coast, we finished up to land on the beach at Studland Bay in the morning. Landing craft mounted with rockets had gone in first and totally scorched everything on the shore, presenting a scene of utter desolation. Remarkably, the area is now a well established nature reserve. We had to drive in quite hard because there was a sand bank which the ship had to be forced over before reaching the beach in a text book landing on quite a steep beach. The bow door went down with a precision of which we could all be proud - and two of the hands rolled a porter's truck ("won" from Southampton Central Station for loading stores aboard) on to the sands - we had all been rather disappointed that there was no load to disembark. This would have been quite funny but for the fact that a lot of top brass observing the landings had gathered on the beach at this spot. Fortunately they had a sense of humour and I was relieved to see the smiles on their faces. They probably knew what we lesser mortals had not been told, that there was never any intention to load us with vehicles and troops.

Following this exercise we returned to Southampton where an incredible array of landing craft and mysterious floating objects were gathering, including great reels of flexible pipline - "Pluto", which were to be laid across the Channel to carry fuel for the invading forces. Tank landing craft were moored alongside the long straight line of the New Docks, if I remember rightly, four abreast. With 38 foot beam each the mass of craft presented a superb bombing target, but fortunately by this stage in the War we had mastery of the air and no raids developed. Ashore, the great transit sheds that formerly handled passengers and cargo from the liners regularly sailing from there, were turned into Naval Depots for storing ships and providing for the needs of their men - post offices, NAAFI stores and canteens. The bustle of activity was ceaseless, and an atmosphere of tense anticipation pervaded throughout. A short leave home, and then we were sealed off into this town the Navy had created: the final briefings were received, from which it was apparent that our flotilla would be the last in "G" force, and we were to be the last ship, with a large break astern of us before the next invasion convoy - the significance of this would be revealed in a few days' time. We were reviewed on a day of bright sunshine by King George VIth, who passed by the outboard line of landing craft aboard the bridge of a "B" type ML. All officers and crews assembled on the outboard craft to "Cheer ship" in the traditional manner. The scene was set.

NORMANDY LANDFALL.

(Reprinted from the summer 1994 edition of "Cruising", magazine of the Cruising Association).

IT had been a choppy overnight crossing from Southampton Water with a fresh, but moderating Westerly wind still whipping up an unpleasant sea; our departure had been delayed from the previous day because the same wind had been blowing at near gale force. However, the weather improved during the crossing, and early that morning, June 6th 1944, the sun was shining on the seaside resorts of the Calvados coast, lighting the straggling line of seaside houses - typical seaside architecture, with a Gallic flavour. As we approached the coast, a little to the East of Arromanches, the seas reduced as we came under the lee of the Cherbourg peninsula. The tide was high, the beaches and seafront looked so deceptively delightful and pleasant - but the waves of aircraft in their black and white striped identity marking, which had been applied secretly at the very last minute, and the occasional heavy "crump" did indicate that this was no yachting jaunt.

Earlier on our cross Channel passage, at dusk on June the 5th we were privileged to have a grandstand view of an unforgettable sight - astern of us through a break in the unending armada of landing craft and escorts, steamed a line of battleships with attendant cruisers and destroyers. Great battle ensigns streamed bravely from their maintops as these dark grey walls of steel ploughed relentlessly Westwards through the waves like some totally irresistable force; occasionally a sea would break over the bows in a seemingly futile manner. Here was the might of the Royal Navy about its business - as I learnt later, to take up positions off the Cherbourg peninsula and pound the defences with deadly accuracy. A miserable evening was transformed by this sight, and the troops we were carrying, who were feeling extremely uncomfortable as we rolled on our way into the night, suddenly lined the rails and broke into spontaneous cheering at this display of British seapower. I am sure none of us realised then that such a sight was never going to be seen again.

We were due to beach at "H" hour, but the beaches ahead were already crowded with landing craft and the rather comfortless signal came back from our flotilla leader - "beach where you can". As the last ship in the flotilla, there was precious little beach left

Mk IV landing craft beaching on D-day, June 6th 1944. As this picture shows, the weather conditions, although moderated from the previous day which caused a 24 hour postponement, were still far from benign. (British Official Photograph)

for us - everywhere there were "drowned" vehicles from previous landings and numerous obstructions - what looked like telegraph poles set at 45 degrees with ominous 88mm shells on top. The Westerly wind was pushing everyone down to leeward, and close to my lee was the end of the beach and the Pointe de Ver. There was nothing for it but to go hard for the last bit of beach left and hope that we would break down any obstacles. The kedge (in truth, our main and only anchor was let go astern and I ran her in hard. Then as the smoke and debris cleared from an almighty explosion forward, from the bridge could be seen the waters of the English Channel through a large hole in the heavy plating of the vehicle deck and the bottom of the ship, blown right through by a mine on the beach. With the help of heavy timber carried as part of our stores we were able to bridge the hole and get the vehicles ashore before setting off for the long slow voyage home - our steering had been damaged on submerged wreckage and we were unable to maintain a reasonable course or speed, but because Tank Landing Craft were a mass of watertight compartments, the damage forward had little effect on our buoyancy or trim.

AFTER D-DAY -
INTO THE CROSS-CHANNEL FERRY BUSINESS.

AFTER repairs at White's shipyard at Woolston, Southampton, we were back on a regular cross-channel ferry run that was to continue through the autumn and winter of 1944/5, but we had to wait our turn for repairs as so many craft had received damage. The delay in repairing the damage forward was frustrating because one felt it important to be keeping up the supplies and reinforcements, but soon after "D" day, a terrible Northerly gale hit the landing beaches. The strong onshore wind and high seas wrecked the "Mulberry" harbour built off Arromanches and wrought havoc among ships and landing craft, some of which became a total loss. After returning to service, only one more trip was made to the British beaches before we were switched to the American beaches. The Americans landing on "Omaha" beach met with devastating fire from the low cliffs overlooking the beach, and suffered terrible casualties to men and equipment. The American built tank landing craft suffered a number of casualties, and in any case, they were really intended for short haul work between larger vessels off shore and the beach; they certainly were not intended for regular cross-channel ferry work, which became the somewhat humdrum existence for the British Tank Landing Craft. Portland became our usual port of embarcation, and the few hours between voyages were always very busy. There were victuals and stores required, and sometimes visits to the base "HMS ATTACK", a steep walk up the hill, to collect new briefings, charts and the like. One could sign in to the officer's mess there, and get a jolly good lunch served by charming Wren stewards. Then one day I repeated this, having been ashore for instruction. There seemed to a lot of khaki shirts about, but it was not until I sat down to eat and saw everyone cut their food up, lay the knife down and eat with a fork that I realised it had become an American officer's mess. No one minded, and I was made most welcome; my first introduction to American hospitality - but you couldn't get a gin and tonic before lunch any more!

LCT 879, late 1944, in Portland Harbour, loaded awaiting convoy. Photograph is of poor quality, but by this time she was showing signs of wear and tear from regular cross-channel trips, often in bad weather.

Apart from Cherbourg, which soon became too far from the front line to be a useful supply port, and had limited facilities for driving off vehicles, it was a long time before the Allies had any useful port facilites available. The retreating German Armies made sure that very effective destruction and blocking was carried out, so all through the Autumn of 1944 we continued unloading our vehicles over the open beaches. The extensive flat sands off the Calvados coast had become very pockmarked as a result of occasional bombing raids, churning propellers and perhaps some natural causes, so that a number of vehicles had taken spectacular nose dives when traversing what seemed to be shallow water between ship and shore.

The order was given that all craft should dry out on the receding tide and wait for clear dry sand to appear before unloading; the troops became very fed up with waiting to get ashore, whilst we were faced with a wait of some six boring hours before floating off again. Without sea water for cooling the generator, this meant no electric light or power for the electric fire, the sole means of heating the wardroom. The mess deck was alright as they had a large coal range for cooking and providing heat. Our motor mechanic (a peacetime mechanic with AEC, the suppliers of engines to London Transport buses) was ingenious, and by rigging temporary cooling water pipes to one of our double bottom tanks which was kept flooded for the purpose, we were able to run the smaller of our two generators all the time we were ashore. It was not long before others were following with similar arrangements - typical of the resourcefulness that so frequently was encountered during the war. Not in any Admiralty manual, the practice would have probably been frowned upon by higher authority had they ever known. It was still tedious, and we tried to organise inter-ship games on the sands; there were other less desirable pursuits - there were vast quantities of ammunition abandoned by the retreating Germans which provided one or two dangerous games. In one, a brass shell case full of explosive complete with percussion fuse was laid on top of a big block of wood (used for chocking up tanks and vehicles against movement in the hold) and a sailor's foot (in heavy Admiralty issue boot) would hold it in place while another would strike the percussion cap with hammer and nail. A spectacular explosion issued from the open end of the shell case, which usually jumped back from under the booted foot. Other games used pieces of lighted cordite, which burnt quite harmlessly when not in a container, but produced a most pungent smell. Why there were no casualties (that I ever heard of) from this horseplay, I really don't understand.

Our cross-channel trips always were made via "Z" area, a great Picadilly Circus South of the Isle of Wight from which coastal and cross-channel swept channels through minefields all radiated. If we were going to Portland Harbour, which we were mostly using for embarcation, the return trip involved a long slog along the beautiful Hampshire and Dorset coasts, past the Purbeck Hills, Lulworth Cove and other such beauty spots. At night, the light house at Anvil Point was switched on at reduced strength for a brief period at intervals (every half hour, I seem to remember). It was a hard trip most times, because the wind was invariably strong from the West, and the flat, punt shape of the bows pounded into the waves, producing a very bumpy and uncomfortable ride. It always seemed ages before we reached the welcome shelter of Weymouth Bay and entered Portland harbour. The convoy would be signalled to "Act independently", which was the start of an unseemly race for the best buoys (nearest to the shore) or to be alongside a "chummy" ship. Normal "Full speed ahead" on our Paxman Engines was 1100 RPM, but "Emergency Full Ahead" of 1350 RPM was only permissible in an emergency and for not more than a limited time (5 mins?). Needless to say, this was an emergency, and black smoke issued from every funnel - diesel engines put under excessive load always make black smoke. I sometimes wonder how we ever won the War!.

Our world was very limited; rarely did we see an up to date newspaper, but I had a personal portable radio with which we received BBC news bulletins on the "AEF

Programme". Sometimes I would listen to other entertainment on this - the inevitable "ITMA" with Tommy Handley, and those wonderful "Music while you work" programmes. These consisted of non-stop lively light music; the signature tune was *"Calling All Workers"*, a lively march by Eric Coates. Nostalgia set in sometimes when they announced this was being relayed from the "Tudor Cafe" Kingston-on-Thames (in Bentall's store) and reminded me of boyhood days when we were taken to afternoon tea in Southend at either Garons or Boots - the two competed fiercely, and both offered appropriate live music with tea. Boots (yes, Boots the chemists!), at the corner of Warrior Square and Southend High Street was probably the better of the two - it had a "Palm Court" atmosphere, under a glass dome. Entertainment was very important in keeping up morale in the forces and on the home front.

At the time, the mood was that we had taken an overwhelming and unstoppable force across to mainland Europe. Initial progress inland was fairly rapid, and much of this was due to the quite remarkable campaign of deception which had kept a lot of the enemy reserves ready for what they believed was to be the main landing in the Pas de Calais area. None of this did we know; indeed many of the elaborate "secret" messages and other schemes have only come to light with the release of secret papers in later years. We only held our own pieces of the jig saw puzzle, but now many of the mysteries of those times have been explained and one cannot but wonder at the overall picture, now all the pieces are in place. By the end of May and even after D-Day, dummy tank landing craft, built of wood and canvas began appearing in East and South East coastal anchorages and harbours from Great Yarmouth down as far as Dover and Folkestone, many of them in the rivers Deben and Orwell.

Without these and many other ingenious schemes, the outcome might have been different. It took a long time to capture Caen, whilst Southwards we could not break through at Avranches and the Falaise Gap, where we found our tanks were outgunned by the superior German "Tiger" tanks. This battle was tipped in our favour by air power, when Hawker "Typhoon" aircraft wrought havoc among the German armour with rockets and cannon - they carried an amazing battery of tank busting weaponry. Little did I know at this time, on hearing of these exploits, that a woman destined to be my wife was heavily involved in the development and testing of these formidable aircraft. None of us at sea, or indeed, the population at large, realised that such desperate efforts were being made to break out of the area immediately behind the beaches; we only heard of the destruction being wrought on the enemy by our air power, without appreciating the strategic significance.

On one trip when we were routed to Southampton instead of the usual run to Portland, I saw an extraordinary small aircraft that buzzed its way across the sunlit sky; such was our isolation at that time that I had not heard of the V1 "flying bombs" with which Southern England was being attacked, but soon after I was able to take a short leave and learn about the war on the home front.. The danger of invasion was clearly receding, and as our armies finally broke out of Normandy and swept up into France, the restrictions on civilians in coastal zones were eased, so late that autumn my family left the rented house in Bray and moved back into our house on the cliffs at Leigh. Slowly, a restricted life was coming back into the town. Techniques for dealing with the menace of V1 pilotless aircraft were proving effective, only to be superseded by another horror, the V2 rocket. This travelled so fast that there was no warning of its approach; it carried an enormous load of explosive which caused serious destruction wherever it landed. These were the enemy's last desperate efforts to break civilian morale at a time when their troops were retreating across France and Holland in the West, and from Russia in the East. I worried somewhat about what I thought to be a premature decision by my parents to move back to the coast, but they did not want to spend another winter away from their own house.

Towards the end of that year, the port of Le Havre had finally been cleared sufficiently to allow some craft to use it, and there was a long slipway over which our loads could be disembarked - a tricky operation, since the tides there rise about forty feet, and on a falling tide, great care was needed to avoid becoming stranded. Although the Allied armies continued to advance, there were still some nasty surprises left, and one had to have a sneaking admiration for the tenacity of the German Army; perhaps we had developed a degree of complacency. In all fields of human endeavour, be it love or war there is no room for complacency. There was the failure of the airborne attempt to gain a crossing of the Rhine at Arnhem, too far ahead of our advancing forces, and then, nearer Christmas, a serious counter attack was mounted through the Ardennes in Belgium, just where they had broken through in 1940. This was also accompanied by the dropping of airborne forces behind our lines to cause havoc in our increasingly long supply lines to the front, and these infiltrations were regarded as such a danger that officers going ashore in Le Havre were ordered to go armed with hand guns - a revolver strapped round the waist made one very cumbersome; they were certainly not the dinky kind of thing one might see in a film.

There was a forces cinema ashore, created from a patched up cinema building that had not been too badly damaged. Both sides had wrought the most terrible destruction on the hotly contested port and there was little else to do ashore. We were able to exchange our sterling with a black market trader at very advantageous prices, and so buy a drink in the few cafes that were open. I favoured one in the Rue Helene, but it was rather more the daughter of the establishment that was the attraction, and I cannot think of a more pleasant way of improving one's French. The whole place was very grim and the port was still a mess - convoys of merchantmen were being routed up the Seine to Rouen, where the port facilities had not been so badly damaged, and goods could be discharged on quays of the North bank. All bridges below Paris had been destroyed by one side or the other, so logistically this was very important for reaching the front line.

Space was at a premium within Le Havre, and frequently we had to lie at anchor outside in the fierce tides whilst waiting for a convoy home. Whilst waiting one day I was grabbing a bit of sleep before the voyage home, when an almighty explosion rocked the ship; I shot outside so quickly that the debris from the blown up bows of a merchantman was still falling in a column of water. Her stern rose out of the water, the propeller still turning and a cloud of steam rose from a fractured steampipe to the anchor winch. This was not the first ship in the convoy coming down from Rouen, but was the unlucky one that detonated an uncleared "acoustic" mine.

War is a very nasty game; early in the War the magnetic mine came along, and this worked on the principle that all ships in use by the Allies were built in the Northern hemisphere and that their keels would be a North seeking magnet, so the mines were detonated by the deflection of a corresponding magnet in the mine when the ship passed over. We overcame that by passing powerful electric loops right round every ship, which reversed their natural magnetism ("degaussing"); it meant that generators had to be kept running constantly unless in a harbour that had been declared safe. So then the acoustic mine was introduced, detonated by the vibrations created in the water from a ship's engines and propeller, and this was not so easy to deal with.

In January 1945, there was a spell of very severe weather and one or two of our crossings were a nightmare, with a lot of fog and frost. There was only the low - powered shaded blue stern light of the ship ahead to follow - no other lights were allowed, and there was constant fear of ramming the chap ahead. On one occasion I was so fed up with the whole thing, I slipped the convoy and made my own way home in dense fog - it was an enormous convoy with little control, so nobody noticed, but with hindsight it was a silly and dangerous thing to do because there were still E-boats prowling in the Channel waiting to pick off isolated craft. In the convoy there were a number of collisions that night. This was quite a nerve-wracking time, particularly as the nights were so long, and I was delighted when my request for repairs was granted. We were leaking badly up forward from the constant battering of the flat punt like bow in the Channel seas, as well as having a defect in one of our two vital generators, and other major engine maintenance was due. We sailed for Poole Harbour on a balmy sunlit day which presaged the onset of Spring and hope of an end of the conflict in Europe, as our armies were again advancing steadily. We were hauled out on a large slipway operated by Bolsons, on the opposite side of the harbour from the main town quay.

This firm (which sadly closed in recent years) were absolutely wonderful and very helpful. Nearby was "The Shipwrights' Arms", a splendid late 18th century pub which served as a good entertainment centre for the crew. This has now been demolished (I wonder how the planners allowed this to happen - surely in post war years it should have been listed?) Being a civilian yard, there were no restrictive naval guards to pass or petty regulations to be adhered to, other than those I laid down myself. My parents and sister came down to stay in nearby Bournemouth, and became frequent visitors. A family tea party was in full swing in the wardroom when the Admiralty superintendent in charge of the work came on a routine visit. I was not sure how he would react to the rather free and easy atmosphere and the unauthorised visitors. I introduced him to the family and offered him tea, at which point my presence was requested on deck to deal with a query, wondering what would be going on in the wardroom on my return. As I returned, my father and the superintendent, Mr Aspinall, were in deep conversation. They had both served in the 10th Armed Merchant Cruiser Squadron, patrolling Icelandic waters in the First World War, and were reminiscing. Suddenly, a good refit at a competent yard became almost magical - lots of mod cons and improvements for the ship and the crew's mess deck. Now fully 21, and full of bright ideas about ship design, I expounded to Mr Aspinall how I thought the power delivered by the Paxman engines was wasted because the propellers were not big enough. To my astonishment, he agreed with me, and had been trying to convince the Admiralty, but their answer was that there was a shortage of manganese bronze (what wasn't there a shortage of at that time!) and bigger propellers were out of the question. However, a pair had been cast for an

Family tea party aboard LCT 879 during refit at Bolson's yard, Poole, early 1945.

experiment which was not carried out following the Admiralty's negative response. "They are in Bristol, and I will have them sent down at once to be fitted before you are re-launched". When we returned to service and that magic signal came to act independently, the others couldn't understand why we always beat them in the race for the best moorings.

After we were relaunched, there was still work to be done, and on another visit, my sister Lorna (by now 14), noticed our small plywood dinghy lying on the vehicle deck. "Could I go for a row?" The dinghy was launched, but there was a pause because only one oar could be found. By the time the missing oar was produced, my sister was half way across the harbour using the one oar in a sculling notch in the transom. The crew, most of whom could probably not row with any great degree of competence, were astonished.

On rejoining the flotilla, the pressure was off and we had longer turn round times between crossings; the news from the front lines was improving and we had over-run the launching sites for the dreaded V2 rockets. By the beginning of May, it was pretty obvious that the war in Europe would be over; we thought we were very clever because for some weeks every visit to the Naval stores included a request for light bulbs, wire and fittings. On VE day (May 9th), we were back in Poole Harbour, in what we knew as "Dorset Lake", and that night every ship's generator was grinding out electricity for the most amazing display of lighting. If we thought we had been clever, you should have seen some of the others - they had been much more daring in their requests. I think the authorities knew what we were up to and turned a blind eye.

TO HOLLAND - UNDER PEACETIME CONDITIONS

W ITHIN a day or so, we were under orders to load supplies for Holland from Southampton. First, they were to have been driven aboard in vehicles, but then it was decided to lower the supplies direct into the hold and cover them (which meant we could carry a much bigger load). Soon we sailed for Rotterdam, in company as a flotilla - but what a difference from those dreary convoys with darkened ships; now showing our full navigation lights, plus lights round the stern deck and from the accommodation - no more blackout - the ships stood out sharp and clear.

Arriving off the Hook of Holland, each ship was met by a Dutch pilot to take us up the New Waterway to Rotterdam. With tears of joy in his eyes, our pilot said we were the first English ship he had piloted since 1940. He took us into the small harbour of Maasluis, halfwayup the waterway, because blockships had been sunk across the channel to prevent the Allies using Rotterdam as a supply port, and it was essential to negotiate these at high water. Our pilot spent the night aboard with us, and we gave him a good meal which made him ill - they had been so starved that their digestive systems must have been suffering from lack of exercise. That evening, he related some of their wartime experiences, and how he and his wife listened to the BBC programmes from London. Asked if he found the news broadcasts good, I was astonished by his reply - "Oh no, we listened to Tommy Handley in "Itma" - very funny". "But if you had been discovered listening to London, the Gestapo would have arrested you" - "We took great care and listened under the bedclothes" For a long time it shook me that a couple risked their lives to listen to comedy programmes, but in later life I realise that these were a lifeline for them, in a grim life overshadowed by fear and short of not just luxuries but of the basics of a reasonable lifestyle.

The next day he skilfully took us right between the mast and funnel of a sunken ship - no wonder they wanted flat bottomed landing craft for this job - and on into the docks at Rotterdam where cranes swiftly unloaded our cargo into waiting vehicles. A crowd of youngsters gathered round the ships, and it was not long before all the ships emergency supplies of unpalatable biscuits had been distributed. Everything we saw told of the destruction and the harsh treatment these people had received, but equally, their joy that it was over and the warmth of their welcome was very touching. None of us went beyond the docks area - there was little to see because of the damage.

Instead of heading for home (I had hoped we might do more of these mercy trips) we were ordered to sail through newly swept channels in the minefields off the coast, to the Dutch Naval base of Den Helder, which had become a major German centre during hostiliies. Here, as in other places we visited, people came with the most extraordinary offerings in exchange for cigarettes. A packet of twenty cost us 6 pence (2.5 pence in current coinage) and for the minimal amounts demanded I bought a bottle of Heidseick Dry Monopole champagne; for a few cigarettes I was offered a Zeiss camera, but did not accept this; for my 21st birthday some family friends had given me a Kodak folding bellows camera - almost impossible to obtain in the shops so I did not need this strange sounding foreign camera! I was, of course very naive in so many things and missed an opportunity to acquire a superb professional instrument. Another ship in the flotilla bought a small steel motor launch fitted for towing, in exchange for cigarettes, and managed to haul the thing aboard over the bow ramp. I never found out what he did with it, or how he explained it when he arrived home.

Our task at Den Helder was to ferry German prisoners of war to Harlingen on the other side of the Waddenzee; they came aboard 500 at a time watched by two Canadian guards carrying Lee-Enfield rifles. They were still well disciplined, but subdued as one might expect of a defeated army. I never really had any explanation of what we were doing, but it seems that there was still a usable rail link at Harlingen by which they could be repatriated swiftly, and the authorities wanted them out of Holland because of the desperate shortage of food. There was a very strict policy of "non fraternisation" in force at this time, which was not unreasonable as these same defeated men had been been shooting to kill only a few days previously.

Next, we had the sad orders to sail for Plymouth in order to pay off, and on a mooring in the St Germans, or Lynher river, with beautiful scenery as a backdrop, we started de-storing. It was all very depressing, as we had been a happy ship, but then I heard, on the bush telegraph, of a job going, to remove equipment from the Channel Islands. I rushed to see the Commander running this operation and volunteered immediately. "Is your ship still fully operational Platt?" - "Yes" I lied, and raced back to tell the crew, who were all for taking part in an interesting expedition - "Use your ingenuity to get our compass back from stores - don't bother about the guns, the shooting's over". I never asked how this was done, but they soon were returning triumphantly with the compass.

After revictualling, we were off - the bliss of this trip, not having to keep station with other ships in the flotilla, full navigation lights during the short period of darkness, and our own navigation, rather than accepting someone else's (which you had to do to stay with the protection of the convoy escorts). It stiffened the resolution I had already made, that when I started boating with my own little ship, I was going to be a "loner" and eschew races, rallies, or anything involving a lot of other boats.

First, we visited St Peter Port, where the pilot asked if I liked lobster - "Yes" (I don't think I had ever had any!), and the following morning there were two lobsters scratching around on deck, in a sack outside the wardroom door. After loading from a ramp in the inner harbour items of equipment for use had our forces met with opposition, we then sailed for St Helier, for a similar purpose. Here, there was another hazard (or was it an opportunity?) Invitations came from mothers of eligible daughters to countless parties and dinners, but I was wary of the situation - an English Naval officer, in their eyes, might be a catch (in spite of the uniform, I was only a very temporary part of the Navy). From Jersey, we went to Braye Harbour, Sark. At that time, few civilians had yet returned; it was beautiful and remote and I loved it. The Germans had built a long, flimsy, pier there which we used, but the weather was good otherwise I think we would have demolished it. After loading at another slipway, on the tide, we sailed to Southampton to discharge our mixture of transport, temporary buildings, and a small launch. This diversion was only a temporary reprieve, and we were ordered back to Plymouth to pay off; on our passage Westwards, we passed a "chummy" LCT with a steam roller in his hold. How he wangled this job, I shall never know, but it was being taken from Devonshire to Kent. It did show the immense peacetime possibilities for such vessels, and indeed, for some time after the war, the "Red Funnel" line had a converted Mark IV TLC as a vehicular ferry from Southampton to the Isle of Wight, complete with a smart passenger saloon over the after end of the vehicle deck.

CIVVY STREET

FOLLOWING a fortnight's leave, I was told to report to "HMS WESTCLIFF" - a combined operations establishment on the promenade between Leigh and Southend, with enormous Nissen buildings actually stradling the kerb between roadway and pedestrian path; a large area of the town was enclosed for accommodation purposes which included several large houses and small hotel buildings. There is absolutely no trace of its existence today. I expected, at the end of this leave, to be sent to the Far East, where we were slowly gaining Pacific islands from the Japanese, who were resisting with suicidal fanaticism. The dropping of the atomic bombs on Hiroshima and Nagasaki brought this conflict to a sudden end in August, and although there have been critics of this action in recent years, the fact is that the sudden termination of what might have been a long and bitter war saved countless lives, of British and Japanese forces, and civilians. The civilian populations of those (and other) Japanese cities had been warned to get out to avoid casualties, by means of massive leaflet drops from "Flying Fortress" aircraft before the bombs were dropped.

My leave was extended, and I was issued with ration books which my mother was delighted to have - food was very severely rationed, and I was able to cycle down to HMS "WESTCLIFF" to renew them. We had obtained permission when I had a short leave earlier to bring "EUONYM" downriver from Bray and re-unite her with her mast and rigging still stored in Bundock's boatyard at Leigh (which by then had been taken over by Parsons). At the time, I was madly in love with a young lady who lived in Kent - I had actually sailed "EUONYM" across the Estuary several times in the autumn of 1945 to meet her; there always seemed to be a frustrating lack of wind. I had also taken my sister away for a few days in the boat, as she had not been well, but it was extremely difficult to buy rationed food away from regular suppliers, and apart from some whale meat steaks which we bought in Gravesend, we lived on very little else. I wonder how much good it really did her.

By this time, it was becoming clear that my father was far from well. The Navy granted me a release from the service on compassionate grounds - they were glad to get me off the payroll, for there were dozens of unemployed officers at that time - and I went into the family textile business. My cherished hopes of taking up naval architecture receded, and I became fully involved in the business, with no training other than how to run a tank landing craft on to a beach! Fortunately my father's right hand man, Howard Banks, was highly efficient and did a lot to teach and encourage me. I bought a boat of my own - "TROJAN", a converted Naval whaler, 27 feet long with about 6 foot beam - she was like a long thin banana. Her accommodation was spartan, and offered comfortable crawling headroom; she was ketch rigged and had no engine. I had bought her while the market was very flat, before the flood of de-mobbed servicemen drove prices of almost anything that floated (and some that didn't) sky high. In my newly acquired ex Naval whaler I managed to sail across to Whitstable, Harty Ferry and other nearby places; in those days it was like sailing to another world, particularly as there was some kind of war going on between the fishermen of Whitstable and Leigh. "TROJAN" was only a stop gap, and I knew that eventually I wanted a boat with a deeper hull and heavier displacement than I had sailed in so far. But more pressing problems began to dominate the scene; the following Spring (1946) "EUONYM" was sold, by which time prices were very much higher.

In August that year, just one year after the War was over, my father died of lung cancer at the age of 55 - he had been a heavy smoker. The family was devastated. My mother was wonderful, but she was made a widow at the age of 49 and it was now my responsibility to see that she was properly cared for.

It was becoming obvious that the temporary premises occupied by the family business on short leases would have to be replaced; not only were they highly inefficient (raw materials had to be carted in hand trucks across the A12 Colchester road at Gallows corner), but the prospect of private motoring returning meant the owners would be needing their premises again. I started exploring the area for premises, or land on which to build - without a car. Fortunately, in Dagenham Borough Council's offices, I met an old friend from 3rd Chalkwell Bay Sea Scout days who was in the surveyor's offices. He explained the new Town & Country planning acts shortly to become law, so that I did not waste time looking at land on which industrial premises could not be built, and as a result, we bought one and a half acres of land from gravel pit owners who had decided they had already worked out most of the available gravel. Some instinct made me want to buy freehold land - a decision often criticised by economists who would say "Are you in the property business or textiles?". With hindsight, over fifty years later I believe the decision was right, but also with hindsight I wish we had bought a lot more land - the owners would have been willing sellers. Hindsight is a wonderful thing, but comes too late for decisions to be made, and I find it galling to find journalists and writers who criticise decisions and strategies of wartime leaders long after the battles are over. I wonder what sort of hash they would have made of it had they been there? Fortunately, I was able to tell my father before he died that we were buying the land. Everything was difficult at that time; all kinds of building materials were difficult to obtain, and even if it was available, there were frustrating controls and permits to be negotiated through a maze of bureaucracy. It was a hard slog, but we were able, at the end of 1946 to move to the new site, built on a former searchlight station and farmland (for some years after we moved there, the Dagenham Horse Show took place on a field at the back of our site). That winter was the coldest for many years; frozen pipes and electricity cuts frequently held up production, transport was blocked by snowbound roads and the railways were in a state of post war crisis; the whole Country almost ground to a halt. Looking back at those times, they were a nightmare only relieved by the fact that the War was over. Little time in all this to think about boats and sailing.

SAILING (& motoring!) STARTS IN EARNEST

IN the Spring of 1947, I sold "TROJAN", with a handsome profit, as boat prices were booming. My friend Michael Beaumont had bought a very attractive boat, "LYNETTE", built at Leigh a year or so before the War, and in the glorious summer of 1947 (nature always tends to balance itself, and this benign period followed on from the terrible winter) we sailed her across the Estuary to the Medway frequently. She had a single cylinder engine built at Leigh, and called a "Leonse" engine. It had little lubricating oil reservoirs with brass taps that needed turning on every so often to keep it running smoothly. Its only trouble was that it did not really run at all, and it was sent back to its makers in Old Leigh High Street for complete overhaul. Ballast was put in the boat to compensate for the loss of weight, and the propeller taken off as there was nothing to drive it. Without the propeller, an already well behaved sailing boat became like magic to sail; it was an instructive lesson in the amount of drag caused by a propeller. We took our summer holiday together, and first sailed her up to Bradwell Quay, where we anchored in the creek - tacking out the following morning, I put her on the bank while Michael was below cooking some breakfast. I dropped my trousers and underpants, jumped overboard, put my back under the transom and shoved her off with sails all set. As she gathered way again, I jumped in the dinghy towing astern and thence aboard again; Michael had taken charge and tacked again before we hit the other bank. During this holiday, we paid our first visit to the River Deben and were completely charmed. There were some boats on moorings at Felixstowe Ferry, just inside the entrance, not more than 4 or 5 in the beautiful Ramsholt reach, rather more at Waldringfield off the beach below the "Maybush", and then some off Kingston Quay ("Kyson" to the locals), the last place below Woodbridge where a boat might lie afloat at low water. Off Woodbridge Town, a few boats took the ground at low water. These idyllic conditions were, of course, long before the great sailing boom, and before the general use of motor cars to reach boats kept far from home. The tranquillity and beauty of the scenery were refreshing to the soul. The river, over fifty years on is still beautiful, but crowded with yacht moorings in nearly every reach.

That autumn, we both spent a lot of time looking at boats for sale; it was fairly heartbreaking as so many had suffered from wartime neglect, and we peered into many cabins that reeked of musty decay. By this time I had acquired a motor car - a 1936 Austin 10, which made travelling around to inspect boats much easier - up to then I had not learnt to drive, but this now became rather important, and I received lessons from a professional chauffeur, who was very keen on "the limousine ride". Achieving this in such a car was not easy, but he told me to imagine I had old ladies with weak necks as passengers! My mother had shrewdly taken out a provisional licence for me during the War, when driving tests were suspended. At the end of the war, full licences were automatically issued to such holders, so I have driven all these years without having passed a test.

Then, I was offered a boat at Brightlingsea by W Fieldgate & Son, shipbrokers and Lloyds Agents in the ports of Colchester and Brightlingsea. Travelling from Leigh to Brightlingsea by car was quite a safari in those days, and we toiled through the winding road from Leigh to Chelmsford via Rayleigh, to join the Colchester Road; after passing through Kelvedon and Feering, we crossed the level crossing that carried the line to Tollesbury pier (then still in use as far as Tollesbury itself), through Colchester and on to Brightlingsea. Here, we found "CAMPION" lying in a mud berth at the yard of James & Co (later to become James & Stone, and now, sadly, defunct). Michael and I liked what we saw; I had engaged surveyors to look at one or two boats, but in those days they struck me as pretty amateur, so why not do it ourselves? We returned for the survey of this 28 foot long gaff-rigged transom-sterned smack yacht, built by Thomas Kidby in 1936, and in fact never put into commission before the War overtook sailing. Sails of pure Egyptian Cotton had clearly never been bent on the spars, and with other equipment, including the anchor winch, lay unfitted in store. It did not take long to find trouble - her smack type matchboard linings were ripe with dry rot and fell apart as we touched them. Below the floorboards was what I can best describe as an iron mine, below which the hull had been cemented in fishing smack style to produce a smooth interior to the bottom. All this discouraged proper investigation in that region; the planking of the hull and decks was in excellent condition. Her engine, which did not really get much scrutiny, was a 4-cylinder Morris "Hotchkiss" engine which once powered a bullnose Morris of 1926 vintage, converted for marine use with a kit supplied by a Bristol engineering firm, A C Whitehorn. There were few marine engines available in those days suitable for a yacht's auxiliary engine, and this kind of adaptation was quite usual. An offer was made based on the survey, and £1075 later "CAMPION" became mine. I commissioned some essential work to be carried out - like mounting the anchor winch, and the fitting of a coal stove complete with a proper deck fitting comprising a water filled safety well. Additional equipment had to be bought, including a large pair of oil navigation lights and an anchor light from Davey & Co in the West India Dock road, Poplar. Their establishment, close to the docks, was in an old chapel packed with traditional marine equipment for ships and yachts; at that time I think they still would have been able to supply all the requirements of a 4-masted square rigger. My joy in finding a suitable boat was somewhat tempered by the fact that the young lady for whom I yearned promptly jilted me; it would be fair to say that the two events were probably not unconnected.

A NEW HOME FOR CAMPION.

(parts of this chapter were originally published in "Yachting Monthly" July 1948)

TOWARDS the end of November came the great moment when three of us - Michael, Peter (of the famous encounter with Southend's tramway system) and myself would sail "CAMPION" to my home shore. The Friday night's complicated train journey to Brightlingsea was itself an adventure; we had to change trains at Colchester, and from there we were put down at Wivenhoe station beneath gas lamps whose light ebbed and flowed with the wind. By this time, when we were the only people on the platform, a Dickensian looking official emerged from the shadows and assured us the train for Brightlingsea would be along shortly. Eventually, an ancient tall chimneyed hissing locomotive drew in, hauling two carriages in matching style. The bewiskered official appeared again, eagerly helping us aboard and shut the door firmly behind us. We knew the distance could not be great, but it seemed to take ages, and at one point, in a weak shaft of moonlight, we could see nothing but water from either side as we clattered slowly along. The carriage, with a Victorian clerestory roof, was lit by gas, which also spookily ebbed and flowed with the wind. "Do you think we really are in the right train?" "I don't know, but that chap was very eager to get us in - may be it's a ghost train". With thoughts like this, we were relieved when we eventually arrived at a dark and deserted Brightlingsea. Later, after a meal and drink in the warmth and comfort of the Royal Hotel (where we had stayed overnight when making our survey), we found

"CAMPION" riding serenely beneath the friendly glow of her riding light, exactly as arranged with the yard.

By nine the following morning "CAMPION'S" decks were a scene of activity as the Essex Yacht Club burgee was hoisted and final preparations made for sea. The mooring was transferred aft to let the ebb tide swing her head into the South-westerly breeze. At last the mainsail triumphantly rose with a clicking of patent blocks, and almost before it was finally set, the mooring was slipped.

I eagerly grasped the tiller and there came an end to the rising tension I had felt, wondering how she would handle and what sort of a job we should make of our departure in a strange ship. She responded easily to my slight touch; there was no need for the panic setting of a headsail, which had been fully prepared for if her head could not be made to pay off. Jib and foresail were set in leisurely fashion, and as the halliards were coiled down there was a wonderful feeling of relief and pleasure, for "CAMPION" was now beating down the Colne in fine style.

By the time we started beating South through the shallow Rays'n channel (leading to the Crouch entrance) the wind had freshened considerably, and at mid-day, as it was near low water, I stood as close as possible to the Dengie shore, and dropped the hook in slightly over a fathom to await more water and pull down a reef if necessary. Then came trouble, when we prepared to get under weigh again. The chain cable did not fit the windlass, and each link jammed in the sprockets of the gypsy (remember no one had ever sailed this boat before and I was now finding out a lot of things the hard way). Inch by inch it came in as we hammered the links into the chain pipe, but as we shortened in, the snubbing became very violent. As I had feared, first the pawl sheared off, followed shortly after by the whole gear stripping. To haul in by hand was out of the question, as the water had become very choppy, and I had to decide whether to slip the whole lot (she only had 13 fathoms of chain anyway) or veer as much as possible and ride the night out.

I was sure the wind would abate by dawn, so veered as quickly as possible to ease the snubbing, and I clapped rope springs on the cable to take some of the strain from the bitts. "CAMPION" rode easily in spite of the choppy seas; we banked up the coal stove and settled down below for a long uneasy winter night at anchor. By dawn the wind had eased to a pleasant Westerly, and there were signs that the sun might put in an appearance to brighten the day. After the inevitable cup of tea we set full mainsail and sailed our reluctant anchor out of the ground.

Beating up the Rays'n, with the aid of the sounding lead, we had a magnificent breakfast of kippers and bloaters. Michael, who was duty helmsman during breakfast, had no difficulty in tacking her single handed and at the same time taking constant soundings, for "CAMPION" sailed herself excellently with the helm lashed very slightly aweather. Reaching the Whittaker channel, and bearing away before a wind that was freshening up, "CAMPION" surged forward with a great white bone in her teeth - we felt like kings, it was so exhilarating. At eleven in the forenoon we hardened sheets to reach past the Whittaker beacon, there being sufficient water over the sand. Once clear of the beacon, we headed up closehauled to slowly tack over the ebb tide up the Swin; to cheat the ebb we stood into the Maplin bight (known as "Abraham's Bosom" to the bargemen) which gives a large area of sheltered water out of the main tide. Close to the SE Maplin buoy, we headed back towards the main channel and promptly ran aground; the sand comes round the bight in a hook. The now rising tide seemed to take an age to float her off, and it was again dark before reaching the deep water, where the rising wind was knocking up a lively sea. As soon as we weathered the W Mouse buoy, which cleared us from the Barrow sands, I hove to and hauled down a reef in the main; we got pretty wet in the process. The wind was a good force 6, but we were now able to make long tacks.

Once we had weathered the Nore Towers, I could see the lights of Southend pier, and beyond, the lights of home were gradually coming into view. We reached Southend pier at about high water - had it not been for that famous structure we could have stood inshore much sooner and obtained a lee from the wind which had now veered to Northwest. Standing inshore, I could see people walking along the front, and "CAMPION "slipped stealthily along in the dark breeze-ruffled waters, lit by occasional shafts of moonlight. But the tide was now ebbing against us, and it took a long time to work up to the Chalkwell shore. Soon after 1030 she touched bottom, and I ran forward to let go the anchor. The sails came down out of the darkness wet and stiff, and although we worked quickly, it was a long job making her shipshape, and by the time we had sorted out our gear below, she was settling down with a gentle list. We dowsed the lights, drew the fire, battened down the cabin and clambered into the dinghy. "CAMPION" became still and quiet as the last of the water lapped round her keel. She had come silently, in the night, to her new home shore.

That winter, in between hard working weeks - business was brisk, but difficult in every other way, for those immediate post-war years were full of difficulties. The railways, in the process of being nationalised, had been bled white by the tremendous strains of coping with war time traffic coupled with heavy damage from air raids. There was little or

A new home for Campion - low water on her drying mooring off Chalkwell, Michael Beaumont standing by port quarter.

no idea of customer service, and goods were constantly being lost or delayed; in truth they were being asked to carry a lot of traffic totally unsuited to carriage by rail, including much of our own, but there was little alternative at that time. At home, rationing was as tight as it had been during the War, but there was at least a meagre petrol ration for my 1936 Austin 10.

"CAMPION" had been hauled out at Johnson & Jago's yard next to New Leigh Station, and I had spent most of my weekends chipping out the cement from her bottom to reveal that all her heavy sawn frames amidships were only fit for mulch on a flowerbed. During the war she had been neglected and rainwater laid in her bilge for the duration; freshwater and wood are not a happy combination, whereas salt water is healthy for wood (and human beings!). Len Johnson who ran the yard was very helpful, and he set a remarkable craftsman on the restoration. Les Harris was of the old school; he always removed his shoes before boarding a gentleman's yacht, so you would find Les working away in the rough bare bilges, in his socks. Stout new heavy sawn frames were accurately fashioned, and the planking

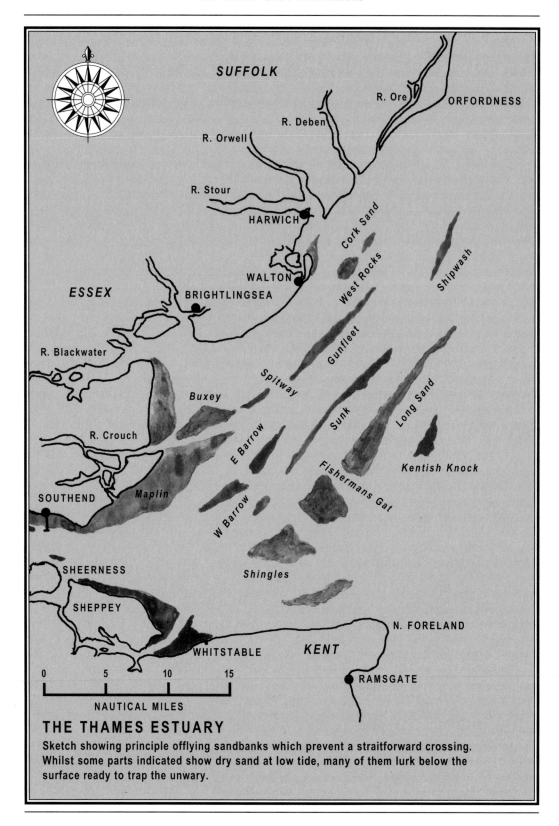

THE THAMES ESTUARY

Sketch showing principle offlying sandbanks which prevent a straitforward crossing. Whilst some parts indicated show dry sand at low tide, many of them lurk below the surface ready to trap the unwary.

refastened to them with galvanised spikes. Miraculously, and certainly not due to any real experience on my part, the bill for restoration came almost exactly to the amount by which I had made my lower offer for the boat, because of her condition. The internal lining was replaced with plywood, but this kind of thing was all within my own limited capabilities as a carpenter.

Externally, the hull was repainted in what became the house colours for all my boats - grey hull and black bulwarks (the first of the "grey mistresses") Of course, I suppose my early knowledge of the Leigh cocklers, and in particular the "Renown" whose loss at Dunkirk made a considerable impact on my young mind was partly responsible, but also, grey is a very practical colour. A wooden yacht is best painted white, because it reflects the sun's heat and reduces the risk of the planking shrinking, but it shows dirt and stains easily, so grey is a compromise. I always think a very dark colour looks good on a well finished hull - it gives such wonderful reflections, but it draws the heat with disastrous results for planking and seams. Black bulwarks give a contrast to the grey, and the two colour finish reduces the apparent height of the topsides.

WOODBRIDGE FOR EASTER
& TO GUERNSEY IN SUMMER

THIS was a kind of slogan, setting a difficult target. The wind always seemed to be in the Northeast whenever a voyage up the coast was planned, and so it was blowing when we anchored out in the Ray, with two of Johnson and Jago's hands still working aboard; the yard launch came out to collect them. The disastrous length of anchor chain had been replaced with proper half inch galvanised chain, calibrated to fit the sprockets in the gypsy wheel of the repaired anchor winch, and anchoring with the big fisherman anchor suddenly became a simple operation instead of the struggle we had experienced on the delivery trip. Once again, Michael and Peter were aboard.

So, that evening, we started beating out of the Thames Estuary against a pleasant whole sail breeze from the Northeast, making slow progress until the tide turned in our favour. Unfortunately, as you progress out of the Estuary, the turn of the tide comes earlier, so you can only count on about five hours help from the tide before it runs against you. The Thames sailing barges never attempted to sail against a Northeaster, anchoring West of Southend pier to await a change of wind. I can remember as a boy counting over a hundred of them trapped by a prolonged period of Easterlies, gently rolling in the swell that developed during the ebb tide.

During the night the wind fell light, and we were making little progress on each tack, and in the morning, the tide turned against us when we were close to the Whitaker buoy - our course lay outside the Gunfleet sands, to put us in a commanding position for making the Deben entrance. Late in the afternoon, a sea fog came rolling in like a curtain and at the same time the wind freshened; our dead reckoning showed we should be able to bear away to run before the wind into Harwich harbour, and with the wind astern, we were careering along like a scalded cat towards the unseen shore. Suddenly, ahead we saw the menacing grey backs of steeply mounting waves - breakers. We were further South than estimated. I threw her about and close hauled away from the danger; twice the aft end of the keel thumped on the bottom, but we were sailing away from what we realised was the seaward side of the Cork sands near their Northern limit. It had been a dangerous way of proving our position! After picking up the penetrating beam of the Cork light vessel, we were able to nose our way from buoy to buoy round Landguard point and clear of the dangerous half submerged wreck of a destroyer - a wartime casualty. A little way above the old Felixstowe dock, the anchor went down in smooth water protected from the East wind (an area now covered by the building of container berths). We were cold, and wanted to light our coal stove, but there was a terrible smell of petrol below. Another lesson about our new ship learnt the hard way - she had been fitted with a car petrol tank, the filler cap for which was below the deck under a removable brass deck plate; heeling to the stiff breeze with a tank that had been filled for the voyage caused spillage. Floorboards had to be taken up for ventilation, bilges pumped dry and all hatches opened wide for some time before we eventually felt brave enough to light up.

The next day we rounded Landguard Point outward bound in good visibility and headed for the River Deben, into which we stormed with a favourable North Easterly wind and a strong flood tide - Easter always coincides with some of the biggest spring tides of the year which run very hard; following those there is a period of very low neap and spring tides, the "bird tides", which enable sea and shore birds to nest on the saltings and coastal margins.   On up to Woodbridge, where we anchored off the promenade and went ashore feeling as if we had arrived in a foreign port. After a drink in "The Boat" inn (now a private house) and purchasing a few essentials, we set off down river and anchored off Waldringfield beach. Our brief visit to the Deben also included a stop at the "Ramsholt Arms", a minute and remote pub run by a Mrs Nunn. Fresh water was drawn from a well with a hand pump, lighting was by oil lamps and the floor was stone flagged.

A falling barometer heralded the end of Easterly winds, but fortunately they were still Southeasterly and our voyage back to Leigh was much easier than the outward passage . In spite of an early start, it was late evening and very dark by the time we passed Southend pierhead. From there, we located the Leigh buoy (known locally as the "Low way buoy) and I looked for the two red lights that were supposed to lead us into the Ray. These red lights were nothing more than red panes in two street lamps on the Leigh Cliffs, put there by the old Leigh Council, long since absorbed into Southend Borough. They were difficult to identify against the blaze of lights, including the red neon sign on the "Coliseum" cinema, but we found them. No sooner had we put her on the transit than we hit the hard Marsh End sand with a sickening crash. The wind seemed to freshen, and a wicked tide swung the bows round to run the boat further up the sand. The sea boiled round us; we rushed to unlash the kedge anchor, and I made ready with the dinghy to row it out. Before we could even load the anchor in the little 8 foot pram dinghy, I lost hold of the boat and was swept away into the night and could not make way against wind and tide however much I exerted myself at the oars, soon losing sight of "CAMPION" in the dark.

At that time there were several of the old sailing bawleys moored in the Ray, and I managed to find my way to one of them, silhouetted against the lights of the shore. Clambering aboard, I secured the dinghy aft, then groped my way into the accommodation forward. After some time groping about, I found an oil lamp and matches, then an anchor lamp, which I lit and hoisted in the hope my friends would realise where I was. They had no idea what had happened to me, nor did I know the fate of my own boat and crew. Below, I found a bunk with a rough horsehair mattress and laid down for an uneasy rest. Later I went on deck - it was almost high water now, and was relieved to see a nearby riding light, and straining my eyes into the dark could just make out the shape of "CAMPION" riding peacefully at anchor. Returning to the horsehair mattress, I slept better, and when the first daylight began creeping in through the partially open hatch (there was no other opening to let in air or light) I went on deck, to meet the fishermen returning to their bawley using the last of the night's tide to row out from Old Leigh. I explained my situation, and gave them five shillings (25 pence) to cover costs of lamp oil and a lamp glass I had cracked on the cabin oil lamp. They were well satisfied, and I jumped in the dinghy to return aboard "CAMPION" where we were all pleased to be reunited, and over a hearty breakfast (probably sausages full of bread and scrambled egg made from dried egg powder) they accused their captain of abandoning ship in a hurry at the first sign of trouble! They had dropped the bower anchor over, and after she floated off on the rapidly rising tide, set the stays'l to move a few hundred yards into deep water. On the midday tide we sailed in to pick up our mooring off Chalkwell station, neither boat nor crew any worse for the experience. The real lesson was that those red panels in the street lamps were leading marks into the Ray when they were first erected in Victorian times, but since then there have been many movements of the sands. It might have been better for us if the "Coliseum's" red neon lights had totally preventing us seeing the transit.

The remaining Spring and early summer saw the boat used for a lot of weekend voyages to places like Harty Ferry, Whitstable and Hole Haven - the latter before it became dominated by oil refineries (now nearly all disused).

The summer of 1948 was boisterous, and I did not start down-channel until too late in the season, by which time the Westerlies have usually set in (another lesson I learnt the hard way!). Early August saw us get as far as Ramsgate, with my old schoolfriend Peter, who was now reading medicine. Rising winds and a gale warning meant we would go no further, and I was glad to leave her tucked away in the shelter of the inner harbour. The following weekend, with a crew of four, which included an Australian cousin, Harold Reader, we ran through the open lock gates under stays'l early in the morning, with a brisk Northwest wind behind us. Sadly, this fine wind soon petered out, and we made slow progress after passing Dover; the combination of a rapidly falling barometer and a Southwesterly right in our teeth

1948 was a boisterous season - more often reefed down than not - "Campion" leaving the East Swale. Photo by H S Newcombe FRPS.

meant we sought the shelter of Rye harbour - a rather lonely and windswept place. The boat was moved up to Rye town, as there was no prospect of going any further that weekend. In those days, after Ramsgate, there were few ports of call for a yacht before reaching the shelter of the Solent - Dover (which now welcomes yachts) did not really want them, Rye is tidal, Newhaven a cross channel port with little provision for yachts and a horrible entrance. Shoreham and Littlehampton have poor entrances, positively dangerous in onshore winds.

In recent years, the advent of Brighton marina, then Sovereign harbour at Pevensey have transformed the prospects for a yacht voyaging Westwards. Now, there is also limited provision for yachts in what used to be known as the "Sleepers hole" at Newhaven, but I have never used it. Rye seemed to be a sticking point, and the wind blew fresh from Southwest for several days. The only boat that left harbour during that time was later towed in by the Dungeness lifeboat. A rising barometer and wind veering to West eventually encouraged us out with only two of us aboard - my old schoolfriend Peter was once again on board, we hoped that we would get away at last from this low lying windswept corner of England.

Clearing from Rye in the afternoon, with one reef in the mains'l, we started a fairly hard slog to windward, with spray lashing across the boat as she breasted the Channel seas. Another welcome change in the coastal scenery came as Fairlight cliff came into view, looking very attractive in the afternoon sunshine; an easing of the wind had caused us to shake out our reef, but at Fairlight it freshened again and we struggled to put the reef back - it was wet and tiring work. As evening approached, I decided we needed a rest and a meal; we would make little progress against a foul tide round Beachy Head so I stood into Pevensey Bay where there was some shelter from the Westerly wind, and close inshore put about onto the offshore tack and hove to. It has always amazed me the transformation between bashing into the seas, and the peace which descends upon a boat when she is hove to, making little progress, quietly dipping up and down in the waves. At dusk, we rigged the navigation lights, and at the stern, set the all round anchor light, suitably screened to show the requisite arc of light astern. Below, a hot meal was prepared, and every now and then we stuck a head out of the hatch to see that all was well. Very slowly, "CAMPION" was drifting away from the shore, but a long way from any shipping route or danger.

Suddenly, out of the dark, came a hail. It was from "SLOR", a classic 8-metre out of Burnham which had left Rye shortly before us. Although this was a racing boat capable of making circles round "CAMPION", the steep Channel seas slowed her down considerably, whereas "CAMPION'S" heavy displacement kept her momentum through the seas. They were going to carry on round Beachy head as a boat like this would not heave to satisfactorily - she was like a thoroughbred racehorse, and built to go, not stand still as we were doing. During our period of rest, the wind eased, and veered to the Northwest, so soon after two in the morning, we were off again with smooth seas and a fair, gentle, wind We never saw our 8-metre friends again; the conditions had become ideal for her and no doubt she was galloping down Channel. The first of the morning sun showed Eastbourne, snuggled in low land to the East of Beachy Head, and then came the magnificent sight of Beachy Head abeam to the North of us, the early morning sun lighting the folds of the chalk cliffs. It seemed a milestone to us - now quite definitely we were off the South Coast of England, with a wind that had veered to Easterly and was pushing us steadily on our way West.

The coast then recedes from the mariner and becomes lower, with Brighton, Worthing and Littlehampton all set in a wide bay on relatively low land. Our next main headland was St Catherine's Point on the Southern end of the Isle of Wight. We were now passing through the "Z" area I had known so well as a meeting area of the mineswept channels during the War. Whatever man may draw upon his charts, one bit of sea looks very much like another without any identifying mark; there was no longer even a buoy to mark the centre of the circle the Admiralty had placed on war-time charts. It was dark before we had St Catherine's Light abeam, and we altered course to head us into Bournemouth Bay. The wind freshened and we were roaring along towards Poole, our immediate destination. Suddenly it became vital to know our distance run and fortunately a good fix at midnight showed us on course and close to our estimated position by dead reckoning. We were heading towards Poole entrance and just beyond the channel lies a nasty man-made line of rocks known as the training bank, designed to keep the channel scoured. Straining our eyes into the darkness ahead, we spotted the welcome light of the Poole Hook Sand Buoy with considerable relief. Just after one in the morning, "CAMPION" rounded the Hook buoy and as we hardened in sheets to reach up the entrance channel, the noise of breaking seas on the sand and training bank served as a sinister warning as to what could have happened had we missed that buoy.

The rest of the night was spent at anchor in Brownsea Road, and the following morning we made our way to Poole Quay, where we berthed almost opposite Bolson's yard where LCT 879 was refitted three years earlier. That same evening we were off again, Michael Beaumont having rejoined us. A flat calm prevailed and we motored into Studland Bay to anchor for the night. There was still no wind and we motored round into Swanage Bay, a little further West, but there was no question of using the engine for long; petrol was precious, rationed, and petrol engines are prodigious users of fuel. Another 24 hours, and we still were able to take bearings from lighthouses on the English coast. The barometer was dropping ominously, so wind was coming. Over 24 hours later, after tacking in light but improving winds, the light of Les Hanois, the Westernmost point of Guernsey was sighted, and we felt that at last we were getting there. By this time, the wind was up to force 6, but North West and we were able to lay the course without tacking; the seas were confused and made hard work of steering as we gradually bore away round the Southern coast of Guernsey. After anchoring at St Peter Port just clear of the cross-channel steamer track into their berth, we sat down to a hearty and (we thought!) well deserved lunch.

The rest of our stay in Guernsey was spent in a drying berth alongside the quay in the old harbour; where, fortunately, we found a berth beside a ladder because the rise and fall of tide is enormous compared with our home waters; very long berthing ropes had to be used, adjusted to come tight just before she took the ground, and with some heavy weight along her starboard side deck to ensure she listed against the wall. At low tide she looked like a pimple at the bottom of the wall. Bad weather and adverse forecasts kept us there for another 4 days, during which time Michael ran out of holiday and had to return on the "ST PATRICK" to Weymouth. The year 1948 was still close enough to the War to see people who had escaped the German occupation returning to their homes, and others who were trapped on the Island leaving to visit friends and relations in the UK. The "ST PATRICK" , a handsome ship built just after the war, was maintaining the service with the St Helier, built pre war for the Weymouth - Channel Islands route. There were moving scenes as families and old friends were re-united, and the arrivals and departures of these ships were almost like those of big liners serving distant shores.

Finally, after favourable weather forecasts, we left St Peter Port on the tide, just before mid-day, and with a spanking wind just North of West stormed up the Little Russel channel on the East, and sheltered side of the Island. Coming clear of the Island's shelter, the seas became confused and lumpy; a strong West going tidal stream actually countered any leeway, and forced us up to windward; rough it may have been, but it was an exciting sail. The same wind brought us late that evening to the English coast, where off Anvil Point we lost the wind and spent long hours working our way into Swanage bay, where we anchored wearily, there now being only two of us aboard. Later in the morning, the wind set in again from the Southwest and we were able to complete our voyage back to Poole Quay, where Customs cleared us before we battened down and left her in a trot of rafted up boats.

Within a few days, I was back again, prepared for a single handed voyage up-Channel. For a single handed passage under sail, I prepared some sandwiches and slipped from Poole quay under power, hoisting sail off Sandbanks, still within the shelter of Poole harbour. That evening, after an uneventual passage outside the Isle of Wight, I sailed close up to the East side for shelter from a strengthening West wind and anchored close inshore off Bembridge. It was soon dark - the evenings were drawing in rapidly, and after ensuring the big fisherman anchor was holding, went below to cook supper in the soft glow of the oil lamps - this boat had no electricity of any kind; cooking and lighting were by paraffin, and the engine was started by hand.

During the night, the barometer had started to fall ominously, and the wind had backed to South-southwest, force 5. Once again, I prepared sandwiches before getting underweigh; before mid-day, we were storming along into the Looe channel South of Selsey Bill. Clear of the shelter of the Island, the wind strength had inreased to force 6, and I reduced sail the easy way by dropping the stays'l and tricing up the tack of the mains'l - an old smacksmen's dodge. The grey clouds got lower and thicker and I lost sight of the coast line in heavy rain. The barometer was now falling rapidly, and although not keen on the place, it had to be Newhaven that night - it was Sunday, and I really had to catch a train to get back to work. By half past four I was off the entrance; the rain eased but the wind continued freshening. I rounded up and lowered the mains'l, but as the steadying influence of the sail was lost, the motion became very violent. I took in the jib and hoisted the stays'l - a much easier sail to set or lower in a hurry. As I turned towards the entrance, out of the murk ahead came a cross-channel steamer, the "S.S. WORTHING", wallowing and rolling heavily in the turbulent seas. As "CAMPION" entered the outer harbour, some shelter was obtained, but even with only the stays'l set, she was going very fast. Although not too familiar with Newhaven, one thing very much on my mind was the fixed bridge across the top end of the harbour, and the need for some powerful brakes before reaching it. I cleared the anchor ready to let go, rigged two of my heavy coir fenders and dropped the stays'l - even with bare poles we were still charging for the narrow part of the harbour. From the pierhead a harbour official shouted "berth number, 7". I was already near it, with a trot of boats rafted up alongside. The anchor went down with a run, I raced aft and put the helm hard over, raced foward again just in time to snub the anchor chain as our bows drew near level with the bows of the boats in the trot. The effect was spectacular, as the anchor bit and the chain tightened - the bows dipped like an American limousine braking hard and she started to catapult round. The occupant of the outside boat, seeing what was happening, also put a fender out just before "CAMPION" arrived fairly heavily alongside, and the blow was well cushioned. Temporary lines were rigged, and I took breath before the next stage of getting lines to the shore. A harbour official warned us that a severe gale was expected, imminent. The owner of the pretty, traditional boat inside me worked hard to help secure the ropes; the top of the jetty was only reached by climbing a steep ladder so I don't know what I would have done without his help; during all this, the rain started sheeting down. Then I had to go ashore and find the local boatyard manager's house to arrange attendance on the boat for the week; it was a harbour rule that boats could not be left unattended.

When I returned aboard, I lit the stove - everything was cold and damp, including me. I invited the owner of the boat alongside, who had been so helpful, to come and share the heat of my stove, and to eat our suppers together. Thus it was I had the pleasure of meeting Quintin Riley, a truly remarkable man. He was on a delivery trip with this newly acquired boat, which he was taking to Tollesbury, and would be continuing the voyage when further crew arrived, early in the week. We realised that we were both soaked to the skin from our exertions in the driving rain, and I rigged lines over the stove to dry our clothes. From having never met before, we both ate our supper totally starkers. It was some years before I met him again; he was a devout Christian, doing much for the Church in Essex, and he loved to recall our first meeting - particularly to the Bishop! Quintin had been meteorologist to the 1930-1931 Greenland icecap expedition, surveying possible landing sites for a proposed air route to America, which in those days would have required several short stages. This expedition also included Augustine Courtauld, who was imprisoned alone in an ice shelter for several months, during which he dreamed and schemed for his ideal boat. As a result, he acquired the yawl "DUET", which is still owned by his son, Christopher, and lent to youth organisations. Sadly, Quintin died some years later as a result of a car crash when he was on his way to join his family on Christmas day, having conscientiously carried out his duties as churchwarden.

Early the following morning, when I said goodbye to him and left for the station, the wind had veered to the Northwest, still very fresh, but the sun was shining and puffy white clouds chased across the morning sky. The following Friday night, by then September the 17th, I rejoined her, with a crew of two - Ron Hunt and Michael Heaton, with a return to our home shore in one go as the objective. The wind was still Northwest the following morning; the engine would not start - I think the damp had got into its bones, so we left the berth under sail; gathering speed down the harbour before a following wind, a wire rose dripping out of the water right across the harbour as they prepared to warp the "LONDRES" round facing seawards, ready for her next voyage. There was no stopping now, and hardly room in the narrow harbour to round up; fortunately somebody saw us, so the wire was temporarily slackened beneath the surface again. We waved our thanks and sped on our way. The rest of the trip, passing through the Dover Straits in the darkness of the small hours, was uneventful, and we picked up our mooring off Chalkwell just after midnight on Sunday night.

The boat was used a lot that autumn before she was laid up for the winter in Johnson & Jago's yard. When cousin Harold Reader, who had been with me on one leg of the trip down Channel returned to Australia aboard RMS "ORCADES", as the great ship majestically came downriver in the darkness, I called her up using an Aldis lamp connected to the battery of my Austin car, and sent him a "Bon Voyage" message. It was all rather exciting to see the brilliant signal lamp beams stabbing the darkness of the two or so miles between us. The message was promptly acknowledged and delivered to him from the ship's radio room.

A RETURN TO THE CHANNEL ISLANDS

D URING that autumn, my sister Lorna had not been well, and the doctor said she ought to go away for a few days in a milder climate, so it was decided I would take her to Jersey for a few days, shortly before Christmas. The Paddington boat train ran slowly right through the dimly lit back streets of Weymouth, glistening from recent rain, right on to the quay, where we joined the "ST HELIER", which I had seen during the Normandy landings as an infantry assault ship. carrying assault landing craft in heavy davits added for the purpose; what this did to her stability I'm not sure. For the night crossing, we had a first class cabin each, and soon turned in after we had watched her leave port. Once clear of the land, we started making fairly heavy weather of it, and I slept uneasily. Eventually, I got up just to see how Lorna was faring, the answer being not at all well. The motion of a small boat in the choppy waters of the Thames Estuary, to which she was accustomed, is very different from the heave and roll of a larger ship in the seas of the Western English Channel, and she was very seasick. A short time after I returned to my bunk, a heavy steel door started crashing with the roll of the ship. There were not many passengers aboard, and I suspect most of them were not feeling too good, so I set off in search of an unfastened door - it was slightly eerie, as there was not a soul about. The culprit was a steel door into the engine room; I looked into the well lit engine room where the steam turbines were humming smoothly, but there was not a sign of human life. After checking it could be opened from inside, I clipped the door securely to, hoping it would not come adrift again; I don't think there could have been anyone down there, as the slamming of the door would have driven them mad.

Early that morning I dressed and went up to the dining saloon on the upper deck, just as we were approaching St Peter Port. Lorna, sadly, and I suspect like most of the other passengers, was not interested in any breakfast, although we were now steaming through more sheltered water. The officers invited me to join them at their table, the only one in use that morning. Some had to leave the table ready for departure from Guernsey, but I had some interesting conversations with them on matters maritime. We left the berth at St Peter Port stern first, at quite a speed, and then made a turn to the South heading for the South West corner of Jersey. As we turned, a combination of wind and an awkward swell made us heel a long way, and although the table was provided with good deep fiddles, there was still quite a lot had to be restrained from causing spillages and other minor disasters. At one point, I seemed to be looking out of the window straight down at the surface of the sea, but she soon recovered and became more stable as we picked up speed for St Helier.

The contrast between the Channel Islands and the UK mainland was an eye- opener - back in the UK, just over 3 years since the end of hostilities, we were enduring a depressing shortage of food and a mass of infuriating restrictions that seemed worse than at the height of the War. Here, where they had been under German occupation throughout , there were plentiful supplies of interesting things in the shops, which had lighted window displays after dark, whereas at home such extravagances were forbidden. This different atmosphere in itself was something of a relaxation, and I hope my sister benefited in spite of the misery of the crossing. Our return a few days later was again in the "St Helier" - I enjoyed being on this handsome small ship again, this time for a daylight crossing to Weymouth in much better weather.

As a family, we decided that Christmas would be spent in one of the local hotels, and after finding the best one was already fully booked, fell back on the second best. Clouds and disappointments nearly always have their silver lining; and another family that had to evacuate from Leigh during the War decided they would like to spend Christmas back in their former hometown. They too were disappointed at not getting into the best hotel, and opted for the second best. So, once again disappointment at not getting the best turned into good fortune, for this is how I came to meet my future wife, and events seemed to move quite swiftly (for those more decorous times) from then on. The two families from pre-war Leigh were delighted to find they were both in the same hotel; the second best quickly became the best for us; its former staid gentility somewhat disrupted by some of our antics. Whilst we did not know each other well pre-war, the two families certainly knew of each other, and as my mediocre performance at school stumbled along, I was frequently told of this girl, Beryl Myatt, who had done so well in every exam and gained a scholarship to Cambridge. I certainly did not enjoy the obvious comparisons being laid before me by my parents. After graduating in engineering, Beryl went in to Hawker Aircraft's design and test department, working on Hurricanes, Typhoons and Tempests. When we met at Christmas she was by then working for the newly formed British European Airways - a very rare type, for as well as her knowledge and skills as an aeronautical engineer, she was warm, feminine, and great fun. She was of course, introduced to the boat, now hauled out in Johnson & Jago's yard. We became engaged in July 1949 and were married in October, but much was to happen during that time.

At Easter, the customary pilgrimage to Woodbridge took place, and proved an easy trip compared with the struggle of the previous year. During the winter a proper bridge deck had been built over the engine, reducing the size of the cockpit and providing the engine with a dry compartment; the engine became far more reliable from then on, although still quite a procedure to start - remove cabin steps to expose the starting handle and " tickle" the carburettor (to prime it with petrol for starting - once running it looked after itself). Leaving Leigh on the Thursday evening, with Michael Beaumont, we sailed through the night in light winds that at times kept us little more than stemming the tide when it turned against us, but by 9 in the morning of Good Friday we were anchored off the Deben entrance awaiting enough water to cross the bar. The sun was gaining strength and burning off a pearly mist which shrouded the Bawdsey cliffs and by the time we entered the river, a beautiful Spring day was developing; the flood tide, together with a pleasant favourable wind swept us effortlessly past the green rural landscape to Woodbridge town. Whilst going upriver, I met George Jones for the first time; from some converted stabling at the back of his mother's Georgian house overlooking the river at Waldringfield, he was running a brokerage business, the "East Coast Yacht Agency".

Our hearts were light and full of the joys of Spring, for that afternoon Beryl arrived; there were still some main line trains from Liverpool Street calling at Woodbridge That evening we went ashore for dinner at "The Crown", where Beryl was staying over Easter. The following day, Michael's fiancee Daphne joined to make a foursome and during the day we made explorations on the river to the "Rocks", a particularly beautiful anchorage overlooked by a low wooded cliff above a sandy beach. It has subsequently become very popular and crowded with boats at weekends, but in those early post war years it was quiet and deserted. Our weekend included a visit to the "Maybush" at Waldringfield, where we photographed each other under the pub sign.

On the Bank holiday Monday, we anchored "CAMPION" at Woodbridge, outside the fairway, where she would take the ground at low water, and every one made their own way home by train. "CAMPION" was sailed home to Leigh the following weekend.

Easter 1949 on the Deben - two courting couples afloat - Beryl joined us coming to Woodbridge by train (there were still some main line trains going through from Liverpool Street), and Michael's fiancee Dahpne joined us. Photo by Michael Beaumont.

A CLOSE CALL

THERE followed a number of sailing weekends, and on one we could not reach our mooring on the Sunday night, so left her at anchor in the Ray. One weekday evening Michael and I borrowed a sailing dinghy from a cousin so that we could sail out to her, rather than row the long distance from the shore. It was blowing quite freshly, and we started to ship quite a lot of spray so that the boat became heavy. Being unfamilar with the boat, we could not see how to lift the floor boards to bail, and as they had been raised higher in the interests of dry feet, it meant there was a lot of water in the boat. Another point we should have checked was the mainsheet, which had no stopper knot on the end, so when it was inadvertently let go, we could not retrieve it, and the boat drifted uncontrollably. Suddenly, as we endeavoured to retrieve it, she went right over and we were in the water. At first the boat sank, although in fact she did come up again later; there were no buoyancy tanks and we then started swimming towards "Campion", not all that far away to windward. We had broken a golden rule for dinghy sailors, which is always to stay with the boat. Swimming into the waves was hard work, and we were both swallowing a lot of water, so we turned and swam with the waves towards the distant Chalkwell shore. It was a low neap tide, and we were now over the mud flats off shore; for a short while we both were able to just touch bottom, but the tide was still rising and an inch or so made all the difference. I had already discarded a heavy jacket containing my wallet; in situations like this priorities are drastically changed and money, boats and all material posessions cease to have any importance compared with survival. Michael, being taller, was still able to touch bottom with a toe. As far as I was concerned, exhaustion had set in and I would slip away quietly. The will to live was going, and I was giving up.

Suddenly I realised that a launch was alongside me, and arms reached under me to haul me into the boat. It was the Essex Yacht Club launch, and there can be no doubt that it only arrived just in time as far as I was concerned; how much longer Michael would have survived luckily was not put to the test. After the water had been drained out of me, I soon recovered enough to express my gratitude to our rescuers who told us that several people ashore had seen our plight and alerted the emergency services, also someone had shown great initiative and informed the Yacht Club, whose launch reached the scene before the lifeboat, which had been launched. The lifeboat recovered the dinghy, which needed a few minor repairs but otherwise had withstood the ordeal well. Happily, I don't think my mother ever knew quite how desperate the situation had been.

More sailing trips followed this episode, now interspersed with trips to see Beryl at Iver Heath. Another voyage was made to Whitstable - I rather like the place, it had a lot of character, and there were still cargoes being handled there. The berth we made fast to was one we had used before with other boats, but the locals assured us that at low water we would break our back - it seems the war between Leigh and Whitstable was still on. The mud in the harbour is about the consistency of a good thick sauce, and cradles the boat level and gently. The wind came up quite fresh from a Northerly quarter while we were there, and on the next tide a laden barge was heading for the harbour under sail; as the barge drew nearer, the mains'l was brailed up, the stays'l dropped and the only sail still driving her was the tops'l. This came down as she approached the pierheads at the habour entrance, and we began to wonder how this ponderous mass, still moving quite fast through the water was going to stop. At this point, a man sculled a skiff effortlessy out from the quay to meet the barge and took a rope from her starboard bow to a bollard on the corner where the harbour turns a right angle. With the assurance that comes of experience, the hand up forward surged the rope and then gradually let it take the strain. At the same time, the skipper spun the wheel hard over to starboard and the barge swung round neatly alongside the quay under the grain silo. It was a remarkable exhibition of seamanship skills.

TO HOLLAND - AND BACK FOR MARRIAGE

(Parts of this chapter were published in "Yachting Monthly, February 1953 issue)

I N July, Beryl and I became engaged; we were both 25 and although she was of age, I still felt it my duty to inform her parents of our intentions. I was shy and somewhat embarassed (although it was actually the second time I had done this!), and Beryl's father who had a colourful flow of language acquired in a German prisoner of war camp in the First World War, was a very sensitive man and put me at my ease with the following well chosen words - "Thank God she's off our hands at last, and if she's anything like her mother, Heaven help you". In print this looks pretty harsh, but the twinkle in his eye and the way it was said put us all at ease, and within no time a bottle of bubbly was produced.

However, a major voyage had been planned for that summer, and this was to go ahead. A crossing to Holland was planned, and because the Southern North Sea was still littered with a lot of dangerous uncleared wartime wrecks, we would cross from Lowestoft to Ijmuiden, where the sea is deeper and there were fewer wrecks. Our start from Leigh on Friday night was marred by fouling the propellor with the mooring buoy rope; "CAMPION'S" propeller shaft emerged from the hull through a shaft log on the port quarter, which meant manoeuvring under power could be difficult, and turning short round easy one way and almost impossible the other; it is not a happy arrangement. After losing an hour while this was cleared, we then started an incredibly tedious voyage in light or non-existent winds. Three times we anchored when the tide turned foul, the last time off Bawdsey cliff by the Deben entrance. Our weekend was running out, but a wind finally came in from a Southeasterly direction, and with all sail including our big fairweather jib, secondhand, formerly part of the wardrobe of an 8-metre) we finally started sailing well. The weather was good, and with great satisfaction watched the coast go by, the water surging round her bows. Orfordness was abeam by one o'clock in the afternoon, then Aldeburgh and Southwold bathed in after-noon sunshine. It is an interesting coast, with low tender cliffs offering their faces to the ever advancing North Sea. At last we felt that Lowestoft was in the bag, and at half past five the engine was started and sails lowered to enter the harbour.

Once in, Mr Stiple, the Royal Norfolk & Suffolk Yacht Club boatman welcomed us and helped us moor up in the yacht basin - mooring was to a buoy forward and iron rings in the wall aft. Our welcome in Lowestoft gave us a very good opinion of the club, and visits many years later continue to confirm this. Having stowed our gear, we were taken ashore by the boatman and set off from Lowestoft Station at about seven in the evening - a remarkable achievement, bearing in mind the frustration of the earlier part of our voyage. A note made at the time records that our journey home to Southend Victoria Station almost equalled the sea voyage in tediousness, and we were still some distance from our homes even when we alighted from the train. No longer were there clanging trams at Southend's Victoria Circus, so I suppose we caught a bus to Leigh.

A week later, I travelled down by train on a sunlit summer Friday evening; there was a restaurant car in which I was able to have dinner while the train sped through

Traditional steam drifter leaving Lowestoft into the North Sea mist in 1949. Within a few years there were none left.

woods of birch, ash, and oak at Shenfield (making the same journey a few years later these woods had all turned into rows of neat suburban housing). It was after nine in the evening before I arrived at Lowestoft, but there was still someone on duty to take me out to the boat; in July the evenings were still light until late; the train journey had taken me through much beautiful East Anglian scenery, enhanced by the lengthening evening shadows.

The next day was spent in getting stores aboard, including 12 gallons of fresh water (The tank held about 15). In those days, water and fuel came aboard in cans - there were two heavy galvanised two gallon water cans to be ferried out, and two two gallon petrol cans, one embossed "Shell" and the other "BP". The engine had been running on "Pool" petrol, which it did not like, but I believe it was about this time some branded petrol began to appear, and the one which seemed best for us was "National Benzole" - what has happened to it - pre War it was widely advertised using a winged Mercury symbol. One of their best advertisements showed a surprised attractive girl in an open sports car looking over her shoulder at the symbol - "Oh Mr Mercury, you did give me a start!". It certainly made starting our formerly reluctant engine even easier. I also advised Customs of our intended departure on Sunday; in those days there was strict customs control over the limited number of yachts going "foreign".

During the misty late afternoon, I saw a traditional steam drifter leave the harbour and took a photograph because I thought her an attractive working ship; like so many things I have accepted as commonplace at the time, I was watching a fading piece of our maritime history, for they were all gone within a few years, and it was as if she was sailing out of the harbour mouth into oblivion. That evening, the crew for the trip arrived -once again, Michael Beaumont and Peter van den Brul (who had relations in Holland, running clothing stores in Holland).

So, the next day, Sunday, we prepared for sea, Customs came aboard, cleared us and gave us certificates for cameras and binoculars - necessary in those days to avoid the risk of their being suspected as imports on your return. When we left harbour mid-morning, the previous day's mist was still limiting visibility, so, making reasonable progress in a light Southerly wind, the coast was soon lost to view and we were in a world of our own. During the night, the wind became light and fickle, but the mist cleared. During the early morning, the wind improved and veered to Southwest, so that we were able to free the sheets and she started to romp along. The fair strong wind brought us to Ijmuiden in the early afternoon, and dropping sails in the outer harbour, our now more reliable engine was started to take us through the sea lock into the North Sea canal. That evening we were secured at Amsterdam in a yacht basin known as the "Sixhaven", now no longer in use - there is nowadays another larger harbour known as the "Sixhaven". This one was very attractive and immaculately kept; in a berth near us was the Dutch Royal Yacht, "PIET HEIN". Close by, a small ferry, the "HEEN & VEER" ran across continuously to the Central Station. The following days can best be described as "Lotus eating". Peter's uncle took us about in his Rover car, on one day to the "Seignpost" restaurant at Scheveningen. After the frugalities and restrictions still encountered in England, our eyes were opened wide, and we chose from a large menu, sitting at a table with a wonderful view of the sea and harbour. Michael ordered a Dover sole, and when it came, the fish hung over the edges of the large plate. "I ordered a sole, but this looks like a whale". Everything we ate was superbly cooked and of gargantuan proportions.

Beryl arrived at Amsterdam on the Friday after our arrival, and I met her at Amsterdam Central station. It is an International station, and she had flown BEA with a discounted staff fare to Brussels (the flights to Amsterdam were fully booked) and the train from Brussels arrived, drawn by an immaculate shining steam locomotive of elderly appearance, still bearing the maker's highly polished brass plate "Beyer & Peacock, Manchester". Beryl stayed at the Victoria Hotel, conveniently close to the station and yacht harbour - in those days it was Amsterdam's best. Superseded by new modern hotels in later years, it went into decline before being upgraded again. It is in a good position, and has a character that many of the more modern hotels lack.

On the Saturday, Michael had to return to the UK, using the night boat from the Hook to Harwich, and Beryl entertained us to dinner at the Victoria. Although things seemed very plentiful in Holland, this particular day, Saturday the 23rd July was deemed by the Dutch authorities a meatless day. The beautifully illustrated menu, over 19" long contained, apart from a vast selection of Hors d'oeuvres, and a variety of fish dishes, had 5 different chicken dishes and two of duck - it seems poultry did not count. We still have that menu.

Apart from one or two day sails into the Isselmeer to the isle of Pampus and other parts long since filled in, time was spent in the shops, where Beryl was spellbound with the great variety of merchandise available. Unfortunately, department stores do not agree with me and I can be known to go a very strange colour, at which point I have to be released into fresh air. However, quite a few items for our new home were purchased before she returned home.

Our trip back home was arduous - strong Westerly winds blew for days on end; after one attempt to get home, we ran back into Ijmuiden after an exhausting night at sea. Our crew was now Peter, who as a medical student got reasonably long holidays, and a Dutchman who wanted a trip across the North Sea. With a rising barometer and moderating winds, plus the fact that our Dutch currency was running low, we eventually sailed against a wind that was still West, but soon veered to the Northwest which enabled us to set a reasonable course home. When it went into the Southeast with a falling barometer, it was obvious another blow was on its way, and I made all possible speed towards the English coast, but by the time we picked up the lights of the Kentish Knock and Galloper lightvessels simultaneously, the wind was veering round to the Southwest and we could no longer hold the course. Soon after midnight the wind flew into the West and went up to at least force 7. By changing tacks every half hour, we did little better than hold our position; the seas were now mountainous and wave tops swept over the decks. At first light I decided to head for Ramsgate as we could just about lay a course, and perhaps the wind would veer, but even so we had to put in a tack to keep us on track. On the 8 am news, there were reports of vessels in distress including a yacht on the Barrow sands, but the wind had eased to about force 6 and we were making quite good progress; the sight of the chalk cliffs of the North Foreland coming up brilliant white on the horizon was encouraging; the cloud that had covered the skies for several days cleared and visibility was good. It was already well into August, and I was desperate to get home - the wedding date by then had been fixed for October. Finally, early that afternoon we entered Ramsgate harbour, but by the time we had cleared customs, battened down, and arranged with a boatman to move her into a safer berth, it was going to be late before we got home. But there was a short cut - it was still the excursion ship season, and I knew the MV "ROYAL DAFFODIL" would soon be calling at Margate en route for Southend. Piling into a taxi, we raced along the coast road with the ship already in sight, and we just made it in time to buy tickets and climb aboard, somewhat out of breath. Less than two hours later we were stepping ashore at Southend pier and only a bus ride from home. I shudder to think what the journey time would have been by rail. The following weekend, I sailed her home from Ramsgate singlehanded in a mixture of light Southerly winds and frustrating calms; in September she was laid up in a mudberth at Johnson & Jago's yard, and I prepared to concentrate on other matters.

MARRIAGE - AND
LA LUNE DE MIEL GASTRONOMIQUE

PRIORITIES, like looking for somewhere to set up home took over, and because my mother was still living in Leigh, and Beryl's parents had decided to come back there from their War time home at Iver Heath, we would set up home near them. A pleasant little house built in the 1920's on land that once had formed part of the Chalkwell Hall estate was decided upon. Not far from the shore and Chalkwell Station, it had a wide view of the Estuary from the upstairs windows, and looked down a road leading to the seafront - we named it "Prospect House", as Beryl's mother's family owned a Regency style house of that name, once owned by Dr Deeping, father of the author, Warwick Deeping. It vanished as part of a modernisation scheme, in spite of efforts to save it. Buying furnishings was not easy - this was the age of "Utility", but to be fair, the furniture was robustly made, although some of the styles were pretty awful - a matter of taste, I suppose. Our resources were certainly not unlimited, but Beryl had inherited some good antique furniture from her grandmother which was a great help. During this time, I was advised that my name had come up for a new car - in those days of shortages, you put your name on a waiting list and forgot it; as a result £500 put aside for setting up home had to go towards the new car, a very advanced design for its day, the new Austin A40. The ageing Austin 10 was traded in just after a last visit to Iver Heath, where the car was garaged in an old barn. Imagine the surprise when the dealer in the smart showroom was showing it to the prospective buyer, and a rat jumped from the top of the petrol tank at the end of what must have been a surprise journey from the barn at Iver Heath. However, I gather the chap was so anxious to buy the car that he was not put off by such minor inconveniences as rats on the petrol tank.

By this time, it was clear that Beryl's father was far from well, and lung cancer was diagnosed. I could see the same fate as my father's awaiting him; both were smokers, although I don't think Beryl's father was as heavy a smoker, but the one thing both had done was to spend most of their working life in London. People talk today of air pollution, but compared with the atmosphere in London today, it was awful. Chimneys belched coal smoke from industrial and domestic grates, plus hundreds of steam locomotives converging on the place with their sooty moisture laden smoke. In winter particularly, during a period of anti-cyclonic calm, fogs of long forgotten thickness and foul colour shrouded the capital and suburbs for days on end. I remain convinced to this day that this atmospheric pollution on a grand scale had a great effect on the health of those who worked in it.

Consequently, a "Quiet wedding" was arranged, with the service at St Saviour's church in Westcliff, where my parents had been married, and a modest reception arranged, this time at the "best" hotel. For our honeymoon, we flew to Paris on BEA staff discounted fares, booked before Beryl officially gave up her job with the airline. It was the first time I had flown on anything more than a very local flight in an ageing DH "Rapide" biplane, and the advanced aircraft we were flown in was a Vickers "Viking". One can still be seen in the museum at Brooklands - it looks so small compared with even the short haul aircraft used today, but this was the first major advance from the ubiquitous "Dakotas" used for passenger transport during and after the War. It was quite a turbulent flight, and out of the window I could see the the wings flexing - "don't worry," Beryl reassured me, "they are designed to do that", and I thought of the nautical saying of wooden spars and the like - "If it bends, it bears, if it doesn't, it breaks" .

Paris was a cultural and gastronomic spree - Beryl was a subscriber to *"Vogue"*, who had just produced an informative gastronomic guide to the city, with recommended restaurants graded by national specialities, price and style. We navigated our way round Paris with this superb guide, and were adventurous with the dishes we chose. At one place, we ordered snails and the waiter produced some strange utensils - we hadn't a clue, and he had to demonstrate how to use them. Remember, this was long before the days of mass travel, and in those days most people didn't agree with "foreign messed up food". We loved it and were ready to experiment.

For our last night, we had planned to go to Maxim's, but it was quite obvious the money was not going to stretch to such an extravagance. It was important in all our doings to keep sufficient money to settle the hotel bill; strict exchange control regulations limited the currency you could take abroad and this was long before the days of credit cards and similar means of spending money wherever you wished. Fortunately, a pound sterling went a long way in the Paris of 1949. We opted for a small Spanish restaurant in Montmartre which was probably far more fun. A brilliant guitarist played a piece imitating peals of bells, swinging the guitar right over his head - all this for a modest priced meal, and to cap it all we won a bottle of champagne in a draw that was probably rigged in our favour since we were naively obvious as a honeymoon couple. The contents of the bottle were shared out in an atmosphere of international conviviality, a good note on which to end our stay and fly back the next day to Northolt, which was BEA's base at that time, before the development of Heathrow as the main airport.

So much did we take to snails that we decided to have some at Christmas, and these were ordered from Harrod's, with whom Beryl had an account. A day or so before Christmas, a telegram arrived from Harrod's advising "24 snails arriving passenger train Chalkwell Station - please meet". Some one had a sense of humour; needless to say the snails were in a tin, within the kind of package that might be expected from Harrods, and which also contained the shells in which they would be cooked - even the garlic butter was included. An early example of the ready prepared meal now in every supermarket? By the time Christmas came, Beryl's father was failing in health and it was the last family gathering where we enjoyed his robust company; by February he was gone.

SAILING AGAIN - TOGETHER,
AND A RETURN TO FRANCE.

ONCE again, Woodbridge was our Easter 1950 destination, and I suppose by now there was already a sentimental attachment to the Deben and Woodbridge in particular. We set off for another night trip out of the Estuary, with Michael Beaumont aboard again. Fortunately it was a calm trip, Beryl's first, with winds that enabled us to lay the course practically all the way, and the following morning we anchored off the Deben Entrance awaiting the flood tide to take us in. The early Spring sunshine lit the Bawdsey Cliff and the countryside within beckoned us. It had also been very cold early in the morning, and we had lit the coal stove which was still alight when we had breakfast - early Spring mornings can be very beautiful, but also chill until the sun gains strength.

We anchored in a hole close to Everson's jetty, where "CAMPION" just lay afloat at low water, and it was during this visit that we made friends with the Eversons, who were to be very helpful to us over many years to come. Their jetty was a useful landing point for our numerous shore excursions, which now became more frequent as we had acquired a dog - "Zulu", since Beryl's parents could not really cope with him. He was a black oversexed good looking mongrel, not terribly obedient and as his main strain was terrier, once he got on a chase, there was no holding him. He was quite a character and we loved him when he was not infuriating us. That Easter, when Michael's fiancee Daphne joined us after our arrival, we renewed acquaintance with familiar haunts, and had dinner at a new, exciting, and romantic one.

Seckford Hall lies in the countryside just outside Woodbridge, and was built by a famous local worthy, Thomas Seckford, who endowed local charities and contributed much to the development of Woodbridge in Elizabethan times. The hall is a beautiful example of red brick architecture, and at the time of our visit had just been restored from the near derelict state in which the army had left it at the end of the War. Soon after our visit, it was acquired by the Bunn family, who have run and developed it as a high quality country hotel ever since, but we shall never forget the thrill of our first visit to this historic house, in the soft light of a Spring evening.

The following weekend, Beryl and I returned to take "CAMPION" back to Leigh with only "ZULU" to help (or hinder, depending which way you looked at it). Fortunately, again, we had reasonable weather with a wind that varied from West to Northwest - off the Essex and Suffolk coasts the latter is the kindest one for the sailor. On reflection, it was

"Campion"

a very good trip, because owing to the tediousness of our rail journey, and being disciplined by the tides, it was Saturday evening before we dropped down river to anchor above Felixstowe ferry. Early the following morning we poured out of the Deben with the first of the ebb tide; there was no wind and our now far more reliable engine started easily to push us along until the wind came. Twelve hours later, we picked up our mooring off Chalkwell station - not bad going for a heavily built smack, in light winds, but the tides were just right for us that day, and although we were slipping through that gateway between the inner Thames Estuary and the outer, the Swin Spitway, at low water; being the neap tides which follow the Easter Springs there was enough water for us. A few other local trips ensued, sometimes with fresh winds, which Beryl did not enjoy; one of these was made with the damaged mast of the crack Essex One Design "NOCTURNE" on deck, for delivery to a spar maker in Whitstable; again there were only two of us on board to sail the boat and off-load our cargo.

Early in June we took the car to France, crossing on a British Rail train ferry to Dunkirk - these steam ferries, with names like "TWICKENHAM FERRY" carried cars on the train deck if there were no trains, but they also had a garage right up on the upper deck and reached via a long ramp alongside the vessel. Needless to say, it was not exactly "drive on, drive off" in the sense of a modern car ferry, but after a sunlit crossing, we headed South and reached a small auberge, "La Grenouillere" which had 3 letting rooms. In peaceful rural surroundings on the banks of the swift flowing River Canche (which flows into the sea at Le Touquet), it seemed a good haven for the night. The cuisine was Michelin recommended, and it seemed natural that we should experiment here with frogs' legs. Compared with escargots, they were disappointing and not so different from chicken, but nevertheless, they served us a magnificent meal and we retired for the night into crisp coarse linen sheets. On this holiday, and on every subsequent visit to France over the years we have used the Michelin guide and found it reliable; it is very difficult for a hotel or restaurant to get into it at any level - we tended to choose the establishments listed as "simple" but having a good table, and "La Grenouillere" was just that. In June 1950, booking ahead was unnecessary, and we always found a room for the night. Things have changed in those 50 years - "La Grenouillere" is now a highly sought after venue with the much coveted Michelin rosette for its cuisine; recently, trying to revisit for sentimental reasons regardless of price, we enquired well in advance, only to find it fully booked on the two nights when we might have stayed there. Now it even is fitted with outlets for connecting your modem, so perhaps it is as well we couldn't stay and have our dream of simple rural accommodation shattered.

Our tour was to last a fortnight; out of our strictly rationed supply of currency we had to buy petrol for the car and pay for board and lodging. In theory, it was not possible, but Beryl was an engineer and had done it before on a Welsh touring holiday with a girlfriend. About 3 nights out of 4 were spent in the car; she knew exactly how to slide the front seats off their rails and turn the whole car into a large bed. For cooking, we had a Primus stove in a biscuit tin, and we carried water in one of the cans from the boat. The whole effect could look rather sordid if you caught us at the wrong moment, but an appearance of respectability was achieved in a very short time; respectable luggage was carried for the other nights when we stayed at an auberge or hotel. It was the rigid control of currency that dictated what you could do (in addition to our own financial strictures!), and we needed plenty of fuel as we envisaged covering fair distances. The irony was that in the UK, petrol was strictly rationed, whereas in France, that had suffered grievously from having been over-run by the German Army, petrol was readily available if you had the cash. There was no problem over buying food, and on the whole we managed to find isolated spots to spend our nights - this was long before the French had developed sites for "Le Camping".

On the 6th anniversary of the D-day landings, on June the 6th, we visited the beaches, and I actually found a track down to the shore almost exactly at the spot where I had beached to unload our vehicles. The remains of beach roadway - a form of linked perforated metal sheets were still visible, along with other rusting wreckage. Up in the nearby village of Ver sur Mer, there was a parade and ceremony at the war memorial. A

British cruiser, the "SUPERB" was anchored offshore, and provided a marines band; we had a front line view from our car, using the sunshine roof as a grandstand. It was all very moving, and the thing that brought a tear to our eyes was a wizened Poilu of the First World War, in his fading uniform, marching diminutively but proudly at the head of the parade.

Emotionally disturbed by all that we had seen that day, we moved on Southwards down the Channel and Atlantic coasts; after a mosquito-tormented night near Rochefort, we moved down into Basque country, and sped through Biarritz which was far too grand for us, to put up at a good hotel in St Jean de Luz. From our bedroom window, we watched with some trepidation as a British registered open green Bentley tourer drew in, from which an immaculately clad couple alighted. Could we live up to this? Later, I met the blazered driver, who in a friendly manner said "careful 'ow you park 'ere - if you don't watch, they'll boomp y're rooddy moodguards". He was being friendly, and I thanked him, but it did rather spoil the effect as far as we were concerned. Due to the somewhat unusual arrangements by which our currency was being stretched, we were able to lash out and indulge ourselves at dinner that night. There were several English people dining there and frugally ordering from the extensive menu; they may well have thought we were in the currency black market.

Turning inland, we visited St Jean Pied de Port, a beautiful little town nestling in the foothills of the Pyrenees before swinging up into the mountains, where, climbing through a mountain pass still thick with melting snow, the only other vehicle we passed, in the opposite direction, was British. After struggling through this difficult rock strewn road, we realised as we rejoined a main road that the mountain road was still closed - in mid June Stopping one evening in a remote hollow a little way off the road, some steak was already in the pan when a thunderstorm broke. The hissing Primus was brought into the car in its biscuit tin; looking back on this episode, there was great potential for either fire or suffocation while the storm and torrential rain raged outside. We survived, helped by a bottle of red wine.

Crossing Eastwards, never far from the Spanish frontier, we reached the Mediterranean coast at Agde, after a night at Carcassonne where we stayed outside the romantic walled town, but dined in a good restaurant deep in the narrow cobbled streets. Our entertainment was provided by two gourmets at a nearby table who discussed every course with a passion and vehemence that had to be admired. Even the coffee was the subject of fiercely held views - "Il n'y a rien que le cafe pur" said one of the elderly gentlemen. "Cafe pur" was, it seems just boiling water poured on the coffee grounds in an earthenware jug; fortunately for us they spoke Parisian French, which made it easier for us to understand, but some of the regional accents encountered on that trip, particularly the Basque, were very difficult to interpret. Whilst in Carcassonne, we visited a stretch of the Canal du Midi - an idyllic tree lined waterway providing a link between the Atlantic and Mediterranean for boats of limited draught and air height.

From Sete, on the Mediterranean, we struck North covering many kilometres effortlessly on empty roads - in those days there were no autoroutes and "peage", but it did not matter. Our last night was spent in the Hotel du Gare at Hazebrouck, not too far from Dunkirk. A small, family run establishment, it was unprepossessing from the outside, but Michelin declared it had a good table. We were not disappointed, it was good, and at the end of the evening, Monsieur, still in chef's overalls, and Madame sat down to eat. The only snag was that early the next morning we could hear from the station loudspeakers "Ici Hazebrouck - le train...".

The holiday was a great success and one we shall never forget; only a year or so later, an English couple doing very much what we had done, were murdered in their car, a crime that was never solved. We never repeated this mode of touring, and on subsequent visits to France always stayed overnight in small auberges, limiting the length of stay to fit our own pockets and the miserly currency allowance.

At the end of July, we took "CAMPION" round to the Blackwater and up to Maldon, lying alongside Hythe quay, and I went up to the office, catching a diminutive "push me pull you" train from Maldon's very grand Elizabethan style East station. The line went through fascinating scenery, with glimpses of the swift flowing Blackwater river, and at one point actually ran through somebody's garden before arriving at Witham, on the main line. There were usually no more than three of us on the train, and I could not see an economic survival for the line. Needless to say, it did close, but I am glad that I had the privilege of travelling on it.

From Maldon, we took the boat round to the river Colne, where we moored head and stern to Wivenhoe quay close by the ferry hard - the ferry, long since closed, was still operating. The ferryman had a boy assistant, Sam, and I always remember Sam being given instructions to secure the boat to a ringbolt with a "long bowline". Use of such a knot means that even though the ringbolt be covered by the tide, you can lift the knot out of the water and release the boat; since that day I have always used a long bowline in similar situations. "CAMPION" was returned to Leigh at the end of the summer, and laid up at Johnson & Jago's yard as usual, for a winter which was to produce greatly changed circumstances.

A FLIGHT TO AFRICA
AND THE SEARCH FOR A NEW HOME

OUR company had been approached by the Colonial Office who wanted to establish kapok exports from Nigeria, in preparation for the colony's independence - they were trying very hard to pave the way for the colony to be commercially independent; no one but me could be spared for the task, which could benefit the firm by providing an alternative source of supply. Early in 1951, Beryl was pregnant and we looked forward to the birth of our first child; although the baby was not due till later in the summer, the prospect of parting, probably for two months at this time, was disturbing.

Early in the year, I flew out from London after spending a night near the airport - I think the hotel was called "The Heston Air Park", and early in the morning I bade my pregnant wife farewell and flew off South in a Handley Page "Hermes". I think we both felt pretty awful inside, but made the best we could of the parting. My flight aboard the BOAC "Hermes" landed at Castel Benito airport (soon after renamed "Castel Idris"), Tripoli, in the late afternoon; as we approached, I was amazed how green and fertile it all looked - not what I had expected. The runway had been very badly bombed during the War, and only patched in a fairly haphazard way, so the landing was very rough. While the aircraft was refuelled, the passengers were taken to the terminal building and given dinner. Take off was not until after darkness had descended, and the air cooled sufficiently to give the aircraft denser air to assist its heavily laden take off for the flight over the Atlas mountains. I was beginning to absorb some of Beryl's aeronautical expertise!

Early the following morning we landed at Kano in Northern Nigeria for a breakfast stop and refuelling. It was Kano that was to be my base for buying kapok; it was an important trading centre although the kapok grew further South. I was first bound for Lagos to make contact with authorities there, but after a few interesting but frustrating days it was obvious no one was really interested, and I flew back to Kano, where I had agents who had already located a warehouse and compound in which operations could begin.

Kano was a strange mixture of old and new; the population was largely Hausa, whose religion was Muslim, and their architecture seemed to be predominantly North African - indeed, I am sure there was Arab blood there, and laden camel trains from North Africa arrived daily. The buildings of the old city were mud walled and frequently had castellated tops to the walls, topped with Eastern style spikes. Modern Kano was more brash, but spaciously laid out; I stayed at the Airport Hotel in a fairly spartan room housed in one of several single storey buildings. Lighting was by a hissing Tilley lamp, although there was electric lighting in the main block containing the dining room and lounge. The airport itself and runways were excellent, by the standards of those days in Africa.

During the day I began receiving kapok from merchants and growers; I had acquired a primitive spring scale on which their sacks could be hung and weighed, but in addition I plunged my arm into every sack. Once or twice a rock or brick emerged - one rock represented a lot of kapok. In matting enclosures within the compound we laid the kapok fibre in the sun to dry, and then a primitive cleaning process was applied by boys beating it with sticks before baling it as best we could, without a proper baling press - the volume of the material meant heavy freight charges. It then was sent by the narrow gauge railway to Lagos for shipment; space was said to be at a premium - whether it was or not, I don't know, but this usually meant liberal greasing of palms before your stuff went anywhere. Once at Lagos, the shipping companies (Elder Dempster and Palm line) usually found space on the next available steamer.

Although I started dealing with various people for my purchases, one man emerged as the most trustworthy and reliable; he would drive a hard bargain, but his word was as good as his bond once the deal had been struck. Momo was a devout Mohammedan and had a dignity and culture that owed nothing to any European influences. After a day's work, I would return to the Airport Hotel for dinner, and after dinner a group of us would sit under the starlit African sky and listen to records. I did not like being away from home, but there were bonuses like this which made it easier.

The kapok season was coming to an end; I tried to establish connections that would give us further supplies in my absence the following year; I still had not really come to terms with Africa, because once I was gone, not another ounce was ever offered or shipped. Later that year, independence came to Nigeria, and although I would not want to enter a political argument, it has been my impression that the place has gone downhill ever since.

So, at the end of February 1951, I began to make arrangements for the return trip home; I had acquired some lengths of cloth from some of the Indian stores (remember clothes were still rationed back in the UK), also a number of raw kapok pods (resembling hard wizened and browned cucumbers). Momo rushed to the compound on almost my last day there with an enormous bowl full of eggs - he had heard that they were in short supply in England and wanted me to take them home! I was very touched by his thoughtful (but embarassing) present. I returned in the cool of the evening and surrounded them with kapok in a big strong cardboard box, together with all my other acquisitions. The following day I airfreighted them home in advance of my departure the next day. I was back at the airport when the Hermes carrying my cargo took off, but all was not well. The aircraft started circling over the control tower while everyone had binoculars trained on it. In Kano, the bush telegraph was pretty efficient, and I heard that he was getting a warning on his instruments that there was something wrong with the undercarriage. Eventually he flew off over the bush to dump his fuel (in those days, high octane aviation petrol). It was evening when he returned to land. A group of us from the airport hotel stood on the grass near the runway, which was a gentle hill. The aircraft dipped out of sight at the far end and then came along the runway perfectly level:- we all thought "he's OK". but as he lost speed, and with it, the support of the wings, he lurched over on to his starboard side - the strut on that side of the undercarriage had failed. The propellers hit the tarmac, a sheet of flame came out behind the engines on that side - and miraculously almost immediately stopped. As the aircraft came to rest, we started running towards it to help people down what was to be rather a long drop; this was long before the days of inflatable emergency chutes, but people began emerging, and some stairs were rushed over there. A great pool of petrol was gathering on the tarmac, still hot from the afternoon sun, but again, nothing happenned.

By the time I was due to fly out at the same time the next day, they had cleared the damaged aircraft off the runway and my large cardboard box flew back to London on the same plane. It had been a slightly un-nerving prelude to my own flight home, which was made without incident. Again we stopped at Tripoli with another very bumpy landing - no wonder the undercarriages on that route were having a rough time. Beryl met me at the airport and drove me home; the route in those days was through central London, but I suspect probably faster than today, round the M25.

On arrival home, the carton of goodies was unpacked - Beryl was thrilled with the fabrics, but when we got to the eggs which I had packed in the cool of the Kano evening, on an early March evening in Leigh-on-Sea they felt warm, if not hot. They were very small eggs, and really an embarassment; Beryl started cracking them open for what was to be a massive omelette, but egg after egg had a well developed embryo chick - they were well on the way to hatching out. We found enough infertile eggs to make our omelette, gave some to the dog who was quite happy to eat embrio chicks, and with some sadness consigned the rest to the dustbin. That night I woke with a start and asked Beryl where the torch was - mystified, she said "downstairs" - I replied "there is no downstairs" After two months in a totally different environment, the speed of my transportation (much slower than today) had not allowed me to adjust to the fact there was a light switch by the bed.

In July our firstborn arrived - a healthy and robust son, Roland, who was 9 lbs displacement on launching - a big baby. He was christened at the church in which we had been married.

Sadly, Beryl's mother had died, and my mother announced she was moving to Hayes, in Kent so we began to look at houses in Essex close to the water, but a very profound remark about where to live came from Maurice Griffiths. Because I had written several articles for *"Yachting Monthly"* we became friends with Maurice and Marjorie, who took an avuncular interest in us, and indeed, had given us a very precious wedding present - a watercolour of "CAMPION" by Winston Megoran, a marine artist who did a number of illustrations for *"Yachting Monthly"*. His advice was roughly that we were looking at houses near the waterfront in Essex, which shortened the journey to your boat, a journey you would make, perhaps every weekend in the summer at the most. What we should think about is the journey that I would have to make every day of the week during my working life - "why don't you look for somewhere between the two"? It was a very profound piece of advice, particularly coming from someone who frequently moved home, although I don't think he moved to West Mersea to stay put until he retired from Editorship of the *"Yachting Monthly"*

Our search area moved, although we were still looking at what in Estate Agent's jargon would be called "a house of character" in Maldon whose only problem was that it (or parts of it) appeared to be moving down the hill. But we were by then in touch with agents in the mid-Essex area around Chelmsford. It was not until 1952 that we were offered a house in Writtle, to the West of Chelmsford. It was love at first sight - the house overlooked a most delightful village green which abounded with "Houses of character" The house was ideal for us; we made an offer somewhat below the asking price as the market was fairly slack at that time. Some time after it had been accepted, we were "gazumped", and were devastated. There was now only one place we wanted to live in - we looked at the few other houses on the market in Writtle, but there was nothing suitable. While we were in a period of abject depression about the whole thing, the agent rang us and said the deal had fallen through, would we be prepared to resume the purchase at the price we had offered? There was only one answer to give.

The boat was not fitted out that season, but in 1952 I took her round to Paglesham where it was more sheltered for getting aboard from a dinghy with a baby. This introduced us to another Essex character - Shuttlewood, the boatbuilder, who also rented out moorings. He had firm views about what a yacht should look like, and it is said that when he was shown the drawings of a yacht with the built up topsides that were becoming popular at that time (largely pioneered by Maurice Griffiths) he snorted and said "I've been asked to build some funny boats in my time, but never a stack barge". After a few weeks, he relented and agreed to build the boat. In most boatyards they had a mould loft where the lines from the drawings would be drawn out on the floor, full size. His shed did not have such a loft, and he would scratch the lines in the dirt of the floor, including those of any ironwork required. Before construction started, they would all be rubbed out, but the boats always came out as designed. He was a master craftsman who knew his job. "CAMPION" went back to a mud berth at Johnson & Jago's at Leigh at the end of the 1952 season; we had signed contracts to complete the purchase of the house on Writtle Green at the end of March 1953. At the same time, we were able to buy a piece of land which gave us a vehicular access to a lane at the back, there being no drive in off the road at the front of the house. This land was being used by a delightful character, Tom Day, who was keeping pigs, geese, and chickens there - it was agreed he would continue to do so and give us some of the products from time to time - no amounts or written agreement, but it worked for quite a few years after we moved in until he decided to give up. By that time, a garage had been built with his help - he was a master bricklayer - then we started creating flowerbeds and lawns.

THE WINTER OF 52-3 AND THE GREAT TIDE

W E were now making serious preparations to move away from the town in which we had both been born and grew up as children. Beryl was pregnant again, but before the baby was due, we should be well established in our new house. Greenbury House, to which we were moving was a house containing several ages of architecture; the title deeds had been destroyed during the war, and our solicitors said that it was not a very good title, containing affidavits from various people who knew the property which had belonged to an estate owning many of the properties on that side of Writtle Green. He said that after we had been in occupation for a few years, it could not be challenged, but it did mean that we could glean little of its history from the deeds. Semi-detached with the grocery shop next door, it was said that the older and more primitively constructed part at the back had been two quite small cottages, but at some time about the middle of the 18th century, gentrification had taken place giving a superior style of accommodation and a facade which brought the frontage to within about 3 feet of the line of the footway beside the road, leaving a small token front garden. Then in 1787 (the date is clearly marked in a chimney breast) a single storey extension was added to the back, to create a kitchen or scullery. The house was then L-shaped with the 1787 projection to the rear, but in 1822 (again the date is clearly recorded in the brickwork) a large brickwork extension was added by filling in the "L" to make a square of the main building.

Before we were due to move in, a great drama was to unfold. On Saturday the 31st January 1953, we had a visit from cousins of Beryl's; I remember it was blowing very hard from about South West. After they had left, Beryl had some pains and contractions, and as a result the doctor was called, and ordered her to rest as he was worried about a miscarriage. On the radio news that evening we heard the first reports of a terrible tragedy to a ferry in the Irish sea - the sinking of the "PRINCESS VICTORIA", a relatively new boat on the Stranraer - Larne route, with a heavy loss of life. Other ships and fishing boats were in trouble in Northern waters.

What the radio reports did not say was that the wind direction in the Northern Irish sea was by then Northwest, and the doomed ship had been struck on the starboard quarter by a severe sea as she turned out of Loch Ryan on to a Southwesterly heading. The force of the sea stove in her stern doors protecting the vehicle deck, allowing a substantial weight of water to flood on to the starboard side, creating a list to windward and making the ship more vulnerable to further inundation. She had left Stranraer at quarter to eight that morning; just after 2 pm that day she finally capsized and sank with a loss of 133 lives. This made a sombre background to the personal concern about Beryl.

After going to bed, I could hear the wind howling round the chimneys, a sure sign it had become colder and veered to the Northwest. My elementary knowledge of local tides was that a Northwest wind raised the height of the tide along our shore, and as this coincided with a spring tide, it was going to be a big one. I wanted to get up and go and check the boat's moorings, but Beryl asked me not to go and we slept uneasily through a boisterous and worrying night. Early on Sunday morning, I got the car out and headed for Leigh Broadway en route for new Leigh Station, which would bring me to the boat without going where there might be flooding.

Outside Leigh church a policeman flagged me down and asked where I was going, and was it urgent? He then told me there had been a flooding disaster, and they were short of vehicles to bring survivors from Bell Wharf to St Clement's Church hall, which had been opened up as an emergency reception centre. After traversing the level crossing into Old Leigh High Street, I headed for Bell Wharf through several inches of water still lying across the road, even though it was not anywhere near high water. At Bell wharf, a makeshift walkway had been created with planking to the point where boats from the Leigh cockle fleet were landing evacuees from Canvey Island. I made several journeys with bedraggled shivering survivors, many of whom had been forced on to the roofs of their bungalows to escape the waters.

Gradually, one or two other vehicles joined in (remember it was still early on Sunday morning), and the task was completed. I then went to Johnson and Jago's yard where "CAMPION" was perfectly alright moored securely in her mudberth, but all around was chaos. A motor cruiser had floated off the slipway where she was being refitted, and drifted across the road to finish with the forward end of her keel on the railway fence. The fence itself was draped with seaweed and other flotsam, whilst blocks of wood and some of the stocks of boatbuilding timber were strewn indiscriminately everywhere. A lot off stuff was drifting about in the creek where the water was so reluctant to retreat. "CAMPION'S" mast had been lying on trestles by the roadway, and was nowhere to be seen, whilst her pram dinghy, along with most of the other dinghies which were stored ashore, had gone. Needless to say, no trains were running, and when the service was resumed, going to work by train you could see seaweed high on lineside trees and bushes as well as the trackside fence.

The mast was never seen again, but the dinghies had been commandeered for service on Canvey Island, so these were all ultimately returned. The enormity of the disaster was slow to emerge, but the floods had claimed 119 lives in low lying parts of Essex alone, not to mention those in parts of Suffolk, Norfolk, Lincolnshire, and as far North as the Humber. The worst affected were, of course, those areas such as Jaywick, near Clacton, and Canvey Island where a lot of the dwellings were bungalows, so the occupants' only escape was on to the roofs. As always happens, there were tales of heroism and tragedy, and the public response in setting up relief funds and contributions of warm clothing was outstanding.

My simplistic knowledge of the effect of Northwesterly winds on East coast tides has, over the years been improved by learning about the causes of storm surges, but in the most authoritive account of the whole disaster, "The Great Tide" by that great Essex historian, the late Hilda Grieve, there is a complete scientific explanation of the causes, which are complex. I have incorporated the title of her book into the heading of this chapter; there is no better way to describe what happened that terrible night .

WRITTLE

A T the end of March, our small house at Leigh was cleared, and when the last removal van left, we went down to the Esplanade at Westcliff where there were a few seafront cafes open all through the winter, had a last meal looking over the Estuary that we had both known all our lives so far (we were both coming up to 30) then left via Rayleigh through to Chelmsford and our new house at Writtle. When an old house has been cleared of furniture and carpets, all the warts show - chipped and cracked floorboards, cracks in the plaster - it does not look its best. As the removal men unloaded our furniture, there can be no doubt they assumed we had fallen on hard times, moving from a smart suburban house into this run down wreck. As a parting shot, one of them said "and I bet it's haunted".

That night, probably about 2 am, I heard a loud creak on the upstairs landing outside the bedroom. I crept out in the dark, not wanting to put a light on, and I could see a dim figure at the other end of the corridor. After standing quite still for a few moments, I moved forward a few paces, and the other figure did the same. It took a few minutes before the penny dropped - it was my own reflection in a large pier glass we had bought with the house. The creaking noise still occurs at some time in the night to this day, and is, I think, the timber framed structure just easing its corsets after the stresses of the day.

Our next door neighbour, Mr Fairhead the grocer was quick to welcome us, and during the first few weeks, ladies of the village called. Beryl went to see the local doctor about the baby due towards the end of July to find that his wife (also a qualified doctor) was due to have a baby in October. He recommended Nurse White as the midwife, and so it was she who delivered Vicky in the large bedroom which had apparently always been known as "the girl's room". One or two structural changes since have made it a bathroom, but it was a bedroom when she was born.

So we had now carried out Maurice Griffith's recommendation to move halfway between work and boat, but the next thing was to move the boat. Early that summer, after a rather perfunctory refit, she was sailed round to Heybridge Basin with the stalwart Michael as crew. On arrival at Heybridge on a rather damp and grey day, I first met Jack

Greenbury House Writtle, to which we moved in 1953. Was it haunted?

Coote, who took a photograph of "CAMPION", with myself and the lock keeper, Captain Thompson, in conversation on the lockside.

To my astonishment, when a print arrived at home, it was in colour. I did not know then that Jack Coote was a leading authority on colour film and photography, a pioneer in that field. He owned a boat called "IWUNDA", a centreboarder originally built at Southend for Harry Garon, the head of the bakery and catering firm which dominated the area. "IWUNDA" was at that time moored in Heybridge basin. To most East Coast yachtsmen, the late Jack Coote was best known as the editor of *"East Coast Rivers"*. the essential yachtsman's guide to this wonderful cruising area I still have a copy of the very first issue dated 1956, which says a lot about the way we cruised in those days. "Ramsholt - a few owners keep their boats at Ramsholt, but there is always plenty of room clear of the moorings for visiting yachts to anchor" Of the facilities - "Mrs Nunn, the landlady at the inn will usually oblige yachtsmen by allowing them to draw water from the pump in her kitchen" The pub is still there, but extended and modernised, offering excellent fare. *"East Coast Rivers"* is still regularly reprinted and up dated, edited by his daughter, Janet Harber, and remains essential reading for anyone sailing those waters. Today, there is little opportunity for a visiting yacht to anchor at Ramsholt as the channel is filled with moorings.

Campion arrives at Heybridge basin following the move to Writtle - author talking to Cap'n Thompson, lock keeper Photo by Jack H Coote.

Heybridge basin, at the seaward end of the Chelmer & Blackwater canal, had been badly hit by the floods that winter. The sea lock gates, built to hold the river water within, open to the tide when the height exceeds the level in the canal. This often happened, but that night, the water just went on flowing in till it became bank high. Before long it poured over the towpath side into the low lying fields (subsequently excavated for gravel), taking several boats with it. As a result of this, the lower lock gate is now a single sliding

The family afloat - Roland & Vicky watch the bow wave

Beryl, Vicky with the dog ("Pog") author steering.

A breezy day - Beryl, Roland, Vicky - Jane Sadd steering.

door which can withstand pressure from either side, and all the embankments on the seaward side have been raised.

That summer saw the safe arrival of Vicky - another big, healthy baby, and Heybridge Basin was to be a useful base for the next year or so, with young children to be embarked; the tidal restrictions are considerable, but this did not matter for the nursery type of sailing that was to be the norm; it was about 25 minutes from home on roads that were not very good, but relatively empty. There was Mrs Boorer's little shop in the attractive row of lockside cottages where the children were always welcome - and sweets could be purchased. Mooring the boat a little way up the canal was a very rural affair for which heavy gardening gloves were required to ward off the stinging nettles and the odd bramble.

Our excursions for the next year or so were usually limited to Bradwell Quay or West Mersea, and "CAMPION" became a floating nursery - her wide decks, steady movements and bulwarks topped by stanchions and guard rail wire, were a great help. She had no external ballast, just a great iron mine below the cabin floor, and whilst such an arrangement may not win you any races, it did make for a remarkably steady ship. There was a beach just downstream from Bradwell off which we would anchor in offshore winds, where the children landed in safety to play and paddle. We were lucky to utilise this while they were young - someone came along later and built an enormous electricity generating station there. We would anchor for the night in the first part of the creek to Bradwell Quay, where there was a hole that kept us afloat at all states of the tide. We continued to lie overnight in this hole even after the power station was built, and I remember going on deck one night at high water when I could see right into the generating hall, from which a quiet hum emerged. Since those days, a marina has been created to the West of the quay, and I don't think a boat at anchor in the channel would be too popular these days, with greatly increased traffic created by the concentration of boats.

Beryl, Roland, & Vicky (facing camera) Mary Dainty steering.

Vicky & Roland enjoy an exhilarating sail, 1 reefdown.

For our summer holidays, we usually managed to make the Deben, with our good friend Mary Dainty aboard. She was a crack helmswoman and experienced yachtswoman, but also the children had a great affection for her. At Woodbridge, we would lie to moorings in Everson's "hole", alongside a local boat, "CLYTIE", and with easy landing on the jetty. There was plenty of entertainment for the children, a boating pool ashore, and in the nearby railway goods yard two great shire horses shunted goods trucks endlessly. In town, there was the Crown Hotel close to the waterfront where we could get a good meal and a shower. Downstream from Woodbridge, there was the all tide landing on the beach with its overhanging wooded cliff, "The Rocks" - these were outcrops of septaria both above and below low water line. Septaria is a form of pressure hardened clay and is the nearest thing to rock that East Anglia can produce - it is not a very hard rock, unless you happen to hit it with your keel, in which case it might just as well be granite. There is septaria in the walls of Orford Castle, but the quoins are of a harder stone and it shows, where centuries of erosion have cut back the face of the septaria, leaving the corners standing proud.

In those early years before the children started school we would take our boating holiday in June, and although there were not very many boats about at anytime, in those days there was hardly any one else on the river in the early summer, but we would usually meet George Jones aboard "PETER DUCK" which he had bought from Arthur Ransome and kept moored off Waldringfield. Usually, "CAMPION" would be left at Woodbridge with Eversons, and I would come back later with a male crew (often Michael Beaumont) to take the boat back to Heybridge.

Life outside sailing had become very full by this time. We had not been in Writtle very long before I was asked if I would stand for the Parish Council - not something I would have ever thought of, but I stood, was elected, and was there for something like the next 17 or 18 years. The Chairman of the Parish Council at that time was a delightful character called Alf Brown; he was also chairman of the local football club, and the village milkman - there wasn't much going on in Writtle that he didn't know about. I also was persuaded to join the Parochial Church Council, and this was to last for about 21 years.

At the same time, I was very conscious of the fact that our family business was very much a one product company. We were being begged to produce a layered form of kapok for clothing and insulation; we had drawings of the machinery needed to produce it, but as we and others knew, it was protected by a patent. Eventually, we contacted some patent agents to investigate the validity of the patent; it was not long before the simple answer came back - "This patent is no longer valid due to non payment of renewal fees in 1943" - a failure to pay a fee of a few pounds during the War had wrecked their monopoly. We set to and a plant was built; we also found cheaper ways of making it and undoubtedly became a thorn in the side of the originators of the process. We were then asked to supply the material ready quilted to fabric, so American built multi-needle quilting machines were purchased; the next few years were very hard work, and the business was to change dramatically.

WALTON ON NAZE DISCOVERED

IN 1956, we had left it until a day in July to bring "CAMPION" back from the Deben and with my old schoolfriend Keith Warren (one of the gang of teenagers with 12 foot sailing dinghies) we set off and cleared the bar to beat along the coast into a freshening Southwester. Off Harwich, the jib sheets parted - this was before the days of synthetic ropes, and you could never be sure when a rope was going to let you down. I decided to go into Walton-on-Naze to seek a replacement, and after anchoring on the windward side of the channel, a little way below "The Twizzle", we went ashore in search of rope which we found at Bedwell's. By the time we got back on board, the wind was piping up and I let more cable out. At that time, most moorings were in the "Twizzle", but some had crept round the corner into the channel leading down to Stone point; we were clear of those and had plenty of room to ride to a generous scope of chain. Our anchor was a big fisherman type anchor; old fashioned and in many ways awkward, but for holding power I think they are unbeatable. The barometer dropped ominously, and by morning a full gale had developed; I veered even more cable and put a rope stopper round it to take some of the strain off the winch, and give a bit of spring to it. "CAMPION", for all her heavy ballast, danced like a dinghy at the end of this great scope of heavy chain which stretched taught like an iron bar. To go forward and inspect the gear, one had to crawl because it was virtually impossible to stand up in the wind. Several boats nearby parted or dragged their moorings, to finish unharmed on the soft leeward bank of the creek.

Walton-on-Naze - a calm morning, looking down the channel towards Stone Point. This mooring was to be our base for some 30 years; the picture (c1958) is from the days when the muddy chain was hauled aboard.

Later in the afternoon, the wind abated somewhat, and the tide was lower so that the banks gave more protection. We donned lifejackets, and set off in the dinghy to row to the hard at the Yacht club; as the wind had veered more to the West we did not have to row dead into the still strong wind. On reaching the shore, we found that telephone lines were down and it was going to be impossible to telephone home. We walked inshore a little way and I met young John Halls for the first time. The Halls were traditional boatbuilders, and John knew how serious this gale had been; the yacht club were friendly and helpful, but their phone, like many others, was out of action. He took me pillion on his motorbike in search of a serviceable telephone, which we ultimately found. When I rang Beryl, she had already rung the police at Walton, who had later rung her back and reported that two men in oilskins had come ashore - everybody seemed pretty certain that the two men were in fact us, but she was delighted to hear from me, and relay a message to Pat Warren that we were safe and sound. They, of course had heard many reports of damage caused and of yachts in serious trouble - a Channel race was in progress and several of the competitors became casualties. One yacht was carried high up on to a South Coast beach, but fortunately without loss of life or serious damage to the yacht. Tucked up in the Walton Backwaters, we could not have been in a more sheltered berth to ride out such a storm. This incident was to be the start of a long association with Walton that was to last for over thirty years, and indeed is not totally severed even now.

When summer came again, I rented a mooring from the Halls at Walton, and from now on this was to be our summer base; it was a longer and at times tedious journey from home, but we were in sheltered waters with a good cruising ground on our doorstep, and a welcoming and friendly yacht club which I naturally joined. Many were the trips down to Stone Point - a "stone" in Essex is always a place with a very steep beach of sand or shingle plunging down into deep water. Stone Point at Walton could only be reached by boat, and the beach was sand, to the delight of our children. It was mainly in the sheltered waters here that both children learnt to row and sail - we acquired a Fairey "DUCKLING" sailing dinghy as our tender and this was a good safe boat in which to learn.

By this time, our holidays were dictated by school holidays, and our main holiday would include visits to the Deben, Pin Mill and other local spots. One year we anchored off Levington creek - there was just room out of the busy fairway, with colliers going up to the power station at Cliff Quay. We rowed ashore up the creek to a spot where the Ordnance Survey map showed a quay; a very optimistic description of what we did find, but the dinghy was secured and we went into the picturesque village with thatched pub and ancient church. From the churchyard there was a wonderful view of the river and Thames barges sailing up to Pin Mill, gathering for the annual barge match. By the time we got back to our dinghy, there was very little water at the "quay", and a lot of muddy pushing and shoving before we could row back. Years later, a marina was to be built on adjoining marshland, which would ultimately become my home base.

At the end of our holiday, we extended the use of the boat by mooring in an empty mud berth (occupied in the winter by Pat Conly's famous old cutter "GOOD INTENT" alongside the yacht club. A gangplank ashore was rigged; there were the yacht club facilities close by and each morning I would rise very early, walk to the station and catch a train to Thorpe le Soken, where I joined a magnificent train, "The Essex Coast Express", hauled by a "Britannia" class Pacific type locomotive, the last type of steam engine built for British Rail. How I wish (like so many other things in my life) that I had taken my camera and photographed this splendid train arriving at the station. Once aboard, I went to the dining car for breakfast, which was not the standard British Rail

The Orwell from Levington churchyard, 1957 - Beryl, Vicky (hidden), Mary Dainty and Roland. Landing was from a 'quay' at the head of the creek

affair - this was still the Great Eastern Railway and seemed to have escaped standardisation. You ordered what you wanted for breakfast, and paid for what you consumed - no set price. There was a club type atmosphere on board; people were friendly and welcoming - after the first day or so you were invited to join in the jar of Frank Cooper's vintage Oxford marmalade that circulated, instead of the pots of British Rail plastic marmalade. As the train ran alongside the river Colne at Wivenhoe I would look with interest at the boatyards of Rowhedge on the opposite bank - the Ironworks was usually constructing some strange craft for use in a remote corner of the World, whilst the Lower Yard always had some interesting yachts to see. Little did I know then that one day I would come to know this interesting village intimately. During this time, we would rent a beach hut at Frinton so that the family spent the day down there, but were always back at the boat by the time I returned in the evening - the sun would still (hopefully!) be shining by the time I got back, but towards the end of this fortnight I would be getting up in near darkness each morning.

In those days, August Bank holiday occurred at the beginning of August, and we would be afloat for the weekend, spending some of the time at Stone Point among a good few other boats (although by today's standards, you would not call it crowded). One holiday, Beryl was still recuperating from a wisdom tooth operation and was to be treated gently, so there were no adventurous plans. Mary Dainty came, and as always was a great help. The weather was benign with gentle Easterly breezes which died away completely by night, and thus we were lying serenely to our fisherman anchor in the small hours, when the ebb tide had just set in. Some instinct told me that something was wrong; there was a kind of tension through the boat, so I grabbed my trousers from by my bunk, pulled them on over my pyjamas and slipped a jersey on. On looking forward out of the hatch, I could see what looked like a forest of masts against the clear starlit sky, clustered round our bows. Mary and Beryl had both woken up by then and volunteered to help, but we insisted that Beryl did not come out as we felt that Mary and I would be able to sort out the problem.

The forest of masts turned out to be no more than two ketches caught across our bows - no wonder our anchor chain was humming with the strain. The owner of one of the other boats was up on deck, started his engine and began to get their anchor aboard. The other boat, a ship's lifeboat conversion had no one on board, and was the cause of the trouble, having dragged into the other ketch, in turn causing her to drag and thus both boats finished up being held by our fisherman anchor. We secured the deserted boat alongside, so that she was at least in line with the stream instead of across it, and hauled in her muddy anchor chain. She clearly had not let out enough cable to hold against a strong ebb tide. I found a suitable tow rope, and with Mary tending the tow, started rowing to tow the errant lifeboat conversion to a new anchorage. Our other friend was by then re-anchoring, and by way of thanks said how patient my wife had been. Platt, who is very naive about these things started to explain that Mary was not my wife, but I think I was just getting deeper in the mire. Rowing was very hard work, towing this boat against the tide, so I had not a lot of breath left for long explanations. When the time came to let the culprit's anchor go, we had to be pretty smart to avoid getting carried back whence we came, so away it went, and I was determined to let out more cable than before, but the chain came to an abrupt halt before I had let out what I thought would be adequate (it was all the boat had), but it held, and a warm sleeping bag was calling. Thank goodness he had secured the end of his cable, or the whole lot might have gone over the side; I took a turn round his post, and noticed we had made a fair old mess on the deck, but was pleased to see a white rag obviously kept for the purpose on the foredeck, wiped up the mud and carefully put it back where I found it.

The next morning, the sun came up in a cloudless sky, and a gentle Northwest wind was blowing - this would later veer to Easterly, as is the pattern in fine weather on the East coast, but all was not well aboard "CAMPION". The captain prepared to dress for the day and collected the pile of clothes carelessly discarded after the night's exertions, but nowhere could he find his underpants. Lockers were searched to no avail, anyway, they would be where I took them off the night before. Suddenly the awful truth came through - white rag on foredeck of errant lifeboat conversion. Of course, they were in my trousers hastily donned in the night and my re-anchoring efforts had caused them to work down the trouser leg over my pyjamas. The knowledge they would be covered in cold black mud was not as bad as thinking of the explanations that might have to be given to the owners if they had returned aboard. Never has a dinghy been propelled so fast, and I made it before any sign of returning owners, grabbed the pants, oozing black mud, and hastily retreated aboard in a rather black mood. The most innocent of nautical operations could be misconstrued so easily.

THE RIVERS ORE AND ALDE

A S the children grew, we started using these rivers (which in fact are one - the Ore as far as Orford, and the Alde above) and we would take "CAMPION" right up above Aldeburgh following the convoluted but well marked channel - woe betide you if you missed one of the marks - to lie off "The Oaks" at Iken, where there was a hole which enabled us to lie afloat through low water. I still have our pencilled sketch of the anchorage, taped with yellowing tape into the relevant page of the original 1956 *"East Coast Rivers"* and one of the marks used was a "green tussock in a cornfield". The children would go ashore on the clean beach below the oak trees (by then they were becoming quite responsible rowing and managing a dinghy) and we would relax from the stresses of life in this peaceful and idyllic anchorage for a few days before moving off elsewhere. In the distance could be seen the great ventilators on the maltings at Snape - they were still malting barley then, but although malting has long since ceased, happily they are still there atop the concert hall into which the old maltings have have been converted.

A pattern was beginning to emerge where I would sail the boat with a friend (often Michael Beaumont) round to Aldeburgh and leave her on a mooring rented from Russel Upson, another East Coast character. The other great character was Jumbo Ward, who lived in a remote cottage above the anchorage at Iken; he was the official river pilot, but I

"Campion" off the Oaks at Iken, River Alde.

think he also had some moorings for hire. Having left the boat there, we would be able to return home by train on a line where the guard had to get out, open a level crossing gate, close it after the train had gone through and rejoin it the other side of the crossing. At Saxmundham, we changed on to a "main line" train. The whole thing was delightfully rural and primitive, but was modern inasmuch as they were using diesel cars. One year we arrived at a deserted Aldeburgh station where the ticket office was closed, but we knew there should be a train, and sure enough there it stood in the platform. Voices could be heard in a room marked "staff", so we pushed the door open to find driver and guard imbibing tea "Yes. the train will be leaving on time, and I can sell you tickets - would you like a cup of tea?" So this was the atmosphere in which we embarked on our 15 minute ride to Saxmundham.

The driver invited us to view the cab; when it was time to go we prepared to leave the holy of holies, but were invited to stay. "Won't you get into trouble for having passengers in the cab?". "You'll get a better view from here, and anyway, I'm retiring next week". It was a very pleasant way to view this extremely rural rail track, over heathland and past rows of wind-sculpted Scots pines which are a feature in this part of Suffolk. We were in fact the only passengers; when we approached the signal box just outside Saxmundham station, the driver surrendered the large token, which gave him sole access on the single line, to the signalman, and in return came a bowl covered with an immaculate white cloth. "His missus makes the best rabbit pies in Suffolk". I count this one of my most fascinating rail journeys, but alas, by the following year the line had closed forever.

On another occasion, we met our friends the Sadds, who had a classic Shepherd yawl, "OSPREY", buit in 1912 by Stone of Brightlingsea (later James & Stone). As they had children of comparable age to ours, this worked very well. "OSPREY" was a thoroughbred, but when you put a mizzen mast in a boat, it does affect her behaviour at anchor or on a mooring, particularly in a wind over tide situation - I was to discover this later when I had a boat built with ketch rig. We were off Slaughden quay, and because it was blowing hard, I think we had both put out two anchors, with the bridle well below the water. "OSPREY" charged about like a racehorse raring to go; the next day the wind had eased and we made ready to go, but the tangle of muddy rope and chain on "OSPREY'S" ground tackle was unbelievable. We were able to veer cable until "CAMPION'S stern was just under her bow, and our low, wide transom stern gave us a good deck to sort it on, washing the filth over the side. It was like undoing a Chinese puzzle with added mud.

The next day, we left the river soon after low water in order to take the flood tide up the coast. John Sadd arranged a pilot - sadly, I do not remember his name (was it Andrews?), but he went ahead of the two boats in his launch, and we followed him closely - as "OSPREY" drew six feet against our four foot six inches, we were perfectly safe. "OSPREY" was bound for the Blackwater, whereas we were returning to Walton; "OSPREY" raced ahead, closehauled and was soon on the horizon as we ploughed our more sedate way. To be fair to "CAMPION", she was a good deal smaller and considerably shorter on the waterline length, which has a lot to do with determining a boat's speed.

BUSINESS AFFAIRS - A TRIP TO PARIS

OUR family textile business in Dagenham was changing in character at this time; we had already put in American quilting machines to quilt the kapok interlining we were producing, and had built a new facade on the rather utilitarian buildings that were forced on us by post war restrictions. There was a battle with the architect, who had produced a striking and imaginative design for the frontage, over the bricks. He wanted us to use a machine made sand faced brick because the regular shape of such bricks made them easier to lay, but we were basically a London firm and wanted the yellow stock brick made by more traditional methods, and which for at least two centuries had been used in London's buildings. In fact, the builders raised no objections when quoting for the building, and so the facade of the building has warm and mellow bricks which harden as they become older.

About this time we were successful in obtaining several large contracts to supply Norwegian Army ski troops with layered kapok to their specification, against strong competition. During this period, the Quartermaster General of the army wished to visit the factory and see their material in production; we were to collect him by car from a Norwegian government guest house in the West of London. Unfortunately, on the day arranged it seemed there was only one car to be spared for this - mine. A poorly disguised groan went up from one or two of the staff, as I was not renowned for keeping cars in pristine condition, but I did make an effort (this was well before the days of automatic car washes) and was quite proud of my car's unusual gleaming appearance. The arrangements all went according to plan, but after we had delivered our VIP back to London, my co-director, Howard Banks said "Stewart, did you realise there is grass growing from the carpet in the back of your car?"

At the same time, there was a constant need to improve production facilities, and we were interested in another type of American quilting machine; arrangements were made for us to see one in operation at a factory on the outskirts of Paris. To save time, I travelled one December evening with our production engineer, James Brown, on the overnight train from London Victoria which delivered you to Paris Nord by 9 am local time. It was a fascinating experience; at platform one, we passed through Customs and passport control to a train of blue Wagons-lits, with a French attendant to greet you at the entrance to each carriage. Right in the centre of these blue carriages was a British Rail restaurant car, in which we had dinner as we sped through the darkened Surrey and Kentish countryside. By the time we reached Dover, we had turned in, but there was little likelihood of sleep as they broke the train in the middle to leave the British dining car on its native tracks, and shunted the two halves of the train into the ferry - one of the same type on which we had embarked the car for our French touring holiday. There were wooden platforms alongside the train which enabled one to disembark into the ship after slipping something warm over the pyjamas and go up to the ship's duty free shop. Of course, I could not resist going on deck to see the ship leave harbour, but it had been a long day and I was soon asleep.

The train was already off the ship at Dunkirk when I awoke again, but the movement of the train quickly lulled me to sleep - it was still dark outside. When I awoke again, it was just getting light, and I was conscious that the train seemed to be hardly moving. I fretted, thinking that at this speed we would never reach Paris at the scheduled time; looking out of the window at the frost covered flat and featureless landscape of Northern France, it was difficult to detect movement of the train. Suddenly, we went through a wayside station, which zoomed past at an incredible speed. Running on welded rails (British trains were still going "diddle de dee, diddle de da" over jointed rails) and with some kind of rubber cushioning built into the wheels, the ride was incredibly smooth and quiet. I stopped worrying about our speed, got up and dressed, and we both went along to the dining car, now at the front of the train, and looking very French. The breakfast menu included a full English breakfast, described in English and French - a splendid piece of marketing.

From Paris, we went to Brussels that evening to see another machine the following day before returning home. Belgium is a small country, and after seeing our machine, it was not a long train journey to Ostend, where we joined one of the Belgian Government's line of cross channel ships - I think she was the PRINCE PHILIPPE, a motor ship with the inevitable Sulzer diesels that were eventually to oust steam from cross channel ships. We were aboard in time to have lunch; although the ship was state owned, the catering was franchised to a private operator. Whereas, at that time, you probably would not have been served until the ship was underweigh in a British Rail ship, they were keen to serve as many customers as possible and we were eating as the ship left. I remember the ship had a very squat, purposeful appearance, dominated by an extremely squat and massive funnel; the crossing was calm, but misty.

At Dover, there was a boat train waiting for us - remember this was still some years before the advent of car ferries, and foot passengers were still the norm. The train was hauled by one of the ex Southern Railways' splendid "Battle of Britain" class of Pacific type steam locomotives, which I was able to admire on arrival at Victoria, although she was now painted in drab British Rail black instead of the green livery of the Southern Railway. Within a day or so of our return from this continental trip, the mist, encouraged by a stationary anticyclone, thickened into one of the last of the great "pea souper" fogs to envelop London and the surrounding counties. People who complain about atmospheric pollution in London either have short memories or are too young to remember them, but fuelled by sulphur-laden coal smoke, they were lethal. During that fog, there was a terrible rail disaster at Lewisham, and the engine of the express train involved was the engine which had hauled our boat train - I think it was the "Spitfire".

A WINTER OF ICE AND SNOW - IMPROVEMENTS TO "CAMPION" - AND MORE OF "ABROAD"

A REGULAR pattern of boating activity had now developed, with "CAMPION" laid up in a boatyard in Downs Road at Maldon for the winter, a mere 20-25 minutes drive from home, and lying to a mooring at Walton in the summer - by now I had a mooring of my own, which the Halls had laid for me. The winter of 1962-3 was a cold one; "CAMPION" was hauled out and laid up ashore under a winter cover, to have some important improvements made. Up to this time, all her ballast was carried inside the boat under the cabin floor, where it took up the entire space. This winter, it was all taken out, cleaned and painted, and at the same time the two pieces of cast iron shoe on her keel were removed - they were protection rather than any kind of ballast. I designed a cast keel for her with a slightly rockered profile, tapering towards the stern so that her draught was not increased, and this one piece casting gave her a strong backbone which the two piece iron shoe had not; the additional weight also enabled me to get rid of some of the internal ballast. It was as well she was out of the water, because a cold spell which developed at the end of January 1963 was so bitter the salty river Blackwater froze over above Osea Island. Successive tides broke up the ice which then refroze to produce a hideous seascape of ice floes; at Maldon it was possible to walk across the river on the ice. The ice pulled caulking out of the seams of

The frozen Blackwater at Maldon - Vicky centre, on ice. The two gravel barges took a fortnight to smash their way up from Osea Island.

boats left afloat, and in some cases they were torn adrift from their moorings. I was very lucky that "CAMPION" was out of the water that winter. Ashore, conditions were also chaotic - there had been very heavy snowfalls, and there were places where strong winds would blow snow off the fields to block the road each night on the country roads I was using to go to work. Some mornings I had to wait while a bulldozer cleared the blocked length of road ahead of me.

At Maldon, two gravel barges were returning light from delivering aggregate to ready mixed concrete depots in the Thames and Medway. One of them had a cut away bow rather like an icebreaker's and took the lead to charge the ice, run up over it and smash a few painful yards at a time. They could, by the time they reached the river above Heybridge, only do this while the boats were afloat on each tide. It took them a fortnight of icebreaking from Osea to finally reach their berth, up by Fullbridge at the effective head of navigation on the estuary.

While "CAMPION" was out of the water, we also fitted a new propeller shaft as the original had become very worn. Many other tasks were completed which could only be carried out with the boat securely on terra firma. In a terrible winter like this one, it is difficult not to get depressed about it, but, of course it always ends and Spring is all the more welcome in such a year. Early in the season, we met George and June Jones in the Walton Backwaters, and moored up alongside "PETER DUCK". George had bought "PETER DUCK" from Arthur Ransome, who did not like her -probably a difficult man to please. Designed by Laurent Giles, she was a pretty motorsailer, and several more were built, although none as pretty as the original - topsides were raised and bow sections filled out a little to gain more accomodation. As I went astern when we came alongside, I suddenly lost all power, and the engine revved up. I had experienced some trouble with reverse gear before, and knew how to deal with the problem, so resolved to leave it until the following morning, in order not to spoil an enjoyable evening together.

When I lifted the cockpit floorboards the next morning, I was horrified to find there was no propeller shaft, but looking over the side, could see the propeller on the end of a long stalk sticking out of the port quarter. Fortunately, the stalwart Mary Dainty was with us, so I lashed the dinghy securely across the stern, Mary and Beryl held the boathook as best they could on the propeller boss while one of them hit the handle with a hammer as I waited below until I could get a grip on the shaft to pull it slowly back into the boat, guiding it into the coupling. The boatyard at Maldon was a pretty slapdash affair, and one of the results of this carelessness was that they had failed to ensure that the propeller was secured in the coupling. As long as you went ahead, fine, it was being pushed in, but the moment we went astern, it pulled itself out of the coupling, and very nearly out of the boat. Apart from the loss of a brand new shaft and the propeller, we also would have had a problem in that the boat might have sunk during the night. I did my best with a hand drill to create a spot on the shaft in which the locking screw could engage, but the following winter insisted on having a pin put right through shaft and coupling.

Further improvements about this time were the replacement of all the hemp running rigging with polyester (marketed in those days under the name "Terylene"). It did not shrink when wet or go hard when it dried out again and was extremely strong, nor did it go rotten. I also had a new suit of tan colour sails made in the same material; again its characteristics did not change whether wet or dry, nor did it absorb water. All this upset my dear friend George Jones, a staunch traditionalist, who thought by using synthetic fibre ropes and sails I was virtually consorting with the Devil.

At about this time we also acquired a small dog - a border terrier, known to some as a border terror. She was small enough to not upset a dinghy or take up too much room below, where she was installed in front of the coal stove - in early Spring and late autumn she thought this was a very good idea. However, she did not like sailing, being used to a floor that was stable and level; her dislike was even greater after some books fell on her from the bookshelf during a boisterous sail. The moment a sail tier was removed, or she heard the clicking of a patent block aloft, she would cower. A sea bed was created for her in a cockpit locker, where she felt safer as no one could throw books or salt spray at her. The moment preparations were made for anchoring, she would emerge on deck, and after inspecting the shoreline would go and sit as close to the dinghy as possible. It could be said she liked "ashore" as much as John Betjeman disliked "abroad". In those less crowded days you could usually find an anchorage near an all-tide landing place to satisfy her needs.

However, a dog can be a handicap; by this time the family were growing old enough to be taken abroad; we went to Venice with Roland, but Vicky contracted chickenpox - and had to be left behind. At that time, I don't think she agreed with "abroad" and didn't mind being left in the house, with someone well known to us, Peggy Smart, and this also solved the problem of looking after the dog. Roland benefited greatly from our time in Venice, and when one evening we sat having coffee under the stars listening to the orchestra at Florians, he decided (at 11 years old) that this was the life. There were the usual excursions to the islands of Murano and Burano, where one was expected to buy lace on one and what we thought was hideous glass on the other - it was a wonder we did not meet with an accident reboarding the boat as we bought nothing - they probably got a commission on any sales.

One day, however, we boarded a working "vaporetto" to take us to the island of Torcello - the fares were absurdly low compared with those quoted by tourist boat operators who did not want to undertake the longer trip to this fascinating and relatively unspoilt island, with no prospect of commission on sales of tourist souvenirs. It was remote, and in places reminded me of the Essex marshes. In the centre was this enormous cathedral, with little of the elaborate gilding and ornamentation found in St Marks and other Venetian churches. The scale of the building and its simplicity were impressive. We returned on the same public service in a "vaporetto" that really was quite a handsome little ship - anything the Italians build has to have style. In spite of all that one is told about the Mediterranean being a tideless sea, Venice, at the head of the Adriatic, does have tides of two or three feet, and on the homeward trip, there were exposed mud banks shining and glinting in the afternoon sun.

Another memorable excursion was made by bus along the littorale to Chioggia. The bus carried people and their luggage, which could be a live chicken in a coop or a thing looking like a bag of laundry. The littorale consists of several long thin islands enclosing the Venetian lagoon, and between the islands a ferry would be waiting. The bus boarded the ferry with the panache and verve you would expect from an Italian driver, and as the rear wheels of the bus reached the deck, the boat was off. Driving off again was executed with equal elan - the man was an artist. Chioggia, a fishing port, was incredibly poor at that time, but we found a simple fish restaurant that produced a good "Fritto misto".

My sister Lorna, who had gone out to Milan to teach English, married Dino Marazzi, one of her pupils, and was living in an apartment block in the centre of Milan, where they had already started to raise a family. Visits to Italy became a regular feature of our life, and we had discovered a wonderful way of getting out there. Once we went by car, on a fascinating trip through France and Switzerland - all these trips were usually undertaken in the children's Easter holidays, and our drive over whichever pass it was took us between cliffs of recently cleared snow. That time both children were left in the care of in the care of Peggy Smart, who was wonderful with them. Our return trip was made via the

The Townsend car ferry "Halladale"- converted from a Naval minelayer

Italian and French rivieras, heading inland at Nice to cross the massif central en route for Calais. The car was carried across the Channel on what I believe was Townsend's first ferry, the "HALLADALE", a former Naval minelayer, which converted very readily into a car carrier. The deck that once carried mines was suitable for cars, which drove aboard over the stern, down one side of the engine room trunking to a small hand operated turntable at the forward end, turning the cars round the tight space so they were ready to drive off. High vehicles such as coaches were accommodated on the open deck aft.

However, after this first venture by car, we found a less time consuming but fascinating way of reaching Milan. It took us under an hour to reach Harwich, where the car would be left in a long stay car park, whence we boarded the night boat, aboard which we would have a de-luxe cabin (it didn't cost a great deal more - I don't think the whole operation was run on very commercial lines) and on arrival at the Hook of Holland, we would board carriages that were to form part of the "Rheingold" express. The carriages you boarded were labelled "Milano", and would take you all the way. The train was complete including dining car and observation car, by the time you reached the Dutch-German border, whence the route lay up the Rhine, through the gorge beneath its many brooding castles and past the legendary Lorelei Rock. As dusk came, the train was rolling down to the North Italian plain in a deep valley, following the torrent of the Ticino River, swollen with melting snow from the Alps. By the time you reached the Swiss-Italian border at Domodossola, it was dark, but all day you had travelled through some of the finest scenery in the heart of Europe. At Milan, Dino would be waiting for us with a car, the whole journey having taken roughly 24 hours from door to door. We were privileged to have been able to use this remarkable route, one of the great railway journeys of the world, which could not be repeated today. In this way, we would spend a week with my sister and her growing family, and then journey onwards, to Rome one year, and Florence another. These visits came to an end when they emigrated and settled in Canada.

THE CRUISING ASSOCIATION - "CAMPION" GOES FOREIGN AGAIN.

I N 1965, Douglas Thompson, who owned a Vertue and was a friend of Michael Beaumont's, invited me to join the Cruising Association. At that time, you still did not come across many sailing people, and even fewer who enjoyed just cruising, but here was a concentration of people interested in cruising, and a mine of information about places worthy of visiting. Douglas had an ulterior motive, and it was not long before I found myself on his "HLR & Boatmen" Committee.

The summer season that year started with some very boisterous weather, but we reached Dover from the Walton Backwaters, after losing the top of the mast, which had snapped off where a bolt had been put right through, causing some unseen internal rot. At

Dover, where at that time yachts were less than welcome, we were put into the enclosed Wellington Dock (now a very well equipped yacht harbour) and immediately contacted the CA boatman, Mr Iverson of Dover Yacht Company. An expert job of scarfing on the broken top of our mast was carried out very quickly. At that time, no one would wish to stay there longer than possible; at one end of the dock they were handling gravel, and at the other, coal. Whichever way the wind blew, you got dust, but variety was provided in that a wind shift brought about a change of colour. In one berth lay a train ferry of the type that once took us to France with our car, and, subsequently, in the overnight train from Victoria to Paris. She was clearly an old ship, and was being painted up on the cheap by her own crew who were virtually throwing the paint at her, and again, another wind shift could have produced some interesting colours into the atmosphere.

Although we were ready for sea, the weather remained vile, with Westerly gales. Then one afternoon, the forecast having indicated a moderation of wind strength, with my old friend Michael Beaumont aboard, we sailed, two reefs down, having fooled ourselves into thinking it was already easing. "CAMPION" shot like a champagne cork out of the Western entrance into a maelstrom of seas, but there was no question of trying to go back and off we went with the wind towards Calais. The seas became a little less confused as we cleared the backwash from the harbour wall, but it was still a roller coaster ride. Fortunately, by the time we were heading up the approach channel to Calais entrance, the wind really did begin to ease, and we entered the harbour at a more modest speed. In the outer harbour, we rounded up and lowered the sails; a local in a rough working skiff pointed out a mooring, and said it was very strong - "big Dutch yacht used it last week". We picked it up, and rove a pennant of stout polyester rope through a large ring at the top of the riding chain. It was getting towards low water, and a large outfall was disgorging torrents of foul smelling water into the harbour; although the wind had eased somewhat, there was still a scend coming in which kept "CAMPION" rolling gently all the time.

I had already started using polyester rope on my mooring at Walton, as an alternative to hauling muddy rusty chain aboard, but there was a lot of cynicism about this from both the professionals and yachtsmen - "wouldn't leave a boat of mine riding to a rope pennant". Having done this for two seasons with no ill effects, remaining the only boat there moored in this way, I was quite confident that this would hold us secure in Calais harbour. After a good hot supper, we turned in to the sounds of a rising wind. As the tide rose, so did the wind, which had backed Southerly, and the swell washing round the harbour turned the gentle rolling motion into a violent roll - I had never known "CAMPION" roll like it before. I went on deck, and several times watched her roll her deck edge under (she did not have a lot of freeboard).

Sleep was fitful that night, but at about six o' clock in the morning, there was an almighty "twang". As I rushed on deck, the thought rushed through my head that the critics were right - "never leave a boat of mine on a rope pennant". It was a bright sunny morning with a very strong Southerly wind. For all her heavy ballast, "CAMPION" was blowing across the harbour like a dinghy, towards a large French cross channel steamer, the "COTE D' AZUR". The cabin steps were pulled away in record time to reach the engine starting handle, the carburettor tickled till petrol appeared and I swung the handle. It was fortunate that by this time we had turned this ancient engine into a pretty reliable piece of machinery; there really was no time to lose, and it fired up immediately. We motored away from the steel topsides of the steamer with only yards left between us, and started steaming up into the wind. While Michael held the boat slowly progressing towards the windward end of the harbour, I hauled the parted mooring aboard. The rope was absolutely fine - no chafe or other damage; the heavy riding chain had parted about a fathom below the mooring buoy. We anchored with our trusty fisherman anchor, hopefully clear of the bottom chain belonging to the mooring that had just parted.

The drama over, we retreated below for a good breakfast, resolved to get out of this hell-hole as soon as possible. At least the rolling had calmed down to a gentle movement - it was again approaching low water. As soon as we were underweigh, we motored over to a pontoon against the harbour wall, where the broken chain and mooring buoy were added to a collection of other accumulated junk. We hoisted sail, with only one reef down and started roaring up the coast, weaving in and out of the labrynth of banks, wrecks, and channels that lie all the way till well North of Dunkirk. The sun shone, and as Calais retreated astern, we began to feel better about things; it was an interesting sail past resorts and casinos, and some very wild stretches of coast with nothing but sand dunes sparsely covered in coarse grass. North of Dunkirk, the French - Belgian frontier was passed, and courtesy flags changed appropriately. Late in the afternoon, flags were changed again as we passed the Dutch - Belgian frontier, and followed the coast round into the Schelde to berth in Breskens on the South bank of the estuary, opposite Flushing.

Breskens is in a small part of Holland lying South of the Schelde and in which Terneuzen is the principal town; it is completely surrounded by Belgian territory on its Southern side, whilst to the North the wide Schelde estuary isolates it from the rest of Holland. To overcome this isolation, the Dutch run a frequent ferry service with large handsome vehicular ferries between Flushing, very close to the station, and Breskens. We arrived to find they had just built a new ferry terminal and put in a long pontoon for yachts in the old ferry dock. There were only one or two boats there, and we had no difficulty in berthing "CAMPION" comfortably, where she was left for three weeks.

On our return, en famille, and accompanied by Mary Dainty, the weather had changed, and we crossed to Flushing to enter the Walcheren canal through Middleburg to the Veerse Meer, in bright sunshine and with moderate winds. The Veerse Meer had only recently been tamed from a fierce flowing tidal gat whence you made a knuckle biting entrance to Veere itself. For us there was no problem as now it was all non tidal, and we entered past the massive defensive tower at the entrance to berth in this quiet haven; once a prosperous port handling many cargoes, but principally wool, and having an active fishing fleet, it was now developing as a tourist attraction after a long period of decline. The merchant's houses and warehouses along the quayside had all survived and were being well cared for - a mixture of typical Dutch styles with their crow-stepped gables. There were still a few fishing boats left, but it was clear that they would not survive long. Whilst there, we saw a handsome looking modern boat called "GLASS SLIPPER", moulded in a new material known as "GRP" - glass reinforced polyester. She was a pioneer in the new boatbuilding technique that was to bring about a transformation to the whole yachting scene. From Veere we went along the length of the Veerse Meer to the impressive new Kats lock which gave on to the tidal Oosterschelde.

As we sailed Eastwards down the estuary, we could see a great construction stretching across the water in our path; our Dutch chart did mention something about a "brug in angebouw" which had not previously registered with us. A mighty bridge was being built across the estuary as part of a plan to damn the estuaries and build good road links between North and South; fortunately several sections were incomplete and we were able to sail through unimpeded to reach the fascinating ancient port of Zierikzee. This harbour still had a large fleet of fishing boats, and there was also some commercial shipping, but we were able to find a berth at the head of the long entrance channel from where it was a short walk into the town. Zierikzee is a large town with many fine buildings; there had been some wartime damage, but sensitive restoration had been carried out in traditional styles. We enjoyed our stay in the pleasant town, but decided we better get back before the bridge was complete - we didn't realise that the design included an opening span, but although work was proceeding fast, there was no problem for us.

Leaving Flushing, we headed for Zeebrugge, where we wanted to enter the big sea lock to reach Bruges and meet some friends. On arrival, they announced that they would not accept sterling, and as we had no Belgian currency, could not pay the lock fees. Beryl raced to a bank, only to find it had just closed for the weekend. However, the Bank manager, who lived over the shop, so to speak, was standing outside and took pity on us; he personally changed enough of our money to get us through the lock. Our Morris Hotchkiss engine quietly pushed us up the canal until we came to a bridge just outside Bruges - it was a lifting bridge, but the gantry across the top still would not allow our mast to pass under, so we berthed nearby at a derelict gas works quay. I do not ever remember mooring a boat in less salubrious surroundings - the derelict gas works buildings, with a slimy quay face which was home to some exotic species of slug. Once darkness set in, there was another problem - mosquitoes. Gradually every opening had to be closed, and we even finished up by stuffing rag in the navel pipe through which the anchor chain passed down to the chain locker. Hundreds were slaughtered on the hot glasses of the oil lamps, which, of course, attracted them. "CAMPION" had no electrics of any kind,.

Returning to Zeebrugge in preparation for return to the UK, Beryl and Vicky went off to Harwich on one of the train ferries which in those days ran from there. A clerk kept a small notebook in which he entered the names for the next departing ferry - they did not run to a schedule. The ships were not licenced to carry passengers, but the rules allowed them to carry up to 12 passengers, and when his book was full, then he started another page for the next sailing. It was a daylight sailing, but Beryl and Vicky were allocated a large cabin with twin beds, and they had lunch with the officers at a very reasonable charge. Provided you were not in a hurry, it was a very civilised way to cross.

"CAMPION'S passage back to Harwich was fast by our standards, with a fair wind from South of East; we arrived early the following morning to anchor in the Customs examination anchorage just above Felixstowe dock. We hoisted our yellow flag and had a good breakfast while waiting for Customs to come off in a launch. When the officer arrived to give us clearance, we discovered it was he who had also cleared the train ferry passengers and remembered Vicky and Beryl. It was only when we were reunited, after "CAMPION" had been returned to her mooring at Walton, we found he had good reason to remember them. Beryl was wearing a blue "John Morgan" type jacket, with strong velcro pocket fastenings. Just as the customs officer bent down to put a chalk mark on a suitcase, she opened her pocket with a loud tearing noise to get her handerchief - it was unfortunate timing, and a very red faced officer thought he had split his trousers in execution of what was then a normal procedure in clearing baggage.

A DREAM BECOMES REALITY

DURING and immediately after the war, I had visions of my ideal cruising boat - remember "CAMPION" (which I owned for 19 years) was bought as a temporary stop gap. My thoughts and drawings had centred round a ketch of about 35 feet overall length, but by now I was beginning to feel if I didn't take some positive action, it would never manifest itself, so early the following year I approached Jack Francis Jones (my friend George's brother) with a view of getting him to design this ship of my dreams. By the time our discussions were finalised, she had grown to 37 feet overall length (the extra 2 feet make a considerable increase in the total size, and also in cost), but draught was to be limited to 5 feet because of her East Coast home waters. A fixed bowsprit 6 feet long was allowed for

- "CAMPION" had a very long one, which with the removal of a stout wooden pin could be run inboard.

During the summer, Jack Jones finished the drawings and full construction details, which were then put out to tender. The contenders whittled down to two - one at Tollesbury (long since closed and now the site of Tollesbury Marina) and the other, Ian Brown at Rowhedge on the banks of the river Colne. The Tollesbury people were somewhat vague about their price, and Jack said "if they get the job either you or I will have a nervous breakdown trying to get the boat you want - Ian Brown is far more businesslike and gave a proper quotation", so the job went to Rowhedge. It was the start of a long association with that salty village.

Meantime, we had a final summer cruise in "CAMPION", and I had arranged for advertisements for her sale to appear in the Yachting magazines while I was away, giving a date after which enquiries could be made, and my office telephone number. When I returned from holiday, a notice had appeared on my door announcing "Selina's Yacht Agency" (The office was situated in Selinas Lane). A queue of potential buyers had jumped the gun, and within a few days I was taking the first and keenest out for a trial sail. It was a perfect day, "CAMPION" sailed her best and the deal was clinched - all over within a fortnight. You would be inhuman if you did not feel sad at parting with this old friend, which had seen me through to marriage, acted as a floating nursery for the family (now growing up rapidly) and with whom we had come through so many adventures safely. At the same time, she had gone to a young man with a family, and who one knew would look after her. He did more than that - he took out the ancient Morris Hotchkiss petrol engine and replaced it with a diesel, after having her sternpost bored to take a centre line propeller and so made her auxiliary engine installation very much more effective.

Friends said after the quick sale "You sold her too cheaply", but my philosophy when selling a capital item like that, is to dispose of it quickly; with all your attention going to the new boat, you will no longer have the enthusiasm to keep her in good order while you wait for the buyer, and if she fails to find one in reasonable time, you finish up with a boat that everyone knows has stuck, and you are at the buyer's mercy. Far better to have a queue!

So, that autumn of 1966, I saw "B 7" (the builder's number for the un-named vessel) gradually taking shape. Her lines had been laid off in chalk on the mould loft floor, from which templates could be made in cheap softwood, representing the transverse sections at intervals along her length. The centre line was already being constructed, and one damp and misty November morning, I went with Ian Brown and Stan, the foreman shipwright, to select a piece of English oak for the stem. Armed with a large plywood profile giving the finished curve of the stem post, we searched a timber yard at nearby Colne Engaine for a large oak limb that would conform to the shape of the stem, ensuring the grain would run true. Everywhere, great oak branches and trunks lay, still in their bark, damp and cold in the November mist. Eventually one was selected and marked up for delivery to the yard at Rowhedge - it looked enormous, and was extremely heavy - oak is a very dense wood, but a lot of wood would have to be cut away before it became the stem post.

Apart from the stern post, which was a straight piece of oak, the keel, hull and deck planking were iroko, a tropical hardwood with many of the rot-resisting properties of teak, and often known as "the poor man's teak". It is lighter than teak, but easier to work, and although teak had been discussed at one of the specification meetings, it appeared that there was no good quality teak in the country at that time, whereas there was plenty of good quality iroko. The coach roof and cockpit coamings were mahogany, and the whole of the coachroof, with plywood top rebated into the mahogany sides, was to be covered in glassfibre fabric soaked and coated in polyester resin. People criticised this, because the joinery work and rich grain of the mahogany looked so splendid - "they ought to be varnished" was the cry. " Will you be there to varnish them every Spring?" - they took the point; there was going to be plenty of varnish work anyway for the enthusiasts, and if you really wanted to see the mahogany grain, it was all there visible from inside the saloon. The cockpit coamings were painted white to match the coachroof, but surmounted by varnished iroko cappings, to match the capping rail atop the bulwarks, and these cappings certainly gave a very pleasing finish.

What did surprise me in Jack Jones' specification, was the choice of larch for the deck beams, except for the mainbeam by the mainmast , and another at the forward end of the bridge deck (which was a valuable strengthener running across the boat between cabin and cockpit) where he put massive beams of oak. Jack Jones had very strong views (about almost everything!), and said that larch was a far more stable wood which did not move. Oak is inclined to twist and move, but where great strength was required, he did allow oak.

In everything that went into that boat, Jack had strong views, largely based on experience gained over many yachts he had designed and supervised. He was almost fanatical about what metals could be used for fastenings - he would not hear of stainless steel for keelboats - there was still a lot being learnt about stainless steel at that time, and in certain conditions where all air is excluded, it can corrode. Keelbolts were to be of "crown iron", heated in the furnace until "cherry red", dipped in pitch and driven while still hot. The cast iron keel, nearly 4 tons of it, was intended to be her only ballast, and as it ran for a considerable length of the wooden keel, would form a strong back bone. I saw the accurately formed wooden template, complete with bolt holes, in the boatyard before despatching to the foundry in Coventry, and on a business visit to Coventry I called on the foundry. By luck, the day I visited was the very day before they were going to pour the molten iron into the mould. It was an educational experience; they had lifted the wooden pattern of the keel out of the fine black foundry sand, and any imperfections were being smoothed out with a small bricklayer's trowel. I was astonished to see that the bolt holes were going to be formed by wooden rods stuck in the sand - "surely the molten iron will burn them away?" was my immediate reaction. But these were people who knew their trade and had done it all many times before; although the wood might char, it would be deprived of oxygen and remain there to preserve the bolt holes. When the great piece of cast iron was finally offered up to the wooden keel, it was a perfect fit, and the wooden keel was then drilled ready to receive the bolts, which came through just where the drawings intended.

The building of "B7" was my first introduction to Rowhedge, and Ian Brown's yard which had formerly been part of Rowhedge Ironworks ("The Lower Yard"). The Brown family bought the yard from the receivers of the Ironworks a few years before I came on the scene, and one of the conditions of the purchase was that the labour force must be kept on - these were skilled men in a yard with a tradition of quality workmanship, without whom there would be little or no point in purchasing the land, buildings and equipment. A large handsome twin screw steel motor yacht, the "MARY FISHER", was hauled out on the biggest slipway in the yard undergoing a major refit. Just under 100 feet long and drawing 8 feet, she looked enormous to me; with her squat yellow funnel looked a real little ship; launched in 1964 by Denny's of Dumbarton and fitted out by James Silver of Rosneath, both famous names, but sadly, no longer existing today, and in fact was the last ship built by Denny's before they closed. The other boats laid up in the yard for the winter were more the size I was accustomed to.

The village itself at that time gave one a feeling of departed prosperity. In the heyday of the larger yachts, Rowhedge provided many of their crews, who turned to fishing or fitting out during the winter. The yachts laid up in Rowhedge provided associated employment in so many fields - crew uniforms, repairs and painting along with provisions, and brought in money to support a number of shops and pubs. There had also been a brewery - part of Ian Brown's yard was known as "Brewery Quay". By the time I knew it, the effects of two world wars and the slump of the1930 era had finished the halcyon days of large yachts; few shops had survived and some of the pubs closed to become private houses. The main yard of the former Rowhedge Ironworks ("The Upper Yard") had become an unsightly scrapyard, which did little to improve the appearance of the village at that time. But in spite of this, there was still a strong sense of community with many thriving village events and organisations, and in particular the Rowhedge regatta. During the time that I have known it, there has been a gradual recovery as the postwar housing boom filtered through, and many of the houses restored - some would scathingly say "gentrified", but the alternative to this is gradual deterioration, and loss of housing stock.

The boatyard itself, once Harris Bros before its absorption into the Ironworks, was full of history, underwent great changes under Ian Brown's management which reflected the rapidly changing yachting scene. During the Second World War, many wooden vessels were constructed for the Navy, and their influence could be seen, particularly in no less auspicious place than the toilet block, put in to serve crews standing by to take over a newly built ship - a typical piece of Admiralty utilitarian architecture, repeated in many boatyards round the coast. Soon after I came to know the yard, Ian dismantled the large slip that had been used to haul out the "MARY FISHER", and replaced it with concrete hard standing - this effectively severed the last connection with large yachts and marked the final end of an era.

Of the pubs that have survived in Rowhedge, the "Anchor" is my favourite; we visited Rowhedge once in the mid 1950s, on a motoring trip in the area, the principal object of which was to visit an antiques dealer in Wivenhoe (from where we bought furniture for our house in Writtle). In Wivenhoe, just upstream from the village, was a dry dock, still in working order in which a steam powered coastal tanker was being refitted. Nearby, in a muddy dock lay the rotting hulk of the "CAP PILAR", the square rigger which Adrian Seligman took on a world cruise. From Wivenhoe, we drove back to Colchester, over the Hythe Bridge and down to Rowhedge, where someone had suggested we could get a good lunch at the "Anchor" - we did, with vegetables grown by the landlord on his allotment. Right on the river bank, it has always been in a premier position, and over the years many improvements have been made so that it has become a favourite eating place for people from Colchester and villages round. At high water, the ships going upriver to the Hythe Quay would pass close by, towering over the pub. Sadly, the decline of Colchester as a port means one is unlikely to see commercial traffic any more, and boating interest will only come from pleasure craft.

The winter of 1966-67 was a busy one at work, at home, and with frequent visits to Rowhedge. The road routes were not easy; none of the by passes on the A12 had been built and Colchester was very congested. The alternative route, which I usually used, was via Maldon, Goldhanger, Peldon and Fingringhoe - a pretty route through villages of character, but tortuous and not really suited to a man in a hurry. Slowly B7 took shape in the large building shed; I was already prefabricating some of the interior furnishings so that they could be "offered up" as soon as the construction was sufficiently advanced. Boats being very three dimensional and all curves in every direction meant that most major fitments had to be trimmed up to fit well. Because this boat was being built to the highest possible specification, all the money was being spent on hull, engine and rig; interior furnishings were a low priority and I tried to do as much as possible myself, using

"Celandine" ready to launch 22nd April 1967.

good quality mahogany faced marine ply, thin mahogany for panelling and strength - and deal where it didn't show. Deckhead, topsides linings and bulkheads were in white formica faced plywood, but there was still plenty of natural wood to avoid a clinical look down below. Our part of the fitting out took on an additional urgency, and Roland and Vicky (now teenagers) both lent a hand. Vicky, almost 14, cut to shape a lot of deal planking to form cockpit locker floors - it was important to have somewhere for stowing gear.

Finally, April the 22nd was agreed as a launching date - the work at Ian Brown's would be completed, and the tides were right. The masts and spars were being built at Maldon in the rather slapdash yard at Downs road, but at that time there was a first class spar maker working there, and it had been mutually agreed to build the spars as a separate contract. A few days before launching date she was hauled to the top of the big shed before being "struck over" on transverse greased wooden ways to the head of the launching slip. Her carved and gilded name boards and sprig of "CELANDINE" on the bows were carved by Mabbitts of Colchester - an old established wood carving firm responsible for much work to be found in churches, and on village or town signs. The name boards were suitably obscured prior to launching.

Early on the launching day, the ever stalwart Mary Dainty joined Beryl to go over to Rowhedge and prepare a large supply of filled rolls and other goodies, all spread out on trestle tables set up in the big shed - there was more room in there after the new boat had been removed. I came over later with my mother, who was to perform the launching ceremony; she had that year moved into a cottage very near us. Not being a lady who had launched a thousand ships - indeed she had never launched one before - she was quite nervous about the whole thing. Approaching her 70th birthday, she dressed very smartly, and as would be expected of someone of that age group, quite naturally wore a hat.

The boatyard was decked out in flags, whilst we managed to put up a temporary stick to enable the boat to be dressed overall with signal flags, topped with a Cruising Association burgee, and Ian presented her with a large red ensign which hung from her ensign staff aft. Somehow word had got round that she was to be launched, and towards the top of the tide (remember, everybody in Rowhedge still thought in terms of high water, even if the connections with smacks and yachts were fading). Upstairs windows in the cottages opposite the yard were flung open and an atmosphere of excitement reigned. A red carpeted launching platform had been constructed near the bows, and an ingenious swinging frame prepared for the champagne bottle - this ensured the aim of the bottle, and was arranged so it would hit the stem just below where the protective steel banding started. Ian was taking no chances with the superb paint finish that they had so diligently applied to the topsides. These men were all craftsmen and proud of the ship they had created. Finally, the cradle on which she now rested was freed of all restraint except for a chain with a large slip link.

My mother said the magic words, which she had nervously rehearsed, loud and

Ian Brown assists mother with the champagne bottle for launching (Essex County Standard Photograph).

clear "I name this ship "CELANDINE", and may God bless all who sail in her". The champagne bottle broke first time, the name was revealed and Stan, the foreman shipwright, smote the slip link on the chain with an accurate blow of the sledgehammer (the silence prevailing made the harsh metallic blow sound all the more dramatic). As she started to roll down the slipway rails, the sounds of *"Rule Britannia"* came out over a borrowed public address system; she floated clear of the cradle to be towed alongside Cat Island quay at the downstream end of the yard. The second grey mistress had been launched

As the tide began to fall away, we left the launching party to take her downstream to a pre-arranged mooring at Brightlingsea. The next day she went up to Maldon ready to receive her spars and sails (by the Maldon sailmaker, Taylor) and where a lot more fitting out work below was to be carried out; Maldon at that time was only 20 minutes or so from home compared with the hour to reach Rowhedge so that valuable time was gained. This same yard had, at that time, bought up the Taylor's paraffin stove business from the original proprietors. In keeping with the general standard prevailing there, these excellent stoves were being spoilt by sloppy attention to detail, so that when the stove was first pressurised for use, paraffin poured out of badly fitted joints. Unfortunately, this was not the only place at that time operating in a slapdash way - failure to attend to important detail was hampering a lot of British engineering at that time. It is no good creating good pieces of equipment if you have not trained the operatives in sound and reliable working practices.

The decision to build "CELANDINE" at this time was, as luck would have it, the right financial moment. Although so many things were wrong in the country at that time, in places like Rowhedge, the skills and pride in workmanship were still to found. But the year she was launched was also the year that a devaluation of the pound was virtually forced on us, and caused the infamous remark by the Prime Minister of the day "it won't affect the pound in your pocket". It didn't - for a few weeks, then costs of imported materials started to rise sharply. Fortunately, practically everything needed to complete the boat had already been purchased and was already incorporated into her. The imported Iroko of which so much went into hull and decks would have made a vast difference in costs, and could have scuppered the whole project. The other financial gain was that purchase tax (on most goods at a rate of 33.3%) was not chargeable on boats, although it was charged on many of the materials going into her construction, but on cost price, not the price of the completed vessel. It was not long before the crafty politicians

"Celandine" underway at last, off the Essex coast.

invented VAT (they didn't invent it, they just copied what other countries were doing already).

Finally, in August, we took her away for her first family cruise, meeting up with George Jones and "PETER DUCK "in the river Alde. The boat sailed and handled like a throroughbred, but there was still a lot to do, and we were still fitting basics like coathooks and galley stowage. The next year I took her over to Holland in early summer, with a crew of chums who had helped me in one way or another - Michael Beaumont, of course, and the manager of Lloyd's Bank in Chelmsford, John Parrish. He was the most unconventional bank manager I have ever met, but a bright star due to rise in the hierarchy. It was a short break, but we visited some well loved places last seen when sailing "CAMPION".

Returning by ferry, we left her over there in the North of Holland and rejoined for a summer cruise en famille, flying from Southend airport in a rather primitive flying machine that was dual purpose - it could carry cars or machinery, rows of seats being installed when it was to carry passengers. The hard usage when carrying freight was apparent from the pieces of adhesive tape patching damage to the fragile lining material of the cabin. It proved a fascinating flight, bound for Rotterdam; there was a fresh Easterly wind blowing and as we flew in clear visibility over the Essex coast, all the sandbanks that I only knew as outlines on the charts very clearly defined, with a fringe of fierce surf breaking on the windward edges. There could not have been a clearer demonstration of onshore breezes caused by the heating of the land mass; by the time we were about 20 miles off the coast, there was no evidence of wind below us (we were probably not flying much more than 5000 feet) and ships were ploughing their way across a sea of glass below us. As our flight approached the Dutch coast, we could see that a fresh North-westerly wind was blowing - straight onshore.

From Rotterdam, we made our way North by train with a change at Amsterdam to a train that terminated at Enkhuizen, where "CELANDINE" had been berthed. After a visit to Medemblik (a place we found almost unrecognisable on a subsequent visit years later - the yachting explosion had caused construction of enormous marinas, coupled with new waterside housing), we made our way South to reach Amsterdam. To proceed through Amsterdam by boat, it is necessary to wait till about 2 am, when you switch your navigation lights on and wait for a gang to appear on the great Central Station railway bridge. Rails and overhead wires are disconnected, and the great bridge swings open. Miss it. and you can spend another 24 hours in Amsterdam, although there is an alternative, and in many ways more attractive route, via Haarlem. By night you continue through a series of bridges, which open in sequence. At one time, there were bridge keepers for each one, but on later visits a team proceeded by car to open the bridges, and this resulted in far longer waits for each bridge. A lot of the continentals are not suited by temperament to this kind of progress, and would race their boats to the next bridge, only to wait all the longer in boats that were not usually good at staying still. A heavy displacement boat is more docile and can be persuaded to keep her position whilst waiting.

The route South we took on this cruise is no longer available to boats with tall fixed masts, but we were glad to have had the experience. Visiting Leiden, we then took a canal that headed South through the suburbs of the Hague; a railway bridge obstructed our passage, and I walked to the nearby station where polite and obliging staff at the booking office phoned for someone to open the bridge for us - it would take about half an hour. The delay meant it was evening as we glided through the suburbs of the Hague, with our navigation lights on, and as we passed the many fine properties with lawns sweeping down to the canal, people enjoying a warm summer evening waved to us, whilst we saw reflections of our boat in their big picture windows. Finally we reached Delft. Undoubtedly, the boat was lying not far from where Vermeer painted his famous view from the sea, although the sea is now quite some distance from Delft. The clever thing that the Dutch do when reclaiming land is to keep the line of the coast or meer with a canal so that good routes are preserved for waterborne traffic. Unfortunately, our romantic view of Delft was somewhat marred the next morning by the sight of a dead dog caught in our mooring ropes. It is in this vicinity that a motorway bridge was subsequently built - high enough for a big barge or small coaster to pass through, but not high enough for a sailing yacht with tall fixed masts. At Rotterdam, Beryl left to return by the night steamer, and "CELANDINE" would sail from the Hook back to Essex. This is a system we have developed over the years; Beryl enjoys being afloat in sheltered waters, but hates open sea passages as she suffers from sea sickness. There is no point in inflicting misery on your loved one, and I always have recruited a crew of keen sailors to undertake this part of the venture. Over the years it has worked well.

WESTWARD HO!

THE year 1969 was to be the first of many subsequent trips in "CELANDINE" down Channel to the West Country and beyond. By this time in life, I had realised that it was a good tactic to make your way down West early in the summer, with long days and short nights, and a better prospect of favourable conditions. Later in the summer, any time in the later part of July or during August, the fierce Westerly winds are likely to set in. There are no hard and fast rules, but the probabilities are there.

So, on a fine June Friday morning we set off across the Thames Estuary with a favourable North Easterly wind. In those days, my route across the Estuary was to go through the Spitway into the Swin, cross by a gutway near the Knock John Tower and then through the Edinburgh channel to the North Foreland. We had left Walton at an early hour, and with the favourable wind made good progress so that by dusk we were past Folkestone and heading for Dungeness, having cleared the Dover Strait in daylight (the place terrifies me, even in daylight!). Dungeness is a dreary place - low lying land to the North and South of it, and a long stretch of featureless shingle out to the promontory. I'm not sure whether the later building of an atomic power station there is an improvement or not. From Dungeness our next target was the Royal Sovereign Tower, a strange looking construction in concrete with an asymmetric platform on top of a cylindrical column. At one corner is the light, above the accomodation and lookout deck, which at that time was fully manned on a watchkeeping basis; in more recent years, it has been converted to a fully automatic function, remote controlled from Harwich. In those days you could rely on a friendly wave from one of the windows if you were reasonably close. By the time we reached the Royal Sovereign, it was getting light, and we altered course to pass clear of Beachy Head; our down channel course passes close to Beachy Head.

Crew for this passage was four strong - my favourite number for a long passage; Michael Beaumont was with us, plus our mutual friends Robert Barlow and George Jones.

George did not agree with the South Coast - "your hand 'll always be in your pocket down there", but he was happy to come because he liked the West Country. With four watchkeepers aboard a routine of two on watch and two off can be kept up, and although to begin with the change from normal shoreside lifestyle can be a shock, it is surprising how quickly the body adapts to the new rythm. Robert was quite amazing with his steady routine that would not be disturbed by bad weather and other minor discomforts - at about half past ten in the morning he would disappear below, to re-emerge with morning coffee, and at 12 noon or soon after he would again disappear below and emerge with gin and tonics complete with thinly sliced lemon - it was our equivalent of the daily issue of rum in the Navy (sadly discontinued). "CELANDINE" was a very seakindly boat with an easy motion, but even so, in a strong wind he must have had to perform some feats of juggling.

As we rounded the South East corner of England, the coast began shielding us from the wind, which had become more Northerly and light, so we were forced to start the faithful Perkins diesel to maintain reasonable progress, and indeed, on this trip we had periods when the wind picked up to fill the sails, only to fail again after a few miles so that the engine had to be re-started. After Beachy Head and the Seven Sisters, the coastline recedes into a deep bay, and is almost continuously developed so that it is not particularly attractive; in those days there were no safe refuges until the Solent. Now, of course there is a marina at Pevensey and another at Brighton which offer shelter - in those days neither Dover or Newhaven offered much for yachts, whilst Shoreham and Littlehampton were unsafe to enter in strong onshore winds.

On this trip, the wind finally failed altogether as we approached Spithead and the afternoon became very hot; dropping the sails, we continued under power alone. As we had used the engine quite a bit, I decided to put in at Cowes to top up our fuel tank; as we headed through the Solent, the P & O liner "CHUSAN" passed by outward bound from Southampton, gleaming in the brilliant sunshine. Refuelling was completed quickly; it was stiflingly hot alongside, without the breeze created by our movement. George had disappeared ashore and returned clutching ice cream wafers - cornets might have been more practical, because by the time we were underweigh again, ice cream was dripping everywhere, and as we passed the hallowed lawn of the Squadron, our behaviour trying to eat these melting goodies was far from elegant. We should have done better, but what do you expect from East Coast sailors?

We pushed on Westward under power, there being no wind at all, and as we passed the Newtown River - a place always described as an idyllic remote anchorage, we lost count at about a hundred masts - of course, it was a fine Saturday evening. Just before midnight, we reached the Fairway Buoy marking the beginning of the Needles channel, but a light wind from Southeast and slack tide enabled us to make progress under sail alone; the off shore approach to the Needles Channel can be a wild and turbulent place, but tonight it was positively benign. The barometer had been falling steadily for some hours, so the fine weather that had brought us so far looked like ending soon. A course was set to take us well clear of Portland Bill, and we sailed quietly on through the early hours of Sunday, with a favourable tide helping to push us steadily Westwards. By four o'clock a misty Portland Bill light was abeam - another big milestone passed. This was coast I had sailed past so many times in my Tank Landing Craft days, although now it was veiled by darkness and a mist which was gathering.

The morning shipping forecast confirmed that the weather was soon to deteriorate, giving strengths of force 5-6 in the Portland area and 6-7 later in Plymouth. As far as we were concerned, the wind was again falling light and our faithful Perkins was once again called to help; it had also begun to rain which surely was an omen. "Rain before wind, then you must your tops'ls mind - Wind before rain then soon may you make sail again." The wind did pick up again later, still from a Southerly point which meant a comfortable sail and enabling us to shut down the engine again, much to everyone's relief. Our next major headland was Start point, at the Western end of Lyme Bay, and just after lunch we got a good radio bearing from the beacon on the lighthouse. This was long before the days of Decca navigation, let alone GPS and one depended on good navigation by dead reckoning - which meant keeping a regular record of course and speed and of the tidal sreams that would influence the vessel's course made good. The rather primitive hand held radio direction finder was pretty basic, and as the signals were only emitted for a short period at a regular interval, obtaining a reliable bearing was not easy - not for me, anyway - some people seemed to manage better.

The mist thickened and the rain continued so that the massive bulk of Start Point was obscured, and it was essential to keep the most accurate record of our progress in order to slot in through the narrow entrance into Salcombe, which was to be our first West Country port of call. The two pilot's quides consulted gave conflicting advice about the depth of water over the notorious bar, but our arrival was with the benefit of a rising tide. The wind was still light, but blowing straight on to the unseen rocky shore; we lowered the sails and motored cautiously in the general direction of the entrance, according to our reckoning. Eventually, we slowed right down as the call of the gulls on the cliffs could now be heard along with the wash of the swell breaking at the cliff foot. Suddenly, we were able to identify two dark masses of cliff and the entrance ahead - a great relief, as these occasions can be very nail biting. The next query was how much water over the bar and through the mist we came past a fisherman at anchor in an open boat - the tide was sweeping into the harbour, and may well have helped in guiding us in. "How much water over the bar" we hailed. In a thick Devon accent, the answer came "Enough for you", and he disappeared in the mist astern.

This was slightly uncertain information, as he did not ask what we drew, but as we were an East Coast boat drawing only 5 feet, he would probably have assumed we were deeper than that. Just at that moment, somebody cried out "Stewart, I can see the bottom". Now to an Essex based sailor used to sailing in silt laden waters, this could be very bad news, but I was not shaken because my eyes had been on the echo sounder for some time - it was giving between 10-12 feet. Once inside, the visibility improved and a weak sun began to filter through.

The following morning saw us weighing anchor by half past eight, and once off shore we were able to ease the sheets for a splendid full sail from the Southerly breeze, in clear conditions. Passing Bolt Tail, to the West of Salcombe I was reminded of the sad case of the "HERZOGIN CECILE" which went ashore here in conditions similar to those of the previous day, back in the 1930s. Without radar and in fog, after a long passage, a small error in navigation could lead to disaster. and I remembered that as a boy I read in the papers of the desperate, but unsuccessful, attempts to save this graceful fully rigged sailing ship - even then, one of the last in commercial trade.

River Yealm 1969 - "Celandine" anchored in the pool.

After a fast passage, we entered the River Yealm soon after midday, with a minimum of 7 feet over the bar. The Yealm is a very picturesque inlet with tree lined cliffs enveloping it all round, and well sheltered once you have cleared the hurdle of a bar that can be dangerous. We anchored in the pool, and went ashore to Robert's House there. It was a family holiday house, and because he had served at nearby Plymouth during his Naval Service, he had strong local connections and eventually retired there. For this one evening, he was reunited with his wife, Betty, and then rejoined for another early departure; I was able to telephone Beryl at Cardiff, where she was on an educational conference connected with her role as a County councillor.

The early morning shipping forecast the next day, Tuesday, was not exactly encouraging - wind South-southwest, force 7, gale 8 later. We tied down 2 reefs, which made "CELANDINE'S" mains'l look very small, motored out over the bar, where it was not long after high water, and stood out on an offshore tack to clear the Mewstone, which prevented a more direct course for Plymouth. "CELANDINE" made good progress through the seas; she had been designed with sharp bows to cope with the short seas of the Thames Estuary and Southern North Sea, but I have to say she went much better in the longer seas encountered down there. It did not take long clawing into the wind before we were able to free the sheets and run for the Eastern entrance to Plymouth - although her gaff ketch rig prevented her pointing as close to the wind as a Bermudian rigged boat, her hull shape and the drive from her loose footed mains'l enabled her to go to windward well in rough weather.

I stayed on the helm to nurse her through the very steep following seas at a breakneck speed; the crew told me not to look behind me - if they hadn't said it, I probably wouldn't have done, but, of course, I did and did not like what I saw - great heaping waves threatening to break over our stern. By half past ten we were passing through the entrance and heading at speed up the harbour, but with a less threatening sea astern. Signal stations were all flying Southerly gale warning cones, and it behove us to find shelter - there was also a lot of water flying about which seemed to be a mixture of rain and spray. In search of shelter, we rounded into the St Germans or Lynher river and just round the corner of Jupiter point found some robust looking moorings off a deserted Naval sailing centre under the lee of a tree covered hill, so we picked up one of these, put two warps on the mooring and thankfully retreated below to light the coal stove, dry ourselves out and prepare some lunch. Later it certainly blew a full gale and the rain lashed us horizontally; we were glad to be so snug on our protected mooring.

The following day, the wind began to ease - summer gales do not usually last very long, and we ventured out and round to Sutton Harbour, where we found a berth alongside, just clear of the fishing boats moored by the fish market, and were able to go shopping for supplies in the old part of the city, the Barbican. Large areas of Plymouth were almost obliterated by bombing in the 2nd World War, but it is surprising how many of the old buildings round Sutton Harbour survived - many of them were dilapidated and derelict, scenes of a a former busy existence as warehouses and chandleries supporting the brisk commercial shipping trade carried on there by trading schooners and ketches. The fish market still thrives, but most of the buildings today are catering for tourism; some people regret this, but it has found a new commercial raison d'etre for the buildings and employment for people, and also enabled restoration of the buildings, many of them historic and of great character. We were lucky to have seen it as it was, but you cannot regret the fact that new trade has been found for the area - it had to have a commercial reason for survival.

The following day, Thursday, and over half way through our week afloat, we set sail from Sutton Harbour at noon, following the long since vanished wake of the Mayflower and the Pilgrim Fathers. This time, we cleared Plymouth via the Western entrance, used by all the larger ships. It was still blowing quite fresh from the South, and we had one reef in the mains'l; conditions were somewhat boisterous, but that was not allowed to disrupt ship's routine - a note in the log from Robert announced "1240, broached new lemon" , indicating the ritual of pre prandial gins was taking place.

The weather was again deteriorating, after the briefest of more benign interludes; by mid afternoon rain and mist were setting in, accompanied by a strengthening wind. We were bound for Fowey, a deep water harbour and busy china clay port, but the entrance is not very conspicuous from seaward, being a mere crack in the high cliffs. Bearing away, we raced towards the menacing cliffs, now shrouded by continuous rain, and hoping we had got our position right. It was impossible to identify the entrance, but we had managed to take a bearing on the conspicuous Gribbin beacon to the West of the entrance. A Southerly gale warning cone was flying from the nearby coastguard station. The trouble with us East Coast sailors is that we are used to low lying coasts - something 50 feet high is a real cliff to us, so that when off a coast with cliffs of 100 feet or so, it looks very near whereas you are still probably all of two or more miles away. For us Essex men, another nerve racking episode was developing as "CELANDINE" charged towards the rugged black cliffs towards an unseen entrance. Suddenly a large freighter slid out from what could have just been a slit in the scenery. It was almost dead ahead and picked out the entrance for us in no uncertain manner, so we held our course with confidence. We picked up a visitor's mooring off the Royal Fowey Yacht Club and went ashore; fortunately there was a running mooring to haul the dinghy away from the shore - as there was a considerable swell licking around the landing slip, our small fibreglass dinghy would soon have been smashed to pieces. Our oilskins were dripping with the continuous rain, but it was cozy and dry inside, where we met a very warm welcome - several pairs of binoculars had been watching our headlong dash into the harbour, and there were complimentary remarks about our ship and her seaworthiness.

The locals advised us to go up to Wisemans pool a little further upriver, where we would find shelter from the swell coming into the outer part of the harbour and they knew there were several vacant moorings. It was sound advice, because we found a mooring there, well sheltered from the wind which became another full gale during the evening. Once again, there was a hasty retreat into the cosy comfort of "CELANDINE'S" saloon.

By Friday afternoon the weather had moderated, and we set off for Falmouth with a fair, but light wind. The sun was shining again, highlighting the rugged coastline, the sea a deep blue and the wave tops sparkling. What a contrast - but sailing is rather like that, you have to take the rough with the smooth, as indeed you do in life. So pleasant were the conditions that a spinner was streamed astern, with no luck - we had been forced to start the engine, and were probably going too fast. Just before seven we entered Falmouth Estuary and the luckless mackerel line was hauled in while Robert served a celebratory gin and tonic. That night was spent at anchor in a deep pool at the entrance to Restronguet creek, with idyllic surroundings.

"Westward Ho" - "Celandine" off St Anthony's Light, approaching Falmouth Harbour.

The next morning, "CELANDINE" was put on a mooring off Falmouth Boat Construction's yard which clung to a steep cliffside at the Northern end of Falmouth town (They have long since moved to the other side of the harbour, at Flushing). A little further out from the shore were two magnificent steam tugs moored ready for use and in steam. Falmouth was dying as a port, and it was obvious they could not survive much longer - the whole place had been devastated by a long suicidal strike at the shipyard which had affected the entire local economy. Falmouth Boat Construction (builders of the well known "Falmouth pilot" cruising yachts) were very helpful and enabled us to store our dinghy ashore in their somewhat restricted premises. The raucous seagulls that wheel constantly over the town bade us farewell as we left in the local train to connect with a main line train at Truro.

The end of July saw us back in Falmouth en famille complete with Jane, the Border terrier, having arrived by car after a start from home in the small hours. In those days, the way West by car was to go through the centre of London and arrive in Falmouth by lunch time - there was no M25 or M4 in those days, but when you got there there were not a lot of yachts either. The sailing oyster boats raced nearly every evening and made a splendid sight, setting every bit of canvas they could muster, with the jumble of buildings that was the centre of the town, clinging to the steep slopes that led down to the water's edge, as a backdrop.

We crossed Falmouth Bay to the Helford River, the first of many subsequent visits. There was room to anchor off Helford itself in those days; when we entered the anchorage, we could hardly believe our eyes, for there amongst the yachts was what looked like a pirate schooner with heavily raked masts, gaff rig, dead eyes and lanyards setting up the rigging, and a picturesquely ballustraded rail round her poop. The Stars & Stripes flew from her ensign staff, and on her counter stern was the name "INTEGRITY" of Padanarum - a small port in Massachusetts. Needless to say, we were intrigued and wanted to know more about this unusual vessel, which we were to find out on a later occasion that summer.

While we were in the Helford river, it came on to blow hard from the South, but we were snugly anchored and went for very attractive walks ashore through narrow steep sided lanes in country known as "The Meneague". On Monday August the 4th, the wind had moderated to a fresh squally force 4-5 from South by West, and we left with one reef down, which was quickly shaken out when we found the wind continuing to moderate. Leaving the shelter of the estuary, there was quite a lumpy sea left over from the strong winds and shortly before bearing away to run with the wind back into Falmouth, Beryl sighted a flare almost dead ahead. Hardening in the sheets slightly, we made for the source of the flare, going like a startled racehorse, and were soon approaching a small motor cruiser rolling and wallowing in the seas, with a very green and miserable looking wife and daughter huddled in the open cockpit; both engines had broken down. I had already prepared a good length of what we still called "Terylene" rope in those days, and prepared to heave to on his windward side to provide a lee, and take him in tow; the light displacement motor boat was making leeway so fast that she was too far away to pass a line by the time I had hove to, so we had to gather way again, bear away and gybe round in order to put myself well on to the lee side of the casualty. It almost certainly meant "CELANDINE" would suffer some damage as he drifted down on us, but it was going to be the only way to pass a towline so we slowed right down under his lee; he insisted on passing me his line as I think he thought it might lessen the salvage claim that I certainly had no thought of making. Miraculously, as the two boats came close together, they both rolled away from each other, and then we had gone past him and the thin piece of coloured polypropylene line stretched like a banjo string. We quickly passed him our stout "Terylene" line and then let that take most of the strain. Bearing away for Falmouth, the casualty snatched cruelly at our stern; a constant watch had to be kept because we were towing our own dinghy astern on a relatively short painter and to let one foul the other could have resulted in an embarassing muddle; we were all kept pretty busy with that boisterous tow. As we passed the Coastguard Station on Pendennis, they called us by lamp, asking if all was well. Fortunately I carried an ex-Admiralty Aldis lamp aboard, which was quickly rigged, but my hands and attention were already very fully occupied, so I flashed back a terse "OK" which satisfied them.

As we reached the shelter of Falmouth inner harbour, we lowered the sails and started the engine, the Lifeboat boarding launch came out to meet us, so we passed the tow to them. The rather jolly character in charge, who turned out to be the permanent lifeboat mechanic asked if we would be around for a little while, as he would like to come and see us. I anchored fairly near the lifeboat mooring, and when he returned he explained that he was also a correspondent for the local paper, *"The Falmouth Packet"*. Apparently the Coastguard had watched us going to the casualty, seen us miss the first time and stood the lifeboat crew by, only to report that we had succeeded in getting the tow, so they were stood down - this meant they missed their "launching money", so, sadly, we had done them out of a job.

A night or so later, the wind had gone round to the East, and we found a very pleasant sheltered anchorage under the cliffs between St Mawes and St Just, where cows were grazing on the steep sloping pastures above the cliff, and the sound of a waterfall could be heard splashing on to the beach. Some time after midnight as "CELANDINE" slumbered on the glassy calm water, I awoke to see a very bright light coming through the cabin portholes. Being in relatively shallow water, I knew we were not about to be run down by a big ship, and our anchor light was burning bright and steady. Then I saw the lifeboat was the source of the searchlight beam; they were looking for two boys who had gone missing in a rowing boat and wondered whether we had seen them. We were not able to help them with any information, but just before they left, a hatch opened and out of the darkness came the rich Cornish voice of our friend the motor mechanic and newspaper correspondent - "we're going to make sure we get to this one afore yew do". The lifeboat went off into the darkness to the sounds of laughter from both boats.

On a Friday morning early in August, Beryl went ashore at Falmouth (with the dog, who disliked being tossed about as much as she did) to start driving Eastwards, with Roland Vicky and myself to take "CELANDINE" to meet her again at Newton Ferrers Our mooring off Falmouth Boat Construction for the length of "CELANDINE'S" stay was finally dropped just before ll am; there was no wind and most of the passage had to be made under power. As we approached the Eddystone light in the late afternoon, a breeze came in from the South, so we hoisted sail, which only helped us for the very last part of the passage. By seven o'clock in the evening, we dropped anchor off the Yealm Hotel, and Beryl and Jane (the dog!) rejoined us. After a day in the Yealm, we found a berth ashore for the car and then sailed for Plymouth, where in perfect conditions an anchorage was found off Earth Hill up the St Germans River for lunch (this was to become a favourite anchorage on future West Country visits) and an exploration ashore. Later that day we returned to the anchorage in the Yealm pool, ready to leave on the Monday morning for Dartmouth - Beryl and Jane by car, the rest of us by boat.

Light airs again caused most of the trip to be made either under power or motor sailing, but we did catch seven mackerel. A shower of rain finished off what wind there was, and sails were stowed before we entered the Dart, where Beryl rejoined us, having found somewhere to park the car. Then we found an empty mooring for the night off Greenaway House (home of Agatha Christie). One of the things we were warned about in the Dart is the daily procession of pleasure boats which causes considerable wash, but "CELANDINE" is a heavy displacement boat, and we were not unduly inconvenienced. However, one went by with someone waving to us - it was Penny, the wife of an old schoolfriend of mine who had settled down in that part of the world; he was in the Customs & Excise revenue cutter fleet and became senior Captain before he retired. She was entertaining visitors, and taking them out on a river excursion.

The next day, my cousin, Jonathon Crowe was due to join us at Totnes, where we would meet him off the train - by good fortune, high water that day was 2016 and the train due at 1805, so after refuelling at Dart Marina, we made the delightful trip upriver on a rising tide, and secured alongside some half an hour or so before the train was due. It was a good tide, so there was plenty of water - unlike our native Essex shore, where Spring tides occur at about mid-day and midnight, down in the West Country, they occur on morning and evening tides.

The highlight of the following day was that the daughter of a longstanding friend of Beryl's she met in her wartime Girton days (the privations of war time conditions at Cambridge forged very firm bonds between those who endured them) was getting married at St Marychurch, Babbacombe. After dropping Beryl to pick up the car, we took the boat over to the Kingswear side of the river and picked up a mooring not too far from the pier. Jonathon rowed Roland and myself ashore, looking slightly out of place in our morning suits. A taxi took us to the wedding, and we returned later in the day by the same route to rejoin the ship and prepare to sail the following morning, while Beryl stayed ashore in a hotel.

Morning suits safely bagged up and stowed below, we set sail the following day, Friday the 15th August for the long haul across Lyme Bay, a crossing of over 40 nautical miles during which the Dorset coast recedes from view until Portland Bill is sighted. The wind was light, but favourable, and conditions pleasant as the Devon coast receded astern; our position that afternoon was determined by radio signals from Start Point astern of us, Roches Douvres in Brittany and the Casquettes in the Channel Islands. By the time Portland Bill was abeam, it was dark, and the light Southwest wind had veered round to a Northerly point, still light, but strong enough to push us along at a comfortable speed. Before first light we had sighted the Needles light, but not until after a minor drama in the small hours of Saturday morning, when the weekend sailors were emerging from the Solent. A ghostly apparition caused by someone momentarily shining a light on his sails appeared on our starboard bow, too close for comfort. Our own lights were burning bright and clear, but no lights at all showed from this mystery vessel; after a few anxious minutes peering into the darkness, we decided he must have got out of the way and we relaxed again. Why do people have to do crazy things like this?

There was no problem with our next sighting - a brightly lit passenger liner heading West from the Needles channel, then when we reached the Fairway Buoy at the entrance to the Needles Channel, making very slow progress due to a strong adverse tide, the Cunarder "CARMANIA" came in from seaward. It was just becoming light, but as she approached us, her name and funnel lights were switched on - rather a nice gesture, we thought, or were they doing it anyway because they were approaching port? The tide was still running foul, and we anchored in Hurst Roads to catch up on some sleep and let the foul tide expend itself.

Later in the day when we resumed our course for Gosport, we saw the liner "CHUSAN" again (previously sighted when we were heading West in June) bound Westwards for the Needles Channel, shortly to be followed by the liner Iberia. Southampton was still a busy port for passenger liners on regular routes, although their days were numbered and soon the only passenger ships would be cruise liners - floating entertainment palaces, rather than a means of travel. We berthed in Gosport at Camper & Nicholson's marina, to be met by Beryl in the car, which made for easy travel home with all our gear. When berthing, we noticed nearby the American schooner "INTEGRITY" which we had seen at Helford. The skipper invited us aboard this pretty and rakish looking little ship, which had been built by a boatbuilder for himself, using woods that all grew in the Massachusetts area, and being something of a purist, he would not allow any synthetic materials to be used in construction or sails and rigging (he would have been horrified by "CELANDINE'S" all polyester cordage and sails). The paid skipper had brought her across the Atlantic, and was awaiting the owner's arrival; we commented on the skipper's lack of American accent - not surprising, as he was a Lancashire schoolmaster on a sabbatical. Down below she was charming and quite simply furnished, but the master's cabin under the poop was rounded to conform to the shape of the stern, and there was a delightful Greek key pattern cornice moulding following the curve of the lining. However, he had strayed from the purist theme by installing a large diesel engine (I don't blame him!)

Sadly, not more than a year or so later, she was abandoned in heavy weather near the notorious Cape Hatteras off the Carolinas, when a rather inexperienced crew were taking her South to the West Indies far too late in the season, and suffered a knockdown. They were taken off by a freighter which inevitably damaged her, but this stoutly built ship refused to sink and sailed herself down there, where she stranded on a coral reef and sank The author Frank Mulville tells the dramatic story of her abandonment, and his persistent but unsuccessful attempts to salvage her, in the book "Schooner Integrity".

A long weekend in the Solent was another new experience for an Essex lad - sailing on Friday from Gosport to Yarmouth en famille - the waters were pretty crowded with yachts who did not seem to keep a very good lookout. We arrived in Yarmouth Harbour, where the Harbourmaster welcomed us - he took a liking to "CELANDINE", and said "You can moor to these piles here, where I can see her from my office". The fore and aft pile mooring was very convenient for getting ashore in the dinghy, but it was not long before boats were rafting up either side of us. On a recent visit to Yarmouth, I found the layout had completely changed from when we were there in "CELANDINE", and the Harbour master's office resited to another quay. The Solent has very attractive scenery and wonderful sheltered waters in which to sail, but it was just hopelessly overcrowded which did not make for relaxation. At that time I could not foresee what the yachting explosion was going to be like, and no doubt by today's standards I would think that the 1969 Solent was relatively uncrowded. Finally, on a Friday evening in mid September, we travelled down by train to Portsmouth Harbour station and took the ferry to Gosport. At that time, there were still some steam ferries operating, built by Camper & Nicholson and powered by a miniature triple expansion steam engine. There was a large open space on the foredeck for bicycles, of which there were many in the rush hour. At least two of those ferries are now operating on the Thames as London sightseeing boats, but their steam power has been replaced by diesel.

No time was lost in getting underweigh, and soon after 7-30 that evening, "CELANDINE" was heading down Spithead under power, there being little or no wind. It was not until half past three in the morning, somewhere off Brighton that a wind came to fill the sails, and we were able to dispense with the services of Mr Perkins. During the night we had passed the Owers Lightvessel, and now had Beachy Head light ahead as our next major mark. Later, heading for Dungeness after passing the Royal Sovereign tower, the wind fell light again, visibility deteriorated with a light drizzle, and our dripping silent progress became so slow that the engine had to be restarted to push us up through the Dover straits - as I have already hinted, not my favourite place as it is full of ferries racing cross channel at 18 knots, the tides are fierce and even on a calm day there is always a jobble, no doubt caused by the ferries and big ships proceeding up and down channel in the constricted waters. In a slow moving boat, it is not the ferry racing for Dover entrance that you worry about, but the one that is a smudge on the horizon which will manifest itself into a very large ship heading for you before your very eyes, probably on a collision course. Discretion is the only policy - keep out of its way, and just as you breath a sigh of relief, you look round to find they have fired another one at you from behind Dover harbour wall. On this occasion, the fog had thinned by the time we got there, but it was still enough to give anxieties.

Finally, as the sun was slipping down to the horizon (it was by now mid September and the days were drawing in rapidly), we entered Ramsgate harbour to secure against the Western arm, which towered above us like a cliff. There was a long ladder which gave us access to the top, and we rigged our warps as slips round the bollards so that all could be let go from on board early the next morning.It was a quiet night - in strong winds Ramsgate outer harbour can be a very restless place - but this night we were rewarded with a peaceful berth, ensuring a good night's sleep.

At five the following morning, we were making ready to leave in total darkness. During the night, an all-night angling contest had developed and a forest of fishing rods hung over the wall, their lines disappearing into the dark abyss caused by bright lights along the roadway on top. There was a considerable chill in the air, and there was little evidence of any anglers - they had perhaps migrated to an all night "caff" for a warming cup. A trot of boats ahead of us meant that we had to leave stern first - fortunately "CELANDINE" handled very well going astern, so it was not a problem. As we gathered way astern, I suddenly saw light on a gossamer thread across the transom, at the same time was aware of a bell jingling agitatedly on a dancing fishing rod above us. A few seconds later, the rod disappeared over the edge into the pitch dark chasm below. It was too late to do anything except complete the manoeuvre, turn the boat round and proceed to sea. The fisherman, when he returned, would undoubtedly be mistified by the complete disappearance of his tackle, but at least would be able to talk about the "enormous one that got away", swallowing hook, line, sinker and rod.

Our early departure caught a favourable tide up to the North Foreland; there was no wind and we were once again motoring through the grey, chilly morning. The outer Thames Estuary is a very large area, and crossing it is a considerably longer passage than crossing the channel - it can be both boring and sometimes very wild, and treacherous, since it has dangerous sandbanks running out a long way, well out of sight of land unless visibility is exceptional. On this mid-September Sunday, it was just boring, but interest en route was created by a large tanker aground in the Edinburgh Channel with three tugs in attendance, no doubt waiting for high water that afternoon to try and get her off.

By late morning a favourable wind had sprung up so we were able to hoist full sail, and shut down the faithful Perkins diesel. Crossing near the Knock John tower (a wartime defence fortification) we headed for a gutway between the East and West Barrow sands into the Swin channel. Now only marked by a buoy, in my early pre-war days aboard "EUONYM" there was a full scale lightship there - the Mid-Barrow. For reasons I am unable to explain over thirty years later, we were heading for Heybridge Basin rather than our mooring at Walton, and this meant that we had to be there at or near high water to get through the lock. By this time, the nuclear power station at Bradwell had become an accepted seamark and good guide into the Blackwater Estuary; we made good progress with a favourable tide and wind that brought us to Heybridge by three o'clock - no time to spare, since high water was predicted for 4 minutes past three that day. Sails were stowed quickly, and twenty minutes after high water "CELANDINE" was in the lock.

LIFE ASHORE TAKES OVER

BY this time in our lives, life at home had become very busy - the business was developing and thriving, but it was very hard work, with fierce competition against many new entrants who took a long time to find out the hard way that it was not as easy as they had thought. At the same time Beryl was becoming deeply involved in her work on Chelmsford Rural District Council - a caring and personal organisation free of party politics - no doubt it had its shortcomings, but a few years later central government was to destroy it and merge it with Chelmsford Borough Council. Government politicians are constantly wanting to make their mark with radical changes, but Westminster has never really understood the needs of local people outside London. Beryl was also on Essex County Council, becoming deeply involved in education. I was still serving on Writtle Parish Council, the Parochial Church Council, The Village Hall Trustees, as well as now becoming involved in Cruising Association matters. In addition, there was the Writtle Society which, with my great friend and neighbour Johnnie Devlin, we had set up in the early sixties. There was also quite a hectic social life - dinner parties at Greenbury House and at the houses of a circle of friends in the area. Looking back on it, I don't know how we coped, but we had the energy and don't remember it being a serious problem. The Lord gives you the strength to do it all at that age, but as I write these words, I do wonder how we managed it all. During this time, the village had been expanded by an enormous development in 1965-6, due to a sudden granting of planning permission by Essex County Council, for a very large area of land which included development on the village's football pitch. The whole thing left a very nasty smell, and the serving County Councillor (an estate agent from outside the village) was not seen again locally. Indeed, this episode was instrumental in Beryl being asked to stand for the County Council. Successful negotiations with the developer finally resulted in a piece of Green Belt land being sold to the village as a playing field, for one shilling (it was easier to do it this way than as an outright gift). Gradually the whole thing simmered down, and only those with long memories will remember some of the acrimonious meetings that ocurred at that time, and the final result was a very much larger playing field than previously. Although this all happened well over thirty years ago, the dangers are still there and a ruthless developer will stop at nothing to change the planning designation of a piece of land; the potential rewards are unbelievable.

It had become the custom over the years to have an end - of - season cruise; in those days small diesel fired boat heaters had not been developed, so few people sailed at that time of year, but both "CAMPION" and "CELANDINE" had solid fuel stoves which gave a wonderful dry heat. The one fitted to "CELANDINE" was more sophisticated than that on "CAMPION" - a "Tor Gem" in smart enamelled finish, with better draught control and capable, when fed with the right sort of anthracite or "Phurnacite", of staying in all night. Equally they were happy to run on wood, and in those days a walk along the shore was always taken with a bucket to fill with choice lumps of driftwood.

So, after a six week break from sailing while other matters were dealt with, we finally locked out from Heybridge Basin late on a Thursday afternoon at the end of October and slipped downriver in the gathering dusk to West Mersea, with Michael Beaumont and Robert Barlow aboard once more. By the time we picked up a vacant buoy it was almost totally dark. The next morning saw us leaving with a pleasant wind of about force 2 - 3 from Southwest and the last of an ebb tide under us. All morning we continued at a steady pace up the Wallet, past Clacton and Walton piers, with a strengthening of the wind helping to push us against the flood tide. Just after half past one the strong tide carried us through the Deben Bar into the river, where we anchored for a belated lunch a little way above Felixstowe ferry. Here we awaited the flood tide to develop before heading upriver to Woodbridge, where we berthed as darkness fell, in the newly developed Whisstock's marina, formed out of the old tide mill pond. Whisstocks had built this marina on a shoestring, although the dredging operations must have been costly. By today's standards, it was primitive, but it was one of the early ones on the East Coast and at last gave a place for visiting yachts to lie close to the town centre without drying out or having to use a dinghy; water was retained by a sill, over which boats passed when the tide had reached sufficient height. Now known as the "Tide Mill Yacht Harbour" it has been improved beyond all recognition, with all the facilities to be expected in a modern marina. Richard Kember, who runs it, once was an apprentice boatbuilder with Whisstocks, and the redevelopment over a number of years is a tribute to the Kember family's efforts.

Early the following morning, Saturday, we were off on the tide, slipping down this most beautiful river in the early morning light, the tree lined banks shrouded in an autumn mist that gave them a strange ethereal quality; so beautiful was the scene that we hardly spoke. At seven o'clock we picked up a mooring off Ramsholt for a slap up breakfast - how wonderful is the smell of frying eggs and bacon on a chilly autumn morning. Later, when the tide was again rising, we pushed out over the bar, and after a walk ashore at Stone Point in the Walton Backwaters, which yielded a rich haul of firewood for our stove, we anchored for the night in Hamford Water, where there was an atmosphere of complete solitude and the only sounds were those of the wild fowl and waders on the marshy fringes.

In those days, we never stayed anywhere for very long, and Sunday saw us heading up the Orwell to Ipswich, where Michael Beaumont was disembarked at a landing place in the New Cut, to catch a train home. Slipping downriver as the light failed, we picked up a mooring off Pin Mill for the night and retreated to the warmth and comfort of "CELANDINE'S" saloon. After a quick trip ashore at Pin Mill to pay our mooring charges, we left on the ebb down the Orwell with 2 reefs in the mains'l, as it was blowing fresh from the South West. With a thrashing beat up the Wallet, "CELANDINE" made good progress with help from the strengthening flood tide, and just before complete

darkness set in, berthed at Ian Brown's yard, Rowhedge, ready to go into her winter mudberth. Laying up is always a sad business and coming back a week later to a boat with no companionable crew aboard, and from which everything has been stripped off and put into store, is like visiting someone who has gone into hibernation for the winter.

Ian Brown's yard at Rowhedge 1971 - all the buildings and slipways along the extensive river frontage have been demolished to make way for attractive riverside "des res". "Celandine's" stern (under winter cover) alongside the quay.

BACK TO HOLLAND AGAIN - AND ADVENTURES WITH BRIDGES.

T HE following year, 1970, we returned to Holland for our main cruise; the family, Roland aged 19 and Vicky 17, were by now experienced crew members and together with their friends were a useful help for passages. Holland, compared with the West Country and beyond, was for us an easier option. In years when we have planned our main summer cruise to Cornwall and Devon, non sailing friends would say "so you're not going abroad this summer?" I then have to point to a map of England and show them the long haul down channel, to compare it with the relatively shorter and easier passages to the near continent. Such passages also avoid my least favourite stretch of water, the Dover straits.

For the outward passage, our friend and ex Naval officer John King joined us, with Vicky and Dave Whitfield, a friend of Roland's who he had met when sailing in the STA schooner "MALCOLM MILLER". For some reason I cannot explain, we sailed from Ian Brown's wharf at Rowhedge at midnight on Friday the 31st July instead of from our mooring in the Walton Backwaters. This meant we had some distance to travel before we could steer for Holland, as the long arm of the Gunfleet sands had to be cleared. Winds were fickle, but kept us going till about 5 in the morning, when the engine had to be started somewhere near the Sunk Lightship. All the way across was a mixture of sailing when the fickle winds served, punctuated by periods of progress under power.

By the afternoon, we were getting radio bearings off points on the Dutch coast. That evening, we hove to, which always has an amazing affect on a boat's motion at sea, even in calm weather, in order to cook a good meal and prepare for another night at sea. As dusk fell, we were sailing along quietly with a Northerly wind that enabled us to lay a course for our chosen port of entry, Ijmuiden. There is an aerial radio beacon there, and we were now obtaining signals from it; air radio beacons were much easier for obtaining a good bearing, since they transmit continually unlike the sea radio beacons which transmitted in groups, at intervals for a limited period. As Ijmuiden was our destination, all we had to do was home in on it, and at 9 o'clock on Sunday morning, "CELANDINE" entered the outer harbour.

There is a thrill about making a successful landfall after any passage out of sight of land - even crossing the outer Thames Estuary, it is pleasing when the North Foreland is sighted, always some time after the low lying Essex coast has vanished below the horizon. After locking into the North Sea canal which leads to Amsterdam, we cleared Customs and phoned my brother-in-law James Myatt, who was a serving as a major in BAOR, Germany, to confirm our arrival - there were to be some complicated family meetings ahead. We pushed on through Amsterdam and into the Isselmeer up to Enkhuizen, and that same evening James and Fiona arrived to collect Vicky, who was to stay with them,while the rest of us left the boat the following morning, securely berthed in the Jachthaven.

We returned to the boat later in August with Beryl (who had to conform to school holidays as by then she had become chairman of Essex Education committee) and Roland, sailing the following day to Medemblik, where our entrance to the harbour was impressive - as we passed through the entrance, the town band struck up! The harbour was quite full, and we made fast outside the "SEVEN KINGS", a Sea Scout boat. For several years I had watched this boat building in a field beside the A12 at Hainault. The enthusiastic troop leader had organised its construction, and it was good to see her in commission at last. A keen young Sea Scout showed us over the boat, of which he was immensely proud and explained how they earned sea time with the hours of work they

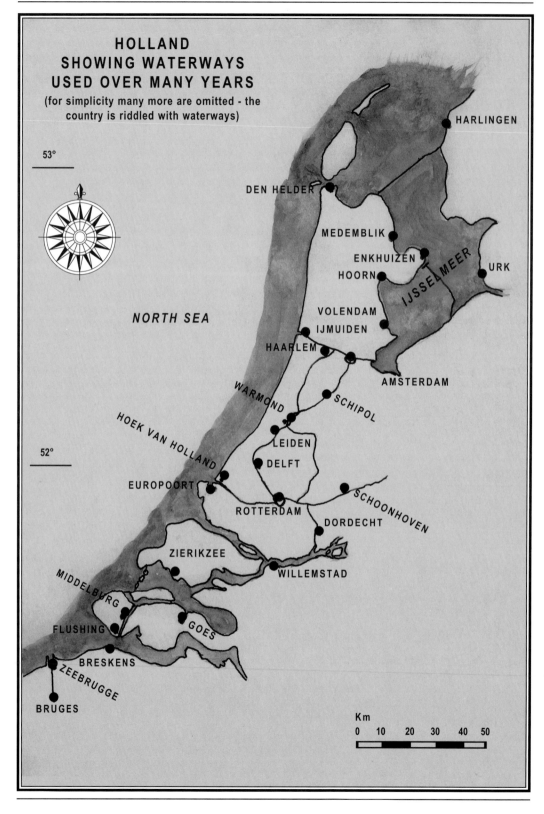

HOLLAND SHOWING WATERWAYS USED OVER MANY YEARS

(for simplicity many more are omitted - the country is riddled with waterways)

53°

NORTH SEA

52°

HARLINGEN

DEN HELDER

MEDEMBLIK

ENKHUIZEN

HOORN

URK

IJSSELMEER

VOLENDAM

IJMUIDEN

HAARLEM

AMSTERDAM

WARMOND

SCHIPOL

HOEK VAN HOLLAND

LEIDEN

DELFT

EUROPOORT

ROTTERDAM

SCHOONHOVEN

DORDECHT

ZIERIKZEE

WILLEMSTAD

MIDDELBURG

GOES

FLUSHING

BRESKENS

ZEEBRUGGE

BRUGES

Km
0   10   20   30   40   50

Brother-in-law James Myatt at the helm off the then island of Urk in the Isselmeer.

contributed. It made me think of my days as a Sea Scout in the Third Chalkwell Bay, but we never had a vessel as fine as this to sail in. Brother-in-Law James had also benefited from being in the same troop, and it was his experience with youngsters coupled with his early days of dinghy racing that made him develop into both a superb ocean racing skipper, and a great force in the Sail Training movement. With his cry of *"Rule Britannia"* youngsters would follow him and knuckle down to the most daunting tasks.

At Medemblik, James and Fiona joined us, bringing Vicky back to rejoin the ship. We sailed in perfect weather to what was then still the island of Urk, with a fishing fleet and related industry; over the years I have seen so many islands in the Isselmeer tacked on to the nearest piece of land, and their fishing industries disappear. After a perfect day's sailing, we returned to Medemblik and the next day the weather broke as a fierce So'wester raged across the flat land and shallow inland sea.

The following day, the wind, though still strong, had abated somewhat and we left Medemblik with 2 reefs in the mains'l and started slogging our way South towards Amsterdam. In the brackish waters, "CELANDINE" was less buoyant than in salt water, and that, coupled with the short vicious sea made it a very wet sail, during the course of which Roland managed to lose a contact lens - there was no hope of finding something the size of a small fish scale in the water running across the cockpit floor from the constant sheets of spray coming over. Gradually we reached the more sheltered conditions at the Southern end of the Meer, passing the Marken light in smooth water.

After the delays one must expect in traversing Holland - bridges, and a lock, we reached the Oude Houthaven (old wood harbour) at Amsterdam some time after 8 in the evening. Passing through another bridge and a lock, we secured to the quayside immediately in front of the great Amsterdam Central Station bridge. This time we were the only yacht Southbound; our navigation lights went on at about 1 a.m., but when the bridge opened shortly before two, an enormous dredging rig, with a tug at each end passed through, and we tagged on close behind. Every bridge opened in quick succession for this outfit, so we stuck to the aft end of this convoy like a leach - the bridge keepers wasted no time in closing down again and we had to hurry through to avoid our mizzen mast being demolished by the closing bridges. After clearing the eight bridges through the sleeping streets of Amsterdam, we could relax and made fast to a quay in order to grab some sleep at the end of a very long and energetic day. The factory nearby really did not need a large sign to tell us it was a chocolate factory - the surrounding atmosphere was heavy with a rich chocolate smell; it was not going to stop us sleeping, and I suppose there are worse smells which can lull you to sleep.

Again, we took the pretty route through Leiden and the Hague, which once again necessitated asking the obliging station booking office clerk to open the railway bridge for us "half an hour and he will be here". Sure enough, within the half hour the bridge was opening for us; this was the last time we were able to use this pleasant route through to Rotterdam as a fixed motorway bridge has been built over it. From Rotterdam, we took the "Spui" running from the New Waterway through to the Haringvliet, where there was a railway bridge to negotiate before we could reach our next port of call, Willemstadt. This bridge had a lifting span, but by the time of our arrival the bridge keeper had clearly gone home for the night; the nearby tide gauge showed 12 metres height above water level, whereas my calculations made my mainmast height 13 metres - probably slightly less. We anchored in the ebb stream, and over supper did some pretty fine tuned tidal calculations which showed that we ought to be able to just get away with it about half past one in the morning.

The whole family turned out, the anchor weighed and we cautiously approached the bridge; the timing was such that there was still a weak ebb flowing against us,which made a slow approach (or quick retreat) easier. The gauge now showed 12 metres plus, but because of weed and dirt we could not clearly see how much plus. I left our Cruising Association burgee flying at the top of the mast as a kind of safety valve - it swivelled on a length of garden cane, and if that broke it would not be disastrous. Vicky was stationed on deck at the bottom of the mast with a powerful torch shining up on to the burgee. As we approached the darkened underside of the bridge, barely moving over the ground, it was pretty obvious we were not going to get under, but at the first light grey painted girder there was a minute gap between the tip of the burgee stick and its sharp shadow on the girder. Fortunately, the surface of the water was like glass - indeed it was a magic night - so the boat had an undisturbed passage through, and we cleared each girder in similar manner. From this anxious moment, it was but a short distance to Willemstadt harbour entrance, not much more than a muddy ditch at low water, and our keel was dragging in the soft mud. Fortunately, it was a little deeper at the town quay, where we thankfully made fast and retreated to our bunks, well satisfied with the success of our venture.

Willemstadt has a picturesque centre, with small ornamental canals and a tree lined central square, whilst the whole town was built within a star shaped fortified wall; on the road leading out of town is a delightful road hazard sign showing a duck and her family crossing the road. Like many old Dutch towns, there is a well preserved windmill at the end of the town quay, a reminder of the way in which water was pumped to drain much of the land on which Holland is built; there is a saying that "God created the world, but the Dutch created Holland". There was no problem in making fast to the town quay in those days; no doubt the tidal restrictions put people off, and anyway, we are still talking of a time before the great boating explosion took off.

Today, they have created a large marina from a meer beyond the old harbour; the Haringvliet has been dammed so there is no tide and we would only get through that railway bridge by getting it opened. Because of the great character of the old town quay, it is extremely popular and surrounded by cafes and restaurants, whilst berths are only available if you are prepared to moor up in a trot of boats alongside each other - "rafting up" as they call it these days.

From here we went through a strongly tidal channel, the "Kramer" (now largely tamed by massive works) through to the Oosterscheldt for a wonderful sail up to the Sas van Goes - a sea lock leading to the short poplar lined canal which takes you to the the

"De Werf", Goes, Holland - the delightful little yacht harbour created by and run by an enthusiastic band of volunteers. The rural entrance is through a hole in the hedge.

town of Goes. In those days, in a small hamlet half way up was a rather flimsy road bridge opened by an ancient "brugwachter". By tradition, as you went through, he would lower a wooden clog on a stick into which you placed a small coin and proceeded. It has now been replaced by an automatic bridge, but I suspect they did not do this until the old man either retired or died - his job was a kind of pension top up. At Goes we were just too late in the day for the last opening of the busy road bridge just before the town, so we secured for the night in barely sufficient water, and went through the following morning to turn hard-a-port into what I can best describe as a hole in a hedge. This leads you into one of the most delightful yacht harbours in Holland, run by the "De Verf" club, a group of keen volunteers who love and cherish the place. "CELANDINE" was made fast alongside a promontory dividing the two parts of the harbour and at the head of which is a whimsical little lighthouse; the base is a W.C., at the back of which is the water hose for refilling tanks or washing down. Showers were available, with honesty boxes for the charge, and similarly, the simply furnished but very comfortable clubhouse has a trap door in the floor from which you could extract cool bottles of beer and pay for them in another honesty box. It was a little walk into town past a busy timber yard with weatherboarded sheds and buildings - now some kind of sheltered housing project which has retained the ancient weatherboarded buildings. Goes is a busy town with good shopping facilities and a big market square, and in more recent times it has become a television centre - one of the prominent landmarks now seen from far off is marked on the charts as a "televisie toren".

Progressing back towards Flushing, we sailed in the Veersemeer right up to the enormous dam blocking it off from the North Sea, where we anchored and proceeded to bathe, first in the North Sea where the dam was faced with a splendid sandy beach (no doubt a protective "spending beach" to absorb the fury of the North Sea waves), and then in the brackish and warmer water of the Veersemeer itself. After a night alongside the picturesque town quay at Veere (in later years well nigh impossible because of the crowds) we went through to Middleburg, where Beryl left and caught a train to the Hook of Holland for joining the night boat back to Harwich.

My old school and dinghy sailing friend Peter van den Brul (by now a consultant anaesthetist) came to join us, with his son Nicky, at this point, and we prepared for the return home on the morrow. Departure the next day from Flushing was early afternoon -

in those days my tactic was to clear one coast in daylight hours, undertake the main part of the crossing in darkness, and then you had a full day's light to see you safely in to port on the opposite shore. A commanding Northerly wind carried us swiftly out of the Schelde estuary through the complex and shallow Duerloo channel - for a small ship, the swiftest and most direct route out into the North Sea from Flushing, but of no use to larger ships. As darkness fell, we were storming along at just over 7 knots, the white foam under our lee bow tinged red from our port light. At the North Hinder light, well offshore, we made a small alteration of course, and after midnight we were passing the Galloper, the first of the British lightvessels on our course. Our luck began to run out at first light as the wind died away and became fickle, while fog began to descend, and progress became slower. At that time there was still the wreck of a wartime destroyer casualty on the bank off Landguard point (HMS Gipsy) - subsequently removed and the bank largely dredged away. Suddenly, we saw part of the wreck in the water close ahead; I threw the boat about on to the tack away from the shore, and just as we completed the turn, touched some part of the wreck, but not very hard and we were sailing away from it. At least we knew exactly where we were! After that there was no difficulty in buoy hopping into Harwich harbour and letting go in the examination anchorage above Felixstowe dock. Later in the morning, the tide being suitable, we were able to go alongside the Town Quay and winkle the Customs out to come and clear us, so that the same tide could be used to sail back to our mooring at Walton, by which time the fog had lifted to give a fine day.

Although there was still some sailing before we put "CELANDINE" to rest for the winter, life was unbelievably hectic back home - Beryl had been heavily involved in persuading The County Council to let Writtle have the use of a redundant house called Longmeads, which had been serving as a hostel for girl students at Writtle Agricultural College, for use as a community centre. The enormous expansion of the village in the late sixties had completely swamped community facilities, and the Village Hall was no longer adequate on its own, whilst the Church had a Victorian corrugated iron building to serve as a hall (affectionately known as the "Iron room"). She fought like a gentle tiger, against a lot of opposition on the County Council, until they finally agreed a scheme that enabled the village to have the former hostel.

On another front, the building of a new school because of the rapid expansion made the former boys' school on the Green, and the girls' school by the church redundant. As the girls' school once had been a church establishment, they were bound to give the church first refusal - as Chairman of the Education committee, she naturally became involved in this negotiation, which had to be settled through an independent valuer - again, after many struggles, the church bought the school back; a lot of it was sodden with dampness (that side of Writtle runs with streams not far below the surface) and had to be demolished, but a fine new main hall was built and the remainder renovated to provide additional accommodation. At the same time, some hideous air raid shelters left over from the war were finally demolished, along with the infamous "Iron room".

Writtle was to have a new, permanent library instead of the visiting affair, and yet another battle took place with the then County Librarian who was determined to demolish the former boys' school and erect a brand new building at vast expense. Again, as Chairman of Education this was within Beryl's realm and she fought (with a good deal of local support) for the conversion of the existing building into a permanent library. All this put pressure on the household; the business was still expanding, and I did a lot of travelling at that time. That year, soon after our return from the Dutch cruise, we had the induction of a new vicar, our third since we arrived in Writtle. The Writtle Society was taking up time, as well as the Parish Council and the continuing busy, but enjoyable social life.

During that winter plans were being drawn up by our great friend and brilliant architect, Patricia Stewart, to effect a major alteration to Greenbury House. Already, a number of changes internally had been made, and enlargements carried out to the garage and workshop, but this one would involve making an enormous hole in the back wall. At the same time, our primitive heating arrangements (a solid fuel boiler) were to be changed, and the lofty chimney which it used would be removed. By then, the house had been listed as grade II, so that any alterations were subject to considerable scrutiny. Patricia designed her alterations to houses with great skill, and always in sympathy with the rest of the building. She would not try to do something that would be unacceptable; the Rural District Council were reasonable in accepting the proposals, and accepted that what we proposed was enhancing the house - it was at the back and did not affect the all important aspect from the Green. It curtailed sailing plans for 1971, but I managed a brief week's trip to Holland, via Ostend in June, before the major work started. With Peter v d B, Michael Beaumont and Robert Barlow we visited Veere and Goes before returning on the Friday.

Fortunately, it was a good summer; the study at the back of the house (which had once been a kitchen) was turned back into a kitchen, and Patricia lent us a 2-hotplate Baby Belling cooker to cook on - an electric kettle and a 2-gallon plastic water carrier from the boat completed the primitive domestic arrangements. It was fortunate we were used to "making do" on a boat, because we had to live like this for several months. The work involved what I airily describe as "the new wing" - the only substantial brick built part of the house, dating from 1822 and using a diamond pattern of blue header bricks in an otherwise red brick wall - this style seemed to be fashionable about then. The area comprised an enormous kitchen, with a quite interesting door and doorcase giving access, and which for some time had been used as the main entrance in preference to the front door, with its very pretty and somewhat grander doorcase.

The work was to be carried out by Maurice Wood, who had carried out work on the house for many years both for us and the previous owners. His family had been builders in the village for many years, and when the big chimney was demolished, a brick was found carved with the initials of one of his forebears. It was only in later years - sadly Maurice had died, but his son Martin continues, keeping the family tradition going - Beryl discovered that an ancestor, Frederick Wood was born in Writtle in 1819, and was a builder who moved first to Clerkenwell in search of more work than Writtle could offer, and then to the newly expanding town of Southend, where he was to become an Alderman of the Borough, and the first chairman of the Highways Committee; Wood was the maiden name of Beryl's mother.

The work involved laying a new gas main to enter the house at the back, where the new gas boiler would be sited in an existing shed attached to the building, to give us the luxury of a gas fired central heating system. The work went on all round us, but by the autumn it was almost complete and we were ready to move into a newly fitted kitchen with a bay window overlooking the walled garden, whilst there was now a separate hallway leading to the door at the side of the house.

Our joy at the completion of this enormous task was marred by the death of Jane, the dog. The whole family had become so attached to this intelligent, affectionate character; it is one of the sad things about such pets that they have a much shorter lifespan than we do, so you know you are going to bid them farewell. She was only an animal, but was part of the family and her going caused us great grief. There has never been a replacement - by then neither of the children were at home during term time, Beryl was increasingly occupied with educational conferences and similar events, whilst I was away at work all day and often travelling away from home.

A WINTER OF DISCONTENT
AND SUMMER OF GREAT CONTENT

THE winter turned into the first of a regular pattern of winters of discontent where trade unions tried to run the Country instead of its elected government (of whichever party), and power cuts were part of the way of life, so we had to run the factory whenever there was power available, and I frequently took a shift on the kapok plant - it was hard work, and moving the heavy bales of raw fibre, I managed to give myself a hernia. Fortunately, Peter Martin, the surgeon, who had already carried out an operation on Beryl the previous year was a sailor and ex naval officer, said he would do it and ensure I was ready for the sailing season.

So with Michael Beaumont, George Jones and Robert Barlow as crew, early June saw "CELANDINE" crossing the Thames Estuary and making her way to the West Country once more - this time mainly against adverse Southwesterly winds - fortunately only on one day were they strong enough to give us an uncomfortable sail, but there were rests on the trip - one night spent at anchor off Margate, well sheltered from the Southerly wind, and another in Rye harbour after a fairly hard sail through my much hated Dover Straits. Another night was spent at Weymouth - a very pleasant town with Regency connections, and it was here that we did some pretty fine calculations to round Portland Bill by the inshore route at exactly the time of tide recommended by the pilot books; it is like catching a train. During the night in Weymouth I felt the boat stirring to a slight swell coming in the harbour. Joy of joys, the wind had come out of the Sou'west! With a good stiff sailing breeze from the East and a fine sunny day, we left Weymouth quay 3 minutes late at 1048, and the tide sped us down the steep East side of Portland Bill, grimly topped by the prison. Soon after mid-day, we were abeam of the light and very close inshore - in this way you pass round in relatively calm water, missing the dreaded Portland race lying further out to seaward. Shortly after clearing the Bill, course was set for Dartmouth, which meant a dead run before the wind in a sizeable sea - not a relaxing point of sailing, and the boom was lashed out with a preventer rope to minimise the risk of an accidental gybe. The 40 mile plus passage passed quickly; it was enjoyable sailing, but the only event of note was a large white gannet flying low over the water. Up till now in my life, "gannet" had only been a naval expression for someone with a healthier than normal appetite, but now, after consulting our copy of Hamlyn's birds, I knew we had seen the real thing; sadly this one failed to demonstrate its spectacular dive after prey.

With the strong fair wind, the sea miles rolled by and the great bulk of the peninsula bounding the Western end of Lyme Bay lay ahead of us, rising higher and higher above our horizon. Soon after half past seven in warm evening sunshine, "CELANDINE" entered the Dart and secured to a vacant visitor's mooring off Dittisham. The following evening, Wednesday, we left the Dart, rounded Start Point and slipped into Salcombe - once you have fought your way down West, there are so many attractive rivers and anchorages within easy sailing distance of each other. Our voyage finished in the Yealm at Newton Ferrers, where she was left on a mooring and we were able to use Robert Barlow's private quay for storing our dinghy.

Another lesson was learnt the hard way when we returned to "CELANDINE". The mooring at Newton Ferrers was affected by a scend coming in from seawards - although well tucked away from the sea, swell from outside tended to ricochet off the steep tree lined rocky banks, and this caused "CELANDINE" to constantly fidget about on her mooring; even after some years of using a rope pennant for mooring (now becoming more readily accepted by the yachting fraternity) I decided to shackle my heavy half inch anchor chain to the mooring. Returning almost three weeks later, I rove a rope pennant as a slip to facilitate departure and with which to shorten the chain and undo the shackle. As I did this, I saw the pin drop out of the shackle and fall into the clear deep water. Three weeks of constant movement had been quietly unscrewing the shacklepin; never since then have I failed to wire a shackle to prevent this happening - it is basic seamanship and I should have known better. I could have caused the loss of this lovely ship, or at least severe damage had she drifted on to those rocky banks. Fortunately I carried a spare large shackle with which to rejoin the main anchor to its cable.

We certainly sailed in those days, and in a short week sailed with Roland and a friend to Falmouth and the Helford River; in Falmouth harbour I fell in love - with a motor yacht named Cardigrae VI, a Camper & Nicholson classic built in 1962, 124 feet long, with a sleek profile and topped by a squat yellow funnel. She had a raised foredeck which faired into her superstructure and bridge, giving the appearance of a purposeful seamanlike ship, and to my eyes, of immense beauty. I had to sail right round her to appreciate this lovely ship. I wonder where she is now, nearly forty years old?

To keep the momentum up, we returned to Newton Ferrers after a quick call into Plymouth Sound - we went up the Tamar and into the St Germans River, where a peaceful anchorage was found for the night, off Earth Hill. This time, on return to the Yealm and the anchor chain shackled on to the mooring, the pin of the shackle was securely wired to prevent it unscrewing itself. In the first weekend of August I returned with two other ex-naval officers, my old friend Robert Barlow and Johnnie Devlin. Johnnie was in the Royal Navy rather than the RNVR, and rose to become a submarine commander; as a youth he had sailed on the square rigger "Joseph Conrad" under Alan Villiers; with some justification he claimed to be the only submarine commander who also had sailed in a square rigger. The "Joseph Conrad" is now preserved in Mystic Seaport museum, Connecticut, USA.

So we finally left the Yealm with this Naval-flavoured crew and sailed for Falmouth via a night in the Helford River, and put her on a mooring rented from Falmouth Harbour Commissioners, ready for a family holiday based on Falmouth. By then, Falmouth Boat Construction had given up their somewhat restricted yard off the main street to concentrate their activities at their other yard over at Flushing; this meant we had no facilities for leaving a dinghy ashore, but we always arranged with the Flushing ferry to pick us up or put us aboard on one of their regular runs, and they were quite happy to do this for the normal ferry fare.

"Celandine" began her return to Essex in mid-September, and after some rather frustrating sailing in light winds, our first night at sea saw a Northerly wind set in to give us superb sailing all the way to Portsmouth, where we dashed alongside the Gosport ferry pier to land Vicky and the son of friends, Oliver Springett, so they could catch a train home - I'm sure we were not supposed to do this, but before anyone could say we couldn't, we were away again and they were on their way into Portsmouth Harbour station. I can't remember who else was left aboard, but for the rest of the voyage we would be short handed, so we picked up a buoy off Gosport for the night to get a good rest. The next day, helped by a wind from just North of West, we sped Eastwards along the South Coast, with cryptic notes thrown in the log - "SS Villandry" passed ahead, bound for Newhaven", and even more exciting -"Bexhill sewer buoy abeam". Finally, we anchored at half past ten that night on the South side of Dungeness, well in towards Rye and sheltered from the Northerly wind. It was a short night's rest - we were weighing anchor again at 7 in the morning to catch favourable tides. The wind was quite fresh and we had one reef in, but there was enough West in it to hold one tack all the way to the North Foreland, helped by strong favourable tides. That night, well after nightfall, we anchored off Osea Island and on the morning tide entered Heybridge basin. It seems strange that we chose to finish the voyage there, but I think it was to save a long car journey down to Walton to pick up a lot of gear, which there had to be ferried ashore in a dinghy. Although some improvements had been made to the A12 road to the East Coast, it was still a formidable journey in those days before all the by-passes had been put in place, whereas Heybridge Basin was still less than half an hour's drive from home.

That season finished with a visit to the site of the proposed Maplin Airport - our last cruise of the season, with Robert Barlow and Michael Beaumont - I can't remember whether George Jones came - he was a vigorous opponent of the proposed airport - but during a bitterly cold weekend at the end of October, we crept through the labrynth of creeks off the river Roach which lead to Havengore - here a shallow draught boat can save a long passage round Foulness by going through the lifting bridge at high water and across the Maplin sands. We anchored in a deep pool not far from the bridge; our coal stove was giving a wonderful warm glow down below, but on deck there were intermittent showers of rain and sleet. Landing in the dinghy, we walked to the Thames Estuary shore just beyond the bridge - the grey sky was reflected in a grey sandy sea whipped up by a cold North-westerly wind. Robert, well known for speaking his mind in no uncertain terms, took one look at the inhospitable scene and said "The sooner they cover this bloody lot with six inches of concrete, the better", and with that we retreated to take the boat back to deeper water for the night, before laying her up at Rowhedge for the winter. Of course, the airport never happened and the only sign still visible to this day is a massive shingle island built on the edge of the sands to make geological and tidal observations.

FEVERISH ACTIVITY ON THE HOME FRONT - AND NORTHWARDS BOUND TO SCOTLAND

DURING the summer, when not sailing, there was great activity on the business front. Although the quilted fabric side of the Company (which I had entered partly because the opportunity was there, but partly because as a one- product company, we were vulnerable) was doing well, the kapok side of the business had been declining for some time and all but one competitor had dropped out. For some time we had an agreement to protect our prices (necessary in a declining market), but this was now illegal - the politicians who decided on this, for very good reasons to prevent market abuse, had never tried running a business in a declining market. So talks were begun to merge our kapok businesses - it seemed sensible. A fifty-fifty arrangement was made, and a lot of time spent in finalising the details, but the whole thing made sense and should make reasonable profits for some years. Two important matters were fixed by the toss of a coin, so that we lost the toss on banks, and NatWest were to be the new company's bankers, but we won on auditors, so our accountants became accountants to the new company. Later, this was to prove of great significance.

At the same time, I was involved in re-structuring the company to separate our property and trading interests. The newly formed property side was also involved with developing a warehouse on spare land we owned at the back of the site, with a company of which a great friend was a director. All this had to be fitted in, apart from the various village activities, with a quite extensive sailing programme. Another matter about which activity in the village was becoming more intense, was the provision of a by-pass which had been promised a long time back, when the route also had been agreed.

Everything on the business front seemed to have been settled by the end of the year, but I decided not to stand for re-election to the Parish Council. There was a lot of

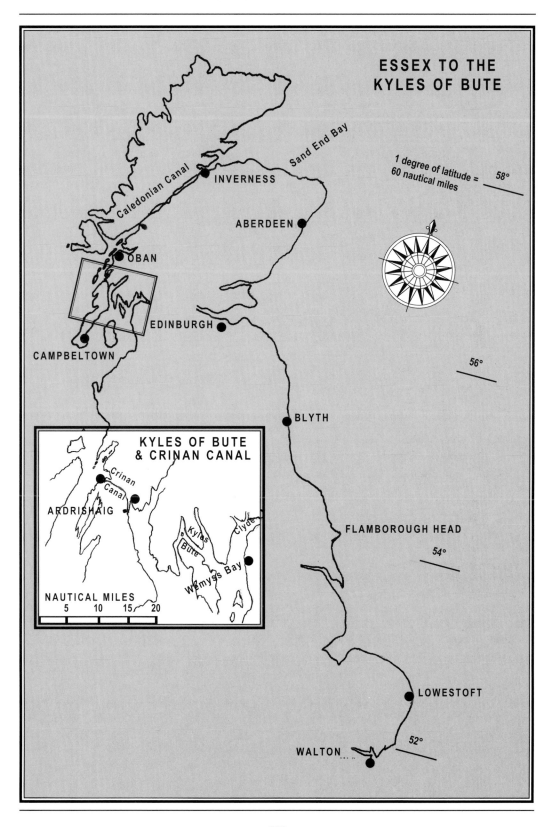

pressure on my time, and after some 17 years felt it was time for some one with fresh ideas to come along. There was also a great upheaval at the Cruising Association, as the lease on Chiltern Court expired at the end of the year, so at the cocktail and rum punch party in mid-December, we bade a sad farewell to these familiar and comfortable surroundings. Negotiations were already in hand for new premises at St Katharine Dock by Tower Bridge, but there was going to be a difficult period until they were ready for occupation - not until early in 1974.

1973 was the year I decided to go North with "Celandine", and visit the Kyles of Bute. I have mentioned that when serving in the "Tuscarora" during 1942, there were two ways of returning to her base at Campbeltown, and that my preferred route was by the Macbrayne boat from Wemyss Bay to East Loch Tarbert. This was a fascinating trip through magnificent coastal scenery, and in those war time days the boat was a vital link serving local communities; I made a promise to myself that one day I would return, in my own boat. Perhaps a rash promise at the time, but now with a powerful and capable boat, I was in a position to fulfil it.

With a crew best described as "ancient and modern" - Robert Barlow and myself as the two ancients, while Pru Sadd and Des Ward were the two young moderns. Both Pru and Des were experienced sailors and in fact it made a well balanced and strong crew for a long passage - nearly 500 nautical miles from Walton to Inverness.

At 10 in the evening on Thursday the 14th of June we slipped our mooring at Walton and left under power until we were in open water, where we hoisted full sail to take advantage of a light Southwesterly wind and favourable tide. By breakfast time we were off Yarmouth, where the wind fell very light and the engine had to be started to maintain a reasonable rate of progress. Our log for that day was full of sightings of long forgotten lightships, now a thing of the past. Cross Sand, Newarp, Haisboro', Dudgeon. With a return of the wind, we were able to sail once again, and course was laid for Flamborough Head. The flat lands of the North Norfolk coast, The Wash, Lincolnshire and the Humber Estuary receded from view, and it was a long haul before we reached Flamborough Head early on the Saturday morning. We had returned to spectacular coast line again, passing well known features such as Filey Brigg, Scarborough Castle - a fortified site since Roman times. The weather as we passed at 10 in the morning was benign, but what did the Roman legionaries posted there think of it? Exposed and wind-swept, how they must have longed for home leave in a Mediterranean climate.

During the course of this day's sailing, as the coast curves round, the Southwest wind came abeam and increased our speed, so I started looking at the charts we would be using ahead. To my horror, we had nothing aboard to cover the crossing of the Firth of Forth, where I proposed a long hop from St Abbs Head , to close the Scottish coast again South of Aberdeen. It was my responsibility entirely to see we had charts to cover our intended voyage, but the Admiralty chart agents in London that I was using at the time had become somewhat unreliable (I think due to financial problems) and although ordered, it was not there in the portfolio. I thought I had checked, but due to the stresses of all the activities at home, had missed it. We would put in at Blyth - it had a good deep safe harbour with one of the oldest and most distinguished yacht clubs in the country - the Royal Northumberland, and I was sure that somehow we would get a chart there, although the next day would be Sunday. "Celandine" was secured alongside their headquarters, a former light vessel, at nine that evening. Thanks to the generosity of a member, who went out to his boat specially, a chart was lent to us that would fill the gap, There were splendid showers aboard the Club of which we all took advantage, so that a well refreshed crew let go the ropes sharp at 9 on the Sunday morning, happy in the knowledge that the skipper's misdemeanour had been overcome, and we were fully equipped for the remainder of our voyage. The day was spent in a mixture of sailing and motoring, with the wind from between Southwest and West, but very feeble at times. It was a beautiful day and the impressive Northumbrian coast line was highlighted for us as it slowly rolled by.

At half past six that evening we were off Berwick on Tweed, and a formal entry went in the log "crossed into Scottish waters". Later in the evening, well offshore of Eyemouth, we hove to for a good supper - the sea was empty, but nevertheless a good lookout was kept until we got underweigh again. Later in the evening, when the distant St Abbs Head was abeam, we laid our course just East of due North and set off on the long open passage. It was late on Monday morning before we began to close the coast South of Aberdeen, and we had crossed tacks with the Sea Cadet training ship "ROYALIST". They were beating South against the same light wind that was pushing us North, but soon after this the wind freshened and backed to the South. We hastily managed to get a single reef in the mains'l, and squared off to run before it. The wind continued to freshen until it was going through force 6 and up to seven - it never seems as bad when you are running before it, but had we been going the other way, it would have been very tough going. As it continued to rise, we brought down the mizzen and stays'l - both easy sails to get in, as she was really becoming a handful to steer in the increasingly steep seas that were rapidly building up. So steep were the waves that at one moment our bowsprit was pointing down towards the deep blue sea at an alarming angle, and the next towards the sky. I decided I would have to stay on the helm until things eased, because at this crazy speed I was very concerned about broaching to and bringing a serious amount of water aboard. North of Aberdeen we passed a sizeable trawler heading South; she was pitching quite heavily and throwing great sheets of white spray right over her bridge and funnel as she fought her way home. In spite of this, we were close enough to exchange a cheery wave.

Two of our stalwart crew went below and managed to knock up some sandwiches to keep us going. Things stayed like this until we passed Peterhead at about 4 in the afternoon, when it became necessary to alter course and follow the coast round Rattray Head and towards the Moray Firth, bringing us on to a Westerly course. A gybe was essential to effect this, so again, the strong crew were a great asset - they knew what to do and managed to swig the mains'l in tight, in spite of the great weight of wind in it. When we did gybe her, it was remarkably gentle - because the wind is always in the sail when gybing, it can slam across with unbelievable force. Now on the port tack, the sail was eased out again and our wild ride continued.

Off Aberdeen, with a freshening wind. Pru, Des (steering) and Robert.

Rounding Kinnairds Head, just beyond Fraserburgh, brought the wind abeam, and suddenly, with the protection of a high rocky coast now acting as a breakwater, the seas went right down and the wind eased. We shook out the reef , rehoisted the sails so hastily dropped when the wind hit us, and I thankfully gave up the helm, having been hard at work on it for some six hours. It all seemed to be going well, but the wind continued to drop until we were forced to start the engine. Everyone was tired from the strenuous sail, and I searched the Admiralty chart for a bay in which to anchor - many of them were too full of rocky ledges for my liking, but Sandend Bay had a good stretch of sandy beach and the rocks were all well to either side of the bay. The anchor finally splashed down at 10 that night - because we were now so far North it was still twilight, but it was not long before we were all asleep in this peaceful open bay with only the very slightest of swell coming from seawards, and not a trace of wind on the water.

It seemed an extremely remote place, and there were no more than a handful of stone cottages visible, but when I returned to Writtle, I discovered that our local garage proprietor and well known village character, Bert Preston had one of those cottages. Every so often he and his wife would drive off from Writtle, and as far as I could make out, only stopped when they got there. Certainly it was a good place to get away from it all, with a beautiful clean sandy beach.

By 8 the next morning, we were underweigh again under power - there was not a breath of wind and it was not worth taking the sail tyers off. In the mist to seaward, I could make out the outline of an Admiralty type "T" class trawler, also making Westwards up the Moray Firth. The Admiralty tended to build smaller ships, for various wartime purposes, that would be easily converted to a civilian use after hostilities ceased. There were the famous "MFVs" which they built because there were simply not enough of this type available for various harbour and inshore duties, so they built them with an eye on their post war uses. How many ever really went into serious fishing, I don't know, but a lot finished up as yachts. The "T" class were coal fired trawlers built for minesweeping duties, and minesweeping gear was not greatly different from that required to shoot a side trawl. Coal burners were very much in favour during the War, because coal was dug up within our own country, whereas precious oil fuels had to be shipped across U-boat infested seas. In the first War, paddle steamers were very much in favour for minesweeping because of their shallow draft, but there were not enough, so they built a whole class, all named after racecourses. Two finished up on the Thames between the wars running pleasure trips from the Medway to Southend pier and the Kent resorts - the "QUEEN OF THANET" (formerly "HMS MELTON") and the "QUEEN OF KENT" (formerly "HMS ATHERSTONE").

This "T" class trawler seemed to keep station on us as we progressed up the Firth, and as our courses came nearer we noticed she was painted Admiralty grey; I remembered that Customs and Excise had one of these in service. She was clearly shadowing us, but they never sent a party to investigate, and eventually lost interest as we approached the narrows at Fort George. At quarter to five that evening, we entered the sea lock and secured alongside in the Muirtown basin at the beginning of the Caledonian Canal.

Here, Pru's parents, John and Barbara Sadd met us as John was to join us, whilst Pru was returning South by train. They had come by car, and John treated us to dinner at the Caledonian Hotel - still then one of the grand railway hotels. Barbara, a keen horsewoman, was going on a pony trekking holiday and then meeting us at Crinan on the West side of the Mull of Kintyre.

From Inverness, the first part of the Caledonian Canal consists of a staircase of locks, some of whose gates were in a fairly advanced state of decay at that time. At the summit of this initial staircase, you look back over the rooftops of the town before proceeding along an artificial length of canal through delightful scenery, with the river Ness flowing swiftly nearby; another lock and you are soon into Loch Ness - a twenty nautical miles long water filled ravine on a Southwest - Northeast axis. The sides are steep and at times precipitous, plunging steeply down to the bottom of this narrow crack in the mountainous terrain. There is no place to anchor because it is so deep, except about

A summit achieved - the top lock at Fort Augustus, entering the highest part of the Caledonian Canal. The waters of Loch Ness lay astern, a long way below.

halfway along its Northern shore, where Glen Urquhart meets the Great Glen, forming a relatively shallow sandy bay. Although we used it on the return voyage, we kept going for the far end; during this time, in the absence of a sighting, we made our own monster from a series of white plastic fenders towed astern, with a face artistically composed from black vynil tape on the leading fender.

At the Southern end of the Loch is Fort Augustus, an attractive town with an Abbey, once a fort, but then in use as a boarding school; to reach the town, you mount through a further series of locks, from the summit of which you look down on the waters of Loch Ness - blue and sunlit on this day. Here we stayed until the following afternoon when we passed through an opening bridge to reach another section of remote canal. At first we were kept waiting because a coaster was coming through, but then news came that she had run aground, so we might as well proceed. Just as we neared the entrance to Loch Oich, there was the red-hulled coaster, and we could hardly believe our eyes - she was the "ANDESCOL" of Colchester, belonging to the London & Rochester Trading Company (which later became Crescent Shipping). There was quite a strong wind blowing which had caught the unladen ship and blown her stern on to a shingle ledge. Our first attempt at plucking him off was unsuccessful, but the skipper then flooded the forepeak with water pumped from the Loch - beautiful sweet fresh water - and this reduced the draught aft, enabling us to pull her off and bring her head to wind away from the shallows so he could drop anchor. With her stern so high out of the water, the propeller had very little bite as it thrashed round more in air than water. We were invited aboard for a cup of tea (although really we would like to have pressed on). The skipper would resume his passage when he had pumped out the forepeak to bring the propeller back into solid water.

Loch Oich, the pip in the middle of the canal, is a facinating labrynth of deep channels and rocky tree girt islets, surrounded by hills and mountains; it is also the highest stretch of water (105 feet above sea level) so thereafter, any locks one passes through are descending again. The navigational channel, from which we did not stray, is well marked. A section of canal passing by Laggan (where a road crosses on a swing bridge) brings you into Loch Lochy, but we stopped for the night at a convenient point before the end of the canal section.

The water in Loch Lochy is said to be so pure that fishing boats passing through from East to West coasts frequently fill their water tanks - without pumping apparatus this would have been very tedious work for us, anyway, our tank was already full of soft Highland water - in contrast to the lime-laden Essex and Suffolk supplies normally found in our tank. The weather was still good, and during our passage through the further length of canal which would bring us to the Western end at Corpach someone entered in the log "Ben Nevis abeam to port". This was a slight exaggeration, but it is so big I suppose it could be construed as being abeam for quite some way, The top was dressed with snow, and I think this was the only time we saw it on our Scottish trip, as it was usually shrouded in cloud.

On the Friday afternoon, we reached "Neptune's Staircase", the series of locks descending to sea level; a magnificent piece of engineering by that giant among engineers, Thomas Telford. A Scot, his work took him to many places in Great Britain, but the Caledonian Canal must be one of his greatest achievements; started in 1803 but not finally open for navigation until 1847. Telford built roads, bridges and canals, but would not take part in the railway boom that was developing, as he felt railways were too restrictive of access and prone to abuse by monopoly interests.

Once out in the waters of Loch Linhe, we headed with a good sailing breeze and bright sunshine down to the Corran Narrows and into the broader waters of lower Loch Linhe, finally to anchor in Duart Bay on the Isle of Mull, where we lay under the protective cannons of Duart Castle (when were they last fired in anger?). The castle and surrounding hills of Mull, were lit by the evening sunshine against a backdrop of deep blue sky. Another scare for us Essex boys took place when, still some way off our desired anchorage, the echo sounder started telling us there was only about 12 feet of water. Mistrusting gadgetry, I hastily pulled out the sounding lead - and could not even find the bottom with it. The penny slowly dropped, and the scale on the sounder was quickly changed, because on the lower scale it had gone right round the clock (60 feet, I think) and were reading 60 feet plus another 12 feet or so over that. Once our mistake was rectified, we went further in to the bay and anchored in three fathoms (18 feet), snug into this deep bay. We simply were not used to such great depths when so near the shore, but I have to admit that in spite of this experience, it has happened again from time to time.

Our time was running out, and the next day, Saturday, we were underweigh by 9 in the morning, encouraged by bright sunshine, puffy white clouds and a sparkling sea - but little or no wind. Later, a pleasant Westerly sailing wind got up, to complete the perfection, and with all sail to No.1 jib flying, we romped South down the coast. The

scenery was spectacularly beautiful as we sped through the Sound of Luing, and then gybed round to sail up Loch Craignish for no reason other than to enjoy the sailing and scenery before heading in to Crinan Loch. Later that evening, after refuelling and taking on fresh water, we locked in to the first basin of Crinan Canal, where we berthed alongside a grassy quay.

An unforgettable sight the following day was the arrival of lunch. "CELANDINE" was getting low on fresh victuals, and we were getting down to using reserve supplies of tinned food. John Sadd generously said he would take charge of lunch; Barbara, having returned from her pony trekking holi-

Sailing in Loch Craignish, en route for Crinan. Robert Barlow in hatchway, John Sadd at helm. When the weather on the West coast of Scotland is good, it is superb - but it can change suddenly and dramatically.

day, was staying in the nearby Crinan Hotel. At lunch time, the head waiter and a waitress, both in full uniform came marching along the canal bank with a cold lobster lunch, all borne on silver salvers complete with salad dressings in silver boats (it normally came straight out of the jar or bottle on board!). Skilfully they brought it below and arranged it on the cabin table, complete with stiff white damask napkins - never will I forget this unbelievable meal which rounded off such a successful trip, starting late Thursday night from Walton and reaching Crinan on the West Coast of Scotland on Saturday afternoon just over a week later.

Early in July, I arranged a long weekend, during which I would make the long promised pilgrimage to the Kyles of Bute. Unfortunately, I have no record of my companions on this trip, nor can I remember, nearly thirty years later, but on a Wednesday evening I flew British European Airways from Heathrow via the London Air Terminal in the Cromwell Road - all these have long since vanished from the scene. How I travelled on to Crinan from what was then called Abbotsinch airport at Renfrew I also do not recall, but by late Thursday morning we were starting our slow (but not unpleasant) progress though the Crinan Canal. Evening saw us racing down Loch Fyne with a stiff Southwesterly wind, to reach East Loch Tarbert by 9 that evening, picking up a mooring belonging to the famous boatbuilding firm, Dickies.

The next morning the wind had gone round to Northwest, force 4 - 5, and the weather still very fair; we rounded Ardlamont Point and entered the Kyles of Bute. At first the scenery is quite wild and sparsely inhabited, but as we sailed Northwards, we began to pass small settlements with some fine houses whose well tended grounds sloped down to the shore. The coast becomes South facing, and because the waters are warmed by the Gulf stream, frosts and snow are a rarity - some of the gardens sported palm trees. One of these delightful places has the almost unpronounceable (for a Sassenach, anyway) name of Tighnabruaich - I so well remember the bustle when the steamer called at their pier in the days when they had no alternative means of transport. The Kyles are shaped like an inverted "Y" with Loch Riddon at the Northern end, and the tip of the Isle of Bute projecting to form the other side of the letter. We rounded this point to sail through the Burnt Islands - not much evidence of burning, they were a riot of rhododendrons in full bloom. It was Clyde Week, and the resort of Rothesay at the head of a capacious bay was crowded with yacht masts and sails out in the bay.

For us, the sailing was exhilarating as "CELANDINE" now sped Southwards, leaving the Isle of Bute astern as the Isle of Aran appeared ahead, a much bigger and more mountainous island. Passing Brodick Bay, I remembered the practice landings we had carried out there thirty years previously, and then rounded Clauchlands Point to enter Lamlash Bay, another large bay, protected to the East by Holy Island. One of the delights of sailing here was that we did not look for a space in which to anchor, but instead, looked for the most scenic part of the shore off which to anchor. There was no sign of habitation in the part we chose, but not long after the anchor had splashed down into the clear water, a lone piper appeared, in full regalia, to parade up and down the lonely strand, the plaintive notes of the bagpipes echoing off the shore.

The following day, after a lazy morning, we sailed North again into the Firth of Clyde; passing Toward Point, the land began to close in on us from both sides. A stiff wind was still blowing, now from the North with just a touch of West in it. On one tack, again in glorious sunshine, we raced up the Firth, the bow wave rolling past in a torrent of sparkling foam, rising and falling as her fine bow drove through the waves, until we reached Dunoon, where we turned back, freeing the sheets off and sailing even faster until reaching the Kyles again. That night, Saturday, we anchored in Caladh Harbour, a natural protected anchorage in a sheltered bay, protected by a small rhododendron covered island lying at the entrance to Loch Riddon, having covered over 42 miles in an afternoon of superb sailing. The evenings are long as far North as this, and we stayed on deck till late, admiring the blaze of blooms and the distant mystic hills.

Our long weekend was coming to a close, and reluctantly the anchor was raised late in the morning, by which time the wind had still failed to appear and we had to motor all the way back to Ardrishaig. Being the end of Clyde week, a number of boats were heading for a cruise in the Western Isles, so there were quite a few of us rafted in the basin that lies beyond the sea lock. Later, a very flash looking racing yacht with large flags of victory flying came crashing alongside the outside of the trot without the usual courtesies. I forebear to mention the boat's name, but we all took an instant dislike to him. He then made sure his numerous racing successes were well known; someone pointed out that we were going to pass through the next lock into the first reach of the canal later in the evening, but he and his crew disappeared ashore, so that when the first canal lock opened, we all passed through, making him fast to the quay as best we could. The lock keeper then went home for the night. It is wrong to feel smug about it, but with a lock between us and him, we would be well ahead when we started off in the morning. The rest of the locks in this very rural canal are do-it-yourself, and call for teamwork and co-operation in getting the boats through. Soon after mid-day on the Monday we were back alongside the grassy bank at Crinan, where once again she was left while we flew home from Glasgow. It could be said we stretched that word weekend about as far as possible!

The experts will always tell you that June and early July produce the best weather in Scotland, and certainly our experience proved them right. This time, Beryl was able to come, and we drove up - the arrangements when boats and cars are involved become complicated. By dint of hiring a car, we managed to leave our car at Inverness and join the boat at Crinan, bringing with us Stefano - our Italian nephew, son of Lorna and Dino. The weather had deteriorated by the time we rejoined in early August, leaving Crinan in mist and rain, the sea a glassy calm. Anchoring for the night in nearby Loch Craignish, the contrast with our previous sunlit sail here on the outward passage in late June could not be greater. Working our way North through the Sounds of Cuan, Shuna and Kereira, there was no wind but the mist and rain had at least cleared; soon after passing Oban we left the shelter of the Sound and were struck by a vicious wind and sea, whilst at the same time the sky cleared. This contrast seems typical of the West Coast of Scotland as I remembered it from my days in the Navy up there. We were bound for Dunstaffnage, at the entrance to Loch Etive where the entrance was not at all distinct and "CELANDINE" headed for a lee shore, but just as I was getting really worried, it suddenly became obvious. There was good shelter here, and only a few other boats anchored off, so selecting a spot to anchor with a good scope of chain was not difficult; unlike Duart Castle, no defensive cannon were visible, but what was there, were superb raspberries. Our own at home were long over, but the Scottish variety are well worth waiting for.

The passage back to Neptune's staircase at the Western end of the Caledonian canal was noted for a mixture of strong winds and almost continuous rain. Leaving the boat at Banavie, at the head of the staircase of locks, we returned our Italian nephew to Italy using the hired car to reach the airport, and staying, with my brother-in-law, James and his wife Fiona, at Auchmannoch House near Troon, where he commanded the Junior Tradesmen's Regiment. Unfortunately, the raising of the school leaving age to 16 caused the closure of this establishment, as well as the Naval boys' training establishment at HMS Ganges, Shotley, where during the War they had tried to turn us Patrol Service ratings into proper sailors. It seems a great pity that the authorities could not find a way of adapting and continuing these excellent establishments; the Country is the poorer for their loss.

The two of us returned to the boat, having turned in the hire car at Fort William, and because I was so taken with the scenery, planned that our transit of the Caledonian Canal would be leisurely. Finally, on a damp and cold Friday evening, after watering ship, we started our passage Eastwards, making fast for the night at a remote and rural berth just below the Bridge of Moy, which would not be opening again till the following day. It was now August the 10th; there was a sharp chill in the air and it was not long before a spiral of blue woodsmoke from our chimney curled lazily towards the grey sky - there was no wind.

Then occurred another of those extraordinary coincidences - three people approached the boat seemingly from nowhere - it was Hubert and Doris Sorrell, with their son, who live so close to our garage entrance gate at Writtle that you could almost pick the beautiful flowers in their garden (and there always are plenty of them) as you drive out. They were camping at an unseen camp nearby, so we had a mutual interest in seeing an improvement in the miserable weather. Writtle is not exactly an enormous place, yet within a short season up in this Northern country of mountain and glen, this was the second Writtle connection we had come across - we folk from Writtle do get about!

The next morning, the sun shone and a gentle breeze dispelled the dank atmosphere, so after passing through the Laggan section of canal, we shut down the engine and ran quietly under bare poles before the Westerly wind into Loch Oich. On Sundays, nothing moves on the Canal and the Locks are not manned, so I was determined we should spend it in an idyllic spot. "CELANDINE" nosed her way out of the buoyed channel to the South side of a small steep and well wooded island, while I kept a wary eye on the echo sounder and a lookout ahead for any unexpected rocks. I cast the sounding lead to get a sample of the bottom - soft silty mud, and we let go the anchor in 2 fathoms (12 feet), 105 feet above sea level and with no tides to worry about. Later, Beryl and I climbed up the hillside on the Southern shore of the Loch to look down on this toy boat lying on the mirrored surface, the wind having fallen away completely. "CELANDINE" had not moved since the anchor went down, and the next morning we awoke to find her still lying in exactly the same position, with the anchor chain hanging vertically from the bow. Saying to myself "nothing moves here on the Sabbath", I rowed over to a sandy spit crested with pine trees, where I stripped and bathed in the soft water with soap that lathered profusely, as it never would have done in our hard water at home. The only problem was the temperature of my bathwater - to say it was invigorating would be an understatement.

After time spent in Fort Augustus, a favourite tourist centre, although not spoilt by it (I wonder what the place is like now as I write, nearly thirty years later?), we sailed in a failing West wind to anchor in the only possible place in Loch Ness (apart from a shallow bay near Fort Augustus). Loch Ness is too deep and its sides precipitous, rendering conventional anchoring impossible. It was late in the day when we reached the shallow sandy bay formed by the junction of Glen Urquhart and Loch Ness; the evenings were by now drawing in, so little was seen of our surroundings. The following morning we awoke to find the steep enclosing hillsides shrouded in a thick damp mist, giving the whole place a sense of mystery. Ashore, we visited the ruins of Urquhart Castle, still shrouded in the clinging Highland mist, and from where we could just discern the outline of "CELANDINE" far below. It would not have surprised us if we saw a ghost - perhaps an ancient Highland warrior. By the time we were aboard again, the sun had dispelled the mist to give another fine day in which to reach Inverness, shut the boat down and rejoin our car for the long drive home.

The final stage of our Scottish saga started when four of us flew up from London to Inverness on Tuesday September the 4th. There had been an exceptional early cold snap, and the tops of some of the mountains had already received a dusting of snow, telling us it was time to head South. We were a strong crew - Roland and his friend from their voyage on the STA schooner "MALCOLM MILLER", Dave Whitfield, and John Hamilton who was taking time off from his job as race director for the Sail Training Association. There was little wind when we cleared the sea lock and stood out into the Moray

Firth; all day we endured a frustrating mixture of motor sailing or just plain motoring in light and fickle winds, and it was not until eight in the evening when a wind came up from the Southeast strong enough to enable our faithful Perkins to be shut down. The wind strengthened and "CELANDINE" was sailed closehauled on the starboard tack, following the coast as far as Fraserburgh where it then begins to curve Southwards significantly, which meant we were gradually standing out to sea on what became a very dark night. Tacking inshore, we were racing towards a rocky shore; as long as we had good shore lights, our position could be checked with cross bearings, but as we tacked Southwards, the coast lacked lights for long distances and we could only rely on accurate timing of each tack to ensure we did not sail her to certain destruction on an unseen dark shore. It came on to rain, which made visibility worse, and the wind veered round further South if not West of South, so that we had to fight for every inch down this unseen coast. It was hard work, but daylight at least brought some relief to the nervous strain of tacking through the blackness of night.

I decided we would put into Aberdeen for a night's rest, but the following afternoon the wind began to fall light again, and once again motorsailing was necessary to maintain a reasonable rate of progress. The harbour authorities could not have been more helpful, and although it was largely a commercial port at that time, they found us a comfortable berth tucked well up into the harbour. Quite a large amount of fuel had been consumed, and in case we were to encounter more fickle winds on our long haul down the coast, it seemed prudent to top up the tanks before we left. The following morning, we proceeded to the fuel berth on our way out of harbour, only to be told they would only supply fishing boats before 9, and as it was only just after 7, we really could not afford to waste so much time. One of the foredeck party pointed out that there was not a fishing boat in sight and they were not doing anything anyway. An abrupt "We'll noo serve you before 9" brought an undiplomatic reply from our foredeck, effectively telling them where to put their fuel pipe. We pushed on seawards and by half past seven when we cleared the entrance, no fishing boats had called for fuel, and the men on the fuel berth were still standing idly around. It was an infuriating example of the bloody minded attitude to be found in those days, both North and South of the border - they could not see a relationship betwen their jobs and the need to bring in money to pay the wages.

The wind was still against us, so we were still tacking along the coast and it freshened enough to force us to take in a reef for a brief period. As if to taunt us, the wind backed into the Southeast, enabling us to lay a course along the coast, but not for long. We clawed our way South with the same pattern of motorsailing interspersed with periods of pure sailing and motoring. With this unsatisfactory progress, we gradually left the coast to cross the wide Firth of Forth overnight and in the small hours picked up the welcome lights of Barns Ness and St Abb's Head from well offshore, closing the coast off the Farne Islands. The wind deserted us during the course of the morning, and by early afternoon the lifeless sails were lowered and stowed.

There was still a long way to go and I was becoming concerned about fuel; the two tanks, port and starboard were each of 25 gallons capacity - the port tank had about 22/23 gallons remaining, and the other only about 9/10 gallons. The weather forecasts began to talk about winds becoming Northerly, but any there was came from the South. I decided to run the Starboard tank as low as was safe without risk of an airlock in the supply, leaving the port tank till we were forced to change. A comforting set of radio beacon bearings was obtained from Tynemouth pierhead and Flamborough Head - at least it felt as though we were progressing Southwards. That night, Saturday, our fourth day from Inverness, the sea was a glassy calm, and although a mist had set in, the powerful light of Flamborough head was sighted abeam in the small hours of Sunday. Sail was rehoisted when the promised Northerly wind came in, too feeble to justify shutting the engine down.

Deciding that I could not risk running the fuel in the starboard tank any lower, I changed to the port tank and then proceeded to spend Sunday morning lying cramped on the cockpit floor to drain the rest of fuel from the starboard tank and transfer it to the port tank, using a large baked bean tin. This was not a pleasant task, but I went on till I had almost got to the bottom of the tank, where the fuel might contain some sediment. Thus, we had an almost full fuel tank to port; barely had the operation been completed before the wind returned sufficiently to help us along with reduced engine speed. Soon after passing the Dowsing lightvessel, we shut the engine down. Gradually the wind increased, coming from just East of North, and we began reeling off the miles. Lowestoft and Southwold lights were passed in darkness; like a horse that knows it is nearing its home stables, "CELANDINE" was romping along in superb sailing conditions. (After all the frustrations of baffling winds and obstinate Scottish fuel suppliers, we surely deserved a break!).

An early breakfast was taken as Orfordness came abeam, bright and clean in the early morning sunlight; by 10 that Monday morning, our sixth day out from Inverness we rounded up into wind and tide to pick up the mooring at Walton under sail, with the contents of our port fuel tank still practically untouched.

The next year, 1974, was eventful, but started with great sadness when our staunch and much loved sailing companion Robert Barlow died. He bore the last days of his life with great fortitude, a gentleman to the last. During the trip to Scotland, when he and I were alone in the cockpit on a night watch, he had calmly said "You know I won't be with you by this time next year" - I found this very painful and tried to forget it, but even then, he knew. It seemed hard to believe that no more would we see his cheerful bearded face coming up through "CELANDINE'S" hatchway.

A HOUSE RESTORED AND A CHURCH ON FIRE

SOON after this sad event, at a Writtle Society meeting, the fate of Number One Lodge Road, a prominent but rather ugly Victorian House in the centre of the village was discussed. Many said it was rotten and should be demolished, but another school of thought said it should be restored. It was not the house which was actually rotten, but its reputation; the owner, an absentee landlord whose death brought about its impending sale had let it to people who turned it into a poor quality rooming house, where the rooms were let to a floating population of tenants, some of whom had extremely doubtful reputations, and stories circulated of police calling at the front door while some of the occupants beat a hasty retreat from a back door. Everybody thought "they" should do it up, but as everyone knows "they" do not exist. I surveyed the property by jumping in the middle of all the floors, and investigating the roof space. The quality of joinery and construction was impressive, the very best of mid to late Victorian standards in materials and workmanship.

The house had at one time belonged to the Writtle Brewery, who had enlarged it in 1895 by adding an almost exact replica of the original house on to the previous frontage; for many years it was let to the Misses Smaile, the village dressmakers who also augmented their income by taking in lodgers. When they had both died, the new tenants then started letting the rooms, and added extra rooms by means of some extremely flimsy partitions that probably would have never been approved by a council building inspector. The indescribably sordid muddle of junk left by tenants over the years disfigured the whole place, and this, with the evil reputation it had managed to acquire, undoubtedly deterred prospective buyers. I acquired the place at a very modest price - I needed to, as a lot of money would have to be spent.

The obvious choice of architect for the job was our friend Patricia Stewart, who had an imaginative breakthrough that transformed the place; we put in new 8-light sash windows to replace the mean looking Victorian windows and created a large size drawing room or lounge out of two smaller rooms, with french windows looking on to the garden. The front door, which was set in an insignificant opening in the brickwork, was transformed by the addition of an open porch - nothing too grand, but it did create a more impressive entrance. The house lay in what had become a conservation area, so the planning application would be closely scrutinised. Fortunately for us, the old Chelmsford Rural District Council still existed, but was due to be replaced in a Local Government reorganisation; the plans came for scrutiny by the planning department of Essex County Council because of its position in a conservation area. Both Patricia and I had discussed every aspect of the improvements we proposed with the County Planners, who were most co-operative and made some useful suggestions. Unfortunately, by the time the plans were finally going through, the new Chelmsford District Council had taken over; I even had to tell them that they had a statutory duty to put a notice on the property to advise the public of our planning application - nothing would have happened otherwise.

My feelings about the new authority imposed on us are best described in a May diary entry - "Pay rates" to which I had added "why? - go sailing instead". As I am not languishing in jail, I suppose I must have relented and reluctantly paid them. The work, by builder Maurice Wood, eventually started later in the summer, after we had removed several skip loads of rubbish - some rooms had several layers of grotty carpet as incoming tenants put theirs on top of earlier ones, whilst a brick outbuilding which was to be demolished had to be cleared of old bikes, rusting mo-peds and similar forms of transport, mostly in pieces. It was hard work.

Because the property stood at cross roads, double glazing was installed by the creation of secondary windows inside the external windows - this system, using about 5/6 inches between the two, gives good heat and sound insulation. I do not remember what form of heating was there before, if any - I suspect each tenant had his own electric heating through a meter heavily loaded in the landlord's favour. We put in an up to date gas fired central heating system which we had up and running before the Writtle Society had their Christmas Party there - a well attended event as many came to see what we had been up to; both inside and out, the house now looked attractive.

The property was eventually sold early the following year, and as the work was financed by a bank loan (interest rates were fortunately low at that time) I was pleased to be rid of the burden. The finances of the operation were so finely balanced that I never really knew how I came out of it financially, but I suspect it was neutral. Having always wanted to renovate a house in danger, I had at last achieved this ambition and had a good deal of satisfaction from the whole enterprise. Not being a naturally modest person, I carved the year of restoration, my initials, those of Patricia Stewart and of Maurice Wood in the brickwork of a chimney in the wall flanking the road through Writtle; nearly thirty years later they are still there quite clearly, beneath the date of an enlargement carried out in 1895.

When I was discussing the plans of No 1 Lodge Road with the County planners, they said "did you know your Church was on fire?", and pointed from their office high in a tower block to a great column of smoke rising above the village, some two and a half miles distant. Our interview was brief and I sped home to find fire engines everywhere

No1 Lodge Road Writtle, after restoration, 1974.

and water being pumped from the village pond. Already the gaunt blackened timbers of the chancel roof could be seen, indicating severe damage, and locals were standing round, unable to help, and in a state of shock.

When a major disaster strikes a community such as exists in Writtle, the response is remarkable, and the following day people were turning up from all over with cleaning materials, and already, a partition was being erected to screen off the severely damaged chancel from the nave, which although badly smoke damged, had been saved by the efforts of the fire brigade. The village had also recovered sufficiently the next day to ask astutely "Did the organ go?" The organ was well known to be near to its last gasp, and was indeed ruined, mainly by water.

A lot of the cost of repair was covered by insurance, but as always, there was an element of betterment in the refurbishment, resulting in a substantial shortfall. A fund was started, and I found myself chairman of the appeal fund. It proved to be a rewarding task because people from far and wide were generous, and we actually had money left in the kitty at the end - of course, in a building 800 plus years old it was not long before this was swallowed up in further repairs and maintenance.

However, there was an unexpected twist in this episode. The fire had been started by a boy of about 13 years who already had a record of arson, and certainly was experienced in knowing how to light a fire. He had arrived in the village the day before, to a children's residential home on the Green, but those in charge were not told of the boy's reputation. This was my first awareness of political correctness; his previous guardians did not want to prejudice his chances in the new surroundings, so nothing was said.

The insurance company decided this was a neglect of duty - insurance companies do not like paying out vast sums of money, and if they think someone can be held responsible for a disaster, they will go for them. For legal reasons, the legal action had to be in the name of the Vicar of Writtle - the headlines read "Vicar sues Essex County Council" The insurance company won.

TREACHERY IN BUSINESS

IF ever there was a year when it didn't just rain, but pour, 1974 was that year. The merger with our competitor in the kapok business was not going as it should; we were rationalising in a declining market, but there was every reason to suppose it should give a number of years' satisfactory trading. We had arranged a modest overdraft facility with the bankers (remember I lost the toss over whose bankers should be used, so we used theirs, Natwest), but I did not think we should need to make much use of it, because both companies had put in a pool of stocks.

Use was being made of the facility; I was unhappy about the cash flow, so I asked our accountants to look at this carefully (remember I won the toss on accountants). During the course of their audit, they uncovered irregularities, and found that the company was supplying heating oil to my co-directors' houses. This was stupid, because the company had every reason to prosper without any need for cheating. I immediately announced my withdrawal from the joint company and requested the remaining directors to find a guarantor for the overdraft to replace me. It was no good continuing with people prepared to do this kind of thing - how much else might be going on?

Immediately, we restarted trading on our own, using the machinery still on our premises - there was no undertaking in our joint set up to prevent either side from doing so. Pressure was brought on them to find a replacement guarantor in my place but nothing happened, the truth being that they could not find one, and it was not long before the bank smelt a rat. They foreclosed, but the overdraft was "Jointly and severally" guaranteed, which means that if they can't get their money from the parties jointly, they go for the easiest target. In this case it meant me, and because it was personally guaranteed, it had to be my money, not our Company's. Although the other part of our business was prospering and had a substantial credit balance at the bank, it could not be used, and I had to arrange a mortgage on Greenbury House with our own bankers, Lloyds - fortunately the property was unencumbered by any other borrowing, but Beryl was not at all happy - no woman likes to feel that her home is at risk.

The other side were by now furious that we were now taking back a very substantial portion of the declining business, so they then decided to get an injunction against our using the kapok cleaning plant, on the basis it belonged to the new company. I had friends in Holland, a country which once had a large kapok industry, who told me of surplus plant we could have in order to clear a factory, for no more than the cost of transport. It was all getting quite unpleasant, and I dislike this kind of thing, but was certainly going to fight for our business, and confronted them with this move.

The whole thing was overtaken by my act of paying off the overdraft - the local branch of Natwest was fairly dim and delayed releasing me until a sharp letter was sent by my solicitors. Once this was resolved I pursued my money, and was advised that the quickest way to obtain it was to issue a 21 day winding up order, which brought things to a head pretty quickly. The injunction was lifted, and I was free to use the machinery again; whereas we could have finished them there and then, because they could not pay, an offer was made to repay over several months, to which we agreed. The son of the family who was then running the business had young children, and would have been in dire straits had we forced the business to close.

A lot of the trouble with the overdraft was that the young man was up to his neck in debt with Natwest, with his father as a co-guarantor, due to a golf course and leisure complex he was unsuccessfully trying to develop. I don't know what happened to them, but their kapok business did not last much longer, nor another enterprise in furniture on which he embarked; every now and then you meet people in this world who have a remarkable ability to turn gold into lead. This was a time fraught with risk and worry, and I mention it to show how much one has to be on one's guard in business affairs; although there has to be a lot of trust in business - it could not function without it - there are always some rogues about.

DOWN WEST AGAIN - AND THE SCILLIES

IN spite of all the problems, we managed yet another trip down West in "CELANDINE", leaving Walton early in June on the principle that you are less likely to encounter long periods of strong Westerlies at that time of year. Unfortunately, nature was not aware of my beliefs and we encountered some fairly tough windward sailing, stopping for frequent rests at Ramsgate, Studland Bay and Weymouth. After leaving Studland Bay with a Northwest wind that was certainly more favourable, as so often happens when at last you get one, it then begins to die on you. Mackerel lines were put out, but then there was a very loud "crr-ummp" that came up through the hull as if it had been hit with a sledgehammer. There are Army ranges nearby, at Lulworth, but no red flags were flying; buoys marking a Naval gunnery area were nearby; we passed a Naval auxiliary Vessel hove to with no one on deck, and we quietly ghosted past her. More explosions followed, and then we saw it. A very heavy projectile hit the water not far from us, sending up a great column of water well outside the area marked by the buoys. Heroism was not the order of the day; the engine was started, mackerel lines retrieved and we steered for Weymouth at maximum speed, leaving more clearly visible falls of shot astern. Presently, the Naval auxiliary vessel sprang into life and gave chase, but it took her a long time to draw level with us in order to tell us we had sailed through a danger area. I replied that it was the first time I had been fired on by my own side, and that their gunnery certainly was in need of improvement. By this time we realised that in the mist, on the horizon, were the outlines of more than one heavy Naval vessel. In the following day's papers bought at Weymouth were the accounts of a NATO exercise in the Channel - I hope that it was not an RN ship that couldn't even get its shot within the fairly large target area.

The following afternoon, we left Weymouth with a reef in as there was quite a fresh West wind blowing, and set off carried by a favourable tide to round Portland Bill on the inshore passage. Under the lee of the highest part of the Portland peninsula, we were struck by a fierce gust that put the lee deck well under water until the top of the bulwarks was almost under. I didn't say much to my crew, but thought "you fool Platt, you should have put in a second reef - if it's like this here in the lee, whatever will we find on the windward side?" In the narrow Channel round the end, we headed up under power into a wind from dead ahead and a very confused sea - this is supposed to be the calm bit inside the dreaded race, but a very short time later we were clear of the headland and squared away under sail to tack inshore; the single reef was perfectly adequate and "CELANDINE" got into her stride, closehauled in seas that were quite moderate. The gust we had encountered was effectively a down draught beating downwards upon the sails - Beryl, with her aeronautical knowledge, knew about these things, known in Greek waters as a "Katabatic" wind.

The wind fell light again as evening approached, and we continued our tacks Westward. The golden Dorset coast was illuminated by the evening sun, and approaching the beauty spot known as The Golden Cap, we hove to. It is a great thing about a boat such as "celandine", where with a little trimming of sails practically all progress ceases and the movement of the hull becomes easy and gentle. At 8 pm dinner was served - shrimp cocktail, steak au facon du Rose, cheeses. All this was carefully recorded in the log, and the meal, produced by Michael Rose, was worthy of mention. There are two crew members named Michael Rose, both living in Writtle, which can be confusing so they are often referred to as "bald" and "thatch" and it was indeed the thatched variety of the species which produced this splendid meal.

We called in to Newton Ferrers on the Yealm, where we visited Robert's widow, Betty, before continuing to Falmouth. From here, nearly a month later, I returned to "celandine" with my old friend George Jones; the Flushing ferryboat put us aboard to leave almost at once and anchor for the night in the Helford River. George had a mission on this trip; he was supervising the re-rigging of a powerful coastal sailing barge, the "LADY DAPHNE", and knew something of her history. I was interested in her, as we were both launched in 1923; she was unusual among barges in that she was built at Rochester by Shorts, builders of the famous "Sunderland " flying boats. Shorts were seeking to expand their riverside site and bought a barge building yard which had a contract to build the barge, so they took the yard over and honoured the contract. Sailing down Channel in the thirties to pick up a cargo of stone from the West Country, she was struck in the night by an Easterly gale which tore some of the canvas, and during the struggle to get her under control, the skipper went overboard. The mate and third hand let off flares, and were taken off by a lifeboat. From there, the barge careered madly on down channel to the Scilly Islands, where she drifted through Crow Sound and rounded up into the wind to beach herself on a sandy stretch of shore at Tresco, undamaged. George wanted to visit the site

Cromwell's castle, New Grimsby Sound, Scillies.

of this amazing event, so we were Scillies bound.

Weighing anchor early the next morning, we rounded the Lizard in perfect conditions - blue sparkling sea, a light Northwesterly wind bearing us towards our destination. Rounding the Lizard, the most Southerly point of mainland Great Britain, the wind obligingly veered a little further round to the North thus enabling us to steer the course for the Scillies, which are almost on the same degree of latitude as the Lizard. The Lizard peninsular can be a wicked place, and is a last resting

place for many fine ships, but this day it was in a benign mood. The coast of Cornwall slipped past, becoming more distant as it receded into the deep Mount's Bay, and by half past seven in the evening we were cautiously entering Crow Sound - the Scillies call for great caution in pilotage due to the many unmarked rocks and strong tidal streams. By the time we had negotiated the Tresco flats, and passed the very beach on which George said the unmanned "LADY DAPHNE" had harmlessly run herself ashore, it was nearly 9 in the evening when the anchor splashed down in New Grimsby Sound, just South of Cromwell's castle (why did Cromwell need to build a castle out here?).

The following day, we prepared rations for an expedition ashore to visit the beach where the barge ran ashore, and the renowned Abbey Gardens. There are no all-weather safe anchorages in the Scillies, but the weather forecast was good and "celandine" in a safe enough anchorage to be left for the day; we landed at about 11 in the morning, not eturning till 6 in the evening. We were intrigued by the gigs - long slim rowing boats manned by (I think 6) oarsmen - and some of the crews are women these days. Fast and seaworthy, they were once the inter-island means of transport, and also used for taking pilots out to ships and boarding wrecks, of which there were plenty; nowadays they take part in fiercely contested rowing matches.

The Abbey gardens are the work of the Dorrien-Smith family, and were started by their ancestor, Augustus Smith. The island was barren and windswept, and right up to Victorian times, the principal source of income on the Scillies was from shipwrecks - they are the first part of the British Isles encountered after leaving the Americas, and woe betide the ship ensnared in this tangle of rocks and islands. Augustus Smith, who leased the island from The Duchy of Cornwall, built the substantial house above the ruined remains of an ancient monastery, planted trees as windbreaks and from thence began to cultivate within the Abbey gardens all manner of exotic plants from all over the world which would not grow on the mainland. The same family, to alleviate poverty on the island (and may be to divert the inhabitants from actively encouraging shipwrecks), initiated the cultivation of daffodils and other crops which would be on the market long before those grown on the mainland. They have been a thoroughly responsible and positive influence on the fortunes of the island; they no doubt would be dismissed today by many a modern sociologist as "paternalistic".

An unexpected exhibition within the gardens was of ships' figureheads once gracing the bows of fine vessels which came to grief here. The most famous and disastrous shipwreck of all was that early in the eighteenth century of Sir Cloudsley Shovell's squadron, returning from Gibraltar. As in so many shipwrecks, they had suffered several days of bad visibility and had no clear idea of their position; in recent years the story of the consequences arising from this national disaster has been re-told in dramatic form by Dava Sobell, in her book "Longitude". In its turn, the significance of the invention of the chronometer has been superseded by the Decca system and then by GPS (Global Positioning System), none of which were available to small yachts in our "CELANDINE" days.

At lunch time we found a seat in a secluded corner and soon were sharing our lunch with a great many birds who clearly knew about picnics. Unfortunately, we had to shoo away the peacocks who, although very beautiful, are an agressive and dominating bird, much given to scrounging - and not past helping themselves from the contents of your haversack.

Within half an hour of our return aboard from this idyllic visit ashore, the anchor was weighed, and we headed back towards the Tresco flats, a shallow stony bar at the Southern end of New Grimsby Sound. There was insufficient depth for us, and the stony bottom showed clearly through the clear water, so we re-anchored temporarily on a very short scope while supper was cooked, finally re-anchoring for the night East of Guthers Island just inside Crow Sound. Again, this anchorage was safe in the prevailing conditions, but would be treacherous should a wind get up from an unfavourable direction - at any anchorage in the Scillies a careful eye must be kept on the weather. Fortunately, we were able to get an extremely good set of bearings from Bishop's Rock, Round Island and a conspicuous well lit TV tower, so there was an accurate check should

Beryl relaxes on deck in Gillan Haven - a gem of an anchorage, but if the wind goes in to the East - get out!.

we suspect the anchor of dragging, or were forced to clear out in the night - but it remained quiet and peaceful.

The wind in the morning was fresh from the Northwest, and after pulling down the first reef in the mains'l, we were away just after 8 and tearing back towards the Lizard, "CELANDINE" showing just how fast she could really travel. After rounding the Lizard, the wind fell light and progress slowed, so that we did not pick up our mooring in Falmouth until 10 that evening.

After celebrating Vicky's 21st birthday in Writtle (she is the only member of our family who can claim to be a genuine native), I went back with Beryl for a holiday pottering in the Falmouth area, during which time we also had visitations from friends as well

"Celandine" in Gillan Haven.

as time on our own, the children now tending to do their own thing. It was during this holiday that we discovered Gillan, lying on the South of the Helford Estuary. This delightful haven, sheltered from the West, but open to the East had an unmarked rock in the middle of its entrance, which would come awash at low water on a spring tide, and I'm sure this put people off. Landing on the beach at St Anthony's, we were greeted by the bells of this ancient church being rung by a group of enthusiastic young people.

On a wet and breezy Sunday, well protected from the rain, we went ashore and walked to the centre of the peninsular between Gillan and Helford to go to church in Manaccan. After the service, we were invited to the vicarage for coffee, which worried us slightly as we were clobbered with oilskins and rigged generally for the indifferent weather. We need not have worried, as the vicarage porch was piled high with oilskins and seaboots, proving that a large part of the congregation were sailing folk. It was here we met the Alder family. He was a lecturer at Reading and their house was there, but they also owned a beautiful cottage "Lamorna" in Helford village. They had a Salcombe yawl, and said they would come round and see us that afternoon, so after an extremely hard sail in this fast and seaworthy open boat, they arrived alongside for tea. There have been many sailing episodes with them resulting from that first meeting.

Another favourite anchorage was at Durgan, in the Helford River, where we would go ashore in this National Trust village, walk up through the sub-tropical garden to the house and pay our garden admission fees in retrospect (latterly we became members and only went up to the house to show our membership cards). We also fell in love with Mawnan church, reached from another nearby anchorage with an accessible beach and path up the cliff. Mawnan churchyard contains the grave of Claud Worth, the great cruising yachtsmen and author of cruising books, also one of the founder members of the Cruising Association. The church itself looks out across the Helford estuary and down the East coast of the Lizard; on the day we visited, the South porch door was open with the sunlight streaming in, the superb view highlighted by the sparkling sea far below.

Towards the end of August, "CELANDINE" was headed East once more; my theory about winds setting in from the West in late summer worked well this time, and the winds bore us swiftly towards the East Coast. Although in those days, I tended to press on, I was not averse to stopping for the occasional rest. This trip we chose to go inside the Isle of Wight, and although I can't remember why, anchored near Wootton creek for the night, before setting off early the next morning to sail through the Looe channel, off Selsey Bill, which is a very useful short cut inside the Owers Banks and popular with small ships. The Westerly wind freshened to give us an exhilarating downhill ride along the South coast, where, after passing Beachy Head, we gybed round as we were beginning to round the corner from South to South East coasts; running before the wind is not a relaxing point of sailing in a fore and aft rig vessel, so late that evening we anchored for a rest in the East road on the North side of Dungeness. It is not a very scenic place, with the long shingle bank dotted with fisherman's huts, various outbreaks of beach huts and other somewhat shanty style development. It did not matter as it was dark, but there was an all pervading smell of fish and chips wafted offshore by the breeze from which we were sheltering - this was soon replaced by a smell of steak and onions from our own galley, a midnight feast.

By 6 in the morning we were weighing anchor and heading up the Kent coast towards that much loved spot of mine, the Dover Strait. The log has an entry made while passing Dover "score - 2 Cross channel ferries outward bound plus one Hovercraft, one ferry inward bound plus one more in distance". Crossing the Thames Estuary, in those days I used to keep well offshore on a course that took us past the Kentish Knock lightvessel; there is a shorter route through the Fisherman's Gat, but it was not marked and is no more than a shallow passage through the sands. Nowadays, with the confidence that Decca and GPS inspire, I have no hesitation in using it; the Kentish Knock lightvessel has long since gone from the scene.

In those days, the Walton channel was not lit (now it is lit, thanks to a combination of the efforts of Walton and Frinton Yacht Club and modern technology) so we entered Harwich harbour to anchor, just before midnight, off Stone Heaps at the entrance to the Orwell. The following morning saw us covering the very last part of our voyage to return to our usual mooring.

Then it was back to the problems with our erstwhile business partners, the continuing refurbishment of No.1 Lodge Road, meetings about the restoration of fire damage at the Church - but also a round of enjoyable social events. Beryl was heavily involved as Chairman of Essex Education Committee in many matters including a fight with central government to retain some very good grammar schools (including the ones from whose good teaching we had both benefited).

The previous year had seen a lot of personal borrowing - planned as far as the overdraft used to restore No 1 Lodge Road was concerned, and secured on the house itself. The loan I negotiated to pay off the overdraft of the merged company from which I made such a quick exit, when I found out the sort of people with whom I was dealing, was totally unintended and secured on Greenbury House. Fortunately, during May I received the final repayment from my erstwhile co-directors, which was a great relief, and also the sale of the restored house was completed, so all my borrowing was repaid; it had all been personal, rather than Company and looking back on it, perhaps I should have been more worried than I was at the time.

Also during the summer, a major competitor went into receivership. We had, in its final years done some business with them, and I suppose we were lucky to have been paid. I had visited the factory, in a delightful part of Hampshire, in the Test valley when it was still thriving and impressive. We bought two Swiss built quilting machines, neither of them very old, and in excellent condition. At the time, we were extremely busy and although we then still owned our own transport, the vehicles were busy and not suitable for collecting such machines, so a suitable open truck was hired and I went down with our transport manager, Mick Buck, who had an HGV licence - I would have happily driven the lorry once, but the advent of the HGV licence requirement put an end to my lorry driving days. Perhaps the roads of this country are safer as a result.

It was a blazing hot day and the countryside looked at its best. Although I was very pleased with our purchases at knockdown prices - the receivers were selling off everything to clear the premises, which probably represented the most valuable residue - it was depressing to see the deserted factory, with weeds growing from the gutters and inside a state of total disorder. There was no means of loading the machines on the truck, but we negotiated with an Irish fork lift truck driver working on the adjacent site to lift them when we had unbolted the machines from the floor - after identifying which machines we had bought. There was no one there taking an interest any more, only someone representing the receiver's interests.

In due course, we summoned our new found Irish friend and started to lift the machine. Alarm bells rang on the fork lift warning of excessive load, while the machines remained firmly in place. We had often used fork lifts to lift similar machines before, and were mystified. In a corner lay a large hydraulic jack, so I commandeered this and proceeded to lift. The machine refused to lift off the floor - standing back, it was obvious the floor was coming up with the machine, stuck to it by the felt anti-vibration pads always used to mount such machines. The floor was not of very good quality, and had been surfaced with a tarry compound - perhaps the hot weather had helped fuse the two together. Now, a sledgehammer was found and quickly used to break the machine clear. Paddy raced the two machines off on to our truck, suitable payment was made and I beat the floor back into a semblance of level with the sledgehammer so that cosmetically it did not look too bad. I went up to the offices, where the telephones were still connected, and phoned Dagenham to let them know we were on our way; scattered about the office were papers with lists of customers (most of whom we already knew) and other information. Once a business closes and the employees lose their jobs, no one is interested any more - it is a depressing atmosphere.

Soon after this episode, another firm closed down, this time in the Highway, East London and not far from where the Times is now produced. Two excellent machines, which I suspect they had never really mastered, were again bought at a bargain price but being so much nearer to Dagenham, the logistics were easier. Of course, we needed these machines to cope with the extra work arising from the closure of competitors. There had been a great increase in entrants to the quilting trade as people jumped on the bandwaggon, thinking it was a licence to print money - although, to be fair the one in Hampshire had been at it longer than we had. A firm from Canada came to the North and let it be known we would all be finished, as using North American production techniques they would undercut our prices. I think they lasted all of two years, but one of the directors admitted in a telephone conversation that they had no idea it was so difficult to make a profit in the UK. Some of the newcomers hurt badly with cheaper prices, achieved by cutting quality, but have not survived.

Meanwhile, in Writtle, the restoration of the fire damage to the church was nearing completion and events were being planned to mark its completion, including a concert by Essex Youth Orchestra, and a performance of the Church's history in Light and Sound (being Writtle, we certainly were not calling it "Son et Lumiere"). This latter was not performed until the following year; its production was hard but enjoyable work over many months for an enthusastic band of volunteers.

MORE OF HOLLAND

A T the end of May, "CELANDINE" went to Holland for a week's cruise. Leaving Walton on Friday afternoon, a favourable but cold wind from Nor'nor'east set us off in good style under full sail. During the night it freshened a little and veered nearer to North; it was bitterly cold, but fortunately one of the crew, Harry Hutchinson, had brought his old thickly padded motor cycling gloves. "CELANDINE'S" wooden steering wheel had an outer chrome rim, which was very cold and each helmsman in turn used these warm comforts for his trick on the helm. Morning saw us awaiting the sea lock at Flushing; as soon as the boat was secured alongside, there was a major priority - to light the solid fuel stove as quickly as possible. Although summer was approaching, we had good stocks of fuel aboard and it was to be alight for the next few unseasonable days.

In those days, one secured alongside the quay on the main canal at Middleburg, which we did in order to make some purchases ashore and cook a good hot lunch - it was that kind of weather. Over the next day or so, we visited Goes, where we once again laid alongside the quay with the quaint lighthouse and renewed aquaintance with some of the dedicated band of volunteers who tended this delightful haven, reached by virtually turning the boat in through a hole in the hedge at the side of the canal.

At Willemstad, although the wind had gone round to Southwest, it remained bitterly cold with rain that sometimes turned to sleet. On the BBC news we heard that snow had stopped play at a County cricket match in the Northwest, our reaction to this being to put more fuel on that stove. In contrast to our earlier visit, when at low water the harbour was a muddy ditch, the tidal rise and fall was now minimal, as the Haringvliet had been dammed off as part of the great delta scheme. When we left, we went through the opening span of the railway bridge - no more scraping under at low water as we once had done. Finally, with the wind back North of West and still very chill, we reached Rotterdam, mooring in the Veerhaven.

Here we were visited by our friend Feico Elhorst, who ran a Dutch firm of kapok brokers with whom we did business; his father had also done business with us in my father's day, but the declining trade meant we met more as friends and less to do business. He also sailed and had a boat, so we had common interests. In addition, we went ashore to meet Beryl, who was staying at the Rotterdam Hilton for an educational conference. By a strange coincidence, our business had completed a contract quilting some very exotic printed material for bedspreads in this relatively new hotel, and she was now in a bedroom furnished with one.

Before our return, the great referendum on whether our country should enter the common market took place. Knowing I was going to be abroad, I had in advance recorded my vote in favour; it seemed then that dropping customs barriers and artificial barriers to trade across a band of European countries was a very good idea, and could remove another of the possible causes of war; had I known what was going to gradually and stealthily be forced on us, I would have voted the other way, but at the time it seemed like a good thing.

The following evening saw us putting to sea again, and Feico came down to wave us off as we motored out into the New Waterway and down towards the Hook of Holland. Our voyage home was another tale of favourable wind patches, calms and interludes under power. The amazing thing about this trip was the dramatic change in weather, and the following day, Friday, was so hot that when we washed down our blisteringly hot iroko decks , clouds of steam came from them. Progress was slow, and proved another of my cynical theories about the weather - "If the wind is favourable, it will fall light, but if it is ag'in you, it will freshen". It was early evening on the Friday before we sighted the Outer Gabbard lightvessel, which is still a long way off the coast. Finally, just after three on Saturday morning, the anchor went down off Trimley hard, sheltered from the Easterly wind - not that shelter from this light wind was needed, but at low water, it ensures that you swing away from the shore. In earlier years, we had anchored just upriver from Felixstowe Dock, but already the deepwater berths at the new and thriving Felixstowe container port were extending up the river Orwell.

At a more respectable hour of the day, we motored over to Harwich Town quay for Customs clearance. As soon as this formality was over, we were away to make the most of the light Easterly wind and sail up the coast as far as Shingle Street at the entrance to the

Alde, just for the sheer joy of sailing in perfect weather past the sunlit coast - beyond Felixstowe the coast is free of beach huts and becomes rural, although at that time the clifftops at Bawdsey still bristled with strange looking radar antennae, some of which we used to call "the nodding men", for that is exactly what they looked like. To prolong our time at sea, we hove to off Felixstowe front for lunch - I am a great believer in heaving to and thus create relaxed conditions for a meal, and if the going is hard, a welcome rest that refreshes the ship's company. However hard we tried, it was impossible to disguise the fact that a good week's cruise was coming to an end - one that seemed to start in winter and finish in summer - and reluctantly headed up the Walton Channel to our mooring. After the somewhat indifferent start, the summer of 1975 turned out to be a scorcher, causing near drought conditions in places, superb sailing and bathing conditions, a bumper fruit crop and a vintage wine year (the former included our garden, but sadly the latter did not!).

After several enjoyable weekend sails to favourite local anchorages, "CELANDINE" headed back towards Holland in mid-July, and very early on Friday the 18th we set off in a light Southwest wind, with a strong crew - Michael Beaumont, Mary Dainty and George Jones - the latter still grumbling about my association with the devil in the form of synthetic ropes and sails. I personally believe they have transformed the running and maintenance of a sailing vessel, but George loved a good argument - we always remained best of friends whatever the argument.

Course was laid for Ostend, taking our departure from the Sunk lightvessel; the wind varied between force 3-4 and almost nothing, but always from the Southwest and there was only an hour during the whole passage when the lack of wind merited starting the engine; good progress meant we were in Ostend harbour by seven in the evening. Things had already started to change there, as the great yachting explosion was gathering momentum and they had created a large marina within an inner harbour. At one time Ostend was a regular port of call, because from Harwich it is an easy passage, and there were suppliers of duty-free wines and spirits who would deliver whatever you ordered within hours of your arrival and no questions asked; I can't remember whether this was still operating on this trip, but if it was, it certainly would be for the last time as rules were being tightened.

Leaving about mid-day the next day, we then started a long run with a favourable wind all the way up the coast, past the conspicuous cranes on the mole at Zeebrugge, and Northwards well offshore from the Dutch coast to pass Scheveningen just after midnight, followed by the Nordwyk light, then the lights of Ijmuiden. It was a well marked route, which followed the coast round until we passed Den Helder, the Dutch naval base, to then enter a minor channel called Mulzwin - one sees a connection with Holland and East Anglia, for we have our own Swin channel. Here the buoyage became very close, and by mistaking one, our keel managed to make contact with an unseen part of Holland for about half an hour - fortunately the tide was rising and we came off the mud to enter the Isselmeer at one end of the great dam that encloses it from the tidal sea, through the "sluis" (lock) at Den Oever. Early that evening, Sunday, we rounded up and dropped the sails to enter Medemblik, at the start of a Southerly progress towards Amsterdam.

Next, we revisited Enkhuizen, after an exhilarating sail in a brisk Nor'norwest wind that drove "CELANDINE'S" fine bows through the short chop of the Isselmeer with great power. I am not a racing man, but have to confess to feeling a bit smug when you seem to be overhauling everything in sight. Each time we returned to Holland, great changes had taken place - the great delta scheme, land reclamation from the Isselmeer, so that former islands became part of the nearest mainland, and a new dam had been thrown right across dividing North from South, and a waterway created between the two, South of Enkhuizen.

Then the wind had became strong from the Southwest, and with a reef in the main and no.2 jib, we thrashed our way down to Hoorn; after a morning in yet another lovely old town (this was our first visit to this one) we pulled down two reefs in the main, and again used no.2 jib, the wind having veered to West to give us a romp Southwards on one tack. It was all good sailing with blue skies and sunshine above, even though some spray came aboard from the brackish waters of the meer (another Dutch word close to our own - "mere"). Finally, as the land closed in on us from either side at the entrance to the Pampus channel, the sails were lowered, not to be used again for a time. Under power, we drove on towards central Amsterdam, and finished that day's progress in theSixhaven. This was not the former Sixhaven in which I had berthed "CAMPION", near the Dutch Royal Yacht, but a larger marina a little further out from the centre, and definitely not so upmarket - the old one was no longer in use. It was still reasonably central, and Michael had to leave at this point, having a reservation on that night's boat for Harwich. The next morning, Mary had to leave, to return on the day sailing from the Hook to Harwich, so I escorted her to Central Station, where after a fairly brief wait, I met Beryl off the boat train. She must have passed Michael somewhere in the North Sea - indeed "CELANDINE'S" crew were giving good business to the Harwich-Hook route. My visit to Amsterdam Central Station was a very slick operation - one crew member away while another arrives within half an hour; the casual observer might have had some interesting thoughts, seeing me putting one woman on a train leaving and meeting another arriving within half an hour later.

That evening saw us once again awaiting the night opening of the great railway bridge, followed by the series of 8 bridges. This was the first time we had been through there since the yachting explosion had gathered momentum, and I noted that we were accompanied on this occasion by "20 other yachts, most driven by incompetent and ill mannered idiots" Each bridge is opened in turn by the same crew driving by car from bridge to bridge, so those who insisted on overtaking, often driving alongside through the bridge, which I would not allow, and had to give way by slowing down. All this madness only meant that they had to wait longer at each bridge, and as they were mainly the sort of boats that cannot stand still, they would be weaving about the place, getting in each other's way. I am happy to say I saw no British flagged yachts behaving so irresponsibly.

After this nightmare, we spent two peaceful nights at anchor, one in the New Meer, and one in the Aalsmeer. In the latter, we enjoyed a spectacular sunset sky over the Meer and canal just beyond - note in log "Venetian lagoon without the smell" By now the weather had become really hot; regular washing down was an enjoyable task, and good for our beautiful laid decks. The water in the meers and canals was fresh, whereas I always prefer salt water for wooden decks - the salt discourages bacteria and rot, whilst always retaining an element of dampness in them,which is good for the wood.

Our leisurely progress Southwards was interrupted by stops to buy victuals from the well stocked travelling shops visiting some of the isolated communities. A favourite stopping place of ours whenever in this part of Holland was the "Petit Cafe Hanepoel", close to the Brassemer Meer, where we could moor alongside in just 5 feet of water. Cafe tables lined the edge of the canal, together with a small ancient road roller filled with

Alongside at the "Hannapoel", near Leiden - Peter Darwent, John Barrington and Roland.

flowers - the Dutch are so good with flowers, they will put them anywhere. The only drawback to the "Hanepoel" is the fact that between your table alongside the boat and the bar is a minor public road along which the occasional traffic speeds. We also met our friends the Elhorsts there for dinner one evening..

Berthing at a pleasant new marina in a rather shabby suburb of Leiden, we said farewell to George Jones and set off back to the Brassemer Meer and Kaag Lakes with their little islands, before returning to the marina, where Vicky was to join us - we were particularly anxious to see her as she was due to leave for Ghana in September for a two year stint as a VSO volunteer, to teach science and maths. Armed with all the railway timetables, we worked out the earliest train she could arrive in Leiden after crossing on the day boat from Harwich. After meeting several trains and no Vicky, we set off back to the boat rather downhearted. There, sitting drinking a cup of tea and enjoying the the sun in the cockpit was Vicky - always resourceful, she had beaten the system and arrived on an earlier train. She knew where the secret key was kept and made herself at home - after all, by that time that boat to her was in many ways an extension of home.

Southward bound, we enjoyed a mixture of sailing in the warm Southeasterly breezes where there were open bits of water, and motoring in the confined spaces, visiting Willemstad, and entering tide water through the Juliana Sluis, near Gouda. Once again, tides were part of the scene - when undertaking sea passages in the North Sea or English Channel, there was always an entry "HW Dover" because it is a standard port from which tidal streams can be calculated - after we had entered the non tidal Isselmeer in the North some wag had written in the log "HW Dover - who cares?", but tides were once again part of the daily routine until we reached the lock at the entrance to the poplar lined canal leading to Goes.

Here, as we entered the lock in sweltering conditions, a Dutch lady on the lockside asked us "How do you like our summer - tropical, not typical?". We have never forgotten this amusing remark, it has gone into the family jargon. Once again berthed in the pretty little yacht harbour "De Werf", Vicky left to catch the day boat to Harwich. By this time, the unused commercial basin in the centre of town had been adapted as a yacht marina, and all the smart yachts were going up there. Of course, it was convenient, whereas "De Werf" was 10 minutes walk from the centre, but nothing would persuade us to use the very urban town basin in preference to this pretty little yacht harbour with its well tended grass banks and shrubs enclosing it from the outside world, and its charming honesty box system for drinks from the cellar under the clubhouse floor and use of the showers. It is a gem.

After a quiet day, which also included re-victualling, the following day, Sunday, Roland joined with two friends, Nick Lugg and Tom Slator, for the voyage home. The day before they arrived there was a hiccup in the weather, with thunderstorms and heavy rain in the evening - still, I suppose, all part of the typical tropical weather, but the next day, when the new crew joined in the morning we were back to warmth and sunshine; setting off down the canal in the early afternoon, we were soon through the Kats lock and into the Veerse Meer, where we enjoyed two days of good sailing in its tideless waters. Each time we returned to the Veerse Meer, one could see the reclamation process still at work; our first visit in "CAMPION" had been not long after the raging tidal streams had been tamed and large areas of mud flat reclaimed. Each subsequent visit, areas that had been reclaimed first had grass covering them, then bushes, and now were beginning to sport considerable areas of maturing trees, whilst some of the isolated mudflats had become green nature reserves for waders and the like. When this kind of major work is undertaken, there is often a great whinge from the "conservationists" who often seem to think more about some problem with the lesser spotted so and so, but after seeing a number of schemes in Europe which are primarily designed to benefit mankind, the answer is that wildlife is remarkably adaptable and after a while you hear no more about it. The Dutch are very sensitive about provision for open spaces and nature, even though land is so hard won and precious to them.

Our enjoyable days in the Meer had to come to an end; returning to Veere to enter the Walcheren canal, we passed the great steel-hulled coastal sailing barge "WILL EVERARD", now out of trade and renamed "WILL". Thames barges once would have been trading to such continental ports, but now she was on pleasure with a charter party. Veere once was a centre for wool trade with British ports, and the ancient quay is lined with what once would have been warehouses and the homes of wealthy merchants; it is sometimes known as "The dead city", because of its erstwhile size and trading wealth. Now, with even the fishing gone, it sleepily relies on tourism and yachts for its income.

Early on Wednesday, we secured at Middleburg alongside the public quay to take on victuals and for Beryl to catch a train to connect with a sailing from the Hook, the station being very close by. By early afternoon we had cleared the sea lock at Flushing and were heading out to sea once more. With light and fluky winds we made slow progress through the Duerloo channel, that short but tricky short cut through the outer sandbanks of the Schelde estuary, followed by a fairly tedious passage back across the North Sea; nearing the coast, we passed the "KONIGIN WILHELMINA" on a reciprocal course - she would have left Harwich at half past nine that morning, and before we reached Pye End buoy, the "ST EDMUND" passed us outward bound for the Hook - in those days there were plenty of sailings in the high season, and several ships employed on the run.

By this time, customs requirements had been simplified - the sheer numbers of yachts made changes necessary, and you left a copy of a form at the yacht club advising your departure and names of crew members, with passport numbers. On return, another copy of the same form was left in the post box provided at the yacht club, and it was no longer necessary to be visited by an officer for clearance, so we spent a night on the mooring after lodging our papers ashore. Still with time left before our week was up, we enjoyed a fast sail up to the Alde and went right up to Iken. Given a wind, "CELANDINE" certainly could cover the distances; the next day we retraced our track, left the Alde and sailed up the Orwell to kill time until there was more water over the Pye sand. Although the Walton channel and adjoining creeks had adequate depths of water, the approach over the sands in Dovercourt Bay was lacking in water at low tide and there is no clearly defined channel into the deep waters of Harwich harbour.

Highlights from the rest of that splendid summer included a trip up to a favourite anchorage of mine off Stutton Ness - a bank holiday weekend when we were the only boat there. On the tide we were able to bathe from the sandy beach, and we bought some fish off a small inshore fishing boat - a large mullet, two small turbot (regarded by many as the finest of the flatfish) and three small plaice for 50 pence.

At the beginning of September, Vicky left for her two year stint in Ghana - two years with no prospect of any leave to come home as VSO, a voluntary organisation, could not fund extra flights. We were proud of her for taking on this task, but sad to think she would be away for so long. Although as the autumn of that year advanced there were some fresher winds, it generally was benign and many local trips were enjoyed, finishing in a cold and misty long weekend with Bill Basham, who also lived in Writtle at that time. On that trip we ventured into the Crouch and Roach before returning to Ian Brown's yard at Rowhedge to lay up. The boat was stripped of gear which was transferred to "J" store in the yard, and after the masts had been taken out, the boat was covered with a strong green canvas cover set over a series of trusses supporting a strong ridge plank - very similar to the construction of a domestic roof. The boat was without the sound of crews enjoying life afloat, and would be a silent hulk for nearly six months.

FIFTY YEARS OF ABBEY KAPOK AND AMERICA IN BI-CENTENNIAL YEAR.

1976 was the fiftieth anniversary of the founding of Abbey (now Abbey Quilting Ltd) by my father, and we were determined to celebrate the half century in style. In 1974, after some frustrating delays, the Cruising Association had moved into Ivory House at St Katharine Dock, hard by Tower Bridge. The headquarters had great charm and character, but although they were leased at an advantageous rate as part of the landlord's planning permission, it was still a larger sum of money than we had been used to paying, and the Association sought to let the premises for events to offset the rent. It was a very fine venue for such an event, set in the historic ambience of the recently restored dock, and in view of my connection with the CA, it was a wonderful opportunity, of benefit to everyone, so there it was to be.

Inevitably, the boat had to be involved in this operation - in the Platt family, if you can bring a boat in somewhere, they will. So, at the end of May, with dear old George Jones and the stalwart Mary Dainty aboard, we set sail from Walton, running before a light Northeast wind up the Wallet to bring up for the night tucked round inside Colne Point. It was just after eleven o'clock that night when the anchor went down, and we were underweigh again just after seven the next morning to take the flood tide through the Spitway - the shallow gate in the otherwise almost continuous line of sands stretching from the Dengie shore out to the North East Gunfleet buoy which is not far South of the approach to Harwich.

The sand banks in the Northern part of the Thames Estuary all reach out like long thin fingers lined up by the direction of the tidal streams, and they present a considerable hazard to the sailor who wishes to cross the Estuary, or from one deep channel across to another; however, there are a few gateways ("gutways") which can be used by small ships. The Spitway is a long used shallow opening leading from the Wallet, which runs along the coast past Walton and Clacton and into the Blackwater, to the Swin, which runs up into Sea Reach of the Thames. Once through, we were borne swiftly upstream by the flood tide and a light Southeast wind, past the historic Blacktail Spit beacon - one of the very early seamarks in the Estuary, marking a prominent spit of sand where the channel turns from Southwest to West past the Shoebury sands, and on past Southend pier.

I do not often visit the shore where my fascination with boats and the sea started, so on the tide, we ventured inshore over the mud flats - steering in towards the "white shelter", and then turning West parallel to the shore before returning to deep water in the Ray and anchoring for the night. At low water, I took Mary into the entrance to Leigh creek where there was just enough water to reach the Crowstone Hard and put her ashore for the night. When I was a boy, there was enough water to lie afloat in a shallow draft boat, but I believe in recent years this has all changed - these mud and sandbanks are for ever on the move. A surprising thing happened when I went to start the outboard on the inflatable dinghy - I just rolled over the side, fortunately before the outboard started . There was about 18 inches of water, so I stood up and got back in the dinghy; something to laugh about, but in a raging tide or strong wind and deep water, it could have been serious.

The next morning, we weighed and on the rising tide motored cautiously up to re-anchor near the moorings at Two Tree Island - another innovation since my young days, giving much more sheltered moorings than off the Leigh foreshore, and accessed by a newly created road across to a landing place; most of the moorings have little depth of water at low tide. At the landing place, we picked up Mary and Beryl, before setting off upriver to London. George had an objective during his trip with us - he wanted to visit the massive coalhouse fort at East Tilbury, an early Victorian fort to guard the Thames against hostile fleets, in the same way as the massive Martello towers scattered along the South East coasts of England - it was still too soon after Trafalgar and Waterloo to become complacent about French designs on our infuriating little country. So, after sailing in a wind that started light, but gradually freshened, we anchored out of the main shipping channel near Mucking no.7 buoy. Mucking is a Saxon name, with the "ing or inge" suffix meaning settlement or place often found in Essex names - we are, after all, the land of the East Saxons - but in today's world Mucking ("Muccas Inge") has unfortunate connotations rather borne out by the bleakness of the outlook there.

A raiding party went ashore to reconnoitre the fort, which was about to receive restoration treatment. Fortunately, we were well prepared in protective clothing, for soon after landing we were struck by a line squall with torrential rain, wind gusting to force 8 or 9 and the odd clap of thunder for good measure. This seemed as good a way of keeping the invader at bay as any, and some of our enthusiasm for history waned - nevertheless, we did see the fort, but everything was closed and access shut off. Today there is regular public access to the restored fort.

The following day saw us resume our progress up the Thames, and after going through the construction work on the site of the Thames barrier, anchored off Wren's magnificent building at Greenwich. The holding was poor, but after two attempts, I thought the anchor was firmly in - it was obvious that there was rock on the bottom - probably chalk from an old sea wall or other construction of long ago. Once ashore, we paid a visit to the Queen's house which had just emerged from a restoration programme; looking out of one of the large sash windows, I caught sight of two masts proceeding down river, and there was only one ship off Greenwich that day with two masts.

Rarely has a group of people raced so hard out of the Queen's House and shot across the busy traffic in the main road, jump into a dinghy and arrive panting on board. We got to her shortly before she would have dragged into a most undesirable looking swim headed rusty lighter full of junk. After re-anchoring, I prepared our fisherman anchor to replace the Danforth, because I thought it would have a better chance on the rocky bottom - there are some places where the old fashioned fisherman anchor is best - but luckily, I think this time I got the anchor down in a better spot where we held till the following morning. Again, we went ashore, this time to see the 1776 exhibition about the War of American Independence - of particular significance to us as we were due to visit America later in the year. In the afternoon we completed our voyage to London, berthing in St Katharines, where she would become a useful base for the forthcoming 50th anniversary celebrations.

The company whose anniversary we were to celebrate had already changed in character from the one my father had founded, and were he to have returned in that 50th year he would have found it difficult to recognise. I had already written a brief book on the subject, but now we had invited a party of customers (some of whom had been with us from the beginning) suppliers and friends to join us at Ivory House. Two delightful young women from Coggeshall did the catering, helped logistically by husbands who worked in the City, and we recruited "Weddy" to serve the wines and generally act as head butler. Genial Mr. Wedlock (a former regimental sergeant major) and his wife were a remarkable pair who hired themselves out as cook and butler to many people in Essex, for private dinner parties, or for official receptions - they were in great demand, because they had a superb flair for doing the whole thing impeccably and discreetly. On this occasion, we only needed the services of Mr Wedlock, who rose to the occasion superbly, and fitted in so well that some people thought he belonged to the Cruising Association and had been there for years. Alas, as I write, Mrs Wedlock died several years ago, and he has had to retire due to ill health - he is greatly missed from the Essex social scene where he had a wonderful ability to make people feel at ease, whilst ensuring that they were properly looked after.

The guests were delighted with the whole affair, and intrigued by this newly restored ancient dock and surrounding buildings (I exclude the Tower Hotel from this part of the description - it would have been more sensitive to produce a building in better taste, and probably better for trade). Our M.P., Tony Newton (now Lord Newton of Braintree) made a delightful short speech (with M.P.s, you are always lucky if you get them due to the uncertainties of parliamentary business).

On the Friday afternoon after the event, "CELANDINE" locked out, and as there was a fair Westerly wind blowing, we immediately rounded up and hoisted the mains'l, under the shadow of Tower Bridge. I suppose a vessel raising a tanned gaff sail is a fairly rare sight in the centre of London, and as we turned to speed down river, became conscious of an audience on the bridge - and a traffic jam. As we went downstream, the other sails were hoisted and, borne on a strong ebb tide, anchored that evening in the Lower Hope, not far from our anchorage of a few days earlier. There were three of us aboard, Michael Thatch Rose and Nicholas Smith who at that time was sales manager to the Company (subsequently to become a director) - it seemed appropriate to have someone from the firm on board, and as he observed, it is not every day sailing (which he enjoys) becomes part of the job.

From there, our trip the next day was a less leisurely re-run of the trip upwards, but I allowed myself the sentimental indulgence of sailing once more close to my native shore, the tide being full. Then we pressed on, to anchor late that evening in Hamford Water, in the Walton Backwaters. The next day, after a brief sail out, we returned to our mooring in the Walton Channel, where the line of moorings was growing longer every season.

Vicky had already departed to do her VSO teaching job in Ghana the previous September, and then on Easter Monday, Roland, who had recently qualified as a chartered accountant, was taken to Kensington High Street to board a green single decker Bristol engined bus whose destination panel read "Kathmandu". An organisation called "Asian Greyhound" was buying old National buses - this one was a former Western National bus which then took young people (only the young could have survived!) to Kathmandu by what I can best describe as the pretty way. Their journey included Paris, Italy, Greece, Turkey, Iran and Irak, Afghanistan, Kashmir, terminating in Kathmandu, Nepal. It is a sad reflection on the world today, nearly thirty years on, that this journey would be impossible.

Beryl had been invited to speak at a conference of the Canadian School Trustees Association being held in Saskatoon that year, they paying her fare across the Atlantic. It was Bi-centennial year, celebrating the 200th anniversary of the American declaration of Independence, and in addition, Beryl's brother, James Myatt, was skippering GREAT BRITAIN II in the Tall Ships race for the leg from Bermuda to Newport Rhode Island. With one half already paid for across the Atlantic, I said "This is the year we must go to America".

Pan-Am were offering a wonderful deal which included the hire of a 6-berth motorhome; I wanted to see some people in New York, so after that Beryl would meet me there, and pick up the motorhome. In those days, airlines were still offering bus connections to their flights from the West End, so I checked in at their terminal not far from Buckingham Palace. I was booking in at the Holiday Inn by the airport for the night, after having seen the business people in the afternoon (remember you arrive in New York more or less the same time as you leave London, after six hours in the air) and Beryl would join me the next day. This was all very splendid, but she phoned to say that Canadian Air traffic controllers had gone on strike. Friends were going to drive her across the prairie staying a night in Winnipeg (where she was immediately invited to a party) before flying out on the last North-West Airlines flight from there before it was blacked, to Minneapolis

St Paul for a connection to New York. I booked in another night at the Holiday Inn and phoned the motorhome company to delay the start of our rental by a day; I would go to the motorhome base and meet Beryl there.

I took a cab to the motorhome office in Queens - a very grotty run - down suburb. Beryl arrived by cab from La Guardia airport; it was slightly disconcerting for her when the cab driver said "You sure you want to go there - have you got the right address?". The people said the motorhome would be ready shortly, which annoyed me because it should have been ready 24 hours earlier. As we sat in their waiting room, we soon were nudging each other whispering "these people are going broke". The excuses of financial desperation are much the same in America as at home. Time was ticking away, and the one thing we had planned early on in this venture was that we would get away from New York before the rush hour - which was exactly what did not happen.

The motorhome was luxurious, and with six berths the two of us were not going to be overcrowded. But it was big - something a little over 22 feet long, with double wheels at the rear; true I had driven the firm's large vans not all that many years back, and still had driven the largest van you could without an HGV licence, but I had driven those on the left hand side of the road. I had often driven a car on the right hand side, of course - but this was a young truck. With Beryl navigating, we found ourselves on an expressway heading North across Throg's Neck Bridge, over the waterway linking the East River with Long Island Sound. We were then on a multiple lane road dense with traffic heading out of town; at certain points we had to change lanes to prepare for a junction, and somehow I became terribly conscious of a lot of square feet of very tender aluminium panelling right behind me. One merciful thing was that, as with all American vehicles, it was an automatic - I don't like automatics, but in America they are better, because you don't have to cope with a gear lever using the wrong hand.

Our first camp site was 100 miles North of New York; luckily the roads became more rural and peaceful just as I was about to become a nervous wreck; it was pitch dark and how we found this camp, at which we had a booking, I do not know, but it is a tribute to Beryl's skill as a navigator. The lady running the site appeared in her night clothes with her hair in curlers, but could not have been more welcoming and kinder. We were complete rookies at this game, and she showed us how to hook up to mains water, electricity and sewage.

The following night, we were booked in at the Hilton at Northampton, Mass., by our friend Juliette Tomlinson, curator of the William Pynchon Memorial Museum in Springfield, Massachusetts. We had given hospitality to her six years earlier when she had come over to celebrate the 350th anniversary of the sailing of the Mayflower from Harwich to America - after being weatherbound in Plymouth before finally setting off to found Plymouth, Mass. The Pynchons were an Essex family, with branches in Springfield and Writtle, and the Springfield Pynchons founded the settlement of that name in Massachusetts, whilst in Writtle church there is a magnificent Pynchon monument. As a serious historian, this was fascinating for her, and although appearing quite a formidable lady, she was great fun and on a subsequent visit to the States, she took us to see "the ball game", and really let her hair down, yelling for her team (I forget whether it was the New York Yankees or the Boston Redsocks). This talented lady was also a lay preacher in the American Episcopalian Church. After seeing the museum and having dinner with her, we set off to see some of the historic villages and houses of New England - Deerfield, Hadley, Wethersfield (settled 1634), before going to stay with an educational contact of Beryl's near Colchester (incorporated in 1698). Everywhere, we were overwhelmed with the hospitality, and although we were happy to be in our comfortable vehicle, they insisted we came into their homes. From Colchester, we were heading for Newport, Rhode Island, when we came across our first real language problem, an example of the two nations divided by a common language. We needed to get to Norwich, but no one seemed to know where it was until the penny dropped with a local - "Aw - you mean Nor-which". We had, of course, been asking the way to Norridge - why do we have some of these illogical pronunciations?

Having been warned by Juliette that Newport was said to be "Wall to wall boats and wall to wall people", we had booked a place at a camp site a little way out of town and got a cab to the waterfront to meet James and the crew of "GB II". He was in the middle of a visit from some of the crew of the Russian ship and was leading them in some robust singing - to our amazement he got them singing *"Rule Britannia"*, in which they were joined by the crowd on the quayside. His great rallying call when there was a task to perform was *"Rule Britannia"* - the youngsters would always rally round and it would all happen. Later we were taken out to the Polish ship, "DA PORMOSA", whose captain was a very popular man and the doyen of the sail training ship captains. From there we went to the Russian ship "TOVARICH" where we were greeted by the political captain (known to James and his friends as "smiler"). The nautical captain had, we believe, been removed from the scene as he was obviously very drunk on the Polish ship. The canapes, if that is what you would call them, offered with the drinks were a complete meal in themselves - I have no idea what they really were, but they were substantial. A thick fog descended on the scene and condensation started dripping from the masts and spars; it was announced that the boat service between ship and shore had been suspended, and we became slightly worried at the prospect of spending a night on a floating part of the iron curtain, particularly as we had been invited to go to a dinner ashore. A young Argentinian Naval Officer was extremely worried, and attached himself to us. However, the resourceful captain of "DA PORMOSA" managed to call his ship on the radio, and they sent boats over which took us ashore to attend a magnificent dinner at Cooks Eel and Pie House - a very up market eatery on the fashionable quayside.

From the exitement of Newport, we moved on to the port of Mystic which has been faithfully restored to represent the port as it was in its heyday. When America does something like this, it is done with great thoroughness so that even things like the old printing works and newsaper offices were reproduced, along with the "CHARLES W MORGAN", an old square rigged whaling ship, and the Joseph Conrad, the ship Alan Villiers took pre-war on a globe encircling trip with enthusiastic young people as crew, including our friend and neighbour Johnnie Devlin who eventually was to become a submarine   commander. To our surprise, we also found an Essex (UK) based sail training boat "MASTER BUILDER" with Bruce Thorogood from Colchester (UK) as skipper. They had moved out from Newport to get a bit of peace and quiet before going down to New York for the parade of sail to be held on the 4th of July.

We hastened Southwards, skirting New York City and visited Princeton, where Beryl had another educational contact. I remember being particularly impressed with their new library, which although clearly modern, had style which curtsied to that of some of the more traditional buildings surrounding it. The weather was very hot by our standards, and as we continued towards Maryland, I could not get over the poles at the side of the road to indicate the depth of snow. We were becoming more experienced in the matter of camping; if you went for the full hook-up to mains services, you not only paid more, but you were also in the more urban and developed area. If the hook-up was not needed, you could choose a pitch in the more remote and rural part of the camp, often totally out of sight of another vehicle; there is land, lots of land in America and their camp sites are very spacious.

Our vehicle had a small hip-bath and shower, and there were two holding tanks -

one for "grey" water and the other for foul water. The rear bumper (fender) contained a flexible length of pipe with which to discharge these tanks at the "dump" point found near the entrance to the site. Electric gauges showed you the state of each tank including fresh water. Being independent of hook ups suited us, it was like living on a boat, but on land. As aboard "celandine", the vehicle had two sets of batteries, one set dedicated to starting the engine only, and the other to providing lighting and services. The gas installation included a heating system, but in the weather we experienced, this was definitely not needed. On the open road we were averaging just under 8 miles to the US gallon (slightly smaller than our imperial gallon), but as it seemed to us they almost gave the petrol away, we were not concerned.

Some friends back home had mentioned us to friends living in a house on a creek off the vast Chesapeake Bay and asked if we could pitch up in their grounds. When we arrived at delightfully named "Canterbury's Manor" Jo and Lloyd Moore insisted we should move into the house where they had a bedroom ready for us. The manor was a genuine colonial style clapboarded house with a wide frontage but little depth, so that every room had good views of the extensive grounds and the creek beyond, whilst the generous sash windows enabled a good through breeze. Every window, and the "porch" (verandah) had very adequate fly screens which were essential if you were to sit out and enjoy the cooler evening air. Outside after dark fireflies filled the air with light; there were many other winged insects which could no doubt happily draw blood samples.

Having arrived on Saturday July the 3rd, the next day was Independence Day. The Lloyds took us by car to their parish church, Old Wye, a brick built gem consecrated in 1720 - although many buildings were, and still are built in timber, by this time bricks were also being used. Inside, it was as one remembered English village churches - we sat in old box pews complete with doors. The book for our communion service was almost identical to the Book of Common Prayer, but, of course, prayers for the Queen were replaced with ones for the President. What you would not have found in an English village church were the fans of palm leaves placed on the seats, to fan yourself in the heat. Most surprising of all was to find the Royal coat of arms of George the Second on the inside of the West wall; it seems no one had bothered to take it down, and had now become a valuable piece of the church's history. After the service we assembled in the churchyard and their Liberty Bell was rung with due ceremony. In the afternoon we watched the impressive parade of sail in New York harbour, on their television.

After this further example of American hospitality, we took to the road again, and crossed the Chesapeake into Virginia by the Bay Bridge-Tunnel. This amazing feature crosses the narrow neck near the entrance where it is about 20 miles wide - not a lot less than the Dover Strait, and was built entirely by private enterprise. Starting on a long pier like structure running across the shallows, you then come to an artificial island with cafes, gift shops and viewing points, and at this point you descend into the tunnel portion which goes under the deep water channel used by shipping. You emerge to another artificial island and resume the crossing on another portion of pier structure. The whole investment and maintenance costs are covered by the tolls, which did not strike us as excessive.

Working our way up the West side of the Chesapeake, we pitched our motorhome on camp sites, very often with Indian names - one was on the banks of the Piankatank River. A visit was made to colonial Williamsburg, another example of how well the Americans pay regard to their history and traditions. Beryl had an introduction to William and Mary University there, and we were invited to see a film they had made about the War of Independence - they, somewhat diffidently, hoped we would not find it offensive. The story was sensitively told, and highlighted the difficulties faced in many families where loyalties were divided. The causes were not difficult to understand, the only communications being through long hazardous Atlantic voyages, and another culture was developing in America that was not understood in London, where no one could see the potential of the Americas, and as providing troops for protection and maintenance of law and order was a costly drain on the British Exchequer, they started imposing taxes that were resented by many Americans.

Working our way Northwards, we visited George Washington's house, Mount Vernon, which was typically early Georgian in style and furnished with furniture probably made in America, but very much in the English style. What did amaze me was that this house was of wooden construction, and the wood cladding of the external walls fashioned to look like stonework, finished with paint containing grit that completed the illusion of massive stonework. Inside, there is reference to the French involvement in the War, and the advice given to Washington by Lafayette, sent by the King to maximise the trouble for les Anglais. Lafayette was so good at this that later he helped in the overthrow of the French monarchy, sending Washington the keys of the Bastille, still to be seen on display in the house.

Next, of course we wanted to visit Washington, but this turned out to be a bit of a disaster. Driving our young truck of a vehicle through the busy traffic, there was an intersection. American road signs are totally different from those found in Europe, and may be alright if you are used to them and understand the directions (another case of "the common language"?). Once committed to the wrong direction, it seemed impossible to get back on the right route to the Capitol, and we found ourselves on a very pleasant parkway going away from the centre. By now our nerves were somewhat shattered and our interest in the seat of American government waned. What finally shattered us was finding we were by now on a narrow road, the Chainbridge road, running alongside the Potomac river; the pleasant shrubs and trees were fine, but there were ominous notices that at 4pm it would become a one way street in the opposite direction, and it was now after half past three. We made it to our main road out of Washington with about five minutes to go.

Our last camp site was still about 100 miles from New York, but there was none nearer. Once again we went into the more rural part away from the civilised hook ups; trees and bushes surrounded us and it was very pleasant. Beryl said how nice it was to hear a nearby running stream. After a while, I had to disillusion her - it was the noise of traffic from a nearby parkway, but it proves that beauty can also be in the ear of the listener.

While we were visiting these historic places in America, Roland was by now at Kathmandu and planning an independent tour of India by buying an all India railway ticket. At the same time, Vicky, with some local leave in Ghana during the school's holiday, was going with a party to Timbuctu - they never reached it because of visa difficulties, but they still penetrated deep into that part of Africa. The Platts were truly scattered about the world, and all sent postcards home.

THE FISHERMEN OF ENGLAND - AND THE JUBILEE FLEET REVIEW

EARLY in 1976 I had bought a small beam trawl, but it was not until our American tour was over that I had an opportunity to try my luck. With her gaff ketch rig "CELANDINE" was well suited to trawl under sail as there were so many variations in sail that could be used to control the speed; scandalising the gaff mains'l (dropping the peak, which reduced the effective part of the sail to a small triangle) - also one could play with the heads'ls and the mizzen to produce a variety of combinations. It was hard work hauling the trawl, particularly if you were unlucky enough to drag in a load of weed. Some trawls yielded mostly crabs, but we would try elsewhere and find lemon sole and plaice in the cod end, and occasionally skate. As complete amateurs, we did not know the right places in which to fish, so our catches varied. They were only modest at best, but it gave a very good feeling for each crew member to go home with something worth eating.

Our trawling grounds were mainly over the sandy shallows of Dovercourt and Pennyhole Bays, lying between the Naze and Harwich harbour, but occasionally we put down our net in the Stour estuary. One weekend at the end of August yielded our most spectacular results; with Beryl, Mary Dainty, her sister Anne and brother-in-law Peter Groom aboard, we were fielding a strong team. We trawled late in the day, and after obtaining reasonable results, put down for a last trawl on the flood tide. It was by this time dark, and I had a rather simple floodlight rigged over the deck aft, contrived from an old car reversing light. Suddenly the heavens opened - fortunately we were in our oilies anyway, because trawling is a wet and dirty job - and an almighty thunderstorm broke almost overhead. I usually hauled the trawl after half an hour, and fortunately the storm was easing just as we were preparing to haul in. The trawl was very heavy, and I cursed because we must have picked up a great load of weed, but the cod end came up absolutely seething with fish - our biggest problem then was finding enough boxes and containers to put them in. There were Dover sole, some quite large, plaice and grey mullet; it was an unbelievable quantity to handle. By the time we had thrown out the crabs and other unwanted detritus, then cleaned the decks up in the light of our primitive deck floodlight (which, of course, totally ruined your night vision), it was time to go and anchor for the night.

When this vast quantity of fish arrived home, there was still a lot even after sharing some of it between us. At that time, we did not posess a deep freeze, but rented space in a neighbour's, the rent being the largest Dover sole in the catch. Large Dover sole taste much better than small ones (and will always be higher priced on the fishmonger's slab as a result). Of course, after this, we invested in a big chest deep freeze, but as Beryl has since ruefully pointed out, never again did we catch fish on this scale; she has even been so rude as to suggest that if we depended on my fishing efforts to live, we would be starving. She was right. In retrospect, there can be no doubt that the fish we caught that night were in some way affected by the thunderstorm - it was bad enough for us on top, but clearly a lot worse below the surface.

That season finished with a trip across the Estuary to Harty Ferry, in the East end of the Swale, and a ditch crawl up to Faversham, where we made fast alongside the "Town Quay", which it probably was a century earlier, but it was pretty ruinous and muddy - the benefit being that it was only a short walk to the centre of this attractive ancient town. We beat a hasty retreat before the tide started to fall, beating back to the Colne the next day against a fresh Northeaster in continuous cold drizzle, which made it quite a relief to get alongside Ian Brown's quay at Rowhedge in preparation for the winter lay-up.

The Silver Jubilee of the Queen's accession was, among other events, to be marked by a fleet review, at which the Cruising Association had been allocated a designated anchorage area. Accordingly, early in June 1977, "CELANDINE" was sailed down South to Portsmouth harbour, and as this was to be achieved in a weekend, it called for some hard work. A Friday evening tide enabled us to take her up to the Walton & Frinton Yacht Club quay, load stores and then anchor for a short stop in Harwich harbour, which we left just after two on Saturday morning.

Knowing we were in a hurry, the wind played up by coming from a Southwesterly direction at strengths ranging from force 5-6 to almost nil, so we had an uphill trip most of the way. At 1230 on Saturday we hove to off Margate to pull down two reefs in the mains'l; by early Sunday morning we are off Dungeness having shaken out all the reefs, and thinking we still had a long way to go. After rounding Beachy Head, the wind backed more Southerly and enabled us to hold the course along the coast. Platt's law about winds applied, in that now it was more favourable, it fell light so progress slowed. It was 1900 when eventually we secured her in Camper & Nicholsons marina at Gosport and fled for the Gosport ferry to catch the last train that would enable us to get a train back to Chelmsford that night. It was a close run thing.

Almost a fortnight later, on the afternoon of Monday June the 27th, four of us repaired aboard - George Jones (ex Lt RNVR), Johnnie Devlin (Lt-Cdr RN Retd), Roland (now almost 26) and myself (ex Sub-Lt RNVR), ready for a Naval occasion. Under power, we sallied forth into Spithead, where the lines of naval ships were already in place. Over in the anchorage allocated to sail training ships we came alongside "Dusmarie" to take her mail ashore, as they were leaving after the Review for an extended voyage. "Dusmarie", formerly a Colchester smack, was converted into a yacht by Cdr Douglas Dixon RN, who took parties of public school boys on expeditions up to the Arctic circle. She was trapped in Northern waters by the outbreak of World War II, and lay deteriorating in Sweden, where she was rebuilt post-war and given a stylish raked stem and a mizzen, making her into a yawl. After his death, his daughter Astrid took over and took parties of girls on sail training voyages. On this occasion, it was too choppy out there to do more than run close enough to hand over the bundle of mail. After surveying the fleet and merchant ships which were now arriving, we headed over to Osborne Bay to anchor for the night; the wind being about force 3-4 from the Southwest, we were well sheltered and had a pleasing view of the well wooded parkland ashore.

Tuesday the 28th of June was the day of the Review by HM The Queen, so we weighed early to get in our designated anchorage close to the Mother Bank. In order to get a good view, we anchored almost on the boundary line, which meant the anchor went down in 9 fathoms - us Essex boys are not used to anchoring in such deep water, but "Celandine" carried 35 fathoms of chain, so our scope of 3 times the depth still left more chain in the locker. It was a bit choppy as we were well off the Isle of Wight shore, but "Celandine" rode comfortably. She already looked pretty smart, but we did go round doing those extra touches to make sure she was really "tiddly" (Naval slang for very smart).

By midday, the 180 major ships were in place - including two tankers, the P & O liner "Manapouri", a car ferry "Viking Valiant" of European Ferries (now P&O) and a humble British coaster, the "Singularity" belonging to Everards. There were trawlers, tugs and other commercial craft, all looking impeccably smart - sales of marine paints must have boomed that year. There were ships from other navies, Commonwealth and foreign. Soon after mid-day, there was another unforgettable sight, which I think left a lasting impression on us all. Sailing smartly by was Essex based Charlie Stock, intrepid sailor and author, who has taken his 16 foot centreboarder "Shoal Waters" into the most incredible places, like Barking Creek, the river Stour at Manningtree, just before it was closed off from the sea for ever - his exploits are legion, and all done under sail or by pushing and shoving. Today, immaculately turned out in reefer jacket, collar and tie, was Charlie, sitting to attention at the tiller - Essex was well represented that day.

Earlier in the day, the assembled ships had been lying at assorted angles, but by noon all were lying in perfect llnes, groomed as it were by the tide - this kind of timing has to be planned in a Naval Review. At 1500 almost exactly, HMY "Britannia" passed us, preceded by the Trinity House yacht "Patricia" - it is a privilege granted to Trinity House, to lead the Royal Yacht on such occasions. As "Britannia" passed, we duly dipped our ensign in salute, and felt we had done things properly. Later, there was a fly past of Fleet Air Arm aircraft and helicopters.

Unfortunately, shore side pressures called, so we were soon back in Camper's marina and heading back for home - which meant missing the illumination of the fleet and a firework display on Southsea Common, but it had been an unforgettable experience and well worth the effort to be present.

AN ELECTION - A NEW BUSINESS VENTURE AND OUR FIRST VISIT TO SOUTHERN BRITTANY

O N the home front, there was another County Council election in 1977; in the days of the non-political Rural District Council, Beryl had sometimes been returned unnposed, but the County Council was run on party political divisions, although they were less nasty and petty than those existing in Chelmsford Borough. By this time, she had become well known for her hard work in Local Government, particularly in education. She was by now also involved in National Organisations for the promotion of maths, science and engineering training - matters to which she was dedicated, convinced that they were essential to the country's interests. She was still Chairman of Essex Education Committee, and was keen to continue the work in which she so passionately believed. It was ironic to think how hard we all worked to secure her re-election - to then work very hard for no financial reward, but it has always been a feature of our country that people have worked hard for voluntary organisations, although as I write, I begin to wonder if their numbers are diminishing. Re-election was achieved with an overwhelming majority.

Within a day or so of the election, I found myself flying out to Norway with a customer. He had been approached by a company offering a revolutionary type of stitchless quilting; when I saw the samples I knew this development had to be investigated, and it was arranged that I should accompany him as a business partner. I was fascinated by the coastal scenery as we flew Northwards - the complicated maze of channels (I believe known as "leads") and islands, all bare of trees but pleasantly green, contrasting with the blue water. Our destination, Alesund lay in a scenically attractive fiord, lush with young spring grass - and a few trees in the more sheltered spots; to reach the factory where this plant was installed, from the small airport, there was a ferry crossing of the busy harbour to be made, which fascinated me. Up here, ships were a very important part of the transport system. Once I had seen this plant, I knew we had to get into this new technology. I made the right noises without appearing to be too nosy - after all, I was engaged in what some people might call industrial espionage. What I could not understand was how someone could operate a plant with a prodigious output of bulky materials in this small town, so far removed from any large manufacturing centres and where the output would mostly have to travel by sea. The plant was clearly American, but if there was a maker's plate, it had either been removed or concealed. Immediately on return, I was on to the Commercial Library of the American Embassy, and after returning from the weekend trip taking "CELANDINE" down to Gosport ready for the Fleet review, I flew out to America with Alan Fosh, our works engineer, to visit the makers of this machine.

Our first night was spent in a colonial style hotel in Williamstown, Northern

Massachusetts; the architecture of this modern hotel fascinated me. It had a grand colonnaded coche portiere under which you arrived in your limousine rather than coach and pair. The windows were eight light sashes, but on examination, the glazing bars were a plastic grid, and the window cleaner sprung them out to clean a single large pane of glass - instant Georgian windows which would cause steam to rise from the head of a British planning officer - the Georgians didn't use plastics because they were 200 years too early. In true American style, a pianist tinkled the ivories in the lounge before we had dinner with the machinery maker's sales manager. It amazes me that you fly out to New York, arriving at the same time as you left London, and then, on this occasion, a short flight in a small aircraft, dinner in the evening, and you are still going, after an extremely long day. Going the other way is always a different story.

Having seen the works where they were building these plants, Alan and I flew down to Carolina in the heart of the American cotton belt, where we were to see the equipment under working conditions. On arrival at check in for the flight South from New York, we were informed apologetically that economy class was overbooked and they had put us in first class - remember this was an expensive time for us to be in America, with the pound standing fairly low against the dollar so there was no grandiose travel at our small company's expense. With our tears well concealed, we were welcomed into first class by the cabin crew, who did not see our status, but it was obvious we were first class - we were both well turned out. As we approached Charlotte airport, the pilot announced there was a violent storm raging right over the airfield, so he was going fly round outside the storm hoping it would abate. Apologising for the delay, he ordered drinks all round; we had already enjoyed a complimentary gin and tonic with generous sized miniatures of gin, so when the steward came round, we both popped the gin into our briefcases. This happened several times, and the cabin crew must have marvelled at the speed with which we downed our gins, and our capacity for same.

Ultimately, he had to bring the aircraft in before the storm had cleared, and it was quite a hair raising experience, ending in a superb landing for which he received a round of applause from the passengers. Then we had to run for the terminal building through torrential rain that was actually hot. Although the airport was in North Carolina, we stayed the night (or what was left of it) at the Carriage House, Lancaster, in South Carolina. The textile complex where we were to see the new machines in operation was bewildering in its size, they did everything from raw cotton to finished fabrics and goods, as well as polyester from fibre to fabric. Two of these machines with phenomenal output were quilting the firm's own printed polycotton fabric on to automatic cutting and stitching machines to produce attractive frilled edge bedspreads (comforters?). The only partly hand operation was in the final packaging of the product. The rate at which these items were being produced was a very clear illustration of the sheer size of the American market; to produce at half this rate would have saturated the British market in a week. But it was convincing; we had to have one of these plants, whose capital cost would stretch our finances severely, but once established in this field the cost and relatively small size of the market would deter any other potential entrant.

Early the following year, the plant arrived and was soon up and running, taking us into an entirely new field of technology where we were all on a steep learning curve. Soon after we were establishing ourselves in this new market, a competitor arrived on the scene; I had been right that it was not possible for the machine in Alesund to survive commercially, and it had arrived in the North of England, to be a thorn in our side for the next two years, but it was in totally incompetent hands and we finished up buying it from the receiver. Amateurish modifications had been made to the machine so there was no point in keeping it intact as we were struggling to sell the product of our own, but did thus acquire a large stock of spares very cheaply, whilst eliminating surplus capacity from the market. Its entrance on the UK market had postponed a move into profitability, which we the family shareholders fully understood - in a public company the shareholders and analysts would be breathing down your neck, but if you can run your business without having to use capital from such people, you are fortunate.

A week after the Silver Jubilee Fleet Review, "CELANDINE" was heading West again. Travelling down from London on the Friday evening with Roland and friends, we were off by half past eight in the evening and motorsailing West through the Solent against a light Southwest wind. It was not until 0800 the following morning when, with fog reducing visibility to about a mile, the wind backed a point enabling us to shut down the engine and sail the course. For a long time we could hear the diaphone of Portland Bill light to starboard as we slowly brought it astern of us. A Naval instructor once described the sound of a fog diaphone as like the sound of a sheep being hit by a golf ball; although I have heard many of the former, I regret that as I don't play golf, am unlikely to ever hear the latter.

All the next day we slowly crossed Lyme Bay, with visibility gradually improving under the influence of a sun that worked hard to burn its way through; at least what wind there was had now gone round into the East and our progress West was a mixture of sailing and motoring. At one point we were sailing quite well and we streamed a couple of spinners, resulting in mackerel for supper that evening as we neared Start Point, now looming clear in the evening sun. I think it was on this voyage that a new, more humane way of killing mackerel was introduced, in which the fish was squeezed behind the gills thus forcing its mouth open; you then inserted a thumb into the mouth, put your index finger over the top of its head and jerked the head back with a vigorous firm movement which broke its neck. It was a quick end; previously we had knocked them out with sheet winch handles - not always effective, and could produce the most incredible mess of blood and fish scales on our pristine iroko deck.

After clearing Bolt Tail, the Western appendage of Start Point, the lights were lit (we were still using large oil burning navigation lights in those days, although our masthead steaming light and stern light were electric), the wind dropped, and under a partially obscured full moon the faithful Perkins engine drove us on towards Plymouth's Western entrance, which I felt was safer to use in darkness as it is well lit and free of offshore hazards compared with the Eastern. Finally, at two o'clock on Sunday morning, the anchor was let go in Jennycliff Bay. What wind there was came from the East, and a good anchorage can be found there, out of the traffic and over a sandy bottom. The last time I had used this anchorage was during those last days in command of LCT 879, after hostilities in Europe had finished, our flotilla had dispersed and we were sailing independent of convoys or escorts. A severe Easterly gale warning had been received and I chose to anchor in Jennycliff Bay; the tank landing craft may have been 185 feet long compared with "CELANDINE'S" 37, but the draft of the two vessels was virtually identical. Later in the morning, "CELANDINE" was berthed in the new Mayflower Marina. This is a very well laid out marina, coupled with an adjacent property development, but like so many of the early marina projects, it encountered financial difficulties, mainly through trying to do too much too quickly, and on a somewhat grandiose scale. The financial vicissitudes have since been overcome, and it is now run on business like lines by its own berth holders - a sort of co-operative.

Late the following Friday, July the 9th, I returned with a crew that could be described as ancient and modern - me at the grand old age of 53, with Michael "thatch" Rose, Geoff Smeed, and George Jones' youngest son Ned, in descending age. Before mid day on Saturday "CELANDINE" was clear of Plymouth Breakwater heading down Channel to clear Ushant, with perfect weather and a light North Easterly wind coming from almost dead astern. (Why am I so cynical about wind directions when in truth it is quite often favourable to our ventures?). The miles quietly slipped past our keel as we settled in to a watch keeping routine. For long trips, as explained before, I like to have four people aboard, so that you can work two on watch and two off, with "dog watches" in the early evening, when the system tends to break down, but it provides a time when we eat, and if the weather permits, all gather for a drink in the cockpit (I can't remember a time when it was so bad that this part of the ritual had to be abandoned!). It also changes the watches so that you don't have to stand the same watch on two consecutive nights.

After our supper, we were settling down for the night watches, sailing quietly along before the Northeast wind on an empty sea, out of sight of any land, when we all jumped out of our skins from an almighty double boom of unbelievable magnitude. Sea birds, of whose existence we had been unaware, all rose screaming from the surrounding waves; what was strange to me about this great crack of doom was that no underwater explosion had been transmitted through the hull - they sound as if the hull has been hit with a sledgehammer. Then suddenly we twigged it - Concorde had flown supersonic over us. Subsequently, I have heard it quite a few times, and although subsequently realising what the source was, it still just as scary each time it hits you. Concorde had only started flying scheduled services the year before, so naturally we were newcomers to the experience; as they only fly at supersonic speed over the sea, it is only we sailors beneath its path will ever hear it.

The next day, Sunday, dawned foggy and we were relying entirely on our dead reckoning position; at noon, with 116 miles on the Walkers patent log, we started altering course round to the South side of Ushant and in towards the unseen rocks guarding the outer approaches to Brest. By early evening, the fog was mercifully clearing and we sighted the Pierre Noire rocks abeam; to get positive confirmation of your position after a long trip on dead reckoning, which requires keeping an accurate record of the boat's progress, is a great relief. The wind became non existent and sails were stowed so that we motored over an oily sea towards Brest, and as dusk fell, the land was closing in on us. Finally, just after ten o'clock (eleven by continental time) on Sunday night we secured alongside in the Port du Commerce.

In those days, a registered British ship proceeding beyond "Home Trade" limits was entitled to bonded stores, the quantity of which would be determined by Customs & Excise at the port of departure. "Home Trade" limits were defined as between the Elbe and Brest, and as this voyage was to take us beyond Brest, we would qualify. I had hoped to pick up the bonded stores on Saturday morning before departure, only to discover that the "Long Room" at Plymouth was not open on Saturday mornings; fortunately someone tipped us off that we would be able to obtain our bonded stores from a firm called Fournier in the Port du Commerce, Brest - although we had not intended calling at Brest, this made a compelling reason for amending our voyage plan. An order was placed with Fournier which included a dozen litre bottles of export gin at about £1-00 a bottle, and a dozen litre bottles of red wine at an absurdly low price, in those returnable bottles marked with three stars, and sealed with a plastic cap covered in foil, which now seem to have gone out of fashion. There was no question of what we were entitled to - Fournier were in business to sell whatever you were prepared to pay for, and I think we did a lot better than had we bought in Plymouth. The case of gin had a chalk mark "No 2 berth Millbay Docks", so like us, it had crossed the Channel from Plymouth. The red wine was of excellent quality, and the dozen bottles lasted no time at all - we should have bought more, and the quality was such that it could have been re-bottled in 75cl bottles with an exotic label, at an exorbitant price!

Sadly, the weather broke somewhat, and after a day of thunderstorms in Brest, where we shopped for fresh victuals, we sailed in the evening to Camaret which is only a short distance, but a good deal more pleasant than the Port du Commerce. The tidal streams of Brittany are fairly strong, and our progress South was now governed by making the most of the tides; our voyage was to take us through the Raz du Sein in between the mainland and the Isle de Sein. so our departure from Camaret was determined by needing a favourable tide through this passage of ill repute among seafaring folk. Anchoring for the night off Ste Evette, Audierne (a stop that we were to use several times over the years), the following day saw "Celandine" slowly progressing Southwards - the winds were light and fickle so there were frequent resorts to motor sailing.

A local had told us that the weather would improve with every headland we rounded, and this certainly seemed to be coming true; that night we anchored in a delightful cove just South of Le Pallais on Belle Isle. The coastal scenery of Southern Brittany is wild and rugged, abounding in off shore rocks and islets, so one must be wary of open anchorages; early the following morning, we were awoken to find "Celandine" plunging and snubbing at her anchor chain with a fresh Easterly wind blowing straight in to our rocky cove. After a hurried departure, we headed for Quiberon Bay (scene of a famous battle between British and French fleets) and called at a former fishing port on the Quiberon peninsula, Port Haliguen. Here we obtained diesel fuel and then secured alongside a fishing boat for lunch; the harbour was gradually changing character to become a yacht harbour with all the associated facilities - on subsequent visits we renamed it "Port Hooligan", and tended to avoid it.

Our destination was The Gulf of Morbihan - an almost landlocked sea approached by a narrow entrance through which the tides empty and refill it twice daily, resulting in racing tidal streams. You take the tide with you, or you don't go. The Morbihan is a labrynth of complicated channels, islands, rocks, sands and marshes amongst which it should always be possible to find a sheltered and secluded anchorage. Some of the larger islands are, of course, infested with a lot of second homes, but that Thursday night we found a delightful little "Anse" (Bay) with a sandy beach on which we cooked some recently caught mackerel, without seeing another soul - even though it was Bastille Day. The following day, we had hoped to reach Vannes, where they were establishing pontoons and moorings for yachts in the bassin close to the town centre, but the water is retained by a gate and we were too late to catch that tide at eight in the morning, so instead we anchored her fore and aft, using the big fisherman anchor aft, off the nearby Isle de Conleau. This was a pleasant spot with an undulating shore line, wooded in parts and an all tide landing place for a dinghy, but not too much swinging room, hence the stern anchor. Arrangements were made with Petit Jean ashore to keep an eye on the boat; although Ned Jones was staying aboard and the rest of us returning home on Sunday, Ned was a very capable sailor (inevitable if you were a child of George and June Jones!), but he was still young and I thought that there should be an adult he could turn to for help if needed.

Saturday was a perfect day, and reluctantly we packed our kit ready for an early morning departure on Sunday. The other three were below, while I watched a yacht drifting down with the tide and a gentle breeze; quietly I said to myself "My God, she's topless". The effect could not have been more dramatic had I shouted "Abandon ship". Remember, we were all naive lads from Writtle, where our womenfolk are demure and modest so had never been exposed to this kind of thing. The result was that three bodies all tried to emerge through the hatchway together; by the time they had sorted themselves out, the boat was almost past us, and I was accused of trying to keep the whole thing to myself. In retrospect, I'm not sure that the object of all this fuss was really worth it.

This was the first of several visits to Brittany over the next few years, and on Sunday morning a taxi took us to Vannes station, where we boarded what I dubbed "The Brittany Coast Express". This train starts at Quimper and then stops all along the coast, including Auray, Vannes and Redon, at each of which places we have boarded it. After a final stop at Rennes, which is a central hub for road and rail in Brittany, it then belts towards Paris at the kind of speeds used on French railways. We would arm ourselves with crusty baguettes, cheese and pates (my favourite being rilettes de porc), a bottle of red wine and some plastic disposable glasses always carried aboard for picnics or barbecues ashore - in France no one would be offended by such eminently sensible precautions against malnutrition.

Another arrangement used on arrival at Montparnasse on this and subsequent trips was to detach the fastest runner (in this case Geoff Smeed) to race ahead and secure a taxi, we following up with his bag. It was always a tight schedule to catch a train at Gare du Nord getting us aboard a ferry at Boulogne that would enable us to reach Chelmsford at not too late an hour. The system worked well, but I learnt from this experience never again to say "Vite" to a Paris taxi driver - I sat in the front, and the crew said that my right foot had made a deep indent in the taxi floor from treading on a non existent brake pedal. Of course, this was all long before Eurostar, which would transform the ease and speed of such a journey today.

A week later, I returned with Beryl to find Ned well and happy, and the ship still moored up exactly as we had left her; the next day Roland arrived in the evening and we raised the stern anchor, to let her swing to a single anchor again. Having had some very good weather so far, it now deteriorated and blew hard from Southwest and West, with accompanying rain. The climate whilst mild, is also wet, as in Cornwall - which it resembles in many ways. Southern Brittany (La Cote Armorique) has many Cornish type names in among the French, and there is a movement for independence from France, just as there is such a movement in Cornwall. These are more sentimental than practical, and unlikely ever to achieve anything other than a flag - some visiting yachts fly a Brittany flag beneath the French courtesy tricolour.

The weather slowly improved - I was anxious that Beryl should enjoy some of the good weather we had experienced, and we were now exploring the Morbihan archipelago, in which there were many attractive anchorages. "CELANDINE" penetrated up the river to Auray, where we anchored fore and aft just below the Quai Benjamin Franklin on the St Goustan side of the river; it was at this quay that Benjamin Franklin landed as the first U.S. ambassador after Independence - it should have been Brest, but the ship was blown off course.

Any information we could glean on depths of water was sketchy and tended to discourage one from going there at all, something I always find a challenge. There was sufficient depth to stay afloat at low tide, and we were not far from a suitable landing place just below the ancient bridge linking St Goustan to Auray which is the head of navigation. Here we met Beryl's brother, James Myatt, Fiona and their family who were camping at a nearby Ecole d' Agricultur - it seemed a rather privileged place to be, but no doubt he knew somebody, and was incredibly good at this kind of infiltration to the best places - an art he used to great advantage when skippering or making plans in Sail Training Races.

It was now almost the end of July, and thoughts turned to the voyage home; we met the Myatts back at our old anchorage at the Isle de Conleau, where we embarked everybody aboard after first purchasing victuals for the voyage home, taking advantage of their Peugot Estate car. Then everybody embarked aboard for the night, the two younger children, Tim and Antonia, sleeping in the cockpit under the canvas cover, which they thought a great adventure. After our shopping venture, we had moved on to a vacant mooring to facilitate a speedy departure early the next morning. Beryl was going home with Fiona and the children in the car via St Malo; it was high water and we were able to go directly alongside a stone landing slip to get them ashore. James came with us, making a good strong crew - Ned Jones and Roland were still with us, so we were four for our passage home.

By half past six in the morning we were underweigh and as we cleared the Morbihan entrance with the ebb tide sweeping us into Quiberon Bay, we listened to the BBC shipping forecast at 0630 (0730) local time. In those days they were still putting it out at that time, although in later years they started to change the timings to suit the artistic feelings of the programmers, who regarded weather forecasts as an interference with what they considered important. There was little wind, and we made our way Northwestwards towards the great Pointe de Penmarc'h. The wind was light and variable, so most of the day was spent motorsailing; a sharp rainsquall came along to liven things up in the afternoon, and after this there was enough wind to sail by, then it obligingly slipped into the Northeast for a time, but remained fickle. Tacking several times after clearing the great Pointe, I decided we would snatch a few hour's sleep, so the anchor went down just before three in the morning, at the   anchorage close to Audierne used on our outward passage. Although it is sheltered from North round to Southwest, otherwise it is a pretty exposed place.

By nine in the morning we were underway again, with a brisk breeze from Northeast which bowled us along in fine style to the infamous Raz du Sein, where a favourable tide swept us through the choppy race. From here, we hardened in our sails to come on to a Northerly course until we could put about and sail in to the Anse de Camaret. Being high tide, we went alongside the town quay (which would dry at low water) in time to shop for more fresh meat, and also carry aboard another 10 gallons of diesel, since the weather outlook indicated more light winds. Anchoring off in the outer harbour for the night, we left at a gentlemanly hour, some time after ten - no point in going earlier, as the North going tide we needed would not start until mid-day. On the outward trip, starting as far West as Plymouth, I had decided to round Ushant, particularly as it was my first time there, but now, starting from the Brittany coast, the shortest way home was through the Chenal du Four, close to the mainland and inside the Ile d' Ouessant with associated islands and rocks. Although the channels through are well marked, and Brittany ferries use it regularly, it is not a place to be taken lightly.

Soon after noon we were passing through the narrows between Pointe de Kermorvan (a typical Brittany name!) and a well marked rock, la Grande Vinotiere, with the tide now in our favour - there is no hanging about here, as if someone blows a whistle and the tidal stream changes just like that. At about this point we exchanged greetings with a Hilliard sloop "DIDICOY" aboard which was my GP from the Writtle medical practice, Jim Pembleton; we neither of us knew the other was sailing in Brittany waters - how the inhabitants of Writtle get about! Sadly, he is not with us any more, but his son, Neil carries on the sailing tradition and is an active member of the Cruising Association. Our wind did not hold, and we were soon motoring, with the tide bearing us northwards on a roller coaster. Gradually the channel widens, after passing another well marked group of rocks, les Platresses - perhaps some primeval Platt females were petrified there?

It was clear that a slow passage lay ahead, and James had to be back for a rather important job interview - he had left the Army, and was to be interviewed as prospective Director of the Royal Bath & West Show (which he did become). Instead of going for the Solent area, I decided Salcombe was the nearest point to make for. After our departure from Camaret on Saturday morning, we finally dropped anchor in Salcombe on Sunday afternoon. The channel crossing was the frustrating mixture as before of motoring, sailing and motorsailing. After a short period sailing before a Southerly wind, in brilliant sunshine and good visibility, with the Devon coastline coming clearer and clearer before us, the wind dropped again; an entry in the log read "wind nil, mackerel nine".

Going ashore, I telephoned Fiona, who would come and rescue her husband that evening, and then I telephoned my old schoolfriend Phillip Andrews to ask if he would come and give us Customs clearance. Phillip had become senior commanding officer in the Revenue cutter fleet, but he had decided to come ashore for his last years before retirement when the post of Customs Officer, Salcombe, became available - his home was not very far from there. So at about six that evening he came aboard and went through the clearance procedure. I should mention that Phillip was a very conscientious officer, and would not have cleared us just because we were old friends, but by half past six when we had satisfied the requirements and obtained clearance, he and his wife, Pen, then became our guests. By seven, Fiona had arrived from Somerset with Tim and Antonia, and we then fed everybody - quite an achievement since we had nothing sophisticated like a refrigerator on board. Onlookers might have noticed the length of time the Customs launch was alongside and thought that we had been caught with something aboard that should not have been.

All our guests, and sadly, crew member James, left later that evening so when we sailed after refuelling the next morning, there were only three of us to keep watches. Our progress along the South coast was not spectacular, but what wind we had was in the right direction at last; the weather was good, and all the great headlands slowly passed - Portland Bill, St Catherines on the tip of the Isle of Wight, Beachy Head, and then put into Newhaven for no other reason than we needed more fuel, where the log reads "1400 went alongside fuel barge operated by nutcase", and then "1600 cleared Newhaven entrance - goodbye Newhaven, good riddance". Two hours to get a few gallons of fuel must be a record. Finally, having left Salcombe on Monday morning, we arrived in the Walton Backwaters on Wednesday afternoon, on the top of a tide which enabled us to go alongside the Yacht Club and offload our gear before putting "CELANDINE" back on her mooring for a well earned rest.

A YEAR STARTED IN FOG
(AND ENDING IN A BLAZE OF GLORY)

THE year 1978 started cold and damp. Before sailing started, I went with Beryl to a concert by the Essex Youth Orchestra - an organisation with very high musical standards, encouraging music and giving youngsters great opportunities for teamwork and confidence building. As Chairman of the Education Committee, she would naturally take an interest anyway, but our enthusiasm for this has continued to this day. The special thing about this concert at Harwich was that it took place in St Nicholas Church, a building familiar to every sailor using the port with its prominent spire serving as a guiding seamark. The evening of the concert was typical of that Spring - cold and damp, the young musicians having to change in a marquee outside the church. St Nicholas Church was built in 1821 to replace the previous building which had become ruinous and had lost the spire which was such a valuable seamark; the heating was on that evening, and was effected by naked gas flames burning in ducts under cast iron gratings - I am not sure what happened if you stood still for too long over one, wearing rubber soled shoes. These ducts were only to be found in the aisles, so I suppose this was unlikely to happen. What did intrigue me were the graceful slender fluted supporting pillars in the nave, and could not resist tapping one with a key to confirm my suspicions - they were made of cast iron, the use of which was spreading as part of the industrial revolution, and started with the first large scale use of the medium for structural purposes in the famous iron bridge over the Severn at Ironbridge in Shropshire.

A month later, "CELANDINE" was launched off the slipway at Ian Brown's yard, after hauling out at the end of her winter slumbers in a mud berth, to be repainted and new anti-fouling applied below the waterline. The weather was still much the same, but we sailed her round to Walton in a thick swirling fog that could be the harbinger of a change in the weather. It was dense enough to totally obliterate the shore, and with the two Michael Roses aboard we navigated almost entirely by the echo sounder which I relied upon to keep me in the sort of soundings I expected. This probably was possible because it was a coast with which I was very familiar; our only sighting until we arrived at Harwich was a glimpse of the top of the tower block of flats at Frinton, bathed in brilliant sunshine against a clear blue sky. I then used a trick used on a somewhat larger scale by Francis Chichester when he was piloting a small aircraft across the Pacific, hopping from Island to Island. By accurately timing his progress from the departure point, he could fix his longitude, but by deliberately flying slightly off course, when he reached the longitude of his destination he flew either due North or South, with the certainty of sighting his goal. So I steered a course that would put me on a collision heading for the long stone breakwater at the entrance to Harwich harbour - it was important to know when we had reached this large and safe haven. Sure enough, it came up ahead, about fifty yards away - so, right hand down to reach the end and enter harbour, where we buoy hopped to an anchorage in the Orwell - by this time the fog was lifting to give a fine evening, and the next day we put her on the mooring at Walton in warm sunshine.

On the weekend of June the 3rd, Beryl was at an educational meeting in Paris (over the years she has acquired quite a knowledge of the elitist French system), and as often happened when she was away, I would slip away on the boat. So we were both away from home when the Queen's birthday honours were announced, with Beryl receiving a CBE. I was thrilled, because although other people clearly valued her services to Essex County and Essex education, I knew better than others just how hard and conscientiously she worked.

When the investiture at the Palace came along in November, Platt felt he ought to open his wallet a bit wider, and I booked a table in the River Room at the Savoy Hotel for a family lunch party. A car was hired to bring my mother up from Writtle as she was by this time severely crippled by arthritis, and, arriving before we had returned from the Palace, the staff at the Savoy could not have been kinder in looking after her until we arrived. Both Roland and Vicky were now back in the Country again and we were joined by James & Fiona. The Savoy did us proud, and after a superb lunch with good wines, I realised that the cost per head came to almost exactly the same as that a few weeks earlier when we had entertained our bank manager to lunch in the Romford area, at a riverside restaurant of some character in Abridge; although it was the best we could do in the area, you could hardly compare it with the Savoy. Perhaps there is a lesson to be learnt here about our perception of London and provincial prices; the establishment at Abridge is now a Chinese! That same autumn, Beryl was a guest at a small dinner party given by the Prince of Wales, who wanted to meet some engineers, and at a small luncheon party given by the Queen. She really was living it up!

There was a scheme afoot to visit Canada this year - to see my sister in her newly adopted country, and to renew our acqaintance with the joys of life in a motorhome. As usual when there was some other major expedition planned, our summer cruise was curtailed to a quick dash to Holland, reached after a not very fast 25 hour passage to

Ijmuiden, locking into the North Sea Canal through the small sluis at midnight, local time. After visiting all our favourite places on our Southwards journey, we stopped briefly at the new yacht haven created at the North end of the commercial quay on the main canal at Middelburg, to re-victual before returning home via Flushing.

In late July we took off from Stansted Airport (half an hour's drive from home) for Vancouver on a charter flight with Canadian Pacific Airways, flying on a great circle route over Greenland and the Northern wastes of Canada. During a busy week with Lorna and Dino in Abbotsford, we visited Vancouver, and Vancouver Island. Victoria, on the latter, is more English than England - the tourist buses are former London Transport double deckers. In a crowded day, a visit was made to the justly famous Buchart Gardens and I also managed to achieve a secret desire of mine to swim in the Pacific. I also met the Cruising Association's Honorary Local Representative, Tony Swain, who extolled the virtues of sailing in the sheltered waters lying between Vancouver Island and Vancouver, with its myriads of islands and benign (but damp) climate - 49 degrees North, as opposed to our 52 degrees North which crosses the River Orwell just above Pin Mill.

From Vancouver we took a chartered 6-berth motorhome (similar to that hired two years earlier in America and in which two people can live in some comfort) then headed up the highway following the Frazer river for a short distance before forking North to follow the Thompson river. Abbotsford lies in undulating downland country, but soon you are in wild and rugged scenery. On taking over the vehicle, there was an axe as part of the equipment - "what's that for - to use on my wife?". "You'll soon find out" was the answer. At our first National Parks camp site on the side of the Thompson valley, we did. These wonderful camp sites, so spacious you are not aware of other people, all have a great pile of logs near the entrance, and you help yourself on the way in. Each parking bay, well shrouded in bushes and trees, has a brick hearth with fire bars, and there is nothing better than cooking your salmon or steak in the open over a wood fire. After our alfresco supper, we went for a walk in the wooded hillside, and almost together suddenly said "what if we meet a bear?" and started talking about who could run the fastest. Not feeling heroic, we turned and walked back to our motorhome at a steady pace.

From here, we continued climbing into the Rockies through scenery of incredible grandeur, coming at times to small settlements. One such was at a place called "Dutch Lake" - a small lily covered lake originally settled by some Germans - "Deutsch", which quickly became Dutch. Nearby, a small river flowed through the woods to suddenly spew out of a cliff face and fall several hundred feet - imagine the shock to an early explorer paddling down the stream in his canoe - you would not survive such a drop. Pressing on upwards, we came to Tete Jaune Cache - about as remote a location as you could expect, but there we found a great supermarket where we stocked up with fresh supplies, but could have bought all manner of agricultural equipment including 10 different sizes of galvanised chain.

Because of the rugged terrain, both road and rail followed close to each other so we were never far from the sound of a train whistle - and became quite hooked on these great freight trains, developing a romantic attachment to them, so much so that we pulled off the highway into a clearing by the railway for lunch one day. The place at which we stopped was beside what in the North American continent is known as a "siding" - a place where the single track line is doubled to provide a passing point. Soon after we arrived, a great freight train, with engines at the front, middle and back pulled into the siding and waited. There did not seem to be signals, but the two drivers must have been in radio communication, and after a while another equally long train went through in the opposite direction, so our lineside wait was well rewarded. Trains carry freight over enormous distances across this vast country, and are an economic way of carrying goods. Passengers fly or go by road for shorter distances (although there are occasional tourist passenger trains). Back home, far too many freight journeys do not justify use of rail for relatively small distances, even if the heavily used lines had the capacity to carry them. Many of those in the "send it by rail lobby" have not stopped to work out the practicalities, or to realise that one rail journey for a consignment equals two road journeys unless it goes from railhead to railhead - a rare eventuality.

Our journey took us to Jasper, near where we bathed in a foul -smelling hot sulphurous lake, said to have great health benefits, then to visit the Athabasca Glacier, the only glacier I am ever likely to see, and where the very deep blue in the crevasses left a lasting impression. The most memorable and highest overnight stop was at Kicking Horse Pass, in a camp site dominated by the Cathedral Crags reaching skywards, and in full view of the spiral tunnel on the Canadian Pacific line. The spiral tunnel, a masterpiece of tunnelling in rock, doubled the distance between two points on the line, but halved the former excessively steep gradient. Watching a long freight train go through, we saw the leading engine coming out at the top as the tail of the train disappeared into the lower mouth of the tunnel. It was early August, and in the morning, after a clear night, there was a touch of frost.

Lake Louise, a well known tourist spot, was spectacular for its blue colour, and then we started our descent from the Rockies, going through the Okanagan valley. The Okanagan is a climatic freak with Mediterranean weather in an otherwise rugged mountain climate. The lake shimmered in the sun, with distant Lombardy poplars completing the effect of Como or Maggiore. Orchards abound, and we went through places with names like Peachtown - and there they were, for sale on its roadside stalls. All too soon we had to return to civilisation - from the sublime to the ridiculous, as within a few days we were standing on Ipswich station wearing bright red "Coca Cola" hats to meet a party of youngsters sponsored by that firm, and going for a week's cruise on the East Coast Sail Trust's barge "THALATTA", having left "CELANDINE" in a drying mud berth at Debbage's yard nearby - not by any means in the most scenic part of Ipswich.

DOWN WEST AGAIN -
FOR THE SPANISH MAIN.

(Parts of this account were first published in the April 1980 issue
of the Cruising Association's Bulletin - now titled "Cruising")

TO make a trip down Channel from Essex, it is important to make a "feeder" trip Westwards before starting the main passage, otherwise you may spend precious time from your holiday in getting well clear of the Dover Straits. So, the tide serving our purpose, we were able to bring "CELANDINE" alongside the Walton & Frinton Yacht Club Quay on a Friday evening in early June to load gear and victuals aboard, before slipping away into the darkness down the (then) unlit channel. That night, we were lucky to find a coaster coming out of Hamford Water - no doubt having come away from the explosives works up Oakley Creek, so we followed his stern light on the principle that where he goes, we can.

To our surprise, he turned seawards over the Pye Sand before I would have done, but this saved time so we followed, keeping a wary eye on the echo sounder. Someone aboard repeated the well-worn joke about the yacht that followed a coaster over sandbanks; the coaster ran aground, whilst the yacht went a little further before running aground herself. After the tide receded, leaving the coaster sitting upright on her flat

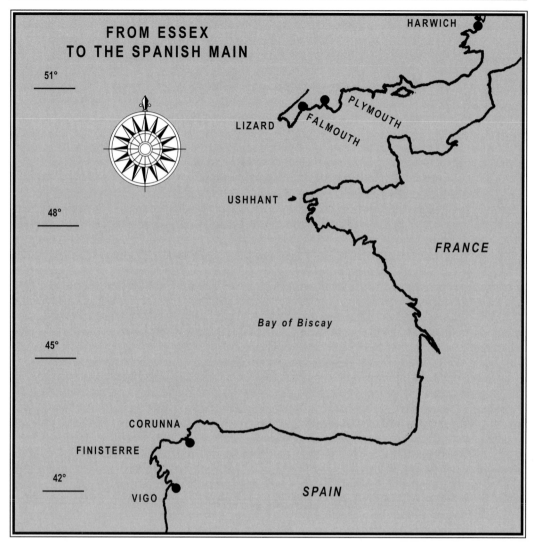

FROM ESSEX TO THE SPANISH MAIN

51°

48°

45°

42°

HARWICH

LIZARD

PLYMOUTH

FALMOUTH

USHHANT

FRANCE

Bay of Biscay

CORUNNA

FINISTERRE

SPAIN

VIGO

bottom and the yacht heeling at a giddy angle, the coaster skipper put a ladder down, and pipe in mouth, strolled over the sand to the yacht - "Good afternoon skipper, I'm here to load sand, what are you here for?".

As soon as we were clear of the sands, full sail was hoisted, and we were sailing closehauled out to the Kentish Knock, to take us across the Estuary clear of offlying shoals and with room to tack. By early morning the wind had fallen away and what little there was came from dead ahead, so sails were lowered and we pushed on under power - we needed to get down West as fast as possible. Past the North Foreland, a favourable tide gathered us in its arms and swept us past the East Goodwin light vessel (long since gone) towards Dover. Visibility was deteriorating, and the ferries were stacking outside waiting to enter harbour. My jaundiced view of this piece of water tells me that usually it is rough, but if it's not, it is foggy. The Navy taught me that Spring and early summer is a time for fog in the Channel - the sea is still cold from the winter, but the atmosphere warm from the strengthening sun, and here was a classic example of these conditions. As we headed for Dungeness, the fog thickened and two long blasts from a ship were heard ahead to port -

"I am underweigh, but all stopped". Soon after, a single prolonged blast came from astern telling us "I am underweigh" - we had passed him unseen, but it was comforting to know that we must have showed up clearly on his radar. "CELANDINE" had two metal octahedral radar reflectors mounted in the rigging either side of her mizzen, because wooden (or plastic) boats do not give good echos to radar signals.

By mid afternoon, we were picking up the fog signal from Dungeness lighthouse fine on the port bow. It was important to get a clear departure point from Dungeness, particularly if poor visibility was to continue, and I was again emulating the Francis Chichester trick of aiming slightly off course - when the great shingle bank loomed ahead, we would do a sharp turn to port and find the point. This dodge worked well, and we were not a long way from the lighthouse when the misty shingle bank loomed ahead; at exactly 1630 we caught a glimpse of the light through the fog, an excellent departure time and position for our next leg.

After darkness, the moon rose, almost full, the fog had dispersed and we were heading for Beachy Head with a light Easterly wind, enabling us to at last dispense with the engine. The night became pure magic, as "CELANDINE" picked up speed, the sails now drawing well to a Northeast wind coming over the starboard quarter, and I took our radio set up in the cockpit to listen to the late shipping forecast. To leeward, the sea sparkled like burnished silver in the moontrack, whilst to windward, Beachy Head and the Seven Sisters shone brilliantly, as if lit by some internal fluorescent source. The chuckle of the bow wave was a suitable accompaniment to the strains of *"Sailing By"* introducing the shipping forecast, which told us the wind would freshen from the East - not bad news for a sailor in a hurry to get down West.

Sure enough, the wind strengthened and an East-going tide was knocking up a lively sea - this happens when wind and tide oppose each other, but a good breakfast was cooked before St Catherines, the Southern tip of the Isle of Wight was sighted in clear visibility and bright sunshine. When the tide turned West going, not only did it join forces with the East wind in speeding us Westward, but the seas went down and we raced Westwards - this was not to last - by mid afternoon the wind had fallen light, clouds formed and soon we were pushing West under engine with rain falling. A motor cruiser came out of the murk and hailed us, explaining they were lost, having come from the Channel Islands, and could we give them a course for the Needles Channel. Some quick calculations on our chart - bear in mind ours was only a "dead reckoning" position, and we gave them a course, clearly indicating that this made no allowance for tide. I hope they found their way in! Later that evening, the weather was clearing; we were once again sailing before a light Easterly wind, and sitting down to a cordon bleu meal created by Michael "thatch" Rose - escalopes of veal accompanied by a suitable white wine. Some will not drink at all at sea, but a bottle of light white wine shared between four people over a good meal will boost morale, feed the inner man (or woman - Vicky was with us for this trip!) and in no way cloud the judgement. Without making too many claims for the benefits of a good meal on passage, the fact is that everything got better; the rain ceased, the wind came back and visibility, which had been clouded by the rain, improved again.

By Sunday afternoon we were in Plymouth, calling at each fuelling point in turn, to find that there was a general shortage of diesel fuel in the West Country, and I was certainly not happy with the prospect of leaving for a long voyage with low fuel tanks. "CELANDINE" was left locked into Millbay Dock, and when I returned by car to prepare her for the voyage, the car boot was filled with 5-litre oil cans full of diesel oil - there was no shortage on our side of the country. Millbay dock was seriously lacking in commercial activity, and quite near our berth they were filling it in- I was assured that we would still find "CELANDINE" afloat when we were ready to go, although she was covered in dust

Alongside Millbay pier, Plymouth, to load victuals and bonded stores

when we returned again to start our voyage.

Early on Wednesday July 11th with myself and three regular crew members aboard - Thatch Rose, Geoff Smeed, and John Aldridge, we locked out of Millbay Dock and secured alongside the pier to take on victuals, water, and bonded stores (our voyage was clearly to take us well beyond "Home Trade" limits. The glass stood high at 1018mb, but was falling slowly; the day was fine and sunny, making us anxious to get to sea. Just after two we finally let go and moved under power out to the breakwater.

The wind outside was light and Easterly; by the time we had cleared the breakwater we had our biggest jib and all sail set, the engine off. Ghosting quietly out to the Eddystone, we took our departure from a point 3 miles West of the light. (When leaving the land, it is very important to know where you started from!). The log was streamed and watches set, the wind picked up and obligingly backed into the North to to push our speed up to 6 knots - we were on our way. The night (a month after our "feeder" trip) was moonlit and clear, and our course 215 degrees magnetic. Next day, the wind freshened slightly to force 5 or 6; "CELANDINE" marched steadily on the course, her knife-like stem cleaving sweetly through the rise and fall of the sea. Those on watch had little to do except steer, read the log, and enjoy the sheer exhilaration of sailing fast for hour after hour over a sunlit sea, while the watch below slept, listened to music or sunbathed.Watches were of 4 hours, changing at 0300 and every four hours until 1900, when we took our two dog watches until 2300 to bring about the daily change of duties. During the dogs, the duties became somewhat merged as our one hot meal of the day was prepared (a certain amount of gastronomic one-upmanship began to develop among the rival Escoffiers) and all hands would enjoy a convivial glass. Before total darkness, and while everyone was still up, the big jib would be taken off and No.1 working jib substituted - heresy to the racing man, but good practice when cruising.

Once again during this trip we suffered a Concorde sonic boom during our convivial pre-prandial drink in the cockpit, and although we now knew about this phenomenon, it still made us all jump out of our skins. During this period, the wind went round to Northwest, and we were making steady progress Southwards, confirmed by radio beacon bearings from Round Island (in the Scillies) and Ushant - before midnight on Thursday we were South of Ushant and into the Bay of Biscay.

The next day, Friday, we ran out of wind and had to start the engine, then a light wind came from West-southwest, causing us to harden in our sheets, whilst a light drizzle set in for a while; by lunch time the sun had come out and the wind veered to West or Northwest, enabling us to shut down the engine again; the barometer was slowly rising, and things looked better, helped by the sighting of a school of Dolphins which playfully swam with us, crossing and recrossing our course close to our bows. But our progress had been slower that day, only helped by mechanical aid at times.

On Saturday morning, I obtained a set of radio bearings from beacons on the Spanish coast, including a powerful Aero beacon sited inland from Corunna which transmitted continuously. By lunch time, a light Easterly wind had set in, and we lunched in the cockpit to the strains of Beethoven and Tchaikowsky. More fixes from radio beacons showed that we were being pushed Westwards by a current, so we altered course to compensate; the wind improved from the Northeast - a note in the log read "Sailing at its very best". A long low swell was running, which we in our small ship hardly noticed, but our course was never far from the shipping tracks, so we were able to see the effect of the swell on larger ships. One minute they would be showing you their decks and hatches, and then a large expanse of antifouling below the waterline; their hulls would be below our horizon one minute, then clearly visible as we imperceptibly rose and fell without the roll from which they were suffering. Our dog watches that evening were full of optimism as rapid progress was made Southwards - perhaps that night might reveal the loom of a powerful light on the Spanish coast. Two sonic booms interrupted our thoughts, still causing just as big a jump as if we had never heard them before.

The barometer had now started to fall, and the forecast that evening gave Northeast force 4 - 5, perhaps 7 or 8 later. Obsessed with the hope of raising the loom of a Spanish light during the night (as if it mattered with good radio beacons to guide us) I stupidly broke my own rule and left the big jib up to speed us through the night - we were storming along at between 7 and eight knots in great style, and comfort. Early the next

Easterly blow in Bay of Biscay, after sail had been reduced.

morning, Sunday, I was off watch and unable to sleep - clearly the wind had risen, and I listened to "CELANDINE'S" straining and tortured hull smashing through the confused seas caused by the Easterly wind and the opposing Westerly swell coming in from the Atlantic. I lazily hoped we might carry on until the watch change at 0700. but just before six, Michael came down to report that it was now blowing a full force seven, the boat was seriously overcanvassed and an immediate reduction in sail needed - so, all hands on deck. A wild scene greeted us as angry seas hissed past, surging through the lee scuppers on every roll and racing off to leeward in a smother of foam. The mizzen and stays'l had already been taken in by the watch - easy sails to handle, but now there was that big jib. First we ran her off before the wind to give a more sheltered foredeck while we smothered the big jib and set the No.2, our smallest, in its place. Then we hove to and put one reef in the mains'l. It made all the difference - she was still doing seven or more knots, but in relative comfort. The operation, which went off quickly and smoothly, was dangerous, but how glad we were to have those wide spacious decks and relatively low freeboard. Wet they may be in those conditions, but you are wearing boots and oilies to deal with that; the important thing is that with low freeboard you are nearer the pivot point of the vessel's roll, whereas out on a longer radius from it you will suffer ever increasing movement the further away from that pivot point. But I had made a foolish mistake the evening before in not reducing sail.

Soon we saw what could be a bank of dark cloud ahead which slowly manifested itself as the Spanish coast, rising high and mountainous. The radio beacon at Corunna confirmed our course (now back to 215 degrees) and we raced Southwards with the great Cabo Prior to the East of us giving some shelter to ease the seas, even though the wind blew with even greater ferocity. Cheese sandwiches in the cockpit served as lunch, and then, sailing in smooth water and lighter wind, we entered Corunna harbour and picked up a vacant visitor's mooring 4 days and one hour after leaving Plymouth, having covered 492 nautical miles from Plymouth breakwater.

Formalities were almost nil, and ashore we were welcomed by the secretary of the Royal Corunna Club, a tall military looking man who offered us the free use of the waterside "new" clubhouse with excellent showers and facilities. A little way inshore lay the "old" clubhouse, with rich dark mahogany panelling - "that is for the people who play bridge, the new one is for the people who sail". He also promised that if we did not mention the matter of the Armada, he would not bring up the subject of Gibraltar. Telephone calls home were made to announce our arrival, and a visit made to the main post office to buy stamps for our postcards. This was an immense grandiose classical building, which to us, after four days at sea, seemed to be gently rising and falling.

.   First, after revictualling we set off, beating against a strong Northeaster to visit the Ria de Ares - Ares looked horrible, all concrete slabs of appartments and half completed villas, so we sailed on to the Ensenada de Redes, to anchor near a peaceful wooded shore not far from the village of Redes, which tumbled down the steep hillside to the water's edge. A good meal, washed down with our newly acquired supplies of Spanish wine presaged a good night's sleep in this tranquil anchorage. Unfortunately it was fiesta or regatta time, and after seeing some fiercely contested rowing races, an outfit calling itself "The Gay Boys" started belting it out from a platform on the village waterfront. Then the fireworks started - the Spaniards are keen on fireworks, and the noisier the bangs, the better. It had been a strenuous day, and we all fell asleep, although I think the festivities lasted until the small hours. The next day saw us back in Corunna, where we picked up Nicholas who had flown out from the office for a few day's sailing in Spanish waters.

Voyaging Southwards, now in light Northerly winds and brilliant hot sunshine we were almost 10 whole degrees of latitude (600 nautical miles) South of our home cruising waters. Leaving Corunna, we took bearings from the Torre de Hercules - a lighthouse built by the Romans, and still in use, to round the great headland of Cabo Villano and that evening enter the delightful Ria de Camarinas, where we anchored off a secluded beach nestling under a pine clad hillside in about 12 feet depth, the rise and fall of tide hereabouts not being very great.

Our next stage was started in dull cloudy conditions, but a fair Northerly wind pushed us Southwards over the great Atlantic swells past the rugged cliffs which rise up almost direct from the Atlantic floor, and against which, even in calm weather, the sea breaks ominously. By the time we rounded the great Cape Finisterre, thought by many before 1492 to be the most Westerly point in the world, the sun had returned. Our next port of call was to be in the great Ria de Arosa, the largest of the Galician rias. It is well protected to seaward by a chain of islands and rocks, with a large entrance for big ships which would have added greatly to our distance, so we opted for a short cut through the Paso de Carreiro, relying on an excellent large scale Spanish chart whose margins not only contained the usual degrees of latitude, but on one side a scale in metres and the other in "yardas". Coming down from the North, we headed up on to an Easterly course which brought the wind abeam and increased our speed just when we would have like to take things more slowly. Racing over the turbulent waters towards an area that looked like a sailor's nightmare, we took constant bearings and found the white tower marking the narrow passage. Apart from the rocks you could see, there were many just below the surface, where tell tale eddies and swirls indicated their presence. We should not have worried - about half a mile from the white tower the wind dropped and the local fishing fleet began returning home so we started the engine and followed them in.

St Eugenia de Riberia was a busy and prosperous fishing port, with not a lot to offer a yacht, but the Cruising Association handbook indicated the one place where a yacht might lie, which is where we went, and the harbourmaster, collecting the very modest harbour dues, confirmed this. The next morning, the crew divided, leaving two aboard while two went shopping - it was Saturday and there was a good street market plus excellent butcher and baker, then I made a telephone call home to confirm we would arrive in Vigo on Sunday. While all these domestic chores were being completed, the crew left aboard watched a large fishing boat turning short round opposite our berth. Suspecting he had not seen "CELANDINE" (or had he?) they started the engine and slipped out of the berth just before he would have clobbered us. It was with some relief that we left the place.

At Vigo we were again made welcome at the yacht club, which resembles a great liner whose verandah decks and saloons overlook the harbour; again, there were excellent showers with the additional advantage of a fine swimming pool. Beryl flew out to meet us, and the valiant crew left for home. The Cruising Association's honorary local representative, Fransisco Steinbruggen advised where diesel fuel could be obtained - from Cangas, on the opposite side of the Ria, and also was helping "JOLIE BRISE", the famous ex Havrais pilot cutter now sailed by Dauntsey's School - she needed anthracite for her Aga cooker! Two girls were acting as cooks, and were heroines, working in a galley that must have been an inferno in this climate.

Vigo was a great contrast to Corunna, much more Latin, whereas the Galicians are of a more stolid and hardworking disposition; the climate is warmer, confirming the view of the Frenchman speaking of Southern Brittany who said "With every headland you round Southwards, the climate gets better". Many of the houses reflect the long influence of the Moorish occupation, with ornamental wrought iron enclosed balconies which could be used by the ladies without having to expose themselves to public view. All supplies were available here, and a nearby laundry returned all the washing beautifully ironed on the next day, for a very modest sum. The yacht harbour was busy, hot and stifling so we were pleased to leave and with only Beryl and myself aboard, set off to explore the ria.

Approaching Vigo.

Puerto Domaya was a favourite of ours, no more than a small indentation in the coast, and a very small village, but with a thriving oyster and shellfish industry - all grown on ropes suspended from crude wooden derricks on rafts - if you half closed your eyes in the shimmer of the afternoon sun, you could imagine them as an ancient fleet of sailing ships. Every day the powerful fishing boats with protective awnings aft would leave to tend the rafts, with large numbers of equally powerful looking fisher lassies aboard; they seemed delighted to see us and all gave us tremendous waves as they went by. The "chief man", Benito Vidal was invited aboard for a drink - with his limited English and our even more limited Spanish, we conversed, and it became clear that they felt honoured that we had chosen to visit their village. After that, when he went by in one of the boats, a net of oysters would arrive aboard. It was quite a long walk to the one and only small shop, which had surprisingly good stocks. Our first big language gaffe occurred here, when we slipped into Italian (after all, it's another latin language!) and asked for a quarter kilo of "burro". They fell about, and it took some time to establish that "burro" is a donkey, whereas what we needed was "mantequilla"; about this time a burly character in a string vest came in delivering bottles of soft drinks and lager from his lorry. He turned out to be a popular local character with a good command of English, having served as a merchant seaman aboard a British ship, and introduced himself as "Cacco", then proceeded to undertake all the necessary translations which made the shopping much easier. We left with great felicitations all round.

Another port of call was Moana - this was a busy fishing town at the head of a deeper bay in the coastline of the Ria. Anchoring off there in the evening, some boys rowed out near us and serenaded us with "English" songs - *My Bonny Lies over The Ocean* and *"John Brown's Body"*. Early the following morning a buzz came from the shore, sounding like a swarm of bees - we were anchored not far from the fish market, where business was in full swing; needless to say, we made good use of it. Also memorable was a visit to a small bar up a somewhat insalubrious back street, where inside all was spotlessly clean but primitive, and we lunched off fresh sardines cooked hard over a charcoal grill with small green peppers. The fish were glistening with sea salt crystals, and washed down with white wine drawn from a great vat on the wall into a large enamel jug, from which we decanted the wine into white earthenware bowls not unlike sundae dishes; drinking elegantly from these was not possible, but I don't think anyone cared.

Before leaving, we stocked up at the local shops, and at the greengrocery and general stores right by the hard where we had landed, the elderly lady in charge wanted to carry the stuff across the road to the hard in a large box on her head. This I simply could not allow - she seemed a good deal older than I was, and so we left again with great expressions of goodwill. As we crossed the road, a lorry pulled up in the middle of the road, and out jumped "Cacco", our friend of a few days earlier. "This is my town, you are welcome here - you must have a drink with me", so we entered a nearby bar, where he was obviously well known (Beryl wondered whether any woman had ever set foot in it before). As we sipped our wine, plates of enormous succulent mussels were produced (I think they may have grown in size with the passage of the years!), and Cacco told us how he and his father ran this business delivering bottled and canned drinks in the area. He had two sons, one at a private school in Madrid, but the other, "he is stupid, and goes to the local school" All this time, the local traffic was doing its best to negotiate the carelessly parked lorry; we felt it time to take our leave, and I tried to buy him a drink, but he would not hear of it. With mutual expressions of goodwill, and our thanks for his hospitality, we left in our Avon dinghy, while he extricated his lorry from the traffic jam it was creating.

There is an inner part of the Ria, reached through narrows over which a high and impressive suspension bridge had been built, a bridge so new that it did not even appear on the charts; the highway either side was still a long way from completion. An apocryphal story was told of the STA Schooner "SIR WINSTON CHURCHILL" bowling up the Ria under full canvas with a following wind and coming across the uncharted bridge; there were anxious moments aboard as they had no information about air height, but it was too late to do much about it. It is a very high bridge, so she passed under with ease.

Once through the narrows, the inner Ria becomes a virtual inland lake with minimal rise and fall of tide, and is relatively shallow. We anchored close under the lee of a deserted sandy shore, in clear shallow water through which we could see our anchor on the bottom. Close by were the Islas Simon, on which a large unoccupied building stood - we decided it had been an isolation hospital, possibly for lepers. In this anchorage, it was very hot and I rigged the cockpit cover as an awning; we bathed in the warm waters either from the boat or the nearby beach. This was an extremely relaxing and enjoyable interlude, but the time came when we had to return to the opressive heat of the yacht harbour, where the return crew was to join. Our friends, the Kings drove out there, and John was joining us for the return trip, while Beryl and Diana were going to return in the car, incorporating a short tour of Northwest Spain which was to include Santiago da Compostella.

Our crew for the return voyage was 5 strong - John King (like myself, ex RNVR), Tony Irving from Truro, Hon Secretary of the CA Section down there, Richard White, filling the gap between school and college by sailing, whom we had contacted through the CA crew list and met down in Plymouth. He turned out to be an absolute natural aboard a boat and had salt water in his blood. The fifth member had contacted me through the CA crew list, which circulates among local clubs and organisations. He rather forced himself on the scene because, having passed all the theory of the Yachtmaster's Exam, he needed a sea passage of over 500 sea miles to qualify (now, I believe, 700 miles), but it seemed that an extra hand might be useful for what I hoped would be a long single leg from Corunna to our home mooring.

After leaving Vigo, we stopped at St Eugenia de Ribeira once more, and then in the bay behind the great headland of Finisterre; our progress so far had been slow, with winds from a Northerly direction. Here we anchored for the night off a beach just North of Finisterre village, sheltered from the Northwest wind then blowing, but I avoided anchoring too close because winds can change, and I had noticed how visibility was now almost unnaturally clear - in home waters a sure sign of rain to come. Sure enough, in the morning a light Southerly breeze was blowing straight onshore and a steady drizzle falling. Heaving to off Finisterre village we sent the dinghy ashore to buy bread, then we were on our way to Corunna.

After a night in Corunna, and a morning spent victualling at a supermarket in preparation for some days at sea, we were off again in the afternoon. There was a shortage of fuel, and we only obtained 26 litres before the supply gave out, so I put in our reserve 5 gallons from a plastic Jerrican - far more easily done in harbour than at sea. Our supermarket shop-up had been quite an expedition in that we lined up three trolleys at the checkout - the manager was so pleased to have such good customers, he bowed and offered to call a taxi, which we certainly needed; the staff were then summoned to load the taxi for us. It was not until we were at sea that all the items were stowed, and there was one quite substantial parcel that no one could remember buying - it turned out to be a type of sliced salami, enough for a sizeable catering establishment. During the ensuing voyage we tried a hundred different ways with salami, but in the end could stand the stuff no longer and it was despatched to nurture marine life in the Bay of Biscay. I don't know about the others, but I have never touched the stuff since.

The first part of our trip was frustrating with light West to Northwest winds, but was blessed with pleasant weather that enabled a civilised style of shipboard life to be carried on. On our second day out, the barometer began to fall, and that night there was warning of strong to gale winds from the Southwest - from Corunna Northwards we were able to receive the BBC shipping forecasts on longwave, whereas at Vigo we were out of range. During the night, we dropped and stowed the stays'l and mizzen - our first, and easy reef. Then early the next morning we pulled down a reef in the main as the wind began to rise, fortunately from a favourable direction that sped us Northwards in the mounting seas. "CELANDINE", with her reduced sail, rode through it all very comfortably, but I was very careful to insist that the main hatch be kept shut except when actually in use for access - I think my crew thought I was being a bit of an old woman about it, but in the light of events that were to unfold a few days later, it became apparent that keeping hatchways shut in bad weather was the right precaution to take. By the evening, a moderation of wind strength and easing of the seas enabled a better than basic hot supper to be served.

By noon on our third day out, we had brought Ushant abeam, and were about to pass into the English Channel. During the previous evening and that morning, I had been keeping a lookout for the "ARMORIQUE", the Brittany ferry that Beryl and Diana were travelling in - the two ships must have passed quite close, but I didn't see her. They had a bad crossing, and their ship was pretty lively in the seas running - afterwards, we said "you should have been aboard a seaworthy ship like ours". That morning, on the 8 o'clock news from the BBC, we were astounded to hear of yachts in difficulty, and large racers at Cowes carrying away gear such as rudders (can't they make vital things like this strong enough?). But now, as we entered the Channel, the seas had gone down, full sail rehoisted, the sun shone, with the Isle of Ushant and its lighthouses showing bright and clear. 24 hours later we were passing the Channel lightvessel marking the shipping lanes, and then making our course for the "Greenwich" buoy sited on that meridian and marking the start of the separation lanes through the Dover straits. "CELANDINE" ploughed on at a steady, but not spectacular speed towards home.

When planning this trip, I had to increase the cruising range covered in my insurance policy, and they had stipulated that the boat should be North of a certain degree of latitude by a certain date - I no longer remember the details, but it was probably about 48 degrees, just South of Ushant, and the deadline about the 20th of August; it was now the 11th of August and we were well North of their limit. Late in the summer, the Bay of Biscay can become increasingly prone to strong winds and seas that are a match for yachts, and there are cases almost every year of yachts setting off too late in the season to cross the Bay, with resulting damage or worse. I don't think it is a place for a yacht in the autumn and winter.

The voyage was certainly going well, but listening to the general weather pattern, it looked as though another depression was on its way, in spite of our rising barometer. With light winds, there were several times when we had to resort to mechanical assistance to maintain a reasonable rate of progress, but at all times the wind was favourable. As we headed for Dungeness, on our fifth night at sea, the visibility deteriorated in a foggy drizzle, but the wind had strengthened to a good sailing breeze; my worry was that we would reach my least favourite piece of water before daylight and in bad visibility - should I reduce sail and slow down? We were sailing fast into a dark abyss - one of the things about fog or mist at sea, particularly after dark, is that you just do not know how far you can see. I decided to keep going.

Dungeness light showed through the murk to give us an accurate check on our progress up Channel, and by the time we were off Folkestone it was getting light and visibility improving; a strong favourable tide swept us on our way past the now clear White Cliffs and towards the Thames Estuary. Although I like going away, equally, I like coming back to my familiar home waters - I never tire of them. By this time, the barometer had been falling ominously for several hours, and it was partly this that had prompted me to carry on through the darkness under full sail. The previous blow came on us in the Bay of Biscay with miles of searoom, but if another was coming, I did not want to encounter it among the outlying sandbanks of the Thames Estuary - a boat is far safer well out to sea than close to shoal and shore.

Meanwhile, at home, some anxious moments were developing as Beryl had also been watching the barometer, and with memories of how much that big ferry had been thrown about in the Bay, knowing we were out there somewhere, naturally wondered how we were faring. She had spoken to brother James, who, becoming equally anxious, phoned back to say "he will have heard those forecasts, and I think will shelter in a South Coast port". She had also been on to Charles Guyatt, the Lloyd's agent at Vigo who had been so very helpful to us out there (and subsequently became the Cruising Association's honorary local representative for many years). He had recorded our departure; Beryl, leaving no stone unturned, talked to Coastguard, who were very helpful, and together they worked out where we might be, coming to much the same conclusion as reached by James. En passant, they said "has he a VHF radio?" and on learning that "CELANDINE" was not so equipped. suggested she buy me one for Christmas!

Early that evening, six days out from Corunna, Richard, the young Cornishman's keen eyes were the first to spot the elusive Pye End buoy, even though he was unfamiliar with these waters (nowadays it is easily sighted, and lit). We rounded the buoy, dropped sails and motored up the channel to our mooring; just after 8 in the evening, I rowed ashore to the Walton & Frinton Yacht Club to telephone home and report our safe arrival.

Beryl asked where I was, thinking I would name a South coast port - she was incredulous to hear we were actually back on our mooring, and Roland, who was with her could be heard in the background exclaiming "Bloody Hell!" with equal incredulity and relief. When "CELANDINE" picked up her skirts, she could make a pretty fast passage and confound the critics of traditional hulls and rig. Not that all traditional hulls are fast, but her lines were very sweet to ensure easy passage through the seas. That night, it blew with full gale force and I was thankful to be in a sheltered spot on a good strong mooring.

The next morning, soon after low water, the wind had eased a bit and I took Tony Irving ashore as he had to get back to Truro. Our fifth member was also taken ashore, but before he went, I had to sign a certificate proving he had undertaken a voyage of over 500 nautical miles - in fact the total distance from Corunna was 738. This would enable him to quality for his yachtmaster's, but I have to say it did not make me too happy. This man was incompetent on a boat, but the others had been very good about it and carried him without complaining.

The end of our Spanish excursion, right where it started from, alongside the Walton & Frinton Yacht Club quay - John King & Richard White help with de-storing.

It was sad that our voyage was over, in spite of my relief at being home before the gale broke - later on the tide, with the wind still blowing quite hard from the West we took "CELANDINE" alongside the club quay to de-store before returning her to the mooring. During the day, news reports were coming in of serious casualties in the Fastnet race fleet down off Southwest Ireland, where they had caught the full blast of this fierce blow. The subsequent report (of which James was one of the authors) showed that some yachts had been abandoned unnecessarily; many had been partially flooded through open hatchways and where insecure washboards in the hatch openings were washed out of place. The modern tendency to design shallow saucer-shaped hulls does not leave much room for bilgewater, and the sight of sea water swilling over the cabin floor can be very daunting.

That winter "CELANDINE" was fitted with VHF radio; like so many things we managed so well without, once you have fitted it the question is asked, "how did we manage without it?".

THE FUTURE OF THE BUSINESS - THE WEST COUNTRY AGAIN AND FIRE IN THE GALLEY

("Fire in the galley" was first published in theDecember 1980 issue of the Cruising Association Bulletin, now titled "Cruising")

ROLAND had seemed to be carving out a good career for himself in accountancy, and was working for Ernst & Whinney (as the firm was then called) in Southampton; he had joined at the point where they had just absorbed a local practice, and so had established himself at a very good moment. He had bought a small terrace house in Liverpool Street which no doubt had once been a railway or dock employee's house, but had been taken in hand and modernised - it was small, and ideal for him.

For some years I had been pointing out to him the snags of running a family business, and that he should not feel under any obligation to come into it. My philosophy was to let it tick over, and then get out, retaining the valuable freehold property, but a few years earlier he had suddenly announced that he felt he should come into it, and this changed my whole thinking - which resulted in my taking the plunge to invest in the new quilting technology - I could not let him come into a dying business. The only way to survive with this kind of business is to plough back most of the profits in new plant and machinery - not on exotic new motor cars.

One of my methods of assessing a new customer's credit worthiness was to pay a courtesy visit - and observe the cars parked close to the offices. A big business may be able to afford expensive cars, but many of the outfits I visited clearly could not support the ostentatious status symbols flaunted in the car park - whose money was paying for these? It was also a likely indication of the directors' lifestyles - probably at their creditor's expense. I have only ever had reasonable "cooking" cars - made in their thousands, they are more likely to be reliable than those only made in hundreds. Of course, I did afford to run a boat - partly by doing a proportion of the maintenance myself, and I kept both "CAMPION" and "CELANDINE" for 19 years each. Cars do not remain a reliable proposition for that length of time. Much also depends on the nature of the business - ours was capital intensive, whereas many of our customers were much more in the merchanting business; of course, a man who travels a lot needs a comfortable, but not exotic car. But it is no good thinking that any business, except the Bank of England, will print money - if it does, you will very quickly have others jumping on the bandwaggon, and that will cut you down to size.

So, in the year of the Spanish excursion, Roland left what had by then called itself Whinney Murray, and came into the business, insisting on going in at the coal face by running a quilting machine himself, before embarking on a much needed modernisation of the accounting system, and introducing computerised accounting. The end result of all this was that we began to know more about our business than ever before - where we were profitable - and where not. To some people, "profit" is a dirty word, but the truth is that no one can run at a loss for very long, whether in business or personal life. Profits are essential if a business is to continue to serve its customers, give worthwhile employment to its employees, pay its bills on time, and pay taxes.

Among new outlets for our output, we were developing a trade in Denmark, and early in December that year I flew out to Aarhuis to meet our agent out there, and visit some of the customers and contacts, flying from Gatwick - infinitely preferable to Heathrow, and served by a fast train service from Victoria. Our itinerary took us nearer to Copenhagen for return, and so we headed there, for what was to be the last flight of the evening back to London. I had not realised how much water there is in Denmark; our journey included a wait at an opening bridge, and a short hop on a car ferry; in spite of all this, I arrived just in time for check in, but had to get my ticket changed for return from Copenhagen. No cash was involved, but the check-in clerk was not very competent, and the minutes slipped away. Finally, some minutes after the last call for the flight, I was racing for the departure gate, steering a direct rhumb line - my only luggage was a large brief case. I had studied the layout of the place, and knew exactly where I needed to head for, but I came to a waist high metal barrier barring my path, so I vaulted over and started running down the corridor to the departure gate - glancing over my shoulder, I realised I had by-passed customs, passport control et al. With no one now on the gate, I arrived on the tarmac to see the plane in front of me, pasenger entrance closed, but there was still a small ladder down from a hatch in the stern of the plane, up which I lept - it was the staff entrance, so to speak. The cabin crew thought I was an official, because of the impressive bulging black brief case (containing overnight gear etc.). Having explained I was actually a passenger, then produced my ticket and boarding pass to be shown to a seat. It was near Christmas, getting late in the day, and was I glad to be in that plane!

The summer of 1980 proved to be a tempestuous one, starting with a tough beat against a strong Northeaster from the Colne up to Harwich to reach our summer mooring at Walton. Then we left for the West country on the evening of Friday the 13th June, but had not gone very far before we were called up on our newly installed VHF radio by another CA boat, "CASSOTIS". He had just picked up a weather forecast that indicated that the Easterly wind would rapidly become Southwest, and force 8 by that night, so we slunk into the Pyefleet for the night.

By the next day it had blown itself out, and we set off across the Estuary in near calm conditions, but were nagged by a falling barometer and forecasts of another blow to come. That night, we put into Ramsgate where we were forced to spend the next day sheltering from another force 8 gale which whipped up the crests of waves to break over the harbour wall. This was to be the pattern of our passage Westwards. After a day in harbour, we were off again with one reef down, tacking laboriously against a fresh wind that made us work hard to fight our way along the coast. That evening, I decided on one of our rests by anchoring tucked well in under the lee of Dungeness for a good meal and break from the slog, before beating through the night and next day along the South Coast towards the Solent. As darkness fell, I headed in towards St Helens Roads to anchor under the protective lee of the Isle of Wight, since the winds continued to blow fresh, now more from a Westerly direction (this was sod's law at work - if they had remained more Southerly as when headed South, we should by now have been making better progress). I was lucky to have a staunch crew for this trip, including Richard White who came through the gale in the Bay of Biscay the year before.

As soon as the anchor went down, Vicky went below to cook a meal while we stowed the canvas and cleared up on deck. Suddenly, a whiff of paraffin smoke told me all was not well, and Vicky called out that there was a lot of burning paraffin in the stove. At the moment I came below, the flexible supply pipe ruptured to unleash a pressurised jet of blazing paraffin. The yellow tongue of fire shot up against the deckhead and licked round towards the coachroof coaming. Somebody passed me the BCF extinguisher from the side of the engine casing, fortunately mounted on the far side from the galley, which was rapidly developing into an inferno. I aimed at the stove, pulled the trigger - and nothing happened.

Things were looking serious; Vicky started to get buckets from the cockpit locker - although water is not the best thing for dealing with an oil fire, it might be all that we were going to have. Geoff Smeed rushed forward and down the forehatch to grab our other BCF extinguisher from the bulkhead; in what seemed an age but was really only seconds I again took aim at the base of the fire and squeezed the trigger. A short sharp burst had a dramatic effect - the fire was completely extinguished. Immediately, I released the pressure from the paraffin supply tank and then cleared out on deck as the pungent poisonous fumes from the BCF spread. All hatches were opened wide, and after about ten minutes the atmosphere was clear enough to go below again.

The galley deckhead was blackened by smoke; over the stove where the fire was fiercest it is lined with stainless steel over asbestos and was easy to clean off. The rest of the galley deckhead was painted with white emulsion paint which was blistering, but it had done its job and prevented any scorching or charring of the woodwork. The plastic casing and diffuser on the fluorescent light fitting had started to melt and buckle, but I was pleased to see that it seemed to be a fire retardant type, and that the light still functioned. A much belated supper was cooked on our great standby and rough weather cooker, the Primus in gimbals.

Next morning we headed for Lymington, the closest point to where Taylor's works were at that time situated, and within minutes of my telephone call they were over to collect the cooker. I had already stripped down the suspect burner and located the cause of the trouble, which had been unsatisfactory from the start of the season, but foolishly thought that I had cured it.

Within two hours, Taylor's had returned the stove after refitting both burners with new parts to ensure a leakproof fit, and a new flexible connecting pipe; the joints subsequently proved absolutely tight and the stove gave no further trouble. I had been using Taylor's paraffin stoves for well over thirty years by then and had complete confidence in them, but paraffin, like any other form of energy, must be treated with respect. Used in an atomised jet of the Primus type, it is extremely economical and burns with a clean flame that can be controlled from a fierce fast heat to no more than a whispering simmer. Out of control, paraffin burns with a hot yellow flame and produces a pungent black oily smoke; our uncontrolled blaze had all started from one small leaky joint.

After a night in the Berthon marina at Lymington, we were off Westwards again, heading into a force 7 from the West with 2 reefs in the mains'l; smashing into the choppy seas soon had us well drenched. It was bright and sunny, which always makes thing seem better, and then the QE II passed about half a mile away, also bound West through the

Needles channel. She looked magnificent in the bright sun, against the blue sea - some wag entered in the log that she was very steady - which we certainly were not. That evening saw us anchoring in another of my "resting" places, Studland Bay, where we were well sheltered from the fierce West wind. The forecast indicated that it would continue West force 7 for the next few days; our objective for the week (it was already Friday) was changed from Falmouth to Poole, and the next day the boat was berthed in Poole Harbour Yacht Club marina. The two BCF extinguishers came home with me for recharging and servicing. This very effective extinguishing medium is now illegal, but we had seen a demonstration of its effectiveness. To a simple mind like mine, it seems they would rather have pollution by uncontrolled fires than from the occasional use of BCF to deal with a potential blaze that could produce great clouds of polluting smoke.

A fortnight later, with Roland and Vicky, we boarded a crowded commuter train at Waterloo in the evening rush hour, but by means of some deft manoeuvring with Vicky in the forefront, seats were grabbed as the empty train came into the platform; when it left, they were standing in the aisles. By 9 that evening we were letting go from our berth at Poole and on our way. Although there was a bit of sea left from a rough period, the weather had taken a turn for the better, and a good Northwesterly wind sent us bowling along. Our new piece of modern equipment (the VHF radio) was used to make a link call home to report progress, which was good; as I said, once you have these modern aids, you wonder how you managed without them (I write these lines a year after the link call service to the shore telephone system was discontinued, killed by the ubiquitous mobile phone). Early afternoon saw us past Start Point and laying a direct course for St Anthony's light at the entrance to Falmouth. Darkness fell as we sailed on towards the dark and mystical Cornish headlands which lay ahead of us; Falmouth is a good safe harbour to enter in darkness, and early on Sunday morning we picked up a vacant mooring off the slumbering town.

Later that morning, we took "CELANDINE" into the new Falmouth Marina sited at the mouth of the Penryn river. Considerable dredging and excavation was needed to create this useful sheltered berthing; dredging itself is not the great problem, but the disposal of the soil can be. In this case it had to be dumped a specified distance out at sea, and as with all these enterprises, it ran well over budget, which often causes the financial downfall of the first proprietors. Falmouth Marina had obtained a fixed price for the dredging contract, and it was the unfortunate dredging contractor who caught the cold. One snag in this marina is the existence of an oil pipeline creating a shallow bar across it, restricting access between the two parts at low water. The pressures of increased yachting activity meant it was no longer as easy to rent moorings down there, and anyway, the convenience of walking ashore instead of having to use one of the ferries was a great advantage. It enabled us to catch a train at Truro and reach home that night.

A fortnight later, on a Thursday, Beryl and I were leaving Writtle by night to avoid the traffic and reach the boat at a reasonable time of day; in the evening we had attended the County Council Chairman's garden party (by this time Beryl had become Vice-Chairman and Chairman of finance). A short rest after getting out of our glad rags, and then we were off. The benefit of having a car on hand facilitated victualling in Falmouth Town centre, a little distance from the marina, and getting it all aboard again - how times were changing! Together, we then spent an idyllic fortnight in this wonderful cruising ground, blessed by weather that had at last become benign.

Several days were spent in Gillan Haven, our very special hidey hole South of the Helford Estuary, where we could bathe from a minute sandy beach enveloped by rocks on either side, walk up the narrow steep and deep lanes to Gillan village, where from a small general store we could obtain the necessities of life, or land on the beach in front of the ancient church of St Anthony with its magnificent brass candelabra. Gillan Haven is in fact the outlet for a small stream; just above the beach by the church is a great shingle bank with a narrow gap through which the stream flows at low water, and through which the tide floods into an inner and almost secret part of this estuary in miniature. Not many boats are kept inside this part, which is shallow and without water for much of the time. A footpath which eventually leads to the village of Manaccan passes by an area of grassy bank set some forty or so feet above the water, with a group of spectacular Wellingtonias reaching for the sky. They are not native trees, although well suited to the mild, wet, and at times windy climate down there.

Friends came down to visit us for a few days, and with them could share the pleasure of this exciting cruising ground. We explore up the Fal to King Harry Ferry and inspect some of the laid up merchant ships - which often included well known passenger liners - we always checked the ships that were there, awaiting sale or the breaker's yard. One year, the former Ryde-Portsmouth passenger ferries were there, having been replaced by more exotic high speed craft. Also important for us were a few days in the Percuil River, where there was still enough room to anchor just upstream from St Mawes Harbour, in a more secluded and sheltered position.

St Mawes presented us with an intriguing mystery, never solved to this day, posed by a very large house probably of late 1930s vintage, with well tended terraced lawns and beds on the hillside close to our anchorage, complete with swimming pool and all that one might expect in a house of this quality. In the years we visited this anchorage, we never saw anybody there, even in the height of the holiday season. Every evening, the curtains of the large lounge facing over the creek would automatically close, but the only signs of life were gardeners or domestic staff. Our excitement rose one year when there was a party at lunch time, with people chatting over drinks on the spacious lawns, and we thought at last there was to be a house party, but by four it was deserted again. Although none of our business, it is fun to speculate about such places, and I suppose we wanted to see people enjoying this lovely house. In recent years I saw it advertised in *"Country Life"*, but I don't think there has been an opportunity since to see if the house is being used to greater advantage.

From our anchorage here we would walk across to Gerrans and Porthscatho on the coast - on one visit, St Gerrans church festival was in full swing and we bought a numbered print of a local scene by East Anglian artist Glynn Thomas - quite a surprise to find his unique style down there. We are very devoted to his style, where he opens up a village or town scene so the houses on one side of the street are shown upside down. In one or two cases, where this style is not needed, he will always put an inverted sheep or other animal discreetly - it is his hallmark. We now have quite a collection of his work, including Harwich, Mistley, and Iken church. They are gems, but although we have caused numerous hints to be dropped, he has failed to do one of Writtle Green, an ideal subject for his style.

Another anchorage often used by us was off the beach above Turnaware point, which afforded good shelter from Southerly winds; a steep climb up an old wartime concrete roadway (there had been a tank landing craft loading hard on this steep shore) was rewarded by superb views across the Carrick Roads and beyond, and to the National Trust property, Trelissick House on the opposite bank. Here, on this 1980 visit, our friends the Alders visited us in their Devon yawl with their three children. We had a slap up convivial meal together that evening, and then somehow managed to find somewhere for everyone to sleep. Piers Alder slept in "CELANDINE'S" cockpit under the cover, and was thrilled with the calm moonlit night that developed after darkness fell.

Later in August, I returned to Falmouth with a keen young crew and sailed on the

Saturday morning, with a light fair wind that encouraged us to set all sail including the big jib; during the day the wind freshened enough to see "CELANDINE" tramping along Eastwards under a blue sky with puffy white clouds. In the afternoon, I settled for an off watch snooze on the lee side of the foredeck in a patch of sun shining between the sails, admonishing the helmsman that I would know if we went off course because my patch of sun would go. When I came to, something had gone wrong - my right fist was clenched and refused to open, but I was due to take the helm and I thought that a vigorous spell on the wheel would get it working again. That night I had planned to spend in Salcombe, to give the crew time to settle in before setting off to get back to Essex in one leg; as my fist remained firmly closed, all the log entries were now being made in another hand except for one or two almost indecipherable sets of hieroglyphics scrawled with my left hand.

After a remarkably good passage, leaving Salcombe on Sunday morning with a fair wind from the South West, we were entering Harwich harbour by nine o'clock on Tuesday evening, to anchor in my usual temporary anchorage at Stone Heaps, in the River Orwell off Shotley. The next day, as we returned the boat to her mooring in the Walton channel, my fist was still clenched and could not be opened. The younger members of my crew were, I suspect, thinking that the poor old boy (remember, I was now approaching my 57th birthday) had suffered a minor stroke - indeed, I was beginning to wonder what had happened. A visit to a specialist confirmed that I had damaged a nerve near my right shoulder - this was undoubtedly caused by lying against the web of a steel bulwark stanchion during my brief afternoon rest on the first day out - a complaint sometimes called "dropped wrist", and sometimes found in drunks who collapse in a peculiar position. There was nothing he could do about it, and I went home with the cheerful news that it would cure itself in anything up to about six weeks.

The one not very useful fact to emerge from this was that I was in fact ambidextrous, but in a most odd way. Writing forwards with my left hand was slow, and the result was a totally different style from my normal handwriting. But if I wrote backwards, I could write as fast as normally achieved with my right hand, and it was recognisable as my writing - but you needed a mirror to read it! Back at the office after this trip, I found that by placing an upturned piece of carbon paper under the top sheet of my desk pad, I could make quick notes of telephone conversations which were perfectly legible, and recognisable as my handwriting by turning over the top piece of paper. For years, I had always used whichever hand was most convenient for jobs such as painting, but had been taught to use the right hand for writing.

ELECTIONS, ELEVATION AND A CALLY RALLY

THE early part of 1981 was a mixture of pleasure and sadness; the pleasure of a visit from my sister and her husband Dino was contrasted with the death of Howard Banks, the man who had helped me so much in those immediate post-war years when I joined the family business straight from the Navy on the death of my father. Beryl was selected once again as Conservative candidate for the Writtle seat; the whole atmosphere had become much more party political, but in a place like Writtle, the sort of person you were, and how you did the job still counted.. Then an event occurred which could not have had a greater effect if an atomic bomb had dropped on the house next door - a letter arrived asking if she would accept a life peerage. Her immense service and duty to the County of Essex and National organisations had been recognised in other places, and my eyes moistened with pleasure that her hard work over the years was being rewarded, even though it was going to entail a new learning curve and round of duty. Of course, the whole thing had to be kept secret until the public announcement, and later that day I walked down the garden where she was doing some weeding, I sang (quietly!) the Gilbert & Sullivan chorus from *"Iolanthe"* - "Bow, bow, ye lower middle classes, ye tradesmen and ye masses". "Shut up - someone might hear you". We Platts are quite resilient and soon recover from shocks like this one.

There followed visits to Garter King at Arms to arrange the design of a coat of arms; Beryl regarded it as a joint affair and brought me into the deliberations, to the extent that, suprisingly they seemed a bit short on anchors, and I was called in to sketch a suitable style of antique anchor - but not of the fouled variety so often found in heraldry - what sailor wants a fouled anchor? Beryl wanted a kingfisher (a favourite bird of hers we used to see by the river in Writtle), so he was perched on the stock of the anchor. A green with little founts of water was incorporated, representing "Writtolaburna", the place of many babbling purling springs, whilst a winged lion held the patriarchal cross (often referred to as a cross of Lorraine) which is to be found in the ancient seal of Writtle Church. She chose as the inscription "Aime Dieu et Tous", which really summed up her whole philosophy of serving God by serving your fellow man (this is my interpretation of her outlook, not hers).

The County Council elections came in May, with Beryl returned by an overwhelming majority; soon after, when the official announcement appeared, she was at a committee in County Hall, at the end of which Bob Daniels Chairman of the Council, decreed there should be a celebration. Beryl told me that that the meeting got through its business in record time, thus proving another of Platt's theories about committees - if you want to finish the business quickly, there is no better way than to have the clink of glasses and popping of corks just audible from the other side of the partition or door. This will usually even silence the bore who brings up some tedious (and often irrelevant) point under "any other business".

Mid June saw her introduction to the House, and within three weeks she was making her maiden speech in a debate on further education. The House is a formidable place in which to speak - you are aware that for any particular subject, all the experts in that field will turn up, and woe betide you if you get it wrong! As an observer at one pace's distance from the whole affair, you could not fail to be impressed with the quality of debate, and the dignified way in which proceedings are conducted. Although divided on political lines, the members are far more independently minded and have no hesitation in voting according to conscience. Unfortunately, partly due to press misrepresentation, where journalists are apt to portray them as a lot of old buffers dressed in ermine, there is a culture of misunderstanding, often among those who should know better, and politicians without knowledge or understanding are now meddling with it, to the detriment of the proper conduct of parliamentiary business. Most of the time I have been privileged to observe the House of Lords in action, one could see the restraining and revising action on ill-thought out or badly drafted legislation, by people who did not have to currry popular favour in order to ensure re-election, but had a deep sense of duty and were not afraid of speaking their mind.

In Writtle some of my friends started a "Gentleman's liberation movement", because whereas the wife of a peer becomes "Lady So and So", it is not the same for the husband of a life peer. This has never worried me one iota, and I get the same privileges as they do, in that I can sit in the chamber and listen to the proceedings in a special area that used to be known as "The Hen Pen", but now is re-named "The Spouse Box". Twenty years ago, Beryl was still one of a very small number of women in the House, and the first time I took my seat in this area, the ladies present looked slightly puzzled - how has this man got in our midst?

The previous year I had been elected a Vice-President of the Cruising Association; there were hints from the organisers of the annual "Calais Rally" that no flag officer had attended for some years, and thus I felt that as my boat was based nearer to Calais than that of any other flag officer, it was my duty to go. As I have mentioned before, this kind of thing is not really my scene, but it was a challenge - there and back over the Spring Bank Holiday weekend - albeit one of Platt's stretched weekends.

On the Thursday night, five of us boarded - did we all go down from the yacht club in one dinghy load? I think there must have been two trips, because there would have also been all the gear and provisions, but "CELANDINE'S" mooring was almost a mile from the club, so someone did a lot of rowing. By this time, a system of self-declaration for Customs purposes was in force, by means of a multipart form on which details of crew and passport numbers were entered and posted in a box by the Yacht club. The form included a brief description of the vessel, estimated time of departure, destination and expected date and port of return. One of the questions to which I enjoyed answering "no" was "Has UK VAT been paid on the vessel and all its equipment?" "CELANDINE", having been built before VAT had been introduced, was perfectly legitimate, but had escaped the impost. Our crew for this trip included our Cornish stalwart, Richard White, Mary Dainty, Elspeth Riddick, General Secretary of the CA, and our Italian nephew (Now a Canadian citizen) Sandro Marazzi.

The mooring was slipped at four thirty on Friday morning, just as it was getting light. With a light Southwesterly wind, we headed out across a cold grey Estuary. Apart from a period when the wind failed us,a good sail was enjoyed under a sky that soon cleared ("The dullest morn often heralds in the finest day"). At eight that evening, we entered Calais and picked up a mooring in the avant port - one hopes better than the one that parted so dramatically when we were there in "CAMPION" sixteen years earlier. Mercifully, the weather was calm and we did not have to endure the awful scend that keeps a boat fidgeting and rolling. On the tide that night, at half past one on Saturday morning, the lock gates opened and we passed into the sheltered waters of the Bassin de l'Ouest.

Sandro left by train for Italy later that morning (to join his father for return to Canada) and Beryl arrived by Hovercraft from Pegwell Bay, Ramsgate (a route long since discontinued). I had already been warned that I would be making a speech that evening in the company of M. J Kelmachter, president of the Yacht Club du Nord de France, and had decided as a matter of courtesy that it would be in French. My French vocabulary and accent are quite good, but my grasp of the grammar abysmal, so with Platt cunning I had already decided that if I roughed it out in draft, Beryl, who is strong on grammar, and Elspeth, a very bright and well educated young lady, "Bien elevé", would between them knock the whole thing into shape. The French were delighted - I think we even managed to insert a little joke - although I am not sure what my compatriots thought of it.

Sunday afternoon saw us locking out again on the tide, and picking up the same mooring again, we pulled down a reef and hoisted sail; a brisk West-southwest wind was blowing, and at five o'clock the twin pierheads were cleared and were romping homewards. By eight that evening we were altering course Northwards along the Kentish coast. Once again, Platt's cynical theory about fair winds was illustrated, as it fell lighter and we shook out the reef from the mains'l, whilst dropping the mizzen. A snag with ketch rig is that when running before the wind, the mizzen takes wind from the mains'l and tends to make it restless and liable to gybe accidentally. By the small hours of Monday, we were ghosting along before a very light wind in the vicinity of the Kentish Knock sand

- by now, a buoy had replaced the light vessel, as about this time, lightvessels were disappearing from the coastal scene. Why the "Kentish" Knock, I don't understand - it is about 20 miles off the Essex coast, on the same latitude as the Dengie peninsula, and being so far out at sea has claimed many fine ships over the centuries.

As we altered course towards Harwich, this brought the wind round on our port quarter which pushed our speed up, helped by re-setting the mizzen after clearing the Northeast Knock buoy - a log entry read "NE Knock buoy closely inspected". This may well have been to read the name - I am not ashamed to go up to an important buoy closely enough to shine a torch and read the name. By seven that morning, the wind had picked up again to give us faster sailing, with the wind abeam, and we were just passing South of the South Cork buoy off Harwich, when she touched bottom - the tail of the Cork sand must have been extending Southwards (the buoy has long since been repositioned). In the cold grey morning light, this was not very comforting, but there was little or no sea running so I let her drive on, and after a couple more scrapes, we were over and into deeper water. By half past eight on that Monday morning we were back on the mooring and waiting for the tide to reach the Yacht club hard in our heavily laden dinghy.

POOPED EN ROUTE TO BRITTANY

CELANDINE" was soon covering the same ground again, this time with a fresh Northerly wind pushing her Southwards to pass our old friend the Kentish Knock at four in the morning, having left the Pye End buoy astern at midnight on Thursday night. The wind veered to Nor'nor'east and freshened to a good force 6 as we passed outside the Goodwins in a lively sea; the sky had darkened, and we were now getting continuous rain. The only good thing about it was the fact we were travelling very fast. South of Dover, the sky cleared and immediately the sun comes out, things look better - but I wanted a time check, opened the cabin doors to look at the clock on the forward bulkhead, and then looked round to see Roland's friend Tom Slator sitting at the wheel, engulfed by water, which poured into the cockpit, broke against the forward end of the cockpit and over on to the bridge deck. Fortunately, the sill on the cabin doors stopped more than a few drops splashing down the cabin steps. The cockpit was flooded to a depth of about nine inches; I think it drained quite quickly, but not quickly enough for me - I was worried about the weight of water reducing her buoyancy aft. This had been a classic case of "pooping", caused by our sailing too fast through the confused seas, but we had no further trouble. We had been three strong, but as Roland had succumbed to severe mal-de-mer, it left only two of us to run the boat.

I decided to anchor under the lee of Dungeness for a rest, and just before two in the afternoon put the anchor down close in for maximum shelter. An hour later, an Army launch closed us to say we were in a danger area from a firing range, and holding up firing practice. That made the decision for me - we went in to Rye harbour on the rising tide, and continued on to moor alongside the Town Quay, where I knew we would be cradled at low water in the softest of ooze. We really needed that rest!

Early the next morning, we motored astern down the narrow Rock channel until we had room to turn - "CELANDINE" was very controllable going astern under power, a great asset. The wind had eased from the previous boisterous day, but was still blowing favourably from between North and East, and that evening we anchored inside East Head, Chichester, well sheltered from the Easterlies. The next day, Sunday, I sailed through the Solent to berth in Lymington Marina - I had originally hoped to get further West, but this was a practical

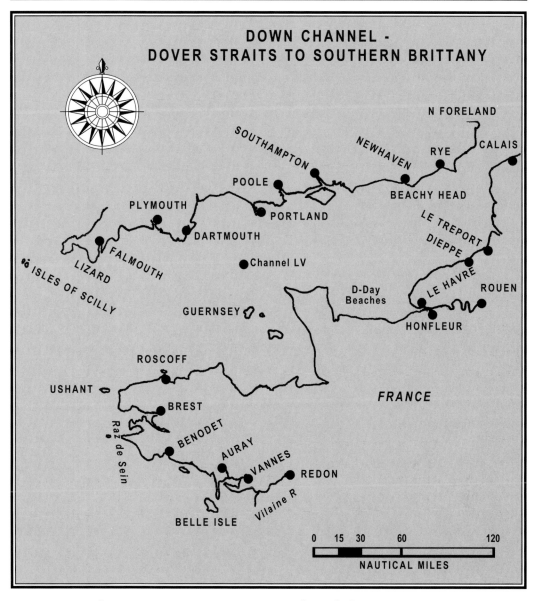

DOWN CHANNEL -
DOVER STRAITS TO SOUTHERN BRITTANY

N FORELAND

SOUTHAMPTON

NEWHAVEN

RYE

CALAIS

POOLE

BEACHY HEAD

PLYMOUTH

PORTLAND

LE TREPORT

DARTMOUTH

DIEPPE

Channel LV

FALMOUTH

LIZARD

ISLES OF SCILLY

D-Day
Beaches

LE HAVRE

ROUEN

GUERNSEY

HONFLEUR

ROSCOFF

USHANT

FRANCE

BREST

Raz de Sein

BENODET

AURAY

VANNES

REDON

Vilaine R

BELLE ISLE

0   15   30   60   120

NAUTICAL MILES

proposition, with a train service to London. Sailing through the Solent on a Sunday is not my cup of tea - too many boats, but we had a fair wind and as always, the scenery beautiful in the bright sunlight.

A week later, we were back in Lymington, having travelled from London on Thursday night. I had arranged delivery of bonded stores for Friday morning, which were put in the Duty free locker and duly sealed with a smart brass padlock - this impressive locker was in fact under one of the foc'sle bunks - which had loose bunk boards! That afternoon, we were underweigh again, but the Easterly winds had gone and we now had to fight our way against a fierce Sou'wester, by evening, we were anchored in Studland Bay - it had been hard work, even getting this far. It was worth the rest, because the next day came misty with the lightest of Southwest winds, but later that day it was freshening again. We rounded Portland Bill on the inshore route past this grim headland, and then were able to lay a good Westerly course across Lyme Bay, before eventually being forced to tack off Sidmouth late that evening - getting down channel can be a very frustrating business! The wind varied, but a period of light wind from Sou'sou'east gave us a useful boost (and the chance to cook a good lunch!), so by seven thirty in the evening we were comfortably berthed once more in Falmouth marina, where we refuelled and bought some essential victuals before sailing at the gentlemanly hour of nine thirty on Monday morning.

That afternoon, we were breasting into quite lively seas South of the Lizard, closehauled and making good progress. There are traffic separation lanes South of the Lizard, and after passing through the Southwest bound traffic lane, we were approaching the up-Channel lane when I was due to go off watch; my priority was to have a snooze - if you are responsible, it is important to get as much rest as possible on a longish passage. As I went below, I told those taking the watch to now keep a good lookout on the starboard bow - "The only thing approaching is a square rigger", pointing my finger at a grey smudge just coming up over the horizon. "Go and get your sleep" they said, "you're having hallucinations". I went below, asking them to call me when she was nearer.

Within half an hour I was on deck again, with my camera at the ready. She was unmistakenly the "LIBERTAD". Argentina's square rigged sail training ship, which I had last seen at Newport Rhode Island. Calling her on the radio I explained we were going to cross her bows in order to get good photographs, knowing we could comfortably do this without danger. The photography was not easy since we had quite a lively motion in the seas that were running - while the "LIBERTAD" proceeded steadily up Channel under almost full sail - there is no finer sight than a large square rigger forging its stately progress through the seas. By the time we had finished our photography session, the cadets were lining the rails; we thanked them and they blew a loud blast of salute on their siren (she was, of course an auxiliary powered ship). Soon after that, they came back to me on the radio with an invitation to a reception on board later that month, at Greenwich - which I was pleased to accept. The Argentinians are basically friendly towards us, and it is sad to think that within a year of this happy mid-channel encounter, the two nations were at war.

Late that evening, the wind fell light, making the sea conditions quieter, but our progress slower and forcing us to resort to motor sail into the small hours of Tuesday, to reach the Chenal de Four inside the Isle of Ushant by mid-morning, when we were once again sailing well under full sail, paying great attention to pilotage through this rock-infested, but well marked area. By evening, we were negotiating the infamous Raz du Sein, which I have to confess, I have never seen in a really angry mood. Another night passsage took us round the great Pointe de Penmarch and across a long open stretch of sea known as L'Iroise, with little to see. It was not until Wednesday afternoon that things began to get interesting again, when we closed the Quiberon peninsula in poor visibility. Rounding the Quiberon peninsula, we once again paused briefly to refuel in our little loved Port Haliguen. By now, we had watched what we had first known as a rather primitive fishing port develop into a very smart and brash marina, and stayed only long enough to take on fuel. Of course, the development had greatly helped the ailing local economy, but it was not our scene, and the name "Port Hooligan" had become fixed in our vocabulary. From here, we once more entered the gulf of Morbihan to proceed up the Auray river and anchor below Auray, off Le Bono and enjoy a late supper, after nearly three days on the move. During the course of this, I was aware of a sharp knocking noise - it was coming from one of the portholes in the topsides, where a swan, perhaps attracted by the light, was looking in and tapping on the glass with his beak. Did he want to come in and join us? More likely, he just knew we were eating and was demanding food - swans in places frequented by yachts become expert scroungers and are very persistent, if not aggressive, in their demands.

The next day, Thursday, we anchored once again fore and aft off the Quai Benjamin Franklin, where sadly, one of our number, John Aldridge had to leave early and return home, using the "Brittany Coast Express" (my unnoficial name), with which we were by now becoming very familiar. In the afternoon, we sailed for our intended target, The Vilaine river. During a casual conversation at the Cruising Association's headquarters, William Hurst, the President, suggested that I would find the Vilaine River an interesting place to visit, and that he was proposing to cruise there this season. Sailing from Auray in the afternoon, we bowled along before a brisk Westerly breeze, but this was bringing us to the shallow Plateau de Dumet too near to low water in the approach to La Vilaine, and I had no wish to bounce the keel on a rock-strewn sandy bottom. We hove to for a while, but the tide rises fairly fast here (although nothing like in the enormous tidal ranges of North Brittany) and soon were in the tidal part of the Vilaine estuary - there was William Hurst's "HOLLY" at anchor, so we rounded up and dropped anchor (it all went very smoothly - rather important under the eyes of the President!).

The next day, after social visits to William and Kathleen Hurst, we proceeded up to the tidal barrage at Arzal; this was a fairly recent development which caused the river to be navigable at all states of the tide, whereas previously it had been a muddy stinking ditch at low water. Locals told us how the conservationists opposed it because of the adverse effect it would have on wild life; in fact, wild life adapted and continued to thrive. As far as the delightful town of La Roche Bernard, the banks are steep and in places rocky, but travelling upstream, the river meanders through a pastoral flood plain, and the hills retreat away from the river. Before reaching Redon, the head of navigation for seagoing boats, we were slightly surprised to find a bridge, but it was clearly of the opening variety, and it was not long after announcing our arrival with a blast on the foghorn that Madame appeared to operate the bridge, which carried a relatively minor road. "CELANDINE" was secured alongside the Quai Jean Bart in the town bassin, which clearly had once been a busy port, but was now almost deserted, the quayside warehouses either empty or being converted for other uses. At one point, there was an access to the Brittany canal connecting Nantes to Brest; it is shallow and tortuous, but would enable a shoal draft boat with lowered mast to miss some very wild and rugged coast - it would take time. The quayside was quite high, but we were able to put her by a ladder because early the next morning we had to make our way to the nearby station and catch "The Brittany Coast Express". Redon was the last stop before the train headed inland for the communications hub of the Brittany peninsula, Rennes, whence it makes its fast journey to Paris.

A week later, Beryl and I travelled out, flying to Paris, and then travelling from Paris Montparnasse first class - an indulgence, but all part of the holiday. The evening journey was an interesting experience - dinner on the train was entirely managed by one stewardess, who served an excellent three course meal in a style reminiscent of airline catering, except that weight was not a consideration, and the specially designed compartmented dishes were of heavy porcelain. She collected our payment, and left the train at Rennes, having put all the packed dirty utensils on the platform, and was met by an official who received the evening's takings from her - all very impressive. It was a thoroughly enjoyable journey through the French countryside, arriving at Redon as darkness fell.

During a relaxing stay within the non-tidal river, Roland came out to celebrate his birthday with us at "Les Deux Magots" - a "magot" is some kind of small monkey, perhaps a chimpanzee, but I have never found a dictionary to explain the difference between "singe" and "magot". After Roland left, Vicky came out, along with Ned Jones, to celebrate her birthday a week later in the same hostelry, in the centre of Roche Bernard. During this time, we were anchored in a convenient small bay upstream from Roche

Bernard, where we dressed ship overall for the wedding of Prince Charles and Diana, and a French-speaking Belgian who had a holiday home there, with boat moored off, hoisted his largest ensign. Later in the day, during which we listened on the radio, he came over and said would we like to see the highlights on television, by invitation of the nearby farmer's wife, so we found ourselves ushered into the spotless parlour; she retreated after we were comfortably seated, wiping her hands on her apron to prove her "paysanne" credentials and had work to do. After the wedding scenes were over, the programme switched to political matters, with a meeting between Margaret Thatcher and Mitterand. Madame had by then re-appeared, and very obviously voiced her approval of Mitterand, but when Margaret Thatcher came on, she uttered "Femme mechante", wishing to indicate clearly where her politics lay. At the end, we thanked her profusely - she had been very kind and thoughtful in asking us - she must have seen our brave display of bunting from her farmhouse and realised we would like to have a glimpse of the proceedings.

Vicky and Ned were joining for the return trip, and John King who had been on our return voyage from Vigo. also came out, while Beryl was returning by train and plane. On our last day in Roche Bernard, Vicky slipped in the showers and cut her eyelid quite badly on the shower head, which seemed to be of a rather unfriendly design. With great difficulty, a doctor was located, and he skilfully put in stitches, carrying out the whole operation in his surgery, and saying that after a few days they must come out.

Leaving the Vilaine estuary too soon after low water, we frightened ourselves by touching bottom, and being quite late in the day when we finally left, swallowed our pride and made for Port Haliguen for the night - it was the most convenient port of call, close to the tip of Quiberon - I wished we had not been so beastly about the place. Our next port of call was another first for us - we entered the estuary of the twin rivers Aven and Belon. Not being quite sure which river to take, we decided to turn to starboard and take the Belon, mainly because we thought it more picturesque, and anchored for the night in a small bay under steep pine covered banks, close to the hamlet of Kerfany. It was a good choice, and we had a clear ten feet of water at low tide in this sheltered bay.

Our next port of call was Benodet, the Cowes of France. It is not a place to my liking, but, of course, has excellent facilities - we refuelled, re-victualled and then went up river a short distance, which transformed the scene. Our anchorage was in the mouth of a small tributary, near Combrit, secluded with wooded banks, and, near a ruined quay where we had a comfortable nine feet at low water. A short excursion up the river Odet had shown it had great charm - and also a number of very grand houses overlooking its picturesque reaches.

From here, we sailed early in the day for Camaret, which was to be our last port of call in France. Winds were light, and visibility was poor, so that we were soon out of sight of land. It was a long hop, and at times the engine had to be called into service, but the wind was fair. During the voyage, we became aware of the sound of very powerful engines near us, and thought it might be high speed french Naval vessels exercising, but the sound stayed with us for a long time, and I began to get the feeling we were being shadowed by unseen vessels. In the afternoon, sailing quietly along Vicky was at the helm, and the rest of us below, when she shouted that an inflatable full of armed men was approaching. As I rushed on deck, she asked "what should we do - we are in international waters?" There is only one thing to do - take their painter and be polite. They were in uniform, and having boarded, announced they were Douane and wanted to see ship's papers and all our passports. They were correct, but stiff and formal as they trooped below where the papers were inspected. We all spoke in our best possible French, and after the first passports were produced, the atmosphere changed. They politely thanked us, I offered drinks and the conversation became personalised - one was about to go on leave and we wished him "Bonnes vacances". They left amid great bonhommie and disappeared into the mist to rejoin their mother ship, now just visible, .

When we arrived in Camaret, their patrol boat was already moored up, but they gave us a friendly wave as we went past them to anchor in the harbour for the night. A few days after our return to the UK, there was an item in the newspapers reporting that a British registered ketch with a polyglot crew had been arrested with oodles of drugs aboard - so they got what they were in fact looking for; their mistake in looking at us was understandable.

That evening, I had the task of removing the stitches from Vicky's eyelid, which I did not enjoy -wielding a sharp pointed pair of scissors so close to your daughter's eyes made me very nervous, but the job was eventually accomplished. It was a bit early to be taking them out, but I wanted to do it before we went to sea. Clearing from Camaret early the next day, we had a slow passage in light but favourable winds, then up to Lymington marina to re-fuel, hand in our Customs forms and buy a few victuals before setting off three hours later to sail for home. Slipping through the Looe channel off Selsey Bill, we headed East before a fair wind falling so light that at times we had to boost progress with the engine. Dawn saw us off Dungeness in deteriorating visibility, which became dense fog in my most unloved stretch of water, the straits of Dover. As we approached the North Foreland, the wind picked up, visibility improved and we were on the home run, passing the Long Sand head, North East Gunfleet and then Stone Banks, on our front doorstep so to speak. I enjoy our voyages, but also get just as much pleasure from arriving back in familiar waters again. At half past seven that Saturday evening, we picked up our mooring in the Walton Channel, having completed a round trip of over 1100 nautical miles.

RETRACING MATERNAL ANCESTRY

THAT September, "CELANDINE" sailed up to the port frequented by my maternal seafaring forebears, the Magubs of Southwold. Leaving Walton early on Saturday, we had a rollicking fast sail with one reef down before a brisk Southwester that brought us to Southwold entrance by two o'clock in the afternoon, with the tide still flooding into the harbour. Roger Trigg, the then harbourmaster had laid on an excellent berth for us, belonging to one of the fishing boats that was temporarily away from the port.

Retracing maternal ancestry - "Celandine" in Southwold harbour.

I was fascinated to visit the churchyard and see the Magub graves - all sea captains of Southwold, once a busy little coastal port. My maternal grandfather, Robert William, did not go to sea, but he did own a "billiboy", the "EVA". and a schooner, the "PEGGY", which I think were mainly employed in bringing coal from the Northeast to unload for use locally and in nearby small towns and villages within the range of horse-drawn transport. He had his finger in many local business affairs, including Adnams, still producing very fine ales to this day, and the Southwold light railway -

which finished as a financial disaster in 1929, an early victim of competition from the internal combustion engine. In its heyday, my mother remembers travelling on the line as a child, and because her father was a director, travelled free. I remember as a boy of six, driving up to Southwold from Leigh in our Austin 16 - 6. (16 horse power, six cylinders) - a car journey of this magnitude took on the aspect of a safari in those days. My father lifted me up to look through a crack in the weatherboarded shed which housed the two locomotives, pronouncing in a voice of gloom that my grandfather had lost a lot of money in this enterprise. In its last hope of operating for another summer season, it was decided to smarten up the rather dilapidated and frail tramcar like passenger rolling stock. Realising that all the platforms were on one side of the trains, and governed by a grave shortage of money, they just painted one side only!

It is still possible to walk along the clearly defined trackbed, but there is not much else to see, except for a short length of track at the end of the "Harbour arm", used for freight traffic. This is now slowly falling down the bank, and will eventually vanish below the water. Southwold is a most delightful old-fashioned place of great character; I have a cousin, Barbara Brown, keeping up the family connection there, and she still has some of those shares in Adnam's brewery, also Daphne, the widow of my old sailing friend Michael Beaumont lives there - she is Suffolk through and through, hailing from nearby Beccles.

The wind that brought us so swiftly to Southwold continued to freshen, and by that evening was blowing a full gale from Southwest, and continuous heavy rain was falling. We were glad to be in harbour, and in the comfort of "Celandine's" cosy saloon. Extra mooring ropes had been put out, and at high water that night there was a certain amount of scend coming in the harbour, but it was really surprisingly sheltered considering how the narrow entrance gives straight on to the open North Sea. We left Southwold two days later, by which time the wind had moderated and veered a little more Westerly; our departure was in darkness and must have been not too long after low water. Slipping from the staging, I then ran her ashore on the mud of the Walberswick side while we hoisted sail and stowed the fenders and mooring ropes; leaving this kind of harbour straight into open sea, I like to have at least some sail set for steadying purposes before hitting whatever may lie outside. Looking back on this departure, it seems we were quite daring leaving early on a rising tide, but the least depth recorded in the troughs of the swell was six feet - we drew five, so there was not really a lot to spare.

Our return trip was via the Alde, and then the Deben, where George Jones left the ship at Waldringfield to go aboard "Peter Duck", whence we went upriver to Whisstock's marina at Woodbridge for a day shopping and generally exploring this characterful town. It blew hard again while we were in the Deben, and the next day anchored off the tiny village of Hemley, where the holding is good and you are sheltered from Southwest winds. At the end of an interesting week, it was still blowing hard and on the Sunday morning we clawed our way back to Walton with two reefs down; we had the benefit of a strong flood tide up the coast and into Walton, but it was rugged and wet going until we reached the more sheltered waters lying inside Pye End.

While I had been away on the boat, Beryl had been on an educational conference, but a week later she and I went blackberrying by boat - an annual event in those days - we always had a good apple crop in our garden, but needed blackberries to complement them, and what better way than to hide ourselves away in the Walton Backwaters to pick them, away from the dirt and fumes of passing traffic. I always maintain that blackberries grown in sea air are tastier!

LUDWIGSBERG - AND THE LAST HARWICH-HOOK VOYAGE OF "ST EDMUND"

ESSEX County Council, of which Beryl was due to become chairman the following year, had a relationship with the Landkreis of Ludwigsberg, with whom they exchanged views on regional and County government, hopefully for the benefit of both bodies. In the Spring of 1982, Beryl went out with the Chairman, Bob Daniels, Chief Executive, Robert Adcock, and other chairmen of main committees to visit Ludwigsberg, and I was to follow at the end of formal proceedings, to hopefully enjoy a few relaxing days out there. I sailed overnight on one of the Dutch ferries from Harwich, taking the car. The next morning, I set off through Holland and on to the South East of Germany - Ludwigsberg is in the province of Stuttgart; it was a very long drive, but having found exactly where I needed to go in Ludwigsberg, I had to turn left into a side road. Turning left on the continent is, of course the equivalent of turning right in the UK. It was just before the summit of a rise in the road, and I managed a head on collision with a Mercedes; my Renault 18 was no match for such a car - rather like a collision between a battleship and a lightly built frigate. Actually, the Renault was pushed backwards by the impact, and this absorbed some of the energy. I was not hurt, but somewhat shaken; damage to my car was limited to the "crumple zone" and with German efficiency, they soon had the spares and we were back on the road in very little time. Meantime, the weather was benign and we enjoyed ourselves in this totally new environment - it is well South, where the people are jolly and lighthearted. Of course, I had driven much too far in one day, and without a navigator it is more difficult to concentrate on both route and traffic. It was a lesson learnt the hard way.

On our return journey (which we broke with a night stop at Heidelberg), we had been invited to dinner at the Residence of the British Amabassador to the Hague - previously we had Phillip (now Sir Phillip) and Elinor Mansfield to stay with us for the wedding of Phillip's sister in Writtle Church. The reception was held in the garden of the Mansfield seniors' home, Chase House; alas, as has happened in so many places, the spacious garden in which the marquee was erected for the reception has disappeared under bricks and mortar. Phillip's appointment as Ambassador was a plum job in the diplomatic service, but the pleasure of receiving this honour had a more serious side to it - his predecessor was shot on the steps of the residence by the IRA.

On finding the address, we were slightly disturbed to find it in what seemed a slightly run down part of the town, and we drove into a rather dark yard, close to which were several Dutch police vehicles. Not surprisingly, the security was strict - as we presented ourselves at the outer door, I was conscious that we were under television cameras. Having announced ourselves over the intercom, the doors swung open without a soul in sight, and we were confronted with a long staircase topped with glass panelled doors, which also swung open as we approached. This was all a bit spooky, but, of course, once we were inside all was warmth, light and hospitality; dinner was served by liveried footmen, the company was congenial and interesting, but we had mentioned to Phillip that we had a booking on the night ferry from the Hook, and might have to act like Cinderella. He told us how long it would take from there to the Hook, but it was difficult tearing ourselves away, and we were slightly worried. Phillip told us not to worry - they would phone the Hook and advise that we were coming.

When we arrived at the ship, which had been held for us, I am sure there was disappointment on the faces of onlooking passengers as we crawled aboard in our Renault 18. They had apologised over the public address for a slight delay in sailing requested by the British Embassy and they really expected something better - at least a Daimler, if not a Rolls. Once aboard the British Rail "St Edmund", the ferry doors closed immediately and we were underway. Having not seen British papers for a few days, we were a little out of touch, but we had heard about the Argentine invasion of the Falklands and were to a certain extent updated by conversations at the dinner party - it was indeed, a worrying situation.

The next morning, we decided to have an early breakfast aboard, and during the course of this heard some interesting banter between stewards and crew members - one said "I'll be Master-at-Arms, you can be quartermaster". I said to Beryl "Surely they can't be sending this, a North Sea ferry out there?" But they did - we had been on what was her last voyage on the Harwich-Hook route, and that very same day, she was sailed to Plymouth for modifications which included fitting a helicopter pad.

What made her an attractive proposition for the job was that she had been built during one of the world fuel crises of the seventies and given extra large fuel oil bunkers; she had the endurance to reach Ascension Island without refuelling, and plenty of capacity for large commercial vehicles as well as cars, plus ample passenger accommodation. I had always thought her a rather fine ship, from the time of her inauguration on the Harwich-Hook run. I don't know what the terms of her service were with the Government, but she emerged from her refit and sailed for the Falklands renamed the "Kerens".

Several years later, I went to speak at a Cruising Association Wessex Section function, held at the Royal Motor Yacht Club at Poole, in which I booked a cabin for the night. My cabin looked over the narrows at the harbour entrance, and as I was just turning in for the night, an outward bound ferry went past. Painted all white she may have been, but this ship was unmistakedly my old friend the "St Edmund" - even if I did see a name, I do not recall what name she was by then sailing under .

TO FALMOUTH FOR ORDERS

L ATER in the summer of '82, the tall ships race was due to start from Falmouth; Brother-in-law James was not skippering a boat in this, but was to be aboard the "Morag Mhor", a twin screw ketch accompanying the fleet and acting as communications vessel. So it was to be Falmouth again this year for "Celandine", and James lost no time in organising us as one of the accomodation units in Falmouth docks to receive crew members awaiting arrival of their boats.

Early in June, we slipped our mooring at Walton and picked up another off the beach just inside Harwich harbour - one of the minor restrictions at Walton, is that the relatively deep Channel, from Crab Knoll inwards, fizzles out and disperses over a wide shallow area in Dovercourt Bay, in the vicinity of Pye End, and "Celandine" could not be taken through this area near low water on most tides. This dodge enabled us to beat the system and start from Harwich soon after low water, in the small hours of Saturday morning. With a strong crew of four, we set off on another of those frustrating voyages with long periods of calm, although when there was any wind, at least it was favourable.

Mike "thatch" Rose was once again in the crew, together with my old schoolfriend Philip Andrews, who had now fully retired from service with HM Customs, and Colin Beveridge. Colin was a vet, but now with a leading pharmaceutical company; during his veterinary days he had practised in Cornwall, so when we arrived in Fowey and picked up a mooring off Polruan, he was on very familiar territory. I knew we were running low in water, but found out how low when the tank ran dry at ten o'clock that evening, and all we then had was our reserve in a plastic can. From our mooring at Walton, we had to go alongside the yacht club quay on the tide and fill with the hose attached to the clubhouse, but if you were working and then setting off as soon as possible, there was not always the chance to top up the tank.

The next morning, Thursday, it was raining hard and we moved alongside the quay to await the arrival of someone to unlock the water supply and serve us with more fuel. The scene was melancholy with not a soul stirring anywhere, but Colin knew there was a paper shop just up the road and volunteered to get a newspaper. He had explained at some length how he once saved a sick cow at a nearby farm and was therefore something of a local hero. When he returned with the paper on this wet morning he described his visit - "They remembered me - I had a full civic reception and they turned out the town band" - this stretch of imagination (some would call it a whopper) cheered up the miserable scene. However, we soon obtained water and fuel and were off for Falmouth before a brisk Southeasterly breeze - at last we were sailing really fast for the last part of our passage West, although the skies remained leaden and we were swept by constant rainsqualls.

It was still only Thursday afternoon when we picked up a mooring in St Mawes harbour, so we enjoyed two more days visiting favourite anchorages in the area; the weather improved and winds came at comfortable strengths from between Southwest and Northwest - all making the whole of Falmouth bay a sheltered cruising ground. We sailed just for the experience of sailing fast in sheltered waters, against a background of impressive coastal scenery. Finally, on Sunday morning, after a superb fast sail with a beam wind from Northwest, we were reluctantly berthing in Falmouth Marina, ready to catch an early afternoon train from Truro. Philip had already left us when we had called at Newton Ferrers to see Betty Barlow - his home at South Modbury was almost within spitting distance.

This year "CELANDINE" had a great deal of use down at Falmouth; the facility of a marina berth made it much easier, so that we could get straight aboard after an overnight drive from home. A weekend trip to revisit Fowey was made with Peter and Ursula Gardiner from Leigh; Ursula was particularly strong on navigation - on such occasions I always feel rather inadequate as mine is so rough and ready. Our return from Fowey was against a brisk Southwesterly wind in driving rain, which reduced visibility considerably, making it vitally important to keep an eye on where we were off this dramatic rocky coast.

The next weekend proved to be quite dramatic in other ways - leaving Writtle at 2 am with an all Writtle crew - Richard Oscroft and Tony Easteal, and with the intention of sharing the driving. We are still talking about pre-M25 days, and the way West lay through central London. Passing Buckingham Palace at about 3 am, we noticed a single light from a window in the facade, and various facetious speculations were made. Little did we know that this was the very night a madman had evaded the security and entered the Queen's bedroom. Our next excitement came at dawn on the M4; I was asleep on the back seat, when there was an almighty "clonk" on the windscreen. I lept up just in time to see a very dead crow fluttering down on to the road astern, together with a windsreen wiper arm! Of course, it did not matter - until it began to rain, but we found a Renault garage at Falmouth who were able to supply a complete new arm.

Fortunately, the weather improved to give us some superb sailing; whilst out in Falmouth Bay, we saw a very large white ship approaching, to heave to off shore, while helicopters plied to and fro - the modern equivalent of the Falmouth Quay punts that used to ferry goods and people between ship and shore in the days of sailing ships, when owners despatched them to the most Westerly safe port in the UK - "To Falmouth for orders" There were times when we had a struggle to get down West, with our fore and aft rig and auxiliary diesel engine; how much worse for a big square rigger with no auxiliary. Falmouth was the gateway to the world for a squarerigger.

This ship was the "Canberra" returning from the Falklands, looking resplendent in the sun, albeit with a few telltale rust streaks that spoke of arduous service in a harsh environment. There had been a general feeling of relief at the successful end to the bullying tactics of Argentina, in which so many vulnerable unarmed merchant ships played their part. It was a great climax to an enjoyable West Country weekend.

The Tall Ships race fleet would be gathering in Falmouth from Wednesday the 21st August, ready to start on the following Sunday, and my plan was to arrive by train, whilst James & Fiona were also coming down that day. I have just described the lift to our spirits following the Falklands affair, but we were still fighting the enemy within, and British Rail were on strike. I had promised to be there and was determined to do so; anyway Roland was already down there with his car. Fortunately, I managed to get a booking on a Brymon Airways flight to Newquay, but my next problem was getting to Heathrow. It was a bit like a game where you had to get from A to B without putting your feet on the ground. Somebody from the office took me to nearby Newbury Park station on the Central London Line (the tube was still running), and after a tedious journey, changing to the Picadilly line, I arrived in good time for the departure at seven fifteen pm.

A fine evening with little cloud cover afforded a wonderful view of the rural English countryside passing beneath us; the distance is comparable with London to Paris. At the simple airport (no formalities as it was not an international airport) within a few minutes Roland had collected me and we were driving across the neck of the Cornish peninsula to Falmouth, to arrive on board just as dusk was falling. The next morning we moved berth into the Falmouth Docks, where we were to remain until the start of the race. Beryl was coming down, but I think she was already with James & Fiona - somehow we managed to scrape everybody together, in spite of the difficulties.

The ships were all arriving, and made a fine sight - of course, although it is called "The Tall Ships" race, there are many more participants than just the big square riggers. A size down were various schooners, tops'l schooners (such as "Sir Winston Churchill" and "Malcolm Miller") and a number of yachts - the main qualification being that their crews must consist mainly of young people. A wonderful spirit of international camaraderie is created, as well as a competitive spirit between crews. Although there is a race, this is not the most important aspect of the event.

Early on the Sunday of the start, we slipped out of Falmouth Docks and sailed over to Helford, to collect the Alder family; it was a perfect day and we watched the start under ideal conditions; practically everything that floated in the Falmouth area was out there. Prince Phillip was due to start the race from "HMS Londonderry", sending off the first class at two o' clock, with the last class leaving at three. The other end of the starting line was marked by the newly commissioned Trinity House yacht "Patricia", a state of the art ship which, although still called a "yacht", was very much a working vessel. She is a practical ship, but in my eyes, not as beautiful as her long serving predecessor of the same name.

The Alder family - Garry at "Celandine's" helm.

Sally (shoulder view!), Lucy, Tim and Piers at start of Tall Ships race, Falmouth. They are all accomplished and intrepid sailors.

Many of these voyages contain accounts of frustration with winds that are adverse or lacking in strength, but this trip, in spite of a hiccup, must rank as a fast one with favourable winds - this was by now, after a wonderful summer cruising in the Falmouth area, late August, and the Westerlies had truly set in. Our stalwart Cornishman, Richard White came along, and all three Alder children, Tim Lucy and Piers. Beryl was worried that I had the responsibility of all three children from one family; I was concerned about Tim, the youngest, taking a night watch, but Sally said most emphatically that he would be very upset if he wasn't included in the watchkeeping rota.

So, we set sail from Falmouth in the early afternoon of Wednesday the 18th August with 2 reefs in the mains'l to cope with a strong and squally Northwester that bowled "CELANDINE" along in fine style; the Walker's log streamed astern clocked up mile after mile so that by seven that evening the Eddystone light was already abeam. Later that evening, a moderation of wind strength enabled us to shed one reef, but our progress Eastwards continued at a cracking pace, so that by midday we had the great mass of Portland Bill ahead of us; it is sometimes referred to as Portland Isle, and stands out like an island in the Channel because the low lying Chesil Bank by which it is attached to the Dorset coast is invisible until you are quite near. By half past two it was abeam and our log now totalled just over 109 nautical miles, 24 hours after letting go from Falmouth Marina.

Up till this point in our voyage, the barometer had been rising, but that afternoon, it began to fall and the wind started backing from North West to a more Westerly point, giving us a dead run up Channel. Although the weather remained fine, the wind began to pick up again so that we were running before a lively following sea - never a happy point of sailing in a fore and aft rigged boat. Away on the horizon to the South one or two of the larger square-rigged entrants in the tall ships race could be seen racing before the brisk breeze towards the Needles channel, heading for Southampton; they had sailed from Vigo on the 14th and were making up for time lost in light and contrary winds at the start of the race.

It was possible, with a little stretch of the imagination, to visualise what the Channel must have looked like in the later Victorian era, when the great square-riggers had reached the peak of their development and could still compete with cargo steamers - the space required for coal bunkers, boilers and machinery cut their cargo carrying capacity considerably, whilst their wage bill was not that much lower than that of the sailing ship, by the time you had paid stokers and engineers as well as the seamen. But as machinery efficiency increased, particularly as oil replaced coal and wages rose, sail's future was doomed, just as the diesel engine finally ousted steam as the most efficient form of propulsion in more recent times.

With thoughts such as these, I lulled myself into a snooze below, aware that we were running dead before the wind. The second sense in me said "this vessel is running by the lee" - a dangerous point of sailing where a sudden lurch from a heavy sea can cause an accidental gybe. Lazily, I thought we must gybe her round - but perhaps I could have another five minutes before going on deck. My mental meanderings were rudely terminated by the sound of the boom slamming across with all the strength of the strong wind behind it, and I ejected myself out on deck like a shot from a canon. A quick inspection showed that the port topmast shroud was slack and that the port wooden spreader, holding the stay out to steady the top of the mast, had a break in it. Young Lucy, a most competent helmswoman and seaman, as are all the Alder family, had been at the helm, and was very upset by what had happened. After getting us on a new course, keeping the sail over on that side to avoid putting too much strain on the weakened side, I then did my best to console her.

The fact is, that as captain, you are responsible for the safe passage of your ship in every respect: it applies as much to the master of a yacht as it does of any other ship. I should have been on deck before the accident happened, and not lazily trying to snatch another five minutes zizz. The same is true of the condition of the ship and all her gear - you as master should know that it is in the best possible order, and be aware of any weaknesses. I was now aware that we were no longer 100% seaworthy, therefore a repair should be effected before continuing up-Channel, and started racking my brain about where to get it done in what was to me alien territory. Already, I was going to pass though the Solent and possibly anchor for a rest, perhaps off St Helens, so I had to find somebody within the Solent area. Suddenly, the penny dropped - Lymington marina, which I had used before, is owned by Berthon Boat Company, builders of the famous "Gauntlet" class of cruiser/racers, and where I had seen traditional boats undergoing refit.

It was half past nine and almost dark by the time we berthed, to enjoy a good night's sleep. By half past eight the next morning, the broken spreader was down on deck, and I took it round to the workshops. Most of the workforce was on holiday, but they were very helpful and realised our urgency - the foreman shipwright said he would do it himself, which was lucky for us, he was a craftsman of the very highest order. They had no suitable oak in stock, but we agreed that iroko would do (and is about the same density as oak). Early in the afternoon, an apprentice came round with the new spreader, and a brace and bit "in case you need to ease the holes slightly to make it fit". So perfectly had it been fashioned that it fitted the first time I offered it up, with no further work required. I gave the new wood a coat of "half and half" - 50% turps and varnish mixture to penetrate and protect the wood until the job could be varnished properly. I am quite sure the hourly rate was high, but always I have found that skilled people on high wages will do the job in far less time, and inevitably with poor craftsmen, you will pay out more at the end of the job. Just after 6 in the evening we were underway again.

The wind was still quite fresh from the West, so we kept one reef in the mains'l and soon were ploughing our way steadily Eastwards again, within the relatively sheltered waters of the Solent. I had already reported to Coastguard our departure from Falmouth, and our need to put into Lymington for the repair, so I called them to report that we were now continuing the voyage. This call produced unexpected results - first a call from brother-in-law James aboard "MORAG MHOR" who said he could pick out our distinctive red gaff mains'l (not a very common sight in this area) ahead, and said "I think we should catch you up by the time we are off Cowes, and I'll call you again". Then a call came through from Rob Bassi, skipper of "DUET". "DUET" was a classic yawl built in 1912 and at that time on loan to the Ocean youth club. She was now owned by Christopher Courtauld, who had inherited her from his father, Augustine Courtauld. We had singled her out for a special send off at Falmouth as at that time I was writing her history, 1982 being her seventieth year. "CELANDINE" and "DUET" were both in Ian Brown's yard the previous winter, Duet having received a very major refit at the hands of Ian's team of first class craftsmen, ensuring that she would go on for many more years.

Nearly two hours later, by which time we had No Mans Fort in Spithead abeam, another cheery call came through from James, who said "you must be going faster than I thought, we haven't caught you up, and we are now going to head up Southampton water" With his great rallying cry of "Rule Britannia" we closed our conversation down. He was in his usual ebullient form, but little did I know then that this was to be the last time I was to hear him as a fit man. By Christmas he was a very sick man, and he was gone in February. A remarkable leader and sailor had been taken from us in the prime of his life; larger than life, young people would follow him to the edge of the world, and he was also a supreme ocean racing skipper. It was he and friends who had done a lot of campaigning in the sixties to raise money for the building of Britain's first purpose built sail training ship, the "SIR WINSTON CHURCHILL". He is still remembered, and there is a Trust Fund founded in his memory to provide bursaries for disadvantaged youngsters to enable them to participate in Sail Training.

Our voyage continued, with the barometer now rising again and the wind falling a little lighter; the reef had been taken out and by six the following morning Beachy Head was abeam; twice we had to start the engine for short periods, but the wind never failed us for long and a little after midnight the anchor was splashing down off Stone heaps, Shotley. The following morning, Sunday, we finished the voyage by picking up the mooring in the Walton Channel and getting ashore from the dinghy at the Yacht Club Hard on the early afternoon tide. (Exactly as planned three months earlier, in spite of the setback - Falmouth to Walton in under five days).

MY CAREER AS A FISHERMAN COLLAPSES - AND A FAMILY WEDDING - AT LAST!

THAT autumn saw several local cruises which involved shooting our small beam trawl; I had been claiming that we were the only vessel on the East Coast trawling under sail, but it had to be said that were were not catching very much - Beryl was unkind enough to say that if we were dependent on my fishing efforts, we would have starved. More successful than fishing were the autumn trips with Beryl, gathering blackberries, sloes - and firewood. Walking along the shore, we would always take buckets and fill them with any pieces of firewood that we found, to supplement our supplies of coal and anthracite - there is great satisfaction in obtaining something useful for free. I remember once, with "CAMPION" anchoring in the Colne off a beach over which the Brightlingsea branch line ran on a low wooden trestle bridge - you could duck under the lines and stick your head up between them. The service was still being operated by a "push me - pull you" steam engine of ancient vintage which we had encountered when I first bought "CAMPION" in 1947; such was the state of this wooden structure that the drivers clearly had orders to proceed at walking pace. They would approach at full speed (probably about twenty miles an hour) and suddenly slow down. When we went ashore to gather firewood, we quickly found a rich seam of coal which probably fell off the bunker as the engine slowed down. We were thrilled to stoke up for the night on free coal, but the next morning our decks and coachroof were covered in black bits - someone described it as British Rail anti-personnel coal.

This particular autumn, after a singularly unsuccessful fishing expedition, some wag (I suspect George Jones) wrote in the log - "net catch - back ache". Without winches with which to haul in the net, it was hard work, and I think there was no more trawling after that - I was approaching my sixtieth birthday and finding it very heavy work, particularly if the main catch was weed. The net was retired to less arduous work and was usually employed to drape on a garage wall with fairy lights when there was a barbecue in our garden for a local charity or organisation.

That December, Roland was married in the country church of Hutton, which was next door to his bride's home. We breathed a great sigh of relief - he was by then over thirty one and we had begun to think of him as a permanent bachelor; the answer was that he had waited a long time for the right girl, and in Louise, a farmer's daughter, he had at last found her.

At the end of 1982, Beryl was approached by Timothy Raison, Minister of State at the Home Office, and asked if she would become chairman of the Equal Opportunities Commission; her reponse was that she was certainly not "womens' lib" However, Willie Whitelaw, then Home Secretary discussed it in depth - the job would demand not less saw her and pressed the case - she was the only candidate they had in mind - he was charming and persuasive. We both discussed the difficulties - the offices were in Manchester, where she would have to spend quite a bit of time each week, and she was expected to assume the Chairmanship of Essex County Council early the following year. Something said years back by Christian Berridge, then Clerk to the County Council and a neighbour in Writtle came to both our minds. Beryl was then representing Writtle on the Chelmsford Rural District Council, and he said "You should widen your horizons and think of the County of Essex, not just your parish". That fixed it - giving up Essex was a great wrench, but this was a National matter. She would be given a three year contract with an option for a further two and would have to become strictly non-political during her term of office.

It was to prove a very daunting five years, and to start with she had an uphill struggle with some of the militant feminist members of the staff, because that was not the way Beryl works - her policy is persuasion rather than confrontation (unless all else fails). Some of the left wing press were less than kind - a woman columnist in the "Guardian" complained after an interview "Silly woman - she is offered a very important highly paid job and is worried about not being able to cook her husband's supper" - her response being "Well. I did". The task was such that she had to stand down at the next County Council election and give up the Chairmanship - her fellow councillors were very understanding and found another Chairman-elect, although they had offered to "carry" her, but this would have been unfair to the electorate.

75TH ANNIVERSARY OF THE CA. - AND THEN TO HONFLEUR.

1983 was the 75th anniversary of the founding of the Cruising Association, and was to be marked by a major rally at the new Brighton marina, so just after midnight on Saturday the 14th of May, we left the quay at Ian Brown's yard and picked up a mooring in the Pyefleet for a few hours - soon after seven we were away on another long haul through my least favourite stretch of water. Vicky came as crew, with her boy friend Rhodri Davies, who was very athletic, but not done much sailing. Our trip was the not unfamiliar mix of passagemaking - one reef down for a stiff Easterly wind to start with, then shaking it out and finishing with a brief period under power before the wind picked up from the East again; what a joy to be passing Dover in bright daylight, but progress slowed, and by the time Dungeness was abeam, it was completely dark - actually I think it looks better like that, when all you can see is the light, which by now was accompanied by lights on the new nuclear power station close by. It is another milestone passed.

At half past two that morning we had another of our ghostly encounters with a yacht sailing without lights. A momentary flash of a torch on his sails warned us of his presence, but it was not long enough to determine his heading so we altered course away from the hazard. Although we were now crossing Rye Bay, which is not so busy, I still cannot understand anyone undertaking a night passage without lights - if anything happened to you, provided you lived to tell the tale, you would be in the wrong. We were going through one of our motoring sessions at the time, so were displaying a clear white "masthead" steaming light as well as port and starboard, therefore giving them a clear indication of our heading. At the unnattractive hour of four Beachy Head was abeam, and the very first light of day beginning to apear; by this time we were slipping quietly along before a light Northeasterly wind in a calm sea. The barometer was now falling, and as it became lighter, the gathering rainclouds could be seen.

A thunderstorm to the Southeast gave a spectacular display, and before long heavy rain was falling. The wind disappeared, and at ten that morning, we lowered our idle sails and prepared to enter the marina. Unable to raise any response on radio, we entered and picked a visitor's berth - at that time there were plenty. The weather improved, and the whole place began to look better - of course, everything was pretty smart and new at that time. The trip had been a relatively uneventful one, and had taken only just over 24 hours from the Colne. Rhodri must have had a favourable impression - the following year they were married, and now together make a very fine cruising team with their own boat and three children. Both our children were late starters in this marriage business, but have made up for it with three children each. Later on Sunday, they both left to return to London whilst I was staying the night to return home the next day. Before they left, I heard a slight scuffle and splash, and Vicky presented me with a fat whiting she had just caught with her hands -"here's your supper" I'm really not sure that you should really do that in a posh

Members of the Writtle Sailing Club in an exposed position off the Normandy coast. L to R - John Aldridge, "Thatch" Rose, Geoff Smeed, Bald Rose.

place like this, but what do you expect from Essex sailors?

The Bank holiday weekend at the end of May was spent in various social events; it was not warm, and Beryl said she would like the stove alight. Could we really light our stove here and belch out smoke in this smart marina, where they might expect yachts to have more sophisticated means of heating? Beryl announced that if I didn't, she would move into the toilet blocks which were warm and luxurious - the stove was lit, and we had a number of visitors from neighbouring boats to share the luxurious dry warmth, with no criticism of the smoke.

A week later "CELANDINE" slipped out of Brighton marina bound for the Normandy coast. A high and rising barometer gave hopes of fine weather for the planned week's cruise - as companions for this trip I had Geoff Smeed and Michael "thatch" Rose; we had met on the Friday evening in the buffet at Victoria Station. The idea was to first slip across to Ouistreham, at the mouth of the River Orne which is canalised to enable ships to reach Caen, and leaving on Saturday afternoon we hoped a night passage would bring us to the Calvados coast by Sunday morning. A night of fickle winds and thunderstorms gave us a slow passage, but the winds were either from North or East, so they were taking us in the right direction. At one time during the night in one of the thunderstorms we were passed by the P & O ferry "LEOPARD", sailing at that time between Southampton and Le Havre. Her lights gave a clear indication of course, and the deck lights showed brightly; I was   fairly sure it was one of the two ships on this run, but when she was quite near a prolonged display of lightning illuminated the blue hulled vessel as if it was daylight.

Finally, it was after 11 in the morning before we secured to a pile mooring; it was low water and would be sometime before we could proceed up the canal, through the famous "Pegasus" bridge and on to Caen. We were on the extreme Eastern flank of the D-day beaches, well to the East of where I had last visited this coast under somewhat different circumstances, in LCT 879. The sun came out, but over lunch we decided, Ouistreham lacked any charms nor did we like the prospect of a long wait to enter the canal towards high water; instead we would take the afternoon flood tide towards the Seine Estuary and slip into Honfleur a day or so earlier than planned.

Winds were light and from an Easterly direction, but a strong tide flooding into the Seine Estuary helped us along past the sunlit coast with the former fishing ports of Dives, Trouville and Deauville, now holiday resorts, and the well wooded Cote de Grace. It was very pleasant, but Honfleur had to be reached before high water because at low water the outer harbour was little more than a muddy ditch, so sails were stowed and we motored on at full speed, to reach the outer harbour just before seven, awaiting the opening of the bridge and gate into the Vieux Bassin. Once in, the harbourmaster directed us to the quay outside the

Vieux Lieutenance, once part of the fortifications, but now housing the harbour master's office. It seems that in his eyes we did not really look like a yacht - indeed, like many others, he did not know what to make of her, and put "CELANDINE" alongside the place designated for fishing boats. Being a fine Sunday evening, the world and his wife were promenading along the waterfront.

The next day, Monday June the 6th and the 39th anniversary of D-day, the crowds had gone and we were able to explore the ancient town in peace, do some re-provisioning, and find somewhere to have dinner that evening. Eschewing the obvious cafes along the tourist trail, we found a small restaurant attached to a commercial or family hotel at the back of the town, and returned that evening to a splendid meal which included soupe de poissons in a great tureen from which we helped ourselves. Years later, on subsequent visits I have searched for this cosy establishment in vain - it seems that it is no more. The

"Celandine" alongside at Honfleur, outside the Vieux Lieutenance.

following day, we sailed North across the Seine estuary past a buoy that in later years was to become like an old friend - the "DUNCAN L CLINCH", marking the wartime wreck of what I assume must have been an American Liberty ship. Rich Americans gave money to sponsor the building of ships to aid the war effort, and would ask for them to be named after a loved one, or perhaps a son who perished in the conflict.

That evening, we berthed in Fecamp. It lacks the charm of Honfleur, but the local yacht club was welcoming - they were shortly locking up, so gave us the keys to help ourselves to showers, and requested that after locking up, we put them through the letterbox. The next morning we were off Northwards again in superb conditions, with a gentle Southerly wind pushing us along past the steep cliffs - "Falaises" - which make a spectacular coastline all the way to Dieppe, entering early in the afternoon, to lie alongside a waiting pontoon before locking in to the Bassin Dusquesne. There was some scend coming in, in spite of the calm weather, and if ever a demonstration of the enormous rise and fall of tide near the Seine estuary and surrounding areas was needed, we had it here. At low water, our crosstrees were level with the top of the quay, whereas towards high water when it was time to lock in, our deck was almost level with the top of the wall. It was a long climb up the ladder at low water, to report to the capitainerie; even more exciting was when the ferry from Newhaven arrived to berth alongside the quay Henri IV. The ship was turned round almost opposite our temporary berth before going stern first in to the car loading ramp - of course, there was room - but not too much!

It was ten o'clock that night before we secured in the Bassin, but we did have the following morning to explore the town. Dieppe is an ancient town; full of character, and some of the shops in the main street would not have looked out of place in a smart Parisian street. On the quay, the fishwives were selling the previous night's catch, whilst along the quay Henri IV were many ancient buildings of great character - somewhat spoilt by the numerous ugly buildings housing offices of the ferry service and railway.

Another long sail that afternoon took us to Boulogne; the Falaises gradually gave way to the low lying marshland of the Somme Estuary; the wind was a good force 4 from West-southwest, and "CELANDINE" bowled along past this now rather less interesting coast. It was a long hop, and it was half past ten at night before we secured alongside a vacant pontoon in the somewhat inadequate provision for yachts in Boulogne. It is quite a pleasant town once you are away from the port area, but we were off again early the next morning, following the ferry "VORTIGERN" out of the harbour; there was little wind and visibility poor in variable patches of mist or fog - but this was the Dover Strait. Before sailing, we had heard the results of the General Election in the UK - there is no record of who won, but it must have been satisfactory as far as we were concerned as there is a note in the log, after anchoring in the Pyefleet at eleven that night that a bottle of champagne was broached - such extravagant consumption of stores has to be recorded. At midnight we settled down to eat, finally crawling in to our bunks at two in the morning. Our week was ending, and the next day, Saturday, with a brisk Southwesterly we slipped round to the Walton backwaters - on our way in, I made a link call home via Orfordness radio, and Beryl was able to meet us with the car when we landed at the Walton & Frinton Yacht Club hard.

AN ASSIGNATION IN ROOM 504 - AND I IMPROVE MY AMERICAN VOCABULARY

A FEW days later I was saying goodbye to Beryl at Heathrow, boarding a flight for New York, while she was leaving within the hour on a flight to Toronto, where she would be speaking to a meeting of the Canadian School Trustees' Association - she was beginning to appear as a star speaker with them. There was a crazy arrangement to meet each other in the hotel bedroom for a cold lunch the following

Monday; when you consider what could have gone wrong, it was not a very good idea.

Some people in New York wanted to discuss with us the possibility of making mattress protectors in the UK for distribution in Europe, and as I was coming out anyway, it seemed an ideal opportunity to meet them. I can't remember where I stayed, but almost certainly it was at the airport Holiday Inn, as I had done in 1976 - cheap and unexciting, but perfectly adequate. There was a regular bus service into the City centre which did not cost a bomb - dollars were still not cheap, although on our French trip a few days earlier we were getting 12 francs to the pound, but it was important to keep down the costs of this trip to our family business.

Dropping off the bus at Grand Central Station, I had a half an hour to spare, so went in to a snack bar for a coffee. Here I received a lesson in American vocabulary as people called in and ordered breakfast; in particular I heard fried egg language - "runnyside, sunnyside up" or - "easy over" particularly come to mind. I duly met the people with the business proposition; they had contacted us because they had found we were the only people in the UK with the ultrasonic quilting machine which would quilt the materials for mattress protectors. It did not take me long to decide I did not like these people; when they sensed this and may be read my thoughts, started issuing veiled warnings that they had a patent on these articles and would vigorously pursue anyone trying to infringe the patent. After parting company, I did a quick tour of New York stores, including Macy's, to see what was selling in this line, and was able to buy one of the very type that we had been discussing; being bulky it would be a bit of a pest to pack, but I had left room for samples.

As soon as I was back in the office, I was in touch with our patent agents who discovered that the patent only covered their method of making the corner fastenings - we weren't going to make them that way in any case, as I think we had a better method. The final word from our patent agents was that the patent did not cover the UK or Europe anyway. Once again, the professionals had earnt their fee!

The next day, Saturday, I flew from JFK to Washington Dulles airport, where my former neighbours in Writtle, the Devlins met me and took me to Hill House, their purpose built house on top of the hill at their 40 acre plot in the Virginian countryside; the stream running round the property was inhabited by turtles. The Union Flag was flying from their flagpole, the weather was superb and I had a wonderful weekend with them. That evening I went to a dinner at which Johnnie was speaking to "The Daughters of the 1812", a rather up market version of the "Daughters of the Revolution". It seems that we had another spat with our former colonies in 1812, but I am weak on the history of this one. I would compare these organisations with the WI in the UK; there is absolutely no hostility about these long forgotten events and we encountered the customary American hospitality. Johnnie started his speech with the sound of church bells played on a small concealed tape recorder - they were certainly not the chimes of Westminster, but I was ashamed that I did not recognise them - they were the bells of Writtle Church. His talk was really about life in an English village, and I am sure they found it as entertaining as I did. Johnnie, as well as having been a sailing companion, was also my fellow founder of the Writtle Society, so he did know something of village life, and was a good raconteur. In spite of becoming an American citizen, he still has the precise clipped accent of a British Naval Officer.

The next day being Sunday, I went to their local Episcopalian Church, where he was by now the equivalent of a Parochial Church Council member. After church, we went for drinks with friends; life out in this part of Virginia is very much colonial style, and many of the people I met were British expatriates, who, perhaps, also found the tax regime somewhat kinder than was the case in the UK at that time, and Johnnie and Peggy had the added draw of two daughters out there. Of course, the weather suits this outdoor entertaining except during a relatively brief winter - which can be quite harsh. Johnnie and Peggy had both acquired US citizenship, and he was doing some selling in real estate (a realtor?).

On Monday morning, they dropped me at the airport and I flew to Toronto, where I arrived bang on ETA at room 504 in the Royal York Hotel (Beryl assures me it was this room number!) for our cold lunch together in a very spacious and comfortable room. I liked Toronto, a lakeside town with attractive park-like offshore islands. The waterfront is attractive, and to add to the pleasure, the replica of "BLUENOSE", one of the famous Grand Banks schooners, was alongside. Those schooners were superb sailing vessels whose decks carried stacks of dories which were launched over the side when the fishing grounds were reached, and the fishermen fished from them with hook and line. The Grand Banks were notorious for fog and abundant supplies of cod. In recent, times the cod fishery has been completely closed because the stocks were being fished to extinction by modern fishing techniques. If they had stuck to the schooners and fishing with lines, perhaps the cod would have had a better chance.

As well as "BLUENOSE", there were many large seagoing freighters to be seen in the docks area, and when you look at the map of Canada and see just how far inland Toronto lies, this is quite remarkable - all due to the St Lawrence seaway. From Toronto, on a clear day, you can look across the lake and see the shores of New York State. Another canal, the Welland, enables large vessels to reach Lake Erie without having to negotiate Niagara Falls - the only people to have done this have always done it downhill, usually in a barrel or similar vessel; I understand the loss ratio is quite high.

After dining with friends that evening, we left Toronto the next morning by bus, to Niagara. The view from the Canadian side is, I am told, the best, and this is what we saw. From our bedroom balcony in the Fox Sheraton hotel (comfortable and adequate, but coming under my designation of "broiler" hotels) we could see the falls (you paid extra for this!) and when we looked out in the middle of the night at this remarkable sight, I observed "they don't turn it off at night". I am glad we went, and have to say the gardens along the front overlooking the river were attractive. But it is a tourist resort, catering largely for honeymoon couples and others that aren't, bordering on my definition of "honky tonk". The next day a public bus took us to Buffalo, across the US border, where there was supposed to be a hire car ready for us. I can't remember which company it was, but they were not properly organised and we transferred our attentions to another who might have a return car shortly. We decided to fly on to Albany, and this company were helpful in that they booked a car to await our arrival there - this was Avis, and I have tended to use them ever since. The weather was good, and we had a good view of the scene passing below, which included the "Finger Lakes"

First, we stayed the night in Williamstown, at the Colonial style hotel with snap-in plastic Georgian glazing bars, first visited on my previous visit to the makers of our ultrasonic plant. After paying them a visit, at North Adams, to get the latest up dates on the equipment, we headed North into Vermont. Of course, the time to go is in the Fall, but it was still very scenic with the trees verdant in their high summer foliage. At a cafe called "The Hundred Mile View" - I don't know whether this was 50 miles in each direction or a hundred miles in one only, but it was outstanding, and here we felt that waffles and maple syrup must be tried. They are very popular, but too sweet and sticky for my taste, at least we had tried them in the very heartland, so to speak.

Moving nearer the coast, we crossed into New Hampshire, where English place names abound, very often repeated not so far away, but the early settlers were limited by poor transport conditions, and they must have been very homesick at times, so not for nothing are these states known as "New England". We stayed at some quite strange places

- no forward bookings and we had to take pot luck; on a previous visit to New England we had been to a town called Essex, I think in New Jersey, and on the coast, but here we found another, and stayed the night in an apartment full of antique furniture, in a house of character that hired the rooms out - no catering on offer. It overlooked a tidal creek so like the creeks and saltings of Essex, we felt quite at home.

At Boston, we met our friend Juliette Tomlinson, curator of the William Pynchon Museum in Springfield, Mass., who invited us to stay at her ladies' club, which catered for married couples. It was very comfortable, and I was relieved to find I was not the only male of the species staying there. The usual attractions were visited - The Quincy Market, and most interesting to me, the USS "CONSTITUTION", a formidable fighting ship in its day. The highlight of this trip was an evening visit to the ball game. Juliette was an enthusiastic, if not frenetic, supporter of the Redsox; she was a regular, and so had good seats. The game is, of course akin to our much simpler game of rounders, but this has so many clever tactics that I became fascinated, even though I have never been very interested in most of the ball games that any decent Englishman is supposed to enthuse over. What also fascinated me was the family atmosphere, which made a well behaved, but enthusiastic and vociferous crowd, of which Juliette was one of the loudest - a totally different side to this austere and learned historian who also was a lay reader in the Episcopalian Church.

From Boston, we flew back to London on a BA flight; we normally fly what the airlines would class as "economy", although they have various ways of making this sound more exciting - we call it "baggage class" - but on this occasion we were offered an upgrade to whatever they were calling the better class at the time - "Club", or "Executive". It is the only time (apart from the short haul flight a few years earlier from New York to Charlotte, when they apologetically had to put me and my colleague in first class) that we have ever had an upgrade, and we made the most of it!

On arrival home we learnt that my dear friend George Jones had died - on the very day that we flew out across the Atlantic. A lovable and at times infuriating character, we had remained great friends throughout, bonded by a common love of boats and the sea, and the East coast waters. Originally he had set up a yacht broking business in Woodbridge, East Coast Yacht Agency, which was very successful but gave him something of a dilemma when his aunts, the Misses Jones of Newney Hall just outside Writtle, bequeathed him the Hall with attached farm. Newney had been in the Jones family for many years, and he felt he should keep it in the family, but was very attached to Woodbridge and the yacht broking firm he had founded. He finally sold the yacht broking business and moved in to Newney, where the farm had lost so much land by compulsory purchase for council house building that it was not really an economic proposition; it was not the only farm in Writtle to have suffered such a fate. The family decided they could not really keep "PETER DUCK" going, and she had to be sold, although she is now back in the family after many years, during which she voyaged to the Baltic and visited Russia.

Among the many enthusiasms which George had was that when Drake and Frost, the boatbuilders in Tollesbury who we dropped from the tendering to build "CELANDINE", came on the market, he wanted me to go in with him to develop it into a yacht harbour. It would have involved selling up the business and re-investing the capital; in spite of his enthusiasm, I was rather lukewarm, and about this time I saw Maurice Griffiths on a social visit. His advice, as on a previous occasion, was very sound - "Keep boating as your hobby, there is a danger of it turning you sour if you become involved professionally, and you certainly wouldn't have the time to do as much of it yourself; to get rid of a successful business and put your money into an unknown venture could be a disaster". His view reinforced my lack of enthusiasm for the idea. And now George, with his endless energy and enthusiasms was gone; Roland went to his funeral on my behalf as he knew how much I would mourn his loss.

THE LONDON RIVER AGAIN

T HAT autumn, "CELANDINE" was away to London again to participate in a further round of celebrations marking the 75th anniversary of the CA. A force four Southeast wind sped her through the Wallet off the Walton and Clacton coast and through the Spitway at near low water, but being neap tides we had a comfortable depth to see us through, even though we had to put in a few tacks to bring us into the deeper waters of the Swin. Once in the Swin, the ancient channel for smaller vessels to come into the Thames, we were able to ease our sheets and bear away. Having slipped the mooring at Walton at 8 in the morning, we anchored for the night in the Lower Hope near the aptly named buoy, Mucking No 7, just before 7 in the evening, as the light began to fail (it was now October).

From here, it seems we took things very gently as we did not get underweigh until the following afternoon, passing through the now fully operational Thames Barrier, under power. After passing from the Eastern hemisphere into the Western, we anchored for the night off Wren's masterpiece at Greenwich - this time, our anchor held first time as opposed to our first visit when we could not get it to grip on a rocky bottom. This stop was dictated by the fact that we could not lock into St Katharine's till late the following morning - the hours for entering are very restricted. It did mean we had the pleasure of waking up to the magnificent scene of The Royal Naval College, the Queen's House and the sweep of grass up to the Old Greenwich observatory, all bathed in the early morning autumn sunlight. The Thames below London is a strange mixture of old buildings such as these masterpieces, derelict wharves and industrial sites, interspersed with modern developments which vary from attractive and sympathetic to awful. Much regeneration had taken place since our previous trip up river six years earlier.

A fortnight later, the benign weather had been replaced by strong winds and frequent rain; the scene as we locked out early Saturday morning was grey and damp. Once again, we passed back into the Eastern hemisphere, and through the Barrier. As we reached the lower reaches, the Southerly wind was vicious, the barometer stood very low, and Thames Coastguard warned of force 8 winds. I anchored close into the Kent shore downstream of Gravesend and veered plenty of our heavy half-inch chain. Soon after we had anchored, DUET came downriver and anchored nearby, having also come out of St Katharine Dock a little later than us. On the early afternoon shipping forecast, there was a barometric pressure difference of over one inch from the South Coast to Scotland, and a little later the Coastguards were reporting windspeeds of up to 50 knots. At half past five they reported their anemometer had broken, but they estimated that it was now storm force 10.

Talking to DUET over the radio, Rob Bassi reported he was going to stay put, as he was expecting a new crew and would be able to get them aboard at Gravesend. I was weighing up the prospects - I like a fair wind, but at the strengths we were experiencing and were being forecast for the next few hours, it would have been foolhardy to venture into the outer Estuary among the many sandbanks, and the Spitway, through which we had to pass on our voyage North would be a mass of broken water, even at high tide - it is only a shallow gateway through to the North Essex coast. "CELANDINE" had to be left somewhere safe, as we all had to get back to work, and there was nowhere other than St Katharines at that time.

Later that evening, we watched a large bulk carrier trying to come head to wind in order to anchor, and it took a long time and a lot of power to finally persuade the ship's head round enough to drop the anchor. At about this time I made my mind up - we would get under weigh before light the following morning and lock back into the dock on the morning tide, so at 5-30, we were getting our anchor and off into the darkness upriver again, locking in to

St Katharine's by quarter to ten, close on high water.

Due to the setback caused by the exceptionally strong winds of mid-October, the return to Essex waters and Ian Brown's yard, was rolled into our end of season cruise, so on the Friday evening a fortnight later, we slipped out of St Katharine Dock. Once again, we were in darkness before getting very far downriver, and anchored in the Lower Hope not far from our anchorage of a fortnight earlier, but with much better weather conditions and a wind from the Northwest. The next day, starting at first light, we got the tides right and just as darkness was falling were anchoring off Stone Heaps, Shotley. Because we had a few days cruising ahead of us, I needed to refuel since the London trip always involves a lot of time under power, and the obvious and nearest place to get fuel was the new marina at Levington - Suffolk Yacht Harbour. Here, as well as taking on 22 gallons of fuel, we embarked Geoff Smeed who had come over from his house in Orford.

This was a brief stop for fuel, but I did begin to use this new facility, particularly when crew changing, as the proximity to the main road from London - by this time, the Orwell Bridge was in use - and the convenience of berthing alongside did make the operation a lot easier. When we had sailed past in earlier years, we all shook our heads as construction proceeded, and said "they'll never keep that entrance open - it can't survive". I suppose there had been a certain amount of anti-marina feeling behind our earlier disparaging comments, particularly as I for one, liked the solitude once you got out to your swinging mooring. But already, one could see that such places had to come in order to cope with the yachting explosion. If you imagine the swinging circle required by a boat on a mooring, there would simply not be enough room to accommodate the thousands of production boats that were by then filling our rivers and creeks. A berth alongside is not good news for a wooden boat, however, as one side will always face the sun so that the planking is likely to open up on that side; at least on a swinging mooring there is a reasonable chance that no one side will be exposed to the sun's rays for too long.

The harbour at Levington had been created out of some long flooded pasture land by digging out and building up the old ruined sea wall with the soil. Digging holes is easy, but getting rid of the proceeds is another matter and can be very expensive. Some marinas built about this time (in particular Brighton, where the CA 75th anniversary had been held that spring) suffered from impossible construction costs - it really was built out into the open waters of the Channel, and although a masterpiece of engineering achievement, the cost could not be justified commercially. After a number of financial failures which no doubt left banks and other financial organisations picking up a nasty cold, it settled when it changed hands at a price compatible with what it could be expected to receive in revenues. That at Levington was started on a modest scale, and successfully built up step by step. Finally we berthed in our winter quarters at Rowhedge, having had an enjoyable autumn cruise back to our native waters; at this time of the year the solid fuel stove was a boon in keeping everything warm and dry below. Crew had come and gone, but Michael (Bald) Rose had been with us from London, also Bill Gordon, at that time a neighbour in Writtle. Michael's daughter, Nicky, had been a member of the crew on the upriver trip.

KEVLAR, ULTRA VIOLET DEGRADATION, HOLLAND AGAIN AND ANOTHER WEDDING

AT about this time, I was introduced to this remarkable fibre, developed from nylon, and capable of producing fabric of outstanding strength. Our firm in Dagenham had been approached by a company developing bulletproof clothing, and they had tried in vain to find a firm that could stitch multiple layers together. They wanted up to 11 layers stitched together, and for this I designed a large demountable frame capable of feeding up to 11 heavy rolls of this material in to a machine normally capable of handling not more than three rolls at a time - the device was little more than ironmongery, but it worked well. The toughness of such a combination presented a problem with the stitching, but we found a certain type of ball point needle that penetrated it with surprising ease. The resultant laminate was capable of stopping a bullet at a given muzzle velocity from a gun at a certain distance - there was no such thing as complete protection, but it would reduce most direct hits to a case of severe bruising or a broken rib, which is preferable to being dead.

As with everything in this world, you don't get something for nothing, and Kevlar was no exception. Of course, it was very expensive, and it had one serious drawback - ultra violet degradation. This has long been a hobby horse of mine, because in the marine environment there is a lot of it about - colours fade, plastics embrittle, and unprotected fair skinned people go a painful bright red before they blister. There was an apocryphal story circulating at about this time, that a tailor working at the experimental establishment in Colchester barracks left a sheet of Kevlar on his cutting table to go to lunch, leaving his big cutting out shears on top of the Kevlar. When he came back after lunch, the sheet had discoloured badly - except under the shears, where the fabric remained its original colour in their outline. So sensitive to ultra violet light was this wonder material, that every evening when the machine was stopped with its multiplicity of fabric rolls, the whole thing had to be covered in black polythene to shield it from morning and evening sunlight.

Kevlar began to be used in reinforcing yacht sails, and although I am sure they were aware of its rapid deterioration in sunlight, I still wonder whether it is practical to overcome this in the marine environment; I have lost touch with it, but they may have overcome some of the problem by introducing modifications to the fibre. As I write some eighteen years later, I read that Kevlar is being used to line the fuel tanks of Concorde to prevent the massive fuel leakage that caused the destruction of a Concorde on take off. In such an application, ultra violet light would not be a problem.

The marine lesson from all this is to watch for ultra violet degradation in sails, ropes, and indeed plastic fittings. Nylon is prone to this problem, but polyester very much less so; I can remember being shocked when the lifeline on a lifebuoy snapped in my hands - I replaced it with polyester. Orange coloured items are very sensitive, and the first of the new breed of mooring buoys I had when changing to the much despised rope pennant system of mooring was a bright orange; within two seasons, the plastic was deteriorating badly, but changing to a more subdued yellow colour made a lot of difference to their durability. The most durable and protective colour is black - motor car tyre manufacturers found this out a long time ago - ever seen a car with orange tyres?

In any year with limited time, we tended to choose Holland and revisit some of our favourite ports of call; this would work quite well as a neighbour had decided to take his new 31 footer from a famous yard on the South Coast to Holland. It was suggested that we accompany him across the North Sea to Den Helder, and whilst this seemed a good idea in theory, I did point out that the North Sea is very big, and keeping together on this long crossing would not be easy. A bright sunny morning in early July found us hove to off

Harwich to make our planned rendezvous with Bob Rowan in "CLEARWAYS", with whom we were already in radio contact. A light Southerly wind suited our agreed course for Den Helder, and soon both boats were sailing quietly towards Holland; fortunately, in the prevailing wind, the boat speeds were similar.

However, there was a problem. Both having confirmed we were on the agreed course, it was quite obvious they were not heading in the same direction, and "CELANDINE" was pointing almost ten degrees South of "CLEARWAYS" heading. Hurried consultations over the radio queried when "CELANDINE" had last been swung, and this was certainly some years ago, but on the other hand there had been no alterations carried out which would affect the compass, and we had a deviation card which showed no significant deviation on any point. I should have asked what their deviation card showed, but this didn't occur to me at the time - and after all it was a new boat from one of our leading builders, so I was worried. I always made little tests at the beginning of a season to make sure an object ahead was where the compass said it should be, and there was also the hand bearing compass on our radio direction finder, which agreed with the main compass.

The two boats were still in sight of each other when the wind began to fail (remember Platt's cynical view that a fair wind will always fail), and we mutually agreed over the radio to start engines and proceed at five knots. Soon after this, an all enveloping fog began to descend, but I had obtained a good departure point from the Shipwash light vessel, where the log was streamed; it is important on such a trip to know exactly where you are starting from, and the further out on your passage this is, the better. Of course, with the advent of fog, both boats were now obscured from each other, and we ploughed on independently whilst maintaining radio contact. Soon after darkness fell, "CLEARWAYS" called us up, and in the background was a most terrible screaming noise - it was the overheating alarm on their engine, and they announced they were shutting it down to cool off. I made a few enquiries to try and help - but being a new boat they were not too familiar with her; there was uncertainty as to whether the beast was direct salt water cooled, or indirect cooled as with "CELANDINE" which had closed circuit freshwater cooling, cooled by a heat exchanger fed from external salt water. The next enquiry was "can you smell hot paint, and does it feel hot?" On hearing "no", my crew (John Aldridge and the two Mike Roses), not always renowned for refined language yelled out in unison while I was speaking into the microphone - "tell them to cut the bloody wires", since it was becoming obvious that this was a fault in the alarm rather than the engine. We agreed to heave to while they allowed the engine to cool, although I was not happy about being stopped in this fog enshrouded world of our own on a glassy North Sea swell. After nearly two hours of inactivity, I called them up to find out how they were faring, but was horrified to get no reponse. What had happened to them - was the alarm part of an ongoing electrical breakdown which had now spread to the radio, or had they been run down?

Whatever the answer, I was not prepared to have us any longer in this hazardous situation, and we resumed course and speed. Later in the night, another attempt was made to call "CLEARWAYS", but still there was no response. At first light, a pleasant sailing breeze returned from the South, and the fog dispersed to no more than a mist; as the light improved we sighted the oil rig "BERYL C" which was marked on the chart as a little way South of our track - it was a good feeling to have the estimated position confirmed, particularly after the time spent wallowing in the fog. It was developing into a beautiful morning, and "CELANDINE" was once again striding along under sail, but we all had this nagging worry - what had happened to "CLEARWAYS"? It was a great relief when they called us a short while later and explained that their batteries were very low so they had turned off their radio. In fact, a modern radio only takes a minimal amount of current and it would not have made any difference, particularly once the engine was running again. It would have been reassuring to have heard from them - in any case, after a short time, they had restarted their engine and were underweigh again while we remained hove to. Our postion was queried, but as it was very obvious where we were - the oil rig displayed its name in very large lettering, and it became apparent that their compass had led them too far to the North of our agreed track, which was laid to clear the Southern tip of an offshore bank. Although they were obviously well ahead, in order to clear the bank they had to put in a dog leg punching into an unfavourable tide. Sighting them just before noon, the two boats then headed towards the Den Helder entrance within sight of each other again; they wanted to visit Texel whereas we were heading South for Amsterdam, so we parted company at that point.

At Den Helder, there was some kind of Dutch Navy week in progress - den Helder is the principal Dutch Naval port; at sunset we were careful to lower our ensign exactly in time with the senior Dutch Naval ship, and the same routine was observed in the morning, but with a loud blast of *"Rule Britannia"* coming from our tape recorder. From Den Helder we sailed to the locks at Den Oever, at the Eastern end of the great dam enclosing the Isselmeer (before its construction, it was the "Zuyder Zee"), to Medemblik, where we met up with "CLEARWAYS" again. An entry in the log reads "first trees since Thorpe le Soken". The wag who entered this was not really making a great statement - there are few trees between Thorpe le Soken and Den Helder, but in a flat windswept landscape, largely reclaimed from the sea, there are not so many trees except where planted in sheltered urban areas, nevertheless, there are also areas such as reclaimed marsh in the Veersemeer area, which we first saw some twenty years earlier soon after it had been tamed from the turbulent tidal "gat" to a tranquil meer, where trees were by now maturing in large areas designated as nature reserves. It is greatly to their credit that some of this land won from the sea at such great price has been thus designated.

Our cruise was to be of a week's duration, leaving the boat in Holland, but in this time we packed in visits to Hindeloopen, Enkhuizen with its twin "Dromedary" towers, Hoorn and then Muiden at the Southern end of the Isselmeer, where the Royal Netherlands Yacht Club has its clubhouse. Finally, we secured "CELANDINE" in the Sixhaven and entrained at Amsterdam Central station to the Hook of Holland; having crossed by night many times on both business and pleasure, this time we made a day crossing to Harwich in one of the Dutch boats. The four of us had a lengthy lunch aboard which took up a fair amount of the six hour crossing, at the end of which entrained to Chelmsford - all four of us were, of course, members of the "Writtle Sailing Club" - you've never heard of it? Neither has anyone else, but on a boat they were the creme de la creme.

From despairing of ever seeing our children married, within less than two years, Vicky announced that she and Rhodri were going to marry - it seems this was getting contagious in the family, although, of course, there were no more after this pair to catch on to the idea. Vicky, as the daughter of a peer and a Commander of the British Empire, had several options available, but to our great delight, she wanted to be married in Writtle church - after all, she was a native of the place. Beryl was by now spending three days a week in Manchester and often further days away on Equal Opportunities business, but with the help of many good friends, all the arrangements were made.

I was thrilled to be giving my daughter away in our own Parish Church, but I'm sure Vicky will forgive me for revealing that I had private worries about taking her to the altar in patched jeans (her, not me!), but that it would not matter (I said to myself). When she showed us sketches of the wedding dress she was having made, we need not have worried, it was a wonderful romantic and demure dress - what father would not be delighted to have taken his daughter up the aisle in this style. Although we had used marquees in our garden for some happy occasions, it was quite obvious as the size of the guest list grew, that we could only get it all in our garden by demolishing a number of trees, including apple trees that contributed to the Platt diet. Anyway, the garden would have to be immaculate - in the middle of the sailing season!

The answer lay in having the reception at the "Writz". This establishment is the refectory of Writtle Agricultural College (now known as Writtle College), and by adding an awning over the patio, we would be able to accommodate everybody, and needless to say, the grounds and flower beds would be immaculate - if they can't get it right, we might as well all give up. I don't know whether we gave them the idea, but subsequently the refectory has been extended over the area that our awning covered. A perfect July day could not have blessed us with a better setting, and the Vicar, Peter Mason, conducted the service with the right mix of solemnity and informality. My mother, who was by now wheelchair bound, was looked after by friends - this is the wonderful thing about a community like Writtle - and was naturally overjoyed to see her grand daughter successfully spliced. My sister came over from Canada, and stayed with our mother, who lived only a few doors away down the Green; apart from the joy of the wedding, I think she knew that it might be the last time she would see her, as mother's health was clearly failing. Rhodri's family are, of course Welsh, and all his Welsh relations made the effort to come over for the occasion; I did even manage a word or two of Welsh in my speech welcoming them (this did call for a good deal of practice!).

Three days later, Beryl and I were crossing the North Sea overnight in the good ship "Prinses Beatrix", and the following evening were heading for the great railway bridge of Amsterdam Central Station in readiness for the once a day opening at about 2 am. Being by now, the end of July, the world and his wife (which includes us!) were afloat, and that night trip through the series of Amsterdam bridges was the comedy as before, only worse. People who think they are on a motorway get to the next bridge long before the brugwachters have arrived in their car, and then get in a horrible muddle - once called a "Horlicks" by a friend of ours. It was with some relief that we let go the anchor in the meer off the main canal at Blauwe Beugel - the great thing about this is that no one else does it, and you can catch up on lost sleep without risk of disturbance. Already, by 1984, the idea of anchoring was fading - if we are not careful it will become a lost art.

From here, we went to Warmond, berthing in the immaculately groomed and well run CIECO marina which we had used on previous visits and run by the Lucas family, who had a very pleasant apartment overlooking the marina and canal. Warmond is a favourite small town of ours, which, in spite of its proximity to Leiden has a number of good small shops, including two butchers - one sadly is now a hairdressers', and a cheese shop selling cheeses seldom seen outside Holland, including an "Oude Gouda" best compared to a mature Parmesan. We met up with "Clearways" again, and dined together in the "Stad de Rome", a gastronomic delight.

A few more lazy days (remember, we had been through quite a hectic period) and then we met up with "Clearways" again at my favourite "Petit Hannepoel" Restaurant, where we were berthed right alongside and enjoyed a totally different meal from that at the "Stad de Rome" - good hearty, but wholesome food. Once more, we met our friends the Elhorsts - Feico had now acquired a boat of his own, so we had plenty to discuss.

Holland has various types of bridge to allow vessels with masts or tall superstructures to pass through - where once there were two such routes from North to South, by this time there was only one, where all the bridges opened in one way or another, either by rotating spans, cantilevered spans, or by lifting the whole span between two tall towers (a "Hefbrug"). As we journeyed South in company, we learnt that the "Hefbrug" at Waddinxveen was closed until Friday - it was now Wednesday, so we found a pleasant small berth to lie alongside just below Alphen-am-Rhin. Alphen is a big busy town, not one of my favourites, but our berth, which had probably once been a small commercial quay, was now part of a small public park. It was pleasant and wooded with shrubs and bushes along the quay face, whilst there were small shops nearby, so here we would wait as we had already heard that boats were crowding together either side of the defunct bridge, which was being replaced.

Soon, we found room for another English yacht, "SHAMAAL", who wanted to get down there on the Friday as he was running out of time; we arranged to keep in touch on Channel 6 - indeed there was now a network of English yachts talking over channel 6. The ANWB authorities in the Hague pronounced that the bridge would open at 1330, but "SHAMAAL" reported from his berth near the bridge (probably about 5 or 6 miles away from us) that he had spoken to the engineers on the job, who prophesied it would not be until 1600. Just before 1400, we berthed alongside the edge of the canal; our headrope was secured to the support of a road crash barrier, whilst our stern rope was on the steel post of a road sign - I think one of the variety that warned you of water ahead.

The whole span of this bridge had been removed, straddled across two barges, and the other had been floated in to take its place in similar fashion; engineers were now working on attaching the lifting mechanism to the new span. The whole operation was a masterpiece of engineering and logistics. Soon after 4, the bridge opened for Northbound traffic - barges and yachts of every description, all of whom were intent on being first through. It was chaos, and there were numerous minor collisions. The bridge was lowered again to let some road traffic through, then re-opened for Southbound traffic - worse chaos. I hung on to our roadside berth for about half an hour and was able to proceed through at my own pace - there was no way I wanted "CELANDINE'S" beautifully finished topsides scratched by some over eager run about.

After visiting Willemstad, we introduced "CLEARWAYS" to the pretty little yacht harbour of "De Werf" at Goes - the one reached by turning sharply through a hole in the hedge - and then on to the Veersemeer. The two boats spent a night at one of the small islands in the meer, with just enough depth of water to lie alongside a slightly marshy spit, where we produced a barbecue - the Rowans on "CLEARWAYS" were well equipped for this, but barbecues are not really in our line of business. That night, Bob Rowan had a strange dream as a result of which he woke up shouting "Stewart hasn't checked the air height". As both boats were stationary under a starlit sky, this hardly seemed relevant.

The next day, we both berthed in the inner part of the yacht harbour at Middelburg, a pleasant place to lie, reached after passing through a small lifting bridge with ornamental ironwork. Either side of the basin was lined with traditional Dutch architecture, and the quays were shaded by avenues of mature trees. On going alongside, Beryl wanted the boat moved astern a short distance to give easier access to a flight of stone steps in the brick quay face, but "CELANDINE" was sluggish and disinclined to move. I checked the depth - were we on the bottom? There was a good 10 feet of water, and there was no evidence of a current to hold her, but with much BF and BI, we coaxed her to the steps. After lunch, someone on an English boat on the opposite side of the basin said "Have you looked up at your mast?" Red faces all round, as I realised that we were bending the large limb of a lime tree back with our mast and crosstrees - Stewart had certainly not checked the air height! As soon as the straining stern rope was released, "CELANDINE" shot forward like a stone from a catapult and a shower of broken twigs and leaves fluttered down on to our decks. When close to trees, people with tall masts should look aloft as well as ahead and astern; by swinging the bows out and coming back alongside the other side of the offending branch, berthing by Beryl's desired steps was made easy.

From Middelburg, Beryl left by train for the day boat from the Hook - on this trip, she could have come with us, but the weather is a fickle thing and I would not want to inflict a bad crossing on her; in the event, this one was as smooth as silk. Ship's clocks were retarded one hour to BST as we cleared the sea lock at Flushing, and by five o'clock in the afternoon, all sail had been set to catch a pleasant light breeze from the Southeast as we set off to go through the tortuous Duerloo channel out of the Westerschelde. As usual, Platt's cynical rule about fair winds applied, and towards midnight, the engine had to be started to assist progress, although towards dawn the wind returned in enough strength to push us along at no more than 4 or 5 knots. It was nearly high water and 24 hours after leaving Flushing when we reached the Pye End sand off Walton , which we crossed close to the ominously named High Hill buoy - somebody added to the log - "where was Pye End?" - we never saw it.

PUBLIC ENQUIRIES AND PLANNING MATTERS

AT about this time, a consortium were making serious proposals to convert a disused boating lake opposite the Walton and Frinton Yacht Club into a yacht marina; the sea wall enclosing it was broken in several places allowing it to become silted so that it amounted to no more than a shallow lagoon at high water. The creek which would give access to it was no more than a ditch at low water, but they were proposing to dredge all the way out to deeper water with a minimum of 6 feet at low water. The entrance they proposed would be right by the starting line for cadet races, and needless to say, Walton was furious about the whole idea. A far more satisfactory marina was being developed off the deep Twizzle channel close by, so this seemed superfluous, particularly bearing in mind the great upheaval that would be caused by the vast amount of dredging required.

A public enquiry was to be held in a hall attached to the Martello caravan camp at Walton - a summer venue, so the heating was not exactly adequate for a mid-winter gathering. I had written my objections, and indicated I wished to speak, but the problem was that so many objectors wanted to do so, that I could not possibly be there for several days awaiting my turn. The Halls agreed to keep in touch with me at work and let me know when it looked as though I would speak; this arrangement made it possible. My main objection was that the cost of dredging and soil disposal would make it unviable, and that the depth to which they proposed dredging their approach channel made the angle of the mud unsustainable - it would take a natural angle of repose very different from the steep banks proposed. I quoted what had happened at Bradwell, where the banks had collapsed inwards; this was dredged again and steel sheet piling put in to retain the bank - and the sheet piling then bulged with the weight of soil behind it. I believe the inspector and his team visited Bradwell as a result.

To the relief of all concerned, the application was rejected, and that was the last to be heard of it. There was quite a party at the Yacht Club when the inspector's verdict was announced. A previous enquiry I had attended many years previously concerned a proposal for one at Stansgate Abbey, on the Blackwater. The applicants had hired a brilliant QC with a great reputation in Essex - the kind of chap you wanted on your side, and in his presence, you had to be very careful what you said. A number of us turned up at the enquiry, held in Maldon, including Peter and Anne Pye ("Red Mains'l" and other very readable books on his cruises) and the Wedgwood Benns who owned Stansgate House which would be next door to the proposed development. One objector was a proper old Essex boy from Mersea - member of a very well known family from that part of the world. He was there to represent oyster interests, and his objection was the fierce tides there, which would give rise to a lot of strandings and damage to oyster beds. He said the tide "runs terrible 'ard there, 4 or 5 knots". He was cross examined, and the great man questioned him on this. He then turned to his assistant who produced a roll of paper with a certain amount of theatrical flourish. "What is this document?" - "an Admiralty chart sir". He then enquired of his assistant "what does this letter in a diamond mean?" Of course, it was a tidal stream point, and the chart showed a maximum of two and a half knots. Demolition of the witness was total; indeed, he left most of us objectors shredded in bits all over the floor, with the result that we departed very dejected; we had lost, surely. But we hadn't, and I believe experienced inspectors know that enthusiastic amateurs are no match for a brilliant QC., and allow for it. The main thing is to say what you honestly believe, and don't exaggerate - "Methinks he doth protest too much".

It was also this year that there was our own brush with the local planners - an event which would never have happened with the former Chelmsford Rural District Council - our friend Patricia Stewart had designed a very attractive conservatory at Greenbury House to replace a rather rickety old shed with a rusting corrugated iron roof. No reply to the application was received within the statutory time, and we began to become restless; no satisfactory explanation was forthcoming, and she suggested I demand an interview with the chief planning officer, saying "they will tell you he is going on leave". This is exactly what they did say, however I said we would prepared to come at any time to suit their convenience, and a meeting was arranged. It transpired that they did not like the line of the gutter and the approval was held up for this. The whole pantomime was absurd, when you consider this was at the back of the house, admittedly a grade II listed building. A slanging match developed between Patricia, who said what she thought, and the planners. The devil entered my soul at this point. With a certain amount of theatre I gathered my papers into their file, stood up and announced that I either was granted planning permission within a fortnight, or would refurbish the corrugated iron shed, and walked out. It was unrehearsed, and I should not have enjoyed this act, but I would be less than honest if I said otherwise; the appalling waste of highly paid officials' time on this minute detail really shook me. Planning permission came very quickly, and the following spring, construction started - it was a worthy addition to the house and totally sympathetic to its character. I am very much in favour of planning controls when properly exercised, but this kind of behaviour brings the whole system into disrepute; the worrying thing is that the bigger the rogue, the more they get away with, while the poor law-abiding citizen suffers from the petty bureaucracy. Most owners of listed houses would not live in them if they didn't like them, and certainly would not do something that spoilt the very character they have paid for in buying it; nevertheless they must be allowed to improve them to suit modern living.

All this happened while Beryl was on her Manchester stint. Writtle is a mixed community, and like any other, there are problem families; they are few, and generally it is a place where most people live comfortably so it is not a place where you would expect to find a great demand for soup kitchens. However, during the time that Beryl was travelling to Manchester, all over the country and, in fact, the world, a number of my friends took pity on me and invited me to their homes for dinner. When Beryl had been discussing the whole project with me, I pointed out that if I could cook reasonably palatable meals on the boat, there was no reason why I shouldn't do it at home. She was usually able to see that the fridge and freezer were well stocked - years of victualling the boat made it nothing new for her, and made me realise just how much she had organised over the years. Sometimes this was not possible, and I then managed to overcome the natural male fear of shopping when necessary.

To refer to my friend's homes as soup kitchens (which I did) was irreverent; I was treated to some wonderful evenings with mouth watering offerings placed on the table. But more than this, it was was the enjoyment of the company of friends, and although I had said I did not mind my own company, that fact is I did not like it for very long at a time. It is sometimes pleasant to get away from everybody for a little while, but I am not good at it for too long. Certainly I would never have made a good singlehanded sailor; occasionally I had taken "CELANDINE" out singlehanded for a very short trip, but apart from the fact I think, although now fashionable, singlehanded long passages are downright dangerous and unseamanlike; they can also involve other people in unnecessary risk and danger. Anywhere within the English Channel and Southern North Sea I like to have two people awake on the boat at night - apart from this, I know that I would soon be craving the company of friends to share in the job of running the ship, and provide conversation. To return to the subject of soup kitchens, a period which lasted five years, it was a downright insult to call them such, and I now take the opportunity to apologise to some wonderful friends. They helped to make that five years shorter.

RETURN TO BRITTANY

T HE year 1985 produced a fairly indifferent summer, with plenty of strong winds, usually from Southwest, and after some local cruises, I once again made use of Levington's Suffolk Yacht harbour, from where we left at first light on a Saturday morning with a light but favourable Northwest wind - my favourite wind, but they never stay in that quarter for very long, usually going into the Northeast. All day we toiled our way across the Thames Estuary and down towards Dover, with a mixture of light winds and calms, eventually becoming dead ahead from the South as we proceeded South down the Straits; the barometer stood very high and at least the weather was pleasant. As we cleared Dover to come round on to a more Southwesterly course, the wind also went round and became a little stronger, so we still had to work hard to claw our way Westward. Beachy Head was abeam at two o'clock on Sunday morning as we motored over a now glassy windless sea.

Nearing the Solent, through the Looe channel, the wind obligingly went in to the East, but it did not last, and we finished tacking through the Solent against a Southwest wind; tacking through the Solent on a Sunday is not my idea of sailing; you not only need eyes in the back of your head, but also a head that can rotate through 360 degrees. That evening, we revisited Lymington Marina where we also refuelled, leaving early the following morning and slipping through the North channel past Hurst Castle; I have no recollection why, but we gave a tow to a boat called "PELICAN II" for about an hour, I think to get him clear of the constricted North channel and into Christchurch Bay, where there was room for us to tack along the coast into the Southwesterly wind, which eventually backed and enabled us to sail our course for Weymouth. The Purbeck coast from Old Harry rocks Westwards to Weymouth posesses some splendid coastal scenery which includes Worbarrow Bay, Lulworth Cove and a range of magnificent cliffs - it is not a coast to be taken lightly as there is no safe haven between Poole and Weymouth, and there are some nasty places like Kimmeridge ledges to ensnare a ship; the beauty is to be admired at a safe distance.

In Weymouth, we secured alongside "GUNNA", a sail training boat of the London Sailing Project - a long established organisation enabling youngsters very often from a deprived background to sail in an atmosphere of adventure with a discipline that has to be observed for the safety of the ship and all who sail in her. It has done some wonderful work over the years, and rescued many a youth from an otherwise meaningless life of aimless drifting. Another vessel I was surprised to meet in Weymouth was the Belgian Sealink "Prins Phillippe", which left just after we made our hurried departure to keep out of the way. This surely was the ship in which I had crossed from Ostend to Dover some twenty years or more ago; I think by this time she was nearing the end of her days, and was employed on the Channel Islands run as a stopgap; the route itself was, I think, becoming something of a Cinderella, with falling demand. Nevertheless, I felt I had met an old friend.

Once again taking advantage of tidal conditions, we swept round Portland Bill and headed into Lyme Bay for another passage involving intermittent periods of pleasant sailing interspersed with motor sailing to keep us moving in the right direction. A tack took us close inshore at Golden Cap - another gem of coastal scenery, but quite different and more gentle than the rugged Purbeck coast. Early in the evening, the wind came round to Northwest and we were able to lay a course direct for the River Dart, where we picked up a mooring shortly before midnight. The next morning, we sauntered up to Dittisham before setting off for Salcombe in a brisk Westerly wind; the next morning we set off in a flat calm to complete the week's passage to Plymouth, where we berthed in the Mayflower marina after refuelling.

Three weeks later we set off five strong - Garry & Sally Alder with their youngest son Tim, Mike "Thatch" Rose, and of course, me. Leaving just before mid-day Saturday, with a steady West wind, taking our departure from the Eddystone light, where the log was streamed. During the night, the wind (for once!) favoured us by veering to Northwest and freshening, so that we began forging our way across the channel, the white foam of our lee bow wave tinged red by the port navigation light. One of the great things about a night passage is that you approach the less familiar distant coast in daylight, hopefully with the whole day in front of you, in fact it was early afternoon before we started picking our way through the trickier parts of the passage between the Isle of Ushant and the mainland, past our old friends "Les Platresses" and "La Grande Vinotiere" Half past six (local time) on a beautiful summer Sunday evening saw us securing to a pontoon in Camaret, the busy fishing port that was also once an outer defence for the great French Naval base of Brest. It was fortified by the great French military engineer Vauban in the late 17th century; judging by the number of "Forts Vauban" one comes across, he must have been a pretty busy chap, and certainly a hero to the French who have many streets and squares named after him.

Sailing South from Camaret at a gentlemanly hour the following morning, a wag (probably "Thatch") entered the wind as "SW, force 1.65". Motorsailing in bright sunny conditions gave us a really good view of the spectacular (if not terrifying) offshore rocks, one in particular having a cathedral-like arch through the centre. Our destination was the river Odet, and the light weather promised a long haul well off shore, crossing the great bay of Douarnenez before reaching the infamous Raz de Sein. By the time we reached it, the wind had veered round to West, but still very light and motorsailing had to continue most of the time. Life was pleasant, the sun shone, and we ate well; at one meal, Sally insisted on showing off her skills as a waitress - in her student days she had done part time silver service waiting. Although it was calm, there is always a swell in open waters and the boat restless; nevertheless she twirled the tray above her head to bring nourishment into the cockpit, and nothing was spilt.

Finally, the wind having failed altogether some time after rounding the great Pointe de Penmarch, we lowered the sails and carefully nosed our way through the darkness towards the Odet entrance at Benodet. My pilotage failed, and we had to make several false attempts before finding the very clear transit leading us in. Although it was dark, there was enough light to see rocks ahead on our mistaken attempts; as a result of these manoeuvres it was after midnight when the anchor chain disturbed the still night as it rattled down over the bow roller. We had anchored a little way up the river, above the motorway bridge, but the next morning had to go alongside the quay at Benodet to re-victual - with five aboard, you can eat your way through a lot of stores - and we needed water and fuel.

After a lunch in the cockpit (as with most of our meals so far this trip) we fled from Benodet, as the place is much too smart for the likes of us, and motored very placidly up this beautiful river, with its steeply wooded banks and some very fine chateaux with well kept park - like grounds. Once away from Benodet it is peaceful and idyllic, with scarce another yacht to be seen. It is fortunate for those who prefer solitude that most yachts, particularly continentals, seem to be gregarious, which concentrates them to leave the places without facilities peaceful and giving room to put an anchor down; the big tidal ranges in this part of the world require a boat to have a long scope of anchor chain.

Another relatively short leg in calm conditions saw "CELANDINE" returning to the estuary of the Aven and Belon rivers, and entering the sylvan bay in the Belon that had so attracted me on our previous visit, found that there was now a visitor's mooring. With plenty of time as we arrived early in the evening an expedition was made ashore, but the following morning an early departure had to be made for another long trip returning Northbound, which turned out to be the mixture as before - some motorsailing and some sailing which was never very fast in the light winds. The barometer which had been high for most of the week had now started a very definite plunge, so our good weather was likely to vanish. Our slow progress back over the same tracks through the Raz brought us to the deep sheltered bay of Morgat with its magnificent sandy beach and caves in the cliffs - surely a children's paradise. The anchor went down shortly before midnight; although this bay would be uncomfortable in a Southerly wind, the winds were from a Westerly direction, and in fact had gone round to Northwest to give us an extremely sheltered berth, with the shore lights mirrored on the calm water.

The morning brought a fresh Northwest breeze, from which we were well sheltered, and we went alongside in the small harbour no doubt to further replenish stores. Early in the afternoon, with one reef down, we raced away to round the Cap de la Chevre at the Southern tip of the Crozon peninsular and then harden our sheets to sail close hauled to clear the headlands on the West side of the peninsula. Camaret is on the North side, just before the entrance to Brest, and by land is no distance from Morgat, but quite a stretch by sea. This time, we were missing Camaret and heading for the great natural harbour of Brest in which whole fleets could lie at anchor - just as well there was plenty of room for them during the years when the British fleet maintained a blockade there in the Napoleonic wars. Once round the Pointe du Toulinguet, the Northwest tip of the peninsula, the sheets were freed and "CELANDINE" raced towards the aptly named Goulet de Brest. It was some of the best sailing in the whole of that week, and we were soon within the great inland basin with its numerous bays and estuaries, to round up off the small village of Roscanvel which lies on the East side of the Crozon peninsula. The "Ros" appears in a number of Brittany place names, and also appears in a number of Cornish names; both places not only have Celtic origins, but their rugged coastal features are also similar. There is also a separatist movement in both, but I think this is more emotional than practical.

The next morning, after a lazy start, we had a splendid romp through the Rade de Brest with a force 5 Westerly wind behind us to the Eastern end of Brest where we secured in the Moulin Blanc Marina. It was now Saturday, and "CELANDINE" was to be left there as we all needed to get back to Plymouth on the morrow. Having checked in advance that there was a Brittany Ferries sailing from Roscoff, we had to find out how we managed this short journey early on a Sunday morning. Although there was a railway to Roscoff, it was only a branch line, and there was no way of making it in time for the ferry; instead, I hired a car just big enough to squeeze in five people and their gear. I think it was from Avis, and the great thing was that they had an office at Roscoff which would not be open when we arrived there, but all I had to do was park the car outside and post the keys through their letterbox. Very early the next morning we were off through the deserted streets of Brest's Eastern suburbs, and reached Roscoff in good time to buy tickets and board the great white ferry. Normally, whereas I often forget peoples' names I never forget the name of a ship in which I have travelled, but this one escapes me, except to say she was a very fine ship.

A beautiful day was developing, and the West wind that gave us such a good sail two days before had disappeared. Probably just as well because whilst this ship looked impressive with her array of saloons and promenade decks, I am not sure how much there was under the water. It was now very much high season, being July the 21st, but to our surprise, the ship was almost empty and we really had the run of the ship. There was a great dining saloon with a superb uninterrupted view ahead, from a very high position. We had a splendid lunch at a table in the forward end; it was served buffet style, and we took our time over it - superb hors d'ouevres, and then to our surprise, they had a typical English roast joint - quite a small one, but perhaps they knew numbers were going to be low that day. As lunch progressed, the first high points of the English coast began to rise from the horizon, and amazingly quickly became identifiable. I suppose we were steaming at a good 18 knots - us small boat sailors are not really used to this kind of travel, nor such height of eye above the water. At the end of this enjoyable crossing, the Alders, who had parked their car in the Brittany Ferries' car park, took Mike and myself to Plymouth station whence they drove off to their cottage in Helford. I arrived home to meet Beryl, who had flown in from Nairobi the day before, having attended a world conference of women in her capacity as Chairman of the Equal Opportunities Commission.

Ten days later Beryl and I were on a flight from Stansted to Paris, and then on to Brest by train; leaving home at a reasonable hour in the morning, we were actually back aboard "CELANDINE" early that evening, ready to do some gentle exploration of this great inland sea. It was during this summer that I began to think about the future of sailing, and keeping afloat till a ripe old age. Would I want to go on sitting in an open cockpit being lashed by rain and spray - thoughts about building some kind of wheelhouse were quickly dismissed as a Phillistine act; were there some kind of planning authority over plans of boats, they certainly would not like such an addition, but neither did I. So thoughts began to evolve around finding some other vessel, and one which I would be able penetrate France's superb inland waterways system. I was also beginning to find the work of maintaining this lovely boat in tip top condition (you couldn't do otherwise) somewhat onerous. She still had her original plough steel galvanised rigging wires, which were inspected and redressed with a linseed oil concoction of my own brew each spring, the wires being draped all over the orchard for the purpose - a true wirescape. The result was they remained as good as new, which would not have been the case had they been of "no maintenance" stainless steel. These thoughts were pushed to the background as we enjoyed our gentle exploration.

After the inevitable refuelling and re-victualling, we first went up the Elorn river, passing under a high motorway bridge, and up this river we found some pleasant and isolated anchorages and excursions ashore. Then there was the Baie de Doulas - almost a fiord - and here we found a delightful spot called Port Tinduff, which was no more than a hamlet, but it had a new stone quay face and clean beach. There were no shops, but there was a fresh water tap behind some public loos on the small promenade. A taxi to nearby Plougastel Daoulas brought us to a small town that could supply our needs (including a copy of the *Daily Telegraph*!) and bring them back to the dinghy on the beach. I surveyed the quay and beach, and found there was no charge for lying there, so on the next early morning's tide, came alongside and prepared to take the ground by putting a line on the mast to ensure she settled lying against the wall and not the other way, particularly as I needed to work on cleaning her rather weedy bottom.

As the tide receded, with the help of copious bucketfuls of water and a scrubber I eliminated the weed - it only grows where the light falls on the hull, the forefoot and deadwood aft, so the areas were not great. It was a sunny and relaxing day; the beach was inviting and we bathed. But by the late afternoon when we refloated, a stiff wind had come up from the Southwest, and soon after we got underweigh, a penetrating misty drizzle shrouded the landscape and made our pilotage more difficult. Entering the Aulne river, we anchored in the first sheltered spot as there was no point in going any further in these conditions. We found a small "Anse" not far inside, and downstream from another high road bridge; we were happy to get the anchor down. Although the banks were attractive, there were some "graveyard" moorings nearby where long discarded small French Naval and support vessels were moored to rust quietly away; they would not look very great even in sunshine, but in this wet misty atmosphere they were depressing, and we soon fled below.

It was still raining when we awoke, but the barometer started to rise, and we went a short distance to another hamlet called Tregarvan (more of the Cornish connection!) where there was a cafe that sold a few limited items of food, while there was a water tap ashore to enable us to take more water out in our plastic cans. Not that just Beryl and myself were great users of the stuff - we had long learned the discipline of economy with water supplies aboard a boat; we swam when we could but otherwise knew how to wash with a minimum. Vicky used to tell of native women in Ghana, when she was on her VSO stint out there, washing themselves clean with a mugful of the stuff, but even we felt that was overdoing it. Our exploration during several days of gales from the Southwest and periods of torrential rain, eventually took us through a sea lock at Guilly Glaz and up to Chateaulin, where we found one of the most convenient of all yachtsmen's supermarkets. We were berthed at the Quai Charles de Gaulle, where right opposite lay a supermarket whose car park was bounded by a quay in which were some ancient stone steps from some previous use of the site. Our shopping trolley went to the quay side, and the contents loaded straight in the Avon dinghy.

Chateaulin, standing astride the canalised river Aulne, is a pleasant place without any great attraction, and we returned downstream to Port Launay, which was a picturesque village flanking the non-tidal river, and having a long quay with both depth and room to moor. The sun was shining as we approached; the wind was probably still blowing fresh at sea, but here we were very sheltered in this deep wooded valley. On the quayside, an artist was working at his canvas, but as we came round the bend in the river, he seized a camera and we were snapped. We berthed near a handsome Bermudian ketch, "GOOD GRACE", whose home moorings are at Ramsholt, on the river Deben, and owned by fellow Cruising Association members Margaret and Gerry Elliot. After a little while, we walked along the quay and discreetly examined the artist's work. To his nearly completed view of Port Launay and its quay in vigorous oils, he was now superimposing "CELANDINE", and a little later we made a discreet approach to see if the picture would be for sale. It was almost finished but he would prefer to let us see it completed before talking of a sale.

Realising that we might be parting company with "CELANDINE" (although it hurt me to think about it) in the foreseeable future, it seemed that we ought to have this picture, and that evening we discussed what our maximum price might be. The next day, he returned, completed it and came aboard for tea and to discuss a sale. The price was probably about double our limit; he explained that he had sold a picture recently to a fellow peer (who Beryl knew well, but we didn't mention this) and he had just written out a cheque. I had made no arrangements, and I was not sure how a cheque for a substantial number of francs would go down with our small Writtle branch of Lloyd's Bank, a few doors up the Green from our house. However, when we talked of payment by cash, his eyes lit up and we finally agreed a substantially lower figure which represented almost our entire supply of the ready; I can't remember now, but we may have thrown in some sterling which he was happy to accept. The picture which he named "L'arrivee de "CELANDINE" a Port Launay" became ours, with the oils still wet - not an ideal thing to carry aboard. He advised that the oil would take about a week to dry if we put it out in the open whenever possible.

We returned to Chateaulin, raced for a bank to change traveller's cheques, and to collect Rhodri and Vicky, who were coming out to join us for a few days, before returning to the idyllic setting of Port Launay for another night. Another few days were spent in this attractive river; the weather was pretty foul and our new picture had precious little time in the open to dry off. Nevertheless, we made a few shore excursions and bathed - Vicky was by now pregnant, but had a very elegant maternity bathing costume and swam with the rest of us (I should say ahead of us, as both she and Rhodri raced through the water like dolphins). Ultimately, we returned to Brest where they left us to do some exploring in France by train and on foot.

The next day, Beryl left by taxi to arrive in the pouring rain so early that the station was not open, clutching the precious oil painting in the specially designed package we had contrived. The paint was till a bit tacky in places, and we covered it first with waxed paper from cornflake packets before adding the outer protection. She returned by train and plane to Stansted, where the Customs officer took considerable interest in the newly acquired work of art. He was unsure about this importation - I suppose it is not every day that someone brings in an oil painting with the paint barely dry. He called his colleague, a lady Customs Officer - Beryl explained it was a painting of her husband's dream ship. After finding there were no duty free cigarettes, she sensed the sentimental value of the picture, and said "Oh, we can't charge her on that", so the picture was in. It hangs in our drawing room, a souvenir of "CELANDINE" and the picturesque village of Port Launay running along the waterfront at the foot of a very steep wooded hill. The representation of the boat has a slight feel of Breton fishing boat about it, but that is understandable. We already had a very good picture of her under sail, in gouache, by the East Coast artist Tony Osler, which captures her character underway, so we felt this was a different sort of picture anyway.

For once, Platt's theories about Westerly winds in late summer seemed to be coming true, and we left Brest at 10 on a mid-August morning with a brisk Southwester blowing and one reef in the mains'l, tacked in the Goulet and brought her into Camaret, which was to be our port of departure. We had all joined the evening before - John Aldridge from Writtle, Ursula Gardiner and her son Richard, now in the Navy. Peter Gardiner could not come this time as he was working; it should be explained that Ursula was the daughter of Howard Banks, who had been very much my "business father" when I joined the firm after my father's early death. Howard had taken up boating later in life, and continued after his retirement until his death. We were a strong crew; the boat had been stored and watered beforehand, but we anchored in the harbour at Camaret to sort everything out and await a favourable tide to sluice us through the Chenal du Four that evening.

After a good meal whilst still at anchor (always a good idea at the start of a passage!) we set off just after seven in the evening and raced out towards the Point du Grand Gouin marking the Northwest side of the anse de Camaret, then closehauled, which slowed us down, to clear the Pointe de St Mathieu marking the start of our passage through the Chenal de Four. It was ten in the evening and getting dark by the time we reached our old friend La Grande Vinotiere, and almost midnight by the time the Le Four light, which gives its name to this short cut inshore of Ushant, was bearing due East, and we began to shape our course more Northeasterly to run up the English Channel. With a freshening of the wind, and the new course bringing it round on to our quarter, "CELANDINE" was charging homeward bound like a racehorse on the final stretch. With the wind now on the opposite side from our outward trip, the foaming lee bow wave glistened green from our starboard light. What a sail!

Early on the following morning, Thursday, there was quite a rainsquall, but the weather was showing no signs of a serious deterioration and the barometer was reasonably high and steady; by eleven that morning the sun was shining brightly again - "Rain before seven, shine by eleven" - it certainly worked this morning. At four in the afternoon, a report from Channel Lightvessel gave the wind as Southwest force 7, but I don't think it ever reached more than the top end of force 6 for us. Certainly, by seven in the evening when we brought the Channel light vessel abeam it was more like force 5, and the tide now being with the wind, the seas became much easier, giving the opportunity to cook a good supper. Our course was now almost dead before the wind - not an easy one to steer, so a preventer line had been put on the boom to prevent it crashing across in an accidental gybe.

Just as we were counting our luck with this strong fair wind, it started to fade, and at five that morning we had to put the engine on to give a bit of boost to our speed, and also to charge our batteries - we now had been at sea two nights with our lights on, and being mid-August, the nights were becoming noticeably longer again. Happily, by mid-day, the wind filled in again a good force 5 - our reef had not been shaken out, because there was every sign that the calmer patch was only a temporary lull; the engine was shut down, we were bowling along under sail and in the afternoon had Beachy Head in sight. It was abeam by six in the evening, then just over an hour later the Royal Sovereign Tower was abeam. This was real express train stuff. There is an annoying entry in the log that we were overtaken by a sloop goosewinging his big heads'l out opposite the main. I am not a racing man, but this was not something I liked; it was almost dark, so we could not properly identify her; she was undoubtedly a bigger boat (that's my story, anyway!).

Although almost full moon, cloud covered most of the sky and we approached the dreaded Dover Strait just after midnight with little help from it; however there was good visibility - it was rather late in the summer for the fogs which bedevil the place in the Spring. By the time we were abeam of the harbour, there was little or no ferry traffic so our passage through was devoid of nail biting worries for once - it seems that half past one in the morning is a slack time in ferry traffic. As we came upon the North Foreland, shafts of early morning sunlight were filtering through the clouds to highlight the chalk cliffs; here is another milestone on the way home as you leave the Kentish shore and head away on the long haul across the Estuary towards my native Essex coast. The wind had veered to Westsou'west, and a tack had to be made to go through a shallow swatchway near the SW Sunk beacon - hanging on to the tack just that little bit too long (how we all succumb to the temptation!) she just touched bottom as we came round , just after low water, and then was away again.

Later in the morning we eased our sheets to head North through the Swin Spitway, the final gate through to the Essex coast. The wind had eased to about force 4; it was the final gallop home for which we shook out the reef and hoisted our big fairweather jib, the sun broke through full and strong to highlight the Essex coast, with the Naze ahead of us topped by its ancient tower.   Although we were now stemming a foul tide, who cares when you have a good fair wind?   It was Saturday, and we began to meet other boats as we closed the coast and entered the Walton backwaters; just before five in the afternoon we were enjoying tea on deck, with "CELANDINE" safely secured to her mooring after just over 69 hours at sea.

HOME AFFAIRS - A NEW BOAT IN EMBRYO AND FAREWELL TO "CELANDINE"

A T home, things had not been too easy, as my mother's condition was deteriorating, due to the failure of her knee joints, which had bowed out to the point where they would no longer support her. I remember a year or so previously driving through the village, going from Dagenham to see Courtaulds at Bocking, when I saw this elderly lady struggling along with her bow legs, and suddenly realising it was my own mother and even then could not see how they could support her. With considerable difficulty, we persuaded her that she must from now on live downstairs, and I'm quite sure that this was achieved just about the last time she could negotiate the stairs. We arranged for someone to come in and provide meals on a rota basis, and when we were at home, could cook in our own house and take a meal round to share with her. I had already been advised to obtain a power of attorney over her affairs, which she readily agreed to as she was not very businesslike.

Lorna came over that summer, and returned to Canada knowing this would probably be the last time she would see her; it was not a happy time. Eventually, the doctor decreed that she must have 24 hour nursing, and I found myself arranging a rota of nurses from agencies to try and keep her in her own home. It was to no avail, and proved impossible to maintain, so we finally found a nursing home between Writtle and Braintree. They were very good, and provided the 24 hour nursing she needed. I used my power of attorney to maximise the income from her modest savings; sadly, I sold the shareholding in Adnams Brewery, severing the last link with Southwold, but the shares fetched a good price and we needed the higher rate of return available elsewhere - interest rates were quite high at the time.

In Writtle, pressure was mounting for the construction of a bypass, promised as a consequence of the building of a large housing estate - of course, we got the estate but not the bypass. An action group was formed, The Writtle Society kept up the pressure; Beryl had campaigned vigorously while on the County Council, but at last we had a starting date. One less serious matter facing the village was that some group (not a village organisation) was pressing us to "twin" with a continental town - it was becoming fashionable. The Parish Council debated the matter without coming to a conclusion, and threw it into the Writtle Society's lap. It was debated at the house of the then Hon Treasurer, Cyril Crane. Cyril had been in the merchant service during the war, and as a result was severely handicapped; he was extremely efficient as treasurer; his contribution to matters under discussion was always brief, but very much to the point. The subject of "twinning" rolled on, and one or two suggestions may have been made, but Cyril brought the debate to a conclusion with one word "Vladivostok"- the meeting dissolved in laughter, and Writtle remains "untwinned" to this day.

During this time, I began to look seriously at my own sailing prospects. Although still only 62, I now began to think about the future of boating activities, developing the thoughts that had gone through my mind on the summer cruise. I had decided that I wanted a boat capable of crossing the Channel, but also able to explore the French inland waterways, and that I wanted a steel hull. Looking for something suitable, I got no further than the advertisements; there were precious few, and none suitable. One or two fishing boats were available, but it was obvious they would not make what I wanted, and I started drawing on scrap paper, finally drawing out sections and waterlines, and a general arrangement on graph paper, making use of some of Beryl's instruments from her engineering days. During the autumn, we had several pleasant cruises including a trip to another Cruising Association event at St Katharine Dock. They were pleasant trips; again, I made use of Suffolk Yacht Harbour at Levington for convenience, particularly as there was no tidal restriction as at Walton; the trips were so enjoyable that I sometimes asked myself what I was planning. The following Spring, 1986, "CELANDINE" was fitted out in the usual way, and once again the annual wirescape appeared in our orchard. The faithful Perkins auxiliary engine was given a thorough overhaul by French Marine Motors; I had overcome the emotional side of parting with the boat I had seen grow from the keel upwards nearly twenty years ago, and was anxious to ensure that when she was sold, she would be in the best possible condition.

Not knowing much about steel construction, I approached someone who did, with a view to getting such a boat built, and this is where Derek Hyde at Plymouth came on the scene; I engaged him to find a builder and supervise construction, he having put my plans into something that could be interpreted in steel. No satisfactory builder could be found, and we came to a hiatus, but I had made my decision that "CELANDINE" was to be sold after an early summer cruise.

In this final fortnight's cruise, we fitted in all our local regular crew members ("The Writtle Sailing Club") and left Walton with the first batch early on a mid-June Saturday morning. Sod's law applied, and the wind was in the Northeast, force 3-4, so there was no easy passage - we were closehauled all the way. By the time we reached the Duerloo channel, the short cut into the Schelde, it was dark, and I funked going into this difficult channel, with numerous unlit buoys, so we backtracked and took the long way round via the Wielingen channel, as used by large ships. The wind dropped away, so the engine was started to push us the rest of the way to Flushing sealocks, which we reached at the hideous hour of three in the morning. At that time, I don't think there was 24 hour operation, and we made fast to a tug just outside, advanced our clocks to European time and grabbed a little sleep until seven, when we locked in to the Walcheren canal; by nine we were secured in Middelburg, whence we pushed on to some of our old familiar haunts.

Our crew for this part included John Barrington, who had become increasingly involved in the nautical scene and was always good company aboard, besides being very practical. Peter Darwent had recently become involved with sailing in "CELANDINE" - he had worked for a long spell in New York, and had a boat which he sailed on Long Island Sound. Peter and Gay were married out there, but had now come to live in a large house just outside the village. He had also owned a Folkboat in the Walton Backwaters; the other member on this part of the cruise was Roland.

At Willemstadt, because it was still early in the season and mid week, we were able to berth alongside the town quay. Whilst preparing supper, a Dutch yacht manned by three comely young ladies came alongside, and there was a definite eagerness on the part of my crew to assist with their lines. At the end of this, briefly thanking us for the help, they all disappeared below without any attempt at conversation. Sitting round the cabin table, the crew fell to discussing their aloofness, and someone came to the conclusion - "A bunch of lesbians". Just a minute said I - "What do you suppose they are saying about us?"

We berthed at Warmond, in our favourite CIECO marina, among its well tended

The end of the last voyage - Mike Rose squared. The bustle of commercial shipping in the background was soon to die, and Colchester is no longer a statutory port.

flowerbeds - the Dutch are very good with flowers. Here. Peter Darwent and John Barrington returned home, and Beryl and Roland's wife Louise came out, with our first Grandchild, Ann, for a very brief weekend. The weather was benign - I don't remember where the wind was, but does it matter when you're inland like this; they left, and new crew arrived - The two Michael Roses (usually known as Mike Rose squared), Geoff Smeed, and John Aldridge. Retracing our track through Holland, we arrived at Flushing on Friday afternoon after victualling at Middelburg.

Locking out at half past four, we were soon able to set the sails, with one reef down, for a wind that was still Northeasterly, as it had been a fortnight earlier - the barometer had remained high for the whole time, giving us good weather. Swift progress was made down the Duerloo channel, but it was almost dark by the time we reached Thornton Bank buoy, well offshore, and where the log was streamed. Steady progress Westwards driven by the freshening Northeast wind brought us to the outlying Galloper lightvessel in the early morning - it was a very short period of darkness, and later that morning we picked up our mooring in Walton, on which was our fibreglass dinghy, for the very last time. I had been using that mooring for over thirty years, it being the one that "CAMPION" had previously occupied. Later that afternoon, with the dinghy in tow, we sailed for the Orwell, because I needed to leave near low water the next morning - there would probably not have been enough depth towards Pye End even though it was a neap tide, and the wind having been from the East for over a fortnight, there would be quite a swell running. Sand it may be, but if you start bouncing on the stuff, it feels like concrete. That night, we anchored off Trimley, where we were well sheltered from the Easterly wind that was now blowing force 6, and had caused us to put one reef in the mains'l.

The next day, Sunday, we had a lie in before weighing just after eleven - an hour before low water, to catch the flood tide up the coast to the Colne Estuary. A little later, whether we had decided the wind had eased, or whether it was a last fling, the reef was shaken out and the big fairweather jib hoisted. "CELANDINE" raced headlong past the familiar coast - Walton Pier, then in no time at all, Clacton Pier. Just before three in the afternoon we were off the Colne Bar Buoy - much too early. We were going to squeeze the last drop of juice from this ship, so we just sailed for the sheer hell of it, roaring through the sea like an express train. Reluctantly, soon after four, we headed up the Colne to lower the sails just before Fingringhoe and motor the rest of the way up to a mud berth in Ian Brown's yard. That morning I had made a radio link call to Beryl, who arrived to meet us with the car. It was a sunny evening, and a bottle of bubbly was opened in the cockpit; the bottle still hangs in my garage alongside the broken one with which she had been launched in 1967.

In an article about the change of boat published in the CA's *"Cruising"* magazine, I said if a long and happy love affair has to be ended, it is best done quickly. One should not be sentimental about an inanimate assembly of wood, copper and steel, but on the other hand, she represented the work and skill of her designer, the craftsmanship of Ian

"Celandine" sails away. The decision to part with her was a painful one- (photo by Geoff Baker)

Brown's team in building her, and the company of all who sailed in her over the years. Our children had gone from teenage to adulthood during that time, now flown the nest, and so many wonderful people had come sailing aboard her - sadly not all with us by this time. It was the end of an era.

The arrangements for her sale were similar to those used 20 years previously for "CAMPION", in that advertisements were to appear in "*Yachting Monthly*" and "*Yachting World*" while we were away, saying "Enquiries after the thirtieth of June", and giving the office address. Needless to say, people had jumped the gun, and there were already several enquiries including a Telex from the Far East, whilst more came after my return on the Monday morning. But someone who had seen none of these, but heard on the local bush telegraph that she was for sale, jumped in and insisted on giving me a deposit, and had already arranged with Ian Brown to have her hauled out for survey. "What can I say to justify my fee?" said the surveyor to Ian - there was a minute piece of soft end grain by the rudder trunk. "What should we do?" - leave well alone, put a bit of Cuprinol on it perhaps". Otherwise, she passed with flying colours, proving that if you build of first quality materials, the boat will last. Down below, some of the joinery was a bit DIY, but all the money went into that hull, which is the part that keeps the water out.

Within a few days, I was out with her again, helping her new owner, Christopher Kerrison, owner of the Colchester Oyster Fishery to sail her to her new mooring in the Pyefleet Creek, off East Mersea, where the Oyster Fishery is based. My second grey mistress sailed out of our lives.

ROUND THE WORLD WITHERSHINS - AND BACK TO THE NEW BOAT.

IT is said to be unlucky to voyage against the sun, and I suppose most round the world sailors start from Britain by crossing the Atlantic from East to West - it's easier that way, if you go far enough South to pick up the North East trade winds from the Canary Islands (having gone through the Bay of Biscay in the early summer, unless you are a masochist or just plain foolhardy). If you fly long distance, it seems much better travelling Westwards, but, of course, if you go to New York on a short business trip you have little alternative but to come back West-East, and that is the trip that usually causes the jet lag. Having said this, that is exactly what Beryl and I did.

A month after the last voyage in "CELANDINE", we were aboard a Singapore Airlines 747 bound for Singapore; this was a new breed of 747s that could make Singapore from London in one tack. Beryl was to be the keynote speaker at an International conference in Honolulu, and was also going to speak for the same organisation in Kuala Lumpur; her club class fares were paid for, and it seemed a wonderful opportunity for me to travel. We negotiated an advantageous deal which meant I came for little more that the standard fare. The plane was superb - the club class was accommodated on the upper deck which had been stretched longer than on the earlier 747s. Flying East from London, in no time we reached the Mediterranean at dusk, and not much later it was getting light again as we reached the other end of the Med. I may be exaggerating slightly, but that's what it felt like to me.

Kuala Lumpur was a bustling place which exuded wealth; also very obvious was the British influence to be seen in the sporting club and other buildings, but the outstanding Railway Station building, by a British architect, looked like a mosque. It was a short visit, but in between official engagements we managed to see the spectacular orchid gardens - the climate lends itself to encouraging burgeoning blooms. After Beryl's main speech, we were taken to dinner at a Chinese restaurant, probably the best one in town and where our hosts were obviously well known. I have to confess that "Chinese" is not my favourite style of eating - perhaps I have been jaundiced by memories of take-away foil packs containing rather bland foods which would be less than piping hot by the time they reached the table. Most people I know seem happy with the stuff, but I have to apologise for not sharing their taste. This one was quite different.

An enormous and elaborate double-decker porcelain stand was placed in the centre of the circular table for ten, loaded with unbelievable delicacies including some remarkable fish - no idea what they were, but they were good. We ate with chopsticks and the meal was washed down with green tea - it may sound awful, but I thoroughly enjoyed it. The Malays are a predominantly Muslim race, so there are fairly strict rules about alcohol, but there is some conflict because there is a large Chinese population (many would probably have fled there from the communist regime in China) who are highly intelligent and industrious, so a lot of organisations tend to be dominated by the Chinese. However, they are making a great contribution to the wealth of the country, so it would be a terrible mistake to try and hamper them in some way. More than anything else that I remember about this meal were the waitresses - lissom creatures in long silk dresses into which they must have been sewn every night - or were they sprayed on?

The next morning, we returned to Singapore where there was to be a four hour wait before our connecting flight. Acting on an impulse, we said "Let's have lunch at Raffles", that legendary hotel of bygone days and famous people. This meant going through immigration procedures, paying a tax and hiring a car with driver. Raffles was old fashioned and steeped in character, but overshadowed by the high rise blocks of flats and modern hotels that had grown round it. It still had pleasant cool gardens, and after the statutory "Singapore Slings", we lunched on a cool verandah overlooking a well manicured garden in a central quadrangle. It was popular and busy, but the service impeccable and the bill reasonable - nevertheless, it must rank as one of the most expensive lunches we have ever eaten. It was one of those things that may seem crazy at the time, but the opportunity had to be taken - an unforgettable experience. Even then there was talk of modernisation, and much as we liked it, there was no way it could continue like that for too much longer. It has since been modernised, and I believe is now one of the most expensive hotels in Singapore.

Our onward flight to Honolulu via Hong Kong took us across the International date line, and I still don't understand whether we got a day younger or older. The conference was not for another week, and we had booked a "condominium" (American for self catering apartment) on the Southeast corner of Kauai, the "garden island". During the planning stage, I had consulted wind charts at the CA to confirm the normal wind direction, and it was obvious that the best place would be on the lee side of the island. The Hawaiian islands are relatively new in geological terms, and stretch out on a Southeast-Northwest axis, with the newest in this series of volcanic erruptions being at the Northwest end. Hawaii is the largest, but the most populated and busiest island is Oahu, with Honolulu and Waikiki beach as the famous tourist attractions. Once off the superb Singapore airlines plane, we then made our way to the local flight terminal, where it was heaving with people - it was the peak of the high season. In what seemed like a totally chaotic departure lounge full of interminable queues, a uniformed angel appeared and led us to a departure gate - we had begun to wonder if we would ever reach Kauai.

The weather was superb, the complex had a private swimming pool surrounded by garden, and from the end of the garden you walked out into a rocky and sandy wilderness of wind stunted trees, with the Pacific ocean swell throwing itself at the rocky shore - not the place to swim. We had a small rental car which got us about - I think it was a Datsun, and was small, horrible and automatic. Small automatics are not very happy creatures, but this one got us about including a visit to the highest point on the North side of the island, said to be the wettest place in the world. It was raining.

The contrast between this idyllic place and Honolulu could not have been greater; Honolulu is a very big city, and we are not really city people. Our arrival at the Hilton on Waikiki beach involved more queuing - sorry, "standing in line" because so many delegates were arriving at the same time, but ultimately we reached our capacious room, with a view over the Pacific and the famous Waikiki beach. It is a beautiful sandy beach, protected by an offshore reef which breaks the Pacific swell into more benign waves lapping on to the beach; to say it was crowded would be an understatement. Nevertheless, we did find that in spite of a programme of organised activities, we had time to swim from this long sandy beach. By walking a few hundred yards from the parking lots, we had it almost to ourselves, and enjoyed a superb bathe in the warm sparkling water.

One of the organised events in the evening was a trip on a "square rigger", which turned out to be some ship hull rigged with three masts and in-mast furling sails, operated by power controlled by someone on deck - I called her a "quare rigger". An excellent buffet type meal was served, and out of harbour, they shut the engines down - we didn't sail, as there was little or no wind, but it saved fuel and in the dark, one bit of the Pacific looks like another. I was glad I was not aboard this ship in bad weather.

However, the one thing about our visit that impressed us both more than anything else in the whole trip was our visit to Pearl Harbour. It is still an active naval base, but the harbour is vast, and an area administered by the national Parks Service is a memorial to those who died in that sudden surprise air attack. Arriving at the visitor centre, you collect free tickets from an office, and wait in a comfortable lounge area with many historic pictures and similar items. The number of your ticket is called, and a large group of visitors is then ushered into a cinema, where a film of the historic event is shown. It contains footage taken from cameras mounted in the dive-bombing Japanese aircraft as well as American film taken at the time; the story is told in a factual way, but the fact one cannot forget is that the Japanese fleet and aircraft carriers were already steaming towards Pearl Harbour while their ambassador was negotiating a peace plan with President Roosevelt, giving perfect cover for the sudden and treacherous attack.

At the end of the film, doors on the opposite side of the cinema are opened, and you embark straight on to liberty boats which take you to the War Memorial itself, approached by a pier straddling over the rust encrusted hull of one of the sunken battleships lying as a silent testimony in the clear water. At the base of the pier, the names of all those who died are inscribed in stone. The whole scene is so moving, we returned to the shore in one of the liberty boats and back to the hotel by taxi, in complete silence.

The devastating blow to the might of America's Pacific Fleet stunned the whole Nation; it was fortunate that some ships were at sea and missed the attack, but the big tactical mistake made by the Japanese was that they did not bomb the repair yards and docks, leaving the facilities in place to repair ships that were not too badly damaged. When the Americans want to get a job done, they go to it, and will not hesitate to use a steam hammer to crack a nut if that happens to be the only tool available. The base continued in use, and ships soon repaired for service - the rest is all history now, but with the impact of this visit still strong in our minds, we left on another Singapore Airlines flight to San Fransisco.

This is an impressive city by anyone's standards, where the new and the old seem to fit easily together. We did all the things one should do - a ride on a cable car, visit the Golden Gate bridge and take a harbour trip to Sausalito, the artist's village - which also has some very good seafood restaurants. On the return trip, I looked along the shore from Sausalito and could not believe my eyes - there was a "Liberty Ship", the British designed, American built wartime cargo ships produced in great numbers to replace the devastating loss of merchant ships, and satisfy the growing need to ship supplies to Europe once the American Army was in the conflict. Handsome working ships with simple, sweet, lines, they were not rivetted, but all welded, and welding techniques were still in their relative infancy, so there were problems with some. This one, I believe the JEREMIAH O'BRIEN, had been preserved by enthusiasts and, still in her wartime grey, kept in working order. On the fiftieth anniversary of D-Day, she actually steamed across the Atlantic with a volunteer crew.

There was no convenient direct flight to London from San Fransisco - all the travel arrangements had been made by the travel agents handling the conference travel, and after a feeder flight to Los Angeles, we boarded a TWA flight. I had heard stories, particularly from my friend Peter Darwent, an experienced transatlantic traveller, that the initials stood for "Try Walking Across" or "Travel With Anguish". Whilst I cannot claim to be knowledgeable about aircraft, I gained the impression that this must have been one of the earliest 747s made. I thought something went wrong on take-off, and became even more suspicious when, instead of heading for the Northern wastelands on a great circle route, we seemed to be flying along the Californian Coast. With humble apologies, it was announced we would be returning to LA, and given a free meal voucher. It was another four hours before we took off in another ancient looking 747 and instead of arriving back at 1215, it was late afternoon before we finally made it. I am not very familiar with the state of world airlines today, and maybe this one has improved out of all recognition, but their peformance did not give the impression of an efficient airline.

Before leaving on our round the world trip,there had been many discussions with Mike French of French Marine Motors, particularly regarding choice of main engine, which would be the heart of the new vessel, and with Derek Hyde over the difficulty of finding a suitable builder; . Derek Hyde, a former superintendent of welding at Devonport dockyard, knew where to find welders in Plymouth and said he would be prepared to enter into a contract to build if we could rent a place in which to build her. A decision on the main engine was soon reached - the heavy duty Perkins six cylinder, naturally aspirated; turbo chargers on marine engines were still giving a lot of trouble at that time, and we didn't need one anyway - it was usually a means of boosting power and fuel consumption.

The boat had the look of a Scottish fishing boat about her - the canoe stern was easily formed, and gave a rounded stern which would make berthing in tight corners easier. Her bow had the fine hollow entry which had been used in "celandine", with a bold flare to give a reserve of buoyancy when dipping into a big one; in this respect she differed from a working fishing boat which needed fuller bows to give buoyancy when carrying a big catch in the hold. Her sheer line was bold - some might think too much so, but it does result in a high bow to throw off the waves.

The search for a shed in which to build proved more difficult, but eventually, some time after our return from the Hawaiian trip, a place was found in a most unlikely situation - a small trading estate on the outskirts of Plymouth. The owner had an empty unit which he intended refurbishing in the next tax year; a beneficial rent was agreed on a weekly tenancy, with the understanding the rent would be paid in cash. Neighbours included, nextdoor, "Rowan's Crash Repairs", and a small engineering firm - several of these people proved useful in their way; as construction proceeded all were intrigued to see how she would turn out, and the bush telegraph brought one or two fishermen from the Barbican area - quite a distance - to have a look.

The base of the keel trough, a massive piece of 12mm thickness steel, was laid early in October and from then on, things moved fairly fast. The whole construction of the hull was in chines, so that the sheets of 5mm steel hull plating were only bent into shape in one plane, and did not have to be formed, which is expensive and requires special plant. The exception was the rounded stem, which had to be sent to specialists for rolling into shape. The plating overlapped by about 2" at each longitudinal join, welded inside and out, which made for great strength.

Visits to Plymouth became an almost weekly affair, usually travelling by car as I needed it once down there, and I quickly found a delightful place to stay overnight - the 14th century Cott Inn at Dartington, which was only a short drive away. All this was happening in the low season, so charges were very reasonable, and I always was able to book a room at short notice. Once or twice, I went by train, which enabled you to go there and back in a day, but did not allow a lot of time on site. Back home, there was a constant round of selecting equipment particularly where it affected construction - the Perkins (no connection with the makers of the main engine) galley stove was a sort of Aga type cooker, fired by the same diesel fuel as used in the main engine and generator, and with a back boiler to provide hot water and central heating. It was a big heavy piece of equipment and special mountings had to be incorporated on top of the double bottom tanks. When people asked what I was building, I would always say "a seagoing country cottage".

The hydraulic anchor winch was ordered from Duerr Engineering of Burnham on Crouch, who were also supplying the hydraulic bow thrust unit; all these things had to be catered for in construction - particularly the bow thruster which required a tunnel through the hull in the forefoot. A visit was made to Cradley Heath in the West Midlands, where I collected the 66lb Danforth anchor (by then known as a "Meon") from Isaiah Preston Ltd., and brought it back in the boot of the car. All this took place against a background of still working, while Beryl was travelling to Manchester and goodness only knows where else as Chairman of the Equal Opportunities Commission.

Christmas in Writtle came as a welcome break in all this feverish activity; in those days the choir would still come round carol singing, finishing with *"Figgy Pudding"*. which we always provided but looking more like glasses of wine, sausages and mince pies. An illuminated cross is hoisted on the flagstaff on top of the church tower and sends the Christmas message out all round the surrounding village and countryside. I would have to clear my study as it would be in use as extra space for entertaining, and the ever growing files on the varied items for the boat all stowed away for a little while; I know all this work was being done for a pleasurable pursuit, but at that time it had become a real chore, particularly when a phone call would announce "so and so have altered the design of this item", necessitating yet another modification.

After Christmas, the hull construction was nearing completion, and it was necessary to arrange for the whole construction to be shot blasted before immediately coating with a primer to protect the steel, but at this point a bitterly cold spell developed, and even in Plymouth there was snow and ice; finally, at the end of January the empty hull was ready to travel to Ian Brown's at Rowhedge for fitting out. The boss of the haulage firm, Debbage of Ipswich drove the lorry himself, and had arranged the statutory police escort, which would have to change at each county boundary, giving plenty of opportunity for delay. After a late start from Plymouth, a friend said he had seen the red painted hull in the early evening, heading East down the A12 near Brentwood, and she was parked in the yard at Rowhedge by eight that evening. Never again would that hull move so fast between Essex and the West country.

A tall telescopic 90 ton crane was hired to lift the hull from the trailer, put it in the water, then lift main engine, generator and the galley stove (a pretty weighty affair) into the boat before she was towed round to the covered slipway on which work would be carried out through the rest of the winter and spring. The cold weather persisted, and although the slipway (used for fitting out lifeboats) was covered, it was still pretty draughty even with the big doors on to the river closed. There was an unbelievable amount of work lying ahead - it is rather like building a house in that the walls and roof all seem to happen quite quickly, but then there is an indeterminable delay while all the services are connected and fittings put in place.

Specialist contractors dressed like men from Mars were brought in to spray the whole of the hull inside, bar the engine room, with 3 coats of epoxy pitch - the most noxious black tarry goo imaginable. One of my tasks was to apply a fibreglass felt quilted between PVC sheeting to the inside of the hull to prevent condensation and consequent corrosion; I used a rubber glue called "Thixofix" which came in very large tins, and although not by design, I discovered the solvent in the glue was also a solvent for the cheap PVC sheet on the reverse of the fibregass matting, and also for the epoxy pitch, as a result of which, both surfaces became slightly tacky and bonded superbly. The solvent in the glue was toxic, and I was careful to come out for a breath of fresh air every so often; when I was working alone in the evenings after coming down from the office, Ian would come round every so often, I think to make sure I was still conscious - it was very thoughtful of him, and anyway, it was nice to see some one for a few minutes. There is no place more lonely than a boatyard late on a midweek February evening. In the engine room, the same glue was used to apply a lining for sound absorbtion which consisted of two layers of fibreglass quilted with a non-inflammable surface fabric, and having a layer of lead sandwiched between - lead is a good sound insulant - if you hit a piece of steel with a hammer, it will vibrate and produce a loud resonant "clang", but the same treatment applied to lead will only produce a dull "thwack".

As the days lengthened, work down there became less arduous, and it all looked more encouraging as fitting out progressed; machinery installations with French Marine working in the engine room and on the Duerr hydraulic equipment, whilst Ian Brown's team worked on the joinery work that would transform this metal shell into something habitable. Steel hulls are not very receptive to the fitting of wooden linings and furnishings so stout wooden blocks and balks had to be secured to the steel frames first, and once this was done things progressed more quickly. Electrical installation was carried out by a Colchester contractor, Central Electric, who had done the electical installation aboard "CELANDINE" twenty years earlier - three separate supplies, with 24 volt DC batteries for most on board services - lighting, refrigerator, oil fired cooker and pressurised water system, a 12volt battery for starting the generator and supplying radios and echo sounder, separate 24 volt batteries solely for engine starting, and a 220 volt AC system to power electric tools and domestic equipment, and to recharge batteries through a large automatic charger.

All this was so sophisticated compared with "CELANDINE", but compared with "CAMPION", it was revolutionary - remember, she had hand starting on the engine and paraffin lighting. A gimballed brass lamp originally fitted in "CAMPION'S" foc'sle, and taken out as a safety measure when the children started sleeping in there, had lain in our garage for many a year, so I set to burnishing off the blackening and dirt of ages so that it could be put in the saloon more for ornamentation than illumination. It was to become affectionately known by my crews as "the ambience". Nothing can beat the soft mellow glow of an oil lamp in a boat's saloon.

All this had been happening against the background of a slow deterioration in my mother's health in the nursing home, which I tried to visit twice a week, and with Beryl and other members of the family at week ends; friends from the village were also very good about visiting her. She was not really ill, but just fading. On Easter Monday, she finally slipped away - the nursing home had telephoned and said they were worried about her, and thought we ought to come over. She died that afternoon while I was holding her hand - you could not have wished a more peaceful way for her to go, thirty one years after the death of my father, after only 24 years of married life. It made one think how short a time that was - by this time we had already been married 38 years. She had always been cheerful in spite of her early widowhood, and had a great many friends in Writtle - as I write, I realise most of these have now gone, but during her last years they were a great help and comfort to her. There is so much to be said for a village community.

A BOAT IS LAUNCHED - A BYPASS AT LAST AND THE GREAT WIND

BY June, the painting of the hull in what had by now become the Platt house colours - grey hull (another "grey mistress!"), black bulwarks and white super-structure - this boat had rather more of that than any of her predecessors - was nearing completion, and a large bronze propeller (33" diameter) had appeared in the aperture aft, so she began to look more like a seagoing boat. A name had been chosen and approved by the Registrar of Shipping, so I prepared name boards in my workshop at home. We chose to continue the wild flower beginning with a "C" theme - "CAMPION" was already so named by another - her original owner, Charles Dearlove, but it was a name we liked and so "CELANDINE" followed. We felt quite romantic about it when the yellow flowers appeared in our garden, but less so when we realised it threatened to take us over. After some thought and research, "CORYDALIS" was chosen for this boat, which would undoubtedly be our last. Almost as soon as we chose the name, some appeared in the garden, but I am happy to say it is more well behaved and shows no sign of taking over.

Finally, on July the 11th, she was launched by Beryl. This was now our second launching at Rowhedge, but because Beryl was working all week, we did not do as much towards the catering as had been the case with "CELANDINE" twenty years earlier, when work on the goodies had started early in the morning. A large crowd of family and friends gathered to watch her go down the ways into the Colne, to then be towed round into the dock where fitting out would continue, and we then tucked in to a buffet lunch once again served

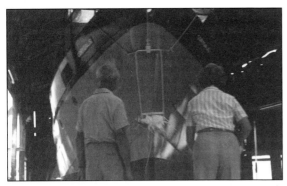

Beryl launches the third grey mistress. With the strength of her throw and the hardness of the boat's steel bow, the champagne bottle had no chance - it broke instantly.

in the big shed - being high summer, it was empty of boats. Although a significant step had been taken, there was still an enormous amount of work to be completed, including stepping the masts in their tabernacles - these wooden masts, made in Ian Brown's yard, were intended for lowering in order to navigate in continental inland water-ways. A picture of the launch was captioned in the local paper as "Splatt".

The engine and generator had been run for the first time when the tide was up - most of the time she was sitting in the deep soft mud. By the beginning of October she was ready for engine trials, and in a force 8 gale she was taken down the Colne, where below Brightlingsea a lively sea was running. French Marine's Mick Collins, who had done most of the engine installation, was hopping up and down the ladder into the engine room, checking that all was well, and doing a certain amount of tweaking. Finally, we dropped the engineers at Brightlingsea, leaving only "Thatch" Rose and myself aboard to anchor her in a sheltered spot awaiting the night tide to return to Rowhedge - there was still a lot of work to do on that boat.

Early in August, well over twenty years after the line for Writtle's Bypass had been agreed, following displays of three options which had been publicly shown to the village - all very democratic - it was finally ready, and Beryl, who had in her County Council days   cam-

"Corydalis" takes to the water.

paigned to get this road built (at times it must have seemed like bashing her head against the proverbial brick wall) was invited to cut the ribbon on Monday morning. Knowing how much Writtle wanted that bypass, Mike Selfe, the County surveyor said that if Writtle wanted to celebrate the event, they could have fun and games on it on the Sunday, but no cars. In the morning a group cycled a multi-pedalled bicycle up and down it, raising money for charity, then a large scale picnic was arranged. I went down on my bike to meet Peter Drew, chairman of the by-pass action committee

to settle on the siting of the picnic. At its lowest point, the new road crossed the river Wid, and we had already thought that if wet, we could picnic on the river bank beneath the bridge, but the day was fine and sunny, so we opted for the road surface on top.

Having established base, so to speak, Peter offered a plastic glass of wine poured from a hock bottle. I had already been to an engagement party, so hock, a fairly weak wine would be just the thing; gradually people arrived on bike or foot - strictly obeying the "no cars" ruling, the Darwents' daughter Tiffany rode in on her white Palamino. They then spread out their picnics in groups with the white line running down the centre; an extremely convivial dejeuner sur le tarmac developed, during the course of which we had several visitations. An AA van arrived - the driver was surveying the new addition to his territory, but as he drew up, a wag pointed to the "AA" on the van and announced it stood for Alcoholics Anonymous. After a friendly chat, he went on his way. Then a security van drew up, thinking we might be some kind of demo, but Peter Drew quickly pointed out Peter Nokes, our Vicar and then Beryl, explaining she would be opening the road tomorrow - "Blime -it's the Baroness" was the retort, and he left the scene convinced of our respectable credentials. Ultimately, the party came to an end, and I mounted my bike to cycle up the hill back home. Unfortunately, the bike seemed to have developed trouble with its steering gear and would not answer the helm properly so steered a rather erratic course back into the village. I later discovered that the wine in that hock bottle was somebody's home made parsnip wine.

The next day, the by pass was formally opened, and Beryl was presented with the scissors by the constructors, Roadworks, an Ipswich based company; these scissors have been carefully kept in a glass fronted cupboard to join other family memorabilia. Every time I use the road, I think of that great event in Writtle's history, and as you pass over the picnic site on the river bridge, heading South, the road sweeps up before you, giving a wonderful view of Widford Church spire on the skyline ahead.

After the first engine trials, we took "CORYDALIS" out for one or two more short trips down-river and back on the same tide, in rather more benign conditions than the first trials and reberthing on Cat Island quay outside Ian's house. On Thursday October the 15th 1987, a fresh wind was blowing by the time Beryl returned home in the early evening from a visit to Birmingham; we both were able to go to a Writtle Society lecture on Georgian Essex, and by the time we returned home it was blowing a gale, while the barometer, already low, was dropping at a spectacular rate.

After midnight, the wind developed into hurricane force, shaking our timber framed house and making a terrifying noise. At about 3-45 in the morning of Friday the 16th, the electricity supply failed, and a little later we received a telephone call from neighbours at the back that our cedar tree had fallen across St John's Road and on to their car. I went out with a torch and saw them out there; there was nothing could be done and I said it was dangerous to be out in such a wind - apart from the difficulty of standing in it, the noise was deafening and many things were airborne - roof tiles, dustbin lids, and whole sheds in some places. As soon as possible that morning, when the wind was no more than a full gale, the Writtle Sailing Club swung into action - "Thatch" Rose borrowed a chain saw from John Aldridge, who was away at the time so he didn't know it, and we worked away to get the road (only a lane) clear. Amazingly, the neighbour's car was not damaged - only the feathery fronds of the tree were on it and almost completely obscuring it. None of the main branches had hit it, which was lucky as many cars were completely wrecked that night where large trees had fallen on them. From our tree we moved on to help Thatch remove a tree resting on his garage roof.

Gradually, the extent of devastation caused by this phenomenal wind, which travelled along quite a narrow path, became known. A cooking apple tree in our orchard was blown over, as were many other trees, complete with root systems and the plate of soil attached to them. The apple crop was still clinging to the tree, and was never easier to pick - no ladders required! At the front of the house, at 7 am, I could see two big lime trees on the green had blown over in a similar way, complete with their root system, while another looked extremely dangerous - in fact half an hour later that one went right over. In the beautiful parkland of nearby Hylands House, many valuable mature trees had succumbed.

Naturally, when the immediate local problems had been dealt with, my thoughts went on to the incomplete boat lying alongside the quay at Ian Brown's. Amazingly, she was perfectly alright, although her decks were littered with wind driven wreckage. October can often be a bad month for strong winds, but this was something very exceptional. Our electricity came back at 3-45 on Saturday morning, almost exactly 24 hours later; we were lucky as some houses quite near had no supply for a full week.

A NEW HOME FOR
THE CRUISING ASSOCIATION

IN March 1988, I was elected President of the Cruising Association, and sadly, one of the first duties was to attend the funeral of my predecessor, Air Vice Marshal John Marson. John was a bluff, genial man who assumed office after a long stint performing many duties at headquarters - not an easy task when you have to come in from Aldeburgh, and finally came to be President late in life at what was developing into a difficult time for the Association, and a stressful one for him.

Ivory House at St Katharine dock was a warehouse built early in the 19th century for the storage of imported merchandise, and in particular, ivory - the tusks were stored on a floor with ample open ventilation. In those days commercial buildings had considerable style, and this one was no exception, with its central tower and large public clock. It was built as part of St Katharine dock, close to the Tower and City of London, securely enclosed against the pilfering that was rife along the Thames, and conveniently close to the commercial centres of London. Unfortunately, the ships soon outgrew the size of the lock entrance, and it declined so that after the Second World War it gradually fell into decay until Taylor Woodrow started a redevelopment of the dock and restoration of the historic buildings. The floor on which tusks were stored became the Cruising Association library and offices, furnished in harmony with the historic building to designs by the Honorary Architect, William Hurst. From the windows one overlooked the dock, which had been developed as a yacht marina and haven for restored Thames barges and other historic craft - the barges were all well maintained and a far cry from the rough working barges I remembered from my childhood at Leigh.

Unfortunately, it was very much "open plan", which meant that if a major event or party was taking place, it precluded the use of the library or cruise planning section for serious study; in addition, there were no facilities for members to stay the night at reasonable cost. The location made access for deliveries restricted and that together with restrictions by the landlords created numerous problems.

Part of the library consisted of some very fine and rare antique books which had been given by early members. The men who founded the CA and formed its early membership were mostly cultured, well educated and successful professional men; ownership of yachts was very much restricted by their high cost, so to that extent it was automatically a somewhat exclusive fraternity. H. J. Hanson, who acted as hon secretary in those early days, and was very much the driving force, suggested that each new member joining might give a book to add to this literary collection, and so antique books that were probably available for ten or twenty pounds were acquired. By the time I became President, these books had appreciated to an astronomic value; their insurance and maintenance had become a serious burden, and ultimately they had to be removed to specialist storage for security.

There was a considerable body of the membership, particularly in the regions without easy access to Ivory House, who felt that these books were irrelevant to the present day Cruising Association; but there were also those who felt that these books were very much part of the Association, and that to sell them off would be to betray the spirit in which they had been given. The yachting scene had by this time totally changed from those early days when boats took up to two years or more from drawing board to commissioning - this represented cost in real terms, and restricted boat ownership. Then came the series production of wooden boats, which immediately reduced the cost, albeit with a loss of exclusivity of design, and then the glass fibre reinforced plastic boat whereby a long production run could be produced from an original "plug". The original still had to be produced by skilled craftsmen, but the volume was produced by less skilled labour. Combined with a totally different social scene where wealth had become far more widely spread, the pleasures of boat owning were opened to a much wider market.

So this was the background to a great debate that was gathering momentum within the CA, and sooner or later had to be resolved. The lease of Ivory House, which had been granted on considerably less than commercial rates as part of the terms of the landlord's planning permission was coming to an end within less than six years, and already the landlords were looking at ways of increasing revenues from their investment. Throw into the mix another group of members who had become attached to the undoubted charms of Ivory House and wanted to stay there, and the ropes were straining in all directions. The landlords wanted us to stay and put up various schemes, but none proved acceptable and at the last rent review (upwards, of course!) with only five years to go, it had become obvious that we would have to move as we were firmly given notice that they would not be prepared to renew, except at a full rack rent which certainly could not be afforded.

The value of those wonderful rare books in store represented the cost of adequate permanent new headquarters of our own, but they could not be sold without approval by the whole membership, so I called for an emergency general meeting at which this issue should be democratically decided, and this meant conducting a postal vote of the entire membership. There was an overwhelming vote in favour of selling the rare books, but to say the meeting at which I presided was acrimonious would be an understatement, and was heavily packed with members wanting their retention. Those in favour of retaining the books felt with great conviction that it would be an unethical step to dispose of them, and could result in the dispersal of this almost priceless collection, possibly abroad.

Finally, because it was grievous to me to see such divisions within the organisation, I adjourned the meeting without a decision being made, but had to point out that we could not ignore the overwhelming vote from the membership at large, and a final decision would have to be made at the AGM in six month's time. It is amazing how there is nearly always somebody who knows somebody or something, and this proved to be the case. When the CA first moved into the large lounge at Chiltern Court, Baker Street, it was because somebody knew the architect to the Metropolitan Railway Estates who built Chiltern Court, and when we moved to Ivory House, it was because somebody knew a friend who told him of the opportunity. Now the same thing was to happen yet again, and a member introduced us to the librarian of Cambridge University library. As a result, a deal was arranged and the books were sold to them, with the provision that they would always be available to CA members on notice being given. Here was an organisation with the facilities to store these books under the conditions they deserved; at the same time there was no risk of their dispersal.

At the AGM. there was little or no opposition to this arrangement, and the CA acquired a large sum of money with which to go shopping; the property market being extremely depressed at this time, there could not have been a better opportunity. One of the parameters for search was defined by the Circle Line, to facilitate accessibility - Chiltern Court (almost part of Baker Street Station) had fulfilled this requirement, and with a little stretch of the legs, so did Ivory House - in fact it was quite a step from Tower Hill Station. A team of us started searching, and numerous properties were considered; an enormous number of buildings with potential were on offer in the Clerkenwell area, and I found myself "kerb crawling" in that part of London - fortunately I was not arrested. It turned out to be a depressing business, but then another one of those amazing breaks occurred.

Somebody had a connection with developments at Limehouse Basin, where

British Waterways were seeking to maximise the value of their land at this derelict dock - once known as Regent's Canal dock, because it gave access to both the Regents Canal and thence the Grand Union Canal, and to the Rivers Lee and Stort via the Limehouse Cut. Plans for refurbishment included a marina for both seagoing and canal boats, and once the introduction had been effected, British Waterways were keen to have us. I was lukewarm at first, because we were moving further out, but the Docklands Light Railway had just opened the extension to Bank Station, claiming six minutes to Limehouse. I promptly caught a train from Bank to Limehouse, timing my journey by their own station clocks, and the journey took exactly five minutes - I was convinced. The contractors were prepared to put up a building to our requirements, including cabins for visiting members, and at the figure we had available.

From that time on, things moved quickly, although my three year maximum term as President expired before the exciting new headquarters were ready for us, and the honour of being at the helm when they were finally opened fell to my friend and successor, Ron Browne. Although some people at those difficult meetings had said we were being too hasty over the need for new premises, in the event, the CA finally moved from Ivory House one week before the lease expired. I was however, able to berth "CORYDALIS" in the basin at the new pontoons for the opening ceremony, although the marina facilities were barely ready. Not only did we dress her overall, but also had lights from stem to stern going right over the two masts. Apart from marking the occasion, a lot of people said they saw her from both the Docklands trains and the Fenchurch Street to Southend trains which share Limehouse Station ("Stepney East" in my younger days).

Still during my presidency, there had been many meetings about its fitting out, and when I felt that some suggestions were getting a little over the top, I quoted from Parkinson's Law a passage that said when an organisation moved into palatial new premises with fountains in the foyer, it was a sure sign of impending decay. Lorna Hammett, the stalwart General Secretary who had seen us through this great upheaval duly noted my words of wisdom, so when I arrived for the opening ceremony, there in the entrance hall was a small pond with fountain playing (loaned by a CA member who ran a garden centre when he wasn't sailing).

TO FRANCE AND THE INLAND WATERWAYS

A WINTER of feverish activity at Rowhedge, which included completion of her full registration in February - all my boats have had full "Part one" registry under the merchant Shipping Acts, which gives a much more authoritative proof of ownership than the short cut "Small Ships' Register", finally saw us off on one or two local trips. During these various minor problems developed and needed correcting, also we swung compasses with our old friend Eric Diggens who had advised on installation of the main magnetic compass - an item which needed care in a steel boat.

Then, on a bright Spring morning towards the end of May, "CORYDALIS" left Woolverstone on the River Orwell bound for Calais. A light West wind was blowing, and once outside Harwich we had all sail set to give a little assistance to the engine. At a steady 7 knots through the water, it was not long before we were lunching aloft on the bridge with the North Foreland ahead, and at half past six that evening entered Calais. It was the weekend of the Calais rally, so there were a lot of boats clinging to a mooring in the avant port - in the same position as the one that had parted so dramatically 23 years previously. There being sufficient water on the rising tide, we lay alongside until later in

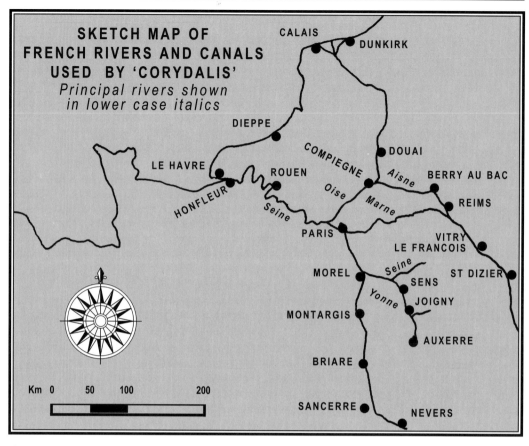

SKETCH MAP OF
FRENCH RIVERS AND CANALS
USED BY 'CORYDALIS'
*Principal rivers shown
in lower case italics*

CALAIS
DUNKIRK
DIEPPE
LE HAVRE
COMPIEGNE
DOUAI
ROUEN
Aisne
BERRY AU BAC
HONFLEUR
Oise
Marne
REIMS
Seine
PARIS
VITRY
LE FRANCOIS
MOREL
Seine
ST DIZIER
SENS
MONTARGIS
Yonne
JOIGNY
AUXERRE
BRIARE
Km 0   50   100   200
SANCERRE
NEVERS

the evening, when we moved through the lock and bridge into the Bassin de l'ouest to join a host of other boats. The crew for this trip consisted of old "CELANDINE" hands - Mike Rose squared, John Aldridge and John Barrington, all members of the Writtle sailing club. Mike "bald" Rose was able to stay, but the rest returned by ferry after a weekend in Calais.

The next day, our generator suddenly stopped within minutes of being started, and I rushed into our immaculate engine room to find the wretched thing had spewed oil everywhere. This was the beginning of a dreary delay in Calais which eventually ended with a replacement being sent out and fitted by an extremely good firm of engineers from Dunkirk.

Underway at last.

The suppliers of the small diesel engine, a well known brand, and claiming to be an international company, had proved unbelievably frustrating to deal with, the details of which are not worthy of repeating, but in a series of Telexes going through the Calais Chamber of Commerce (who were most helpful) there was one gem which I should have kept and framed - this asked if I would deal with their Paris office direct as I spoke "good French". My French, particularly on a technical level, is not that good, and I could see myself becoming involved in big company internal politics, so I rejected such a proposal out of hand. It totally disillusioned me about this company, and within a year or so I threw out this noisy piece of ironmongery in favour of something a little more sophisticated (but not to prove a lot more reliable). Marine generators seem to cause more problems on anything from our 20 tons to one of 20,000 tons.

Delay caused by this forced us to change plans; Mike Rose had to return to the UK, but not before he had done some great work in completing the galley fittings - the completion of this boat was an ongoing saga. Mike was an architect with skilled hands, so when he designed an item, he would then set to and make it - we were still carrying quite a stock of timber and hardwood trim aboard, and made frequent visits to "Bricolage" (DIY) centres. When he left, Beryl arrived by Hovercraft, having just completed her five year stint as Chairman of the Equal Opportunities Commission.

We had also been joined in Calais by my recently widowed cousin Pam Coombs, who had done a lot of sailing when she was younger, but little since she was married. When we were not working on the boat, there were some diversions, like dining at a very good restaurant privé called L'Assiette, and one day the Cruising Association's Honorary Local representative visited to see how we were getting on. He drove us up to a viewing point at Cap Blanc Nez, because there was exceptional visibility that day; we could see the masts and upperworks of a ferry emerging from Dover, and watch the hull gradually come into view - if ever a demonstration of the Earth's surface curvature was needed, this was it.

Finally, a replacement diesel for the generating set was fitted by the engineers from Dunkirk, the masts lowered and secured on their inland waterway cradles - the butts on a strong hardwood beam across the rails forward and the tops on a cradle bolted to the mainsheet fitting on the wheelhouse roof. At high water, we passed through the lock gates into the outer harbour and into the bassin Carnot. The scenery passing through the back end of Calais was not particularly inspiring, but after a short distance, we came to a very low automatic opening bridge - our first experience of a system widely used in French inland waterways. A radar detector signals the bridge mechanism; a notice on the bank tells you (in French, of course) that if you have been detected, a flashing light shows. After a few minutes wait, while traffic barriers went down, the bridge quietly opened and we were through.

Calais presumably exists as the nearest point to Dover, but the River Aa which we soon joined flows into the sea at Gravelines through a rather shallow tidal harbour. Gravelines, a place of some character has been squeezed by the Westward expansion of Dunkirk, which has always been a big commercial port, served by main canal and road routes - it is only in recent years that access to the motorway system has reached Calais. The Calais canal is pretty grotty, but once you join the Aa, not only is the canal better, but the scenery improves. That afternoon, we joined the Grand Gabarit from Dunkirk, busy with commercial traffic and on which we were able to increase speed for the first time since entering the system at Calais. After an overnight rest at Arques, we then came upon the Fontinettes Ecluse, with a lift of 13.3 metres (over 40 feet). Our lack of experience in this kind of thing meant there was some confusion of ropes. We learnt from this that you must use a bight of rope and keep on shifting it to a higher mooring point - many modern locks used by pleasure boats have either floating bollards or pontoons with mooring points, but this was mainly for commercial traffic of which there was plenty.

Although we skirted several large industrial towns, our main view was pastoral, as we passed through pleasant gently rolling countryside - more hills, of course, meant a greater frequency of locks. Unfortunately, the pleasure of this countryside was marred by a black thought that I could not erase from my mind - we were looking at countryside drenched with the blood of young men in the First World War, when the youth of Europe was slaughtered. It was not until we penetrated South beyond the Picardy countryside that I was able to obliterate these thoughts from my mind.

After a day spent in Douai, an attractive but quite large town, we became spectators of what I would call a barge match (not to be confused with the sailing barge events held on our own East Coast!). A laden gravel barge was slowly turning short round - in the path of a huge Belgian barge, and this produced an entertaining flow of language all round; there was no collision. We waited for the waterway (and air) to clear before letting go and pressing on Southwards into country that was becoming increasingly undulating and pretty - which brought us to our first tunnel. Controlled by traffic lights, as there was only one way navigation, we waited at a staging until they turned in our favour, and we entered the Ruyalcourt Tunnel for over 4 kilometres of serious concentration on steering; there was dim lighting in the tunnel, but our portable searchlight also proved useful. The hill through which the tunnel passed was quite steep, and rose spectacularly before us as we entered, and behind us as we left.

Each night we found somewhere to moor, although this wasn't always easy, in Peronne, we found a very convenient quay where we were able to stop for victualling and have lunch before pressing on towards our next tunnel, the Souterrain de Panneterie - this one only just over 1.5 kilometres long, had an instruction to sound our horn. This we did (it makes quite an impressive noise) and the traffic lights changed to green before our very eyes - we never did see how this operation was controlled, but it worked very well. That night we stopped at Noyon, where Pam left to return to the UK, Noyon being on the railway, before joining the Oise at Pont l'Eveque and passing the junction with the Aisne to reach Compiegne.

Compiegne had a quiet and picturesque bassin de plaisance out of the main channel, and here we stayed for a few days. Compiegne is a historic town, complete with a chateau beloved by French Royalty (and Napoleon) as a base for hunting in the forest. Nearby, in a forest clearing is a replica of the railway carriage in which the November the 11th Armistice was signed when the Germans surrendered. In the second World War, Hitler had it sent to Berlin to put on show, but it was subsequently destroyed during Allied bombing raids. The other major event to take place before we left was the Milk race, which passed along the riverside boulevard before great crowds.

During our stay, Beryl developed a bad back (caused, I think, by five years' travelling to Manchester et al with briefcases weighed down with paperwork) and we found a physiotherapist who worked on it with good effect; he would not take payment, so later we sent him a bottle of whisky, in response to which we had a charming letter of thanks. With Beryl's back greatly improved (we were by now just a two man crew) "CORYDALIS" was again headed South, heading up the River Aisne between well wooded banks between the forests of Compiegne and De Laiques. There was not too much commercial traffic - just a few gravel barges - and the travelling was peaceful, so in relaxed mood, we berthed alongside a small pontoon at the Auberge au Bord de l'Eau, Port Fontenay in the late afternoon in time to enjoy a walk ashore in the late afternoon sun. That evening, we enjoyed good provincial cuisine in the Auberge with a view of the river and our own boat in the evening light.

The next day we reached Soissons - a fine town, but our mooring for lunch and some shopping was right in the busy centre, with a large industrial silo complex on the opposite bank . The great thing about Soissons was the lavomatique, at the top of the steps up from the quay, so our dirty linen, of which there was plenty, was put in a machine and left to wash while we had lunch. I don't ever remember a more convenient place for this boring but essential domestic chore. In the afternoon, we pressed on to moor to the river bank just upstream from the double lock of Celles, at which point you leave the diminishing river to enter a canalised section. Just after we had moored, a smart Belgian

In the peaceful River Aisne, alongside the pontoon of "Auberge au Bord de l'eau".

barge, the "GRACIOSA", approached the lock at about twenty past five; he slowed down only to see the lock keeper shut the lockhouse door and stroll away in full view. The barge moored, the young skipper smiled and said philosophically "This is the terminus!"

From here, we followed the canal to Berry au Bac (which we called "berry with the ferry"), and at which point we were to branch off on a canal that would take us to Reims and the canalised Marne . Our canal maps showed that there were berthing pontoons there belonging to a hire boat company. When we arrived, two out of the three long spindly pontoons were wrecked and the hire fleet was all ashore with long grass growing among the neglected motor cruisers. Securing to the remaining sound pontoon, I took a line to a strong point ashore as I didn't like the look of the fragile pontoon. It had started raining, adding to the gloom - I hate to see failed enterprises. The next morning, our pontoon was twisted and distorted, and at the shore end I had to negotiate a platform that had broken off, in order to let go the rope to the shore.

By three in the afternoon, we were mooring up in the well designed port de plaisance in the centre of Reims. It was barely deep enough, so there was a bit of ploughing to get her right in the berth. The great cathedral was close at hand, but it was noisy with a fair replica of spaghetti junction crossing and recrossing the canal close by.

The next day, we were just approaching the lock at Sillery which was closed for lunch, and had a stern rope ashore when the throttle cable to the upper steering position snapped and the uncontrolled engine shot up to maximum revs. Beryl had a turn round a bollard - I shut the engine down immediately before the rope was whipped through her hands; we now had no control over the engine from either steering position. The skipper of a barge moored astern was very helpful, and had a friend running a repair business at nearby Vitry le Francois who came out that afternoon to effect a temporary repair. This gave control at lower speeds (which was all we were using), and restored control of the gearbox; arrangements were made for us to call at Vitry on our return journey to fit a new cable, which I ordered from home to be sent direct to him.

Continuing Southwards after this delay, we encountered our third tunnel, The Mont-de-Billy, where there was a telephone by the waiting staging with which to announce arrival; the charts said we might wait an hour, but the lights turned green within a very short time and we were on our way through 2.3km of tunnel. At Conde sur Marne, we joined the canalised river, which would take us through Vitry, where we would be returning to have the new throttle cable fitted.

We came to the town of Chalons sur Marne, at which we stopped next at a very pleasant tree lined quay; arriving early on a sunny afternoon so had time to enjoy the place, and met a charming couple, Pierre and Patrice Bieri who we invited aboard for a drink that evening. He brought a bottle of champagne, and it turned out he was in the trade; the champagne was from one of the less well known houses of which there are many; he explained that on the underside of a cork from any genuine champagne producer is a rocket or shooting star, and that many of the less well known marques are as good as the famous houses - and, of course, cheaper. After Chalons, we came to Soulanges, a delightful village with a grassy quay with plenty of room to moor, but sadly we shopped at the village shop which was closing down two days later - the story of so many villages.

While we were there, I laid the foundations for our next disaster by washing down the topsides on one side, leaving the wash deck valves open and capping off the hose connection with a view to berthing round the other way at our next stop. Without realising it, I had flicked on the bilge pump switch, and when we reached the next lock I looked in the engine room because things did not seem quite right. A horrifying sight greeted me - there was deep water and a noise of fast running water. I stopped the engine, then realised what had happened. The pressure from the bilge pump had nowhere to go, burst the connection up to the deck fitting and started flooding the engine room. Beryl used the emergency phone, and the lock keeper who was in charge of several locks in that stretch arrived fast in a white van. We manhandled "CORYDALIS" out of the lock and then set about getting rid of a vast volume of water. I changed the valve gear to the "pump bilge" position, but knew that there was no hope of power pumping for a while until the drive belt was clear of the water - I did not want Beryl to be involved, but she insisted on doing her stint on the hand pump, which we worked with our feet in the water. It was very hot work, and looking back on the episode, if the pump was working to fill the boat, would it not work to empty it? I didn't want to run the engine with all that water down there, so we pumped by hand until a reasonable level was reached, when I restarted and put the power pump on. Fortunately, the level had not reached a height where it could enter the sump or gearbox, and the water was clean and fresh.

It was a salutory lesson, and always since then, after using the wash deck facility, I have immediately changed the valves to the "pump bilge" postion. You never know when you might need to pump out, but washing down is not an emergency situation. After this drama, we were underweigh again within four hours, after lunch and a rest from our labours; at Vitry, we encountered a terrifying railway bridge whose air height must have been right on the minimum 3.5 metres (11.4 feet). Our height is an inch or so over ten feet, but because this bridge carried a junction, it was very wide, which made it look lower, and the decking on which the lines ran was an open grid so you looked up at the underside of the tracks. We were lucky a train didn't pass over, the noise and view of the train's underbelly would have been a frightening experience.

At Vitry, we entered the Canal de la Marne a la Saone, which is a route through to the Mediterranean, but the locks are not mechanised and the authorities have difficulty in recruiting enough lock keepers, particularly to cover holiday periods. At one lock, the lock keeper was a young student living in the primitive lock house; she clearly liked doing this job and for her it was a break from normal work. A well dressed lady was there, and to our surprise helped operate the sluices and gates. I guessed the situation, asking if she was the éclusiére's mother, complimenting her on her appearance and how like her daughter she was. She definitely took to this, but Beryl began to think this flirtation was going too far; little danger, as we were already moving out of the lock.

That afternoon, we entered the small yacht harbour "La Double Ecluse" at St Dizier, where we were to leave the boat for nearly a month; there was good security, which is very important, and M and Mme Debiere who run it were most kind and helpful, arranging for their son to run us to the railway station when we left to return home. Just as we were leaving, they gave us a spare key to the main gate in case we arrived back after they were closed.

Our return to the boat was on Sunday the 31st July, and in spite of leaving Writtle quite early to catch a 10 am train from Victoria; our train from Paris reached St Dizier at 2030, so we certainly needed that gate key to get back aboard. The following evening, we were invited to dine with M and Mme Debiere at their characterful ancient cottage in the town, enjoying French traditional cooking and interesting conversation on running boatyards. Our welcome there had been such that we were sorry to leave this pleasant place.

Retracing our track Northwards, we reached the Chantier Cornu-Garnier, where our friendly mécanicien fitted the new throttle control sent out from the UK. After a day in Vitry the job had been completed and paid for, so just after four in the afternoon we were underway with full engine controls from both steering positions. Within 18 months, the same thing happened again, and the whole matter was taken up very strongly with the manufacturers. The control was very simple in that there was only one lever which engaged the gear and acted as a speed control, but this involved a complicated piece of mechanism down below. In the end, an agreement was reached for the supply of a more robust replacement, with separate levers to operate gear and throttle; although it had their name on it, I gathered that these controls were Japanese and supplied for use aboard fishing boats where they needed to be strong; certainly they have proved trouble free.

Our return trip was to take us down the Marne to Paris, and at Conde sur Marne, where we had joined the Canal du Marne from the Aisne (and Berry au Bac with its crazy pontoons) we carried straight on to arrive for the night at Tours sur Marne. The route from Vitry is canalised, but the natural course of the swift flowing Marne is never far away. Tours was a delightful ancient small town, where we lingered to set off for a late start at nearly ten in the morning; we were still not going to push hard, but the pace of our travel had increased, and although there had been thoughts of a visit to Epernay, the weather was very hot and we looked at the shimmering tower blocks through the heat haze and decided to give it a miss. The visit would have involved a detour in what the canal maps describe as an "embranchement", whereas in fact the town lies on the true course of the Marne, which the canal joins some 5 km below Epernay.

The river, which at this point is quite wide, runs through countryside that is less undulating so flows more gently and with fewer locks to be negotiated. Our voyage was still taking us past rural and at times well wooded scenery, even though we were nearing the Paris basin, and our next night stop was at Dormans, where we moored to a good quayside near a campsite on the opposite bank from the town. Our mooring point was close to a bridge to the town, which was sited on quite a steep hillside and offered very good views over the river. The next day, after a brief stop at Chateau-Thierry, where there was no mistaking the name of the place - along the public quay a steep embankment had the town name writ large in flowers. It was Sunday, and the well tended riverbank gardens leading up to the ruined chateau were full of the world and his wife enjoying the mid-day sunshine. The town was also keen to tell you that it was the birthplace of "Le Fabuliste Jean de la Fontaine".

That evening, just over 40 km downstream from Dormans we secured to a rural quay close to an attractive looking auberge, just below a road bridge leading to the small village of Charly. The countryside here was well wooded, and to our delight, we found over 2 metres depth at the quay. So many places have depths where our 1.5+ metres draught requires a ploughing match to get right alongside, with clouds of mud and silt thrown up in the surrounding water. A group of young people were diving from the road bridge (quite a high one) which seemed rather adventurous to us; we dined in the excellent auberge that evening, and the maitre d', immaculate in professional attire, turned out to be one of the people we had seen diving from the bridge earlier.

With fewer locks and the wide river which enabled us to use more power, we were able to cover thirty or forty kilometres in the morning and spend an afternoon exploring ashore; at St Jean les deux Jumeaux we moored near the lock, where the forest came almost to the river, and the next day visited Meaux. Another historic town, complete with ancient ramparts and a cathedral in the flamboyant Gothic style found in so many parts of France, it lies on a large ox-bow in the river, where just downstream from the "Halte de Plaisance" the river cascades over a very uninviting barrage of rocks. Continuing the next day, we entered another canalised section where at one point the natural course of the river veers quite a distance from the more direct line of the canal; the river is also quite shallow and swifter, flowing through more undulating terrain. A short tunnel and two locks put us out on the main river again; less than 20 km from the centre of Paris, the riverside scenery was becoming more urban and industrial so we pressed on.

The navigation once again enters a canalised section at Vaires sur Marne for a short distance, to rejoin the river at Neuilly sur Marne, where we stopped for the night for convenience, not scenic beauty. We were now in the Paris basin, and the river meandered through the flat land in enormous curves, one of which is cut off by a short cut through a tunnel to the lock at St Maur. Here, the last lock before reaching Paris, there is quite a fall; I was expected to go ashore and present ship's papers (which I don't think they understand), and imagining the boat had reached somewhere near the end of the drop, I went up the long iron ladder ashore. A few minutes later, I heard an urgent series of blasts on the horn, gathered up the ship's papers and rushed outside to see her with a considerable angle of heel, suspended by the single mooring rope amidships. Beryl had got a riding turn on the bollard, and both ends of the rope were totally jammed; in fact, in a descending lock there is little turbulence and the boat can be held without a turn, but here we had an emergency. Beryl dived below and grabbed the breadknife from the galley; as she attacked the rope, it suddenly went with a bang and the boat was free, but then I had to be recovered from the bottom of the iron ladder, clutching the precious ship's papers. The lock staff had all conveniently disappeared and offered no help whatsoever, but we were now only 5 km from the centre of Paris, and this incident reinforced my view that you should not judge a nation by the attitudes of people in its capital city.

After this unfortunate hiccup, we still reached the Paris Arsenal port de plaisance in time for lunch. Conveniently situated in the Bastille area, it is well served by metro lines - so much so, that lying in your bunk at night, you can hear the noise of trains rumbling by transmitted through the hull. Before leaving for home, I checked the amount of mooring fee I would be paying after three weeks' stay there; they did not take credit cards and I asked the name of their bankers so that I could transfer the money. This would not be necessary, they assured me - to my surprise they would accept my cheque.

Before setting out from home, I checked with my bank to say there would be a cheque going through for about four thousand French francs, and they were quite happy about this. In fact, when I returned to the boat and tried to pay my berthing fees, they were quite adamant that they would not accept my cheque - of course, the person who told me they would was nowhere to be seen. I had only brought out sufficient currency to pay for victuals and casual berthing fees, and it would have taken time to organise a transfer of funds; there was a fairly tight schedule ahead, and I needed to get that boat out through the lock the following morning. No body was really interested, and this is one of the things that can be so infuriating when things go wrong over there, when the attitude seems to be "get lost".

Their bank was quite near, so I walked round there, and saw a charming assistant manager who listened to my problem. We had an interesting conversation during which she asked me what I thought of the new opera house. Confessing ignorance on this subject. she then told me it was being built very near the Arsenal marina. "Oh, is that the vast concrete construction I see from there?", mentioning we had wondered what it could be - one of my crew said perhaps they were rebuilding the infamous Bastille. She thought this a huge joke, as it was quite clear she did not like it and considered to be another Mitterand folly.

It was well worth the conversation - she returned to my problem and asked if I had an American Express card - "go to their branch near the Opera, and they will cash your cheque" It was quite a distance, by metro and some walking, but I "stood in line" (Americans don't queue) and without any problem got enough cash to pay the berthing fees plus a bit extra. I raced back to the Capitainerie at the Arsenal, paid my mooring fees, breathed a sigh of relief, and took my young crew out to dinner at a newly opened restaurant in the gardens attached to the marina - it was not up to much, but it saved cooking aboard at a busy time while we stored up and generally prepared for the voyage home. For the trip down the Seine, I had Adam Blackstone, who is the grandson of my first cousin, so he is a cousin, but I am no expert on the varying types of cousinship and can do no better than describe his relationship in the way that I have. With him, came Siriol Davies, who is a sister of my son-in-law, so we were a crew of three as far as Rouen, where we would be joined by the stalwart Pam, then there would be a further crew change at Le Havre when members of the Writtle sailing club would be joining.

At half past nine the following morning we locked out and started downstream through the centre of Paris on what was developing into a beautiful day. Notre Dame, on the Isle de la Cite, was bathed in an early morning sunshine which was dispelling a slight lingering mist, giving a spiritual quality to the scene. Beyond the centre, however, like so many other large cities, there are some very uninspiring scenes of waterside urban decay, interspersed with grander projects to revitalise these areas. One interesting building just outside Paris, and looking rather run down, is the Bleriot Aircraft establishment, with the name clearly proclaimed on the brick facade. The building is probably rightly listed as a monument, but it is no doubt difficult to find a modern commercial use that will pay for its maintenance.

Within the hour, we were passing the Isle de Seguin which is entirely occupied by a Renault car factory; I don't know what sort of appearance it presented when approached from the shore side, but the river side was scruffy and poorly maintained. Over the next few years we were to pass it regularly, looking worse and worse each time, and finally abandoned and derelict - no doubt production had moved to a more spacious and better laid out site, but on moving out and leaving the place to dereliction, you would have though they might have taken the name down - the building was hardly an advertisement for anything. I believe that recently a rich benefactor has given money to turn part of it into an Art Centre.

The first lock below Paris is at Suresnes, an efficiently run lock in a most depressing and run down suburb, although on the opposite bank is the famous Bois de Boulogne giving a break in the otherwise industrial scenery. As one approaches Argenteuil, the site of several famous Monet river paintings, there is a vast dock complex, a power station, foundry, storage tanks - you name it, it will be there - not much sign of Monet's peaceful scenes with sailing boats in view. That evening at a little after six in the evening, we berthed for the night at Limay, where there is a "halte de plaisance" - these are generally pontoons with a gangway ashore, and in theory, electricity and water available. The electricity supply is almost invariably vandalised, and you wonder whether it was worth the expense of installation, whilst the water supply varies - at this, had we wanted water, it would have meant someone holding a spring loaded tap down, always presuming you managed to get your hose connected to the strange outlet in the first place. It was in a quiet backwater with tree lined banks, and across the river a view of Mantes-la-Jolie, dominated by its great church tower and spire; just upstream was a busy road bridge, and you were not far from a large power station plus a dock complex. In spite of this, it is one of the first stops, 109 kilometres and three locks downstream from Paris, with a less urban ambience than any other of the infrequent haltes to be found further upstream.

From here, our voyage the next day took us through far more rural and wooded

Halte de Plaisance, Limay, in a sheltered backwater.

scenery; the Seine is a well used waterway and one must expect still to find industrial sites taking advantage of this useful highway. The river flows through relatively flat land, so that locks are not too frequent - only six between Paris and the tidal part of the river, a distance of just over 200 km, but it meanders lazily round great ox-bows. In the lower reaches before reaching tidewater, there are some spectacular limestone and chalk cliffs -"falaises", but the river still winds its way through a flat plain, sometimes sweeping in very close to them. They look as if cut by man in some places, to facilitate navigation, but they are natural, and a geologist would have some interesting observations on their formation. That night, our second out from Paris, we found a quiet little quay at Poses, in a backwater leading down to the great barrage at Amfreville which separates tides from the non tidal part of the river - you could say "The Teddington of the Seine", but it is all on a much vaster scale. Our next day's

Raising masts in the Bassin St Gervais- a convenient place for the operation, but scenically, totally depressing.

voyaging took us through the smaller of the three locks at Amfreville, and just after noon, we were entering the Bassin St Gervais just downstream from the very centre of Rouen, where there is a pontoon for yachts to raise their masts. By the time Pam Coombs joined us that evening, we had the masts up and Cruising Association burgee flying from the mainmast, instead of from the tiny "motorboat" mast used on the inland waterways. Just as well, since it was low tide and she was only just able to see our Cruising Association burgee from her taxi (the driver must have wondered why a nice girl like her wanted to go to this God-forsaken spot) The bassin St Gervais is a neglected, rat infested, derelict portion of Rouen's extensive docks, from where nearly all the former quayside warehouses have been cleared to leave a total wilderness. But there is no passing traffic and it is totally sheltered, so that the boat is absolutely still while the tricky part of the raising and lowering operation is in progress.

This bassin is not somewhere to linger, useful as it was to us, and after our third night out from Paris, we left at

"Bonne heure" to proceed down to the sea. At that time, Corydalis was still new to me, and I was not sure of her ability to push against the strong flood tide, so we secured to a large ship's mooring by putting Adam on to it, and reeving a rope on a return for ease of letting go. In subsequent years, I have found her power ample to push over it, and the flood is of relatively short duration, so this manouevre was not really necessary. Lunch was eaten in peace, and at two in the afternoon we let go and pushed on downriver, soon picking up the powerful ebb tide. Swiftly we were borne downstream. under the Pont de Tancarville (at that time the most Westerly road bridge on the river), past Honfleur and down to the open estuary, passing what was to become a familiar landmark over the following years, a group of buoys marking the wreck of the "DUNCAN L CLINCH" - the wreck itself was under the waves, but I'm sure she was an American liberty ship, a casualty of the War.

That evening, we berthed in the port de plaisance at Le Havre, four nights and 380 km or 205 nautical miles out from Paris. Adam and Siriol left to catch a ferry home, whilst Michael "Bald" Rose and John Aldridge were there ready to join us for the last stage of our homeward voyage.

Sailing before light the following morning - it was now nearing mid-September, and at just after half past four, it was still dark - we had changed the ship's clocks to BST the night before. Once we had turned Northwards for a long day's run up the Normandy coast, we hoisted sail in the moderate Westerly breeze to steady us and help our speed. By the afternoon, the Normandy falaises had been replaced by the low lying lands of the Somme and Canche estuaries, whilst the coastline receded from our view in the deep bay before the high headland of Cap d'Alprech rose above the horizon before us. It had been a long day's voyaging, and it was quarter to seven before we entered Boulogne, where we made fast alongside the fuelling berth as there was no where to lie on the inadequate pontoons - it was still a ferry port, and yachts were not a big priority, but they have probably improved the facilities since the ferry traffic ceased. I have never been back to see.

The following morning we were breasting into a force 6/7 wind from the West, and a little time after we left Dover Coastguard were putting out a strong wind forecast. It was a pretty rugged punch across the Channel and the shipping lanes, but by mid-day we had reached the sheltered water of the Downs, where we took advantage of the smoother progress to eat lunch, before losing the shelter of the North Foreland and setting off across the Thames Estuary. A violent squall with lashing rain hit us as we approached the Edinburgh Channel, but as so often happens, this took the sting out of the wind, which veered to Northwest - dead ahead. Threading our way through to the Swin Spitway, we then made for the Colne estuary, where we anchored for the night in the Pyefleet at seven, thirteen hours out from Boulogne. We were back in the cradle of our home waters again.

THE END OF AN ERA, AND RETIREMENT

THE next day, on the tide we took her to a mudberth in Rook bay at Ian Brown's yard, where a few modifications were made as a result of experience in service, and finally filled with diesel oil before leaving the yard at Rowhedge, which had been such a part of life for over twenty years, for the very last time. Ian had announced that he was closing down and retiring; although running a boatyard like that would never furnish you with a great pension, he was sitting on some very valuable riverside land, and it was this that would provide him with a pension. There was a very loyal band of supporters who had been well served by this yard, and towards the end of November, a well attended reception was laid on for Ian and Pat Brown at the Colne Yacht Club in Brightlingsea. A few days later, the contents of the yard were auctioned, but due to Cruising Association commitments, I could not go and John Barrington went with one or two other members of the Writtle Sailing Club, buying some useful pieces of mahogany that had come out of yachts. I am glad I could not go, I think I would have found it very depressing, for it was the end, not just of an era in my life, but of ship and boatbuilding that had been carried on for centuries in Rowhedge. Its heyday was in Victorian and Edwardian times, when many big and famous yachts laid up there for the winter, while the crews would either go fishing or be involved in maintenance and fitting out. On Saturday October 1st, we let go from the yard at Rowhedge for the very last time. A few days later we took "CORYDALIS" round to the Tide Mill Yacht Harbour at Woodbridge for the winter.

September 1st 1988 was the official date of my retirement, and of course my 65th birthday. In the morning, Beryl asked me if I felt any different - of course I didn't (you don't feel any different inside - it's only the outside that ages) - "I feel like an eighteen year old". "And you're not having one" was her swift reply. Anyway, that evening she treated me to a highly romantic dinner at the Savoy, to mark this great occasion.

Immediately you reach retirement age, instead of paying vast sums in insurance premiums, they start paying you, and you start drawing the old age pension, so financially I found the going easier, helped also by the fact I was no longer paying out large sums for the completion of "CORYDALIS". Additions were still to continue, such as the fitting of an autopilot to our hydraulic steering system, but this kind of thing was relatively modest and could be phased over a period.

Although I continued to take an interest in the family business, I had made it clear to Roland that he was now in charge. I would give my advice and opinion on things, whether asked for or not, but advice (from any source) is there to be accepted or rejected. Once you cease being involved closely with the day to day affairs, it is remarkable how quickly you become out of touch, and I had known of family businesses where a father will not give up the reins and always thinks he knows better - often with disastrous results. Roland was now 37, a qualified chartered accountant who, in his practising days had experienced dealing with a variety of businesses, whereas I was only 23 when I suddenly got pitched in at the deep end, and had only really been trained how to run a landing craft up on a beach. In the event, I don't think we have ever disagreed on any matters of policy.

The other thing that I now had time for was the Presidency of the Cruising Association - I have already described how the attempts to remain at Ivory House proved futile, but only after many time consuming meetings. I visited the Southampton Boat Show as part of the duties - the CA always has a stand at these shows, but have to say they are not really my scene; the thing I found pleasurable was that a young lady discreetly asked if I was over 65, which I was - just, and offered me a concessionary entry charge. She explained some people resented this and would prefer to disguise their age, but not me - nobody could insult me with money. There was the most enjoyable Clyde Cruising Club dinner to attend - there has always been a very good relationship between the two organisations, and on this, my first, Beryl had another irrevocable commitment, so I went alone, by train; I enjoy long train journeys, they are such a wonderful way of seeing the country as well as enabling you to relax and read as you are borne to your destination.

Shortly after ending her five year stint as Chairman of the Equal Opportunities Commission, Beryl had been invited to join the board of British Gas, so she was still kept very busy as she is not the kind of person to take a job on without putting all she has into it. She was now among fellow engineers, with whom she always had a rapport; the Chairman, Sir Denis Rooke was himself an engineer, a man with great vision and integrity. There were numerous site visits up and down the country, in which Beryl enjoyed talking to staff on the ground. Such commitments meant she was not always available for CA events, but whenever other duties permitted, she would be there giving support.

We had arrived at Woodbridge as orphans from the closure of Ian Brown's; the choice was partly because we all like Woodbridge as a town, the river Deben is a delightful river, and the Tide Mill Yacht Harbour was being steadily transformed by the Kember family. For undertaking fitting out, there was my old friend Frank Knights, who although retired, still lived on the premises and continued to take an interest, and had a thoroughly competent and likeable man in charge of day to day running, Keith Cutmore. Whisstocks, who at one time had been leading boatbuilders on the East Coast had suffered a change of direction which meant they threw out all their traditional repair and building work to concentrate on building large and exotic yachts only; they still retained their slipway which was needed to launch their products, and were perfectly happy to hire it out. Thus, in the Spring, we were able to slip "CORYDALIS" using their facilities, whilst Frank Knights' team carried out the work, their premises being adjacent.

Woodbridge retains many specialist shops of the type that have all but disappeared from so many High Streets, and with rising property values, many run down buildings and yards off the main street have been transformed into attractive small shopping precincts. There is even a really old-fashioned Woolies; numerous little teashops can be found, and, sometimes important for us sailing folk, a launderette. The opening of a large aggressive Tesco's at Martlesham Heath (a place Beryl still sometimes refers to as the Empire Test Pilots' Flying School - it was a major RAF airfield) must have affected some of the trade, and the butchers' at which we bought meat and fresh milk in those far away "CAMPION" days is no more, but there still are an excellent butchers' and greengrocers' as well as a good small super-market in the town centre. If you live near the town centre (which can mean being aboard your boat at the Tide Mill) you do not need a car to go shopping.

Over the next few years, we began to take little winter trips downriver, visiting the various hostelries, the Maybush at Waldringfield, (once the haunt of the late cartoonist Carl Giles), under whose riverbank sign Beryl and I were photographed in our courting days, and the Ramsholt Arms - transformed from the primitive stone flagged pub I remember from early days on the Deben, by various additions and up datings. During these winter excursions, you were assured of a welcome and lack of crowds.

At this time, "CORYDALIS" had no regular mooring place; I had given Halls at Walton the mooring occupied by my two previous boats, "CAMPION" and "CELANDINE"; CORYDALIS was just too large for it, and anyway, I had decided that boarding from a dinghy was not something to be carried on into old age. I had the winter berth at Tide Mill, and used the Marina at Woolverstone on an irregular basis - a lot of time was spent in a very nomadic mode. I also used the Neptune Marina in Ipswich Dock, although there were at that time severe tidal restrictions which made it inconvenient.

The first trip to Holland started from Woolverstone, but as we were due to make an early departure, I moved downstream late in the evening and picked up one of the moorings off Levington Marina. I remember looking ashore in the last of the evening light and thinking how attractive the scenery was there, and also how much nearer the sea it was - was this not the reason we had picked up the mooring?

The mooring was let go at twenty past four, and being late May, the sun was already just beginning to lighten the sky in the Northeast - which was also where the wind was coming from, almost a dead noser all the way to Flushing. Although relatively light at first, it soon became a very fresh wind and we started breasting into substantial seas; her high and well flared bows pushed the spray aside, but the strong wind blew it straight back again, and punching into it at seven and a half knots we threw up sheets of spray up that soon covered the whole boat, and every now and then some solid water would run down the lowest part of the side decks. I was interested to see how the hull was standing up to the punishment we were giving it; there was not the slightest evidence down below of any of the creaking that goes on in a hull that is flexing as the internal joinery is distorted by the hull movement - if anything, this hull had been over engineered. The engine pushed us on at a steady pace, the big deep set propeller thrusting us forwards at steady revs. If the crew could take the punishment, the boat certainly could, but even though the hull lines eased her movement fighting her way forward, it was tiring work.

During the afternoon, as we approached the Dutch coast the seas began to moderate; one of the innovations on this boat was the Decca Navigator, and on an open sea crossing of well over 80 nautical miles, this was a great comfort giving confirmation of your position to ensure an accurate landfall after being thrown around by a fairly angry North Sea for some hours. At twenty past five, exactly 13 hours after leaving the mooring off Levington, we entered the sea lock at Flushing before continuing on the glassy waters of the Walcheren Canal to Middleburgh. From here, we continued at a gentle pace visiting all our our familiar ports of call; the outward crew, Peter Darwent and John Aldridge returned to the UK, whilst Mike "bald" Rose and Jean joined.

Warmond was revisited, berthing in our old friend the "Cieco" marina before making our way to Amsterdam. One of the advantages of this boat was that, from the upper steering position, your height of eye was sufficient to see over the canal banks. As we passed Schipol we could actually look down on the airport and see into the big maintenance hangars (an entry in the log records "near miss from 737"). That night saw us once again passing through the Central Railway Station bridge at half past two in the morning, to make fast in the Sixhaven half an hour later. On this trip, we paid a visit to Volendam - I last visited this picturesque (and it knows it!) fishing village cum tourist attraction when Peter van den Brul's uncle drove us around in 1949 - so this was my first visit by boat. There was plenty of room to berth, as it was still only the end of May.

Our berth lay outside a fishmonger rejoicing in the name "Platt". Business was not very brisk and every now and then he would stand outside and shout "qualitat". Nextdoor was a greengrocer, run by a very pretty and slightly voluptuous young lady. Every so often they would both emerge from their establishments, have a quick cuddle and disappear inside again. It reminded me of those barometers (I think they are barometers) where either a woman or man would emerge from holes in the wooden case. Our berth also was by a lamp post to which a litter bin was attached. Clearly Mr Platt sold a lot of smoked fish, whose skins tended to end up in this bin, and equally clearly the local herons knew about this, so that even when we were on deck, they would swoop down to extract the delicacies. Dutch herons are very urbanised.

We returned to Medemblik to find the whole place changed - a big new marina in what I remember as a playing field on a previous visit in "Celandine", with a new housing development in traditional Dutch style overlooking it. Here on the Isselmeer, we were able to play with our Decca - this was a new toy as far as we were concerned, and Michael has always taken an interest in navigation - a natural development from his architectural training - and in perfect visibility with closely spaced buoys marking the channels, we put it to the test. He became quite obsessive about the whole thing; after visiting Enkhuisen and Hoorn, we entered the harbour of Muiden, home of the Royal Netherlands Yacht Club, where, eyes glued to chart and Decca display, he announced "there should be a large castle on your port beam". There was - less than a hundred yards away.

Returning to Amsterdam, Mike and Jean left on Monday, whilst Beryl crossed by the night boat on Wednesday (what a wonderful service those night boats offered - she had been at a meeting on Wednesday, but arrived at Amsterdam Central Station just after half past nine on Thursday morning. From Amsterdam, we cruised Southwards at a leisurely pace, passing through a motorway bridge near Haarlem just before 1300 - the next opening would be at eight that evening - which enabled us to berth for the night in Haarlem, where our friends the Elhorsts visited us. This route enables the journey Southwards to be made in daylight hours, avoiding the night transit of the Central Station Bridge, but great care has to be exercised in studying bridge opening times from the Dutch almanack, or you may be in for a long wait. We were in no hurry, and made our way to the Kaag lakes, where we anchored close to one of the numerous islands; not many people do this, but it does ensure you are on your own and cannot slip ashore to go shopping.

Warmond was revisited, where our friends Peter and Anne Groom (she is Mary Dainty's sister) joined us, having travelled out by car - Peter is a great driver. It was just as well, because Beryl had taken a fancy to an armillary sphere (an upmarket sundial) she had spotted lying somewhat neglected in a garden centre. This was a formidable piece of ironmongery, with a band representing the equator crossed with another band representing the greenwich meridian and pierced centrally with a sharp tipped arrow to act as the shadow pin. The whole thing was mounted on a heavy cast base, and the thought of having to ship this lot back to the UK, with a full crew aboard for the return passage, did not thrill me. Fortunately, the Grooms had come in a capacious estate car and offered to take it home for us; this was a great kindness, and at least with it tucked well away at the back, neither of them were likely to be impaled on the steel arrow. I have to say it has made a pleasing ornament in the garden, where I was careful to ensure the North-South alignment of the arrow. It has illustrated the difference between sidereal time and that shown by our watches - they only seem to coincide at about the time of the solstices.

Now we had a boat with a powerful engine, instead of continuing Southwards when we reached the main waterway upstream from Rotterdam, we headed East, up the Lek or Issel. Here kilometre posts informed you how far from Basle you were, but we settled for Schoonhoven - the town of the Silversmiths, a typical historic old Dutch town with an imposing ancient gateway on to the river, narrow back streets and a tiny small boat harbour. We found a yacht marina that was really part of a caravan site, but there was a berth near the entrance with sufficient depth and a staging (stieger) strong enough to take us. I don't think this place often saw boats as deep and substantial as "Corydalis."

Our leisurely progress continued through some of our old favourite places (all getting increasingly crowded), while our return crew joined in dribs and drabs; the indomitable Pam joined us somewhere deep in Holland, and finally we visited my favourite, the little harbour "De Werf" at Goes (the one entered through what almost looks like a hole in the hedge, and run by the delightful bunch of volunteers, all, sadly, ageing). Here, John Barrington and Peter Darwent rejoined, while Beryl left, and we started on our way to the sea via Middleburg and Flushing. This time, we were going back to London to see the start of the Tall Ships' Race, so we crossed the Schelde to Breskens. What a difference from the place I had visited in 1965 with "Campion"; it had become a vast impersonal marina, where, to pay your dues you walked a long distance to the offices - nobody did anything as convenient as coming round to collect them. Resolved never to visit again, we left at half past five the following morning.

A COWBOY ON THE THAMES

BECAUSE we were heading for the Thames Estuary, I did not use our usual route through the Duerloo Channel, but took the more Southerly big ship channel. A stiff North-northwest wind and grey skies greeted us, and some steadying sail was set for what was a beam wind on the course we were taking; not only did this steady us, but it was also a positive help to progress. Gradually the clouds dispersed, and it all began to look better as the wind slowly veered to become more favourable, so that by three in the afternoon when the sunlit white cliffs of the North Foreland were clearly visible, it had gone round to North-northeast and we hastened on our way through the Princes channel.

Finally, after a fifteen and a half hour passage in which we put over 110 nautical miles behind us, the anchor went down inshore of the West Leigh Middle Buoy, where we were well sheltered from the Northeast wind, which had fallen light inshore at the onset of dusk - further out it was probably still blowing quite hard. Gradually, the long line of lights along the shore stretching from Leigh all the way to Southend began to show, gleaming in the calm water along the edge of the Ray Bank, and I spent a little time on deck picking out some of the familiar spots remembered from my boyhood.

The next morning saw us underway by half past eight, taking the flood tide all the way upriver - once again past the aptly named Mucking - actually an ancient Saxon name (Essex is the land of the East Saxons). "Ings" abound in Essex, particularly near the coast or rivers which the ancients would have used for transport, and the word means a settlement. This one would have been "Mucca's" Ing, and among the other Ings is Messing, between Kelvedon and Colchester - it is a lovely little village, and Mucking may well be, but from the river it looks desolate. Shell did a series of advertisements before the War which played on place names - hence "Mucking and Messing in Essex - but not with Shell".

Approaching Greenwich reach, I saw a small passenger boat coming across the river, so I moved positively over closer to the starboard bank, so that we would pass "red to red" as is laid down. He continued on his course over to what was the wrong side of the river for him. To avoid a collision course, I moved even nearer the starboard bank, but he persisted and I could go no further in for fear of running aground; when I could do no more to pass to starboard of him, emergency action was required to avoid a collision, and we would have to turn to port. The danger here is that if you both panic together, there will still be a collision, so I gave two blasts on the horn - "I am directing my course to port", and immediately swung over to port, which I think was what he was trying to force me to do. The vessel, which was a wooden hulled launch of doubtful vintage, on which a rather home made saloon had been built, probably had about forty people aboard, and had there been a collision with our strongly built steel hull, the result could have been very serious. Only a few weeks after this incident, news came through of the terrible "MARCHIONESS" disaster.

Since that tragedy, there has been a general tightening up of procedures, and the passenger boats are required to report their movements by radio. If there had been radio contact at the time of the near miss that we encountered, he might have told us of his intentions - even if only to say "push off aht o' me way". On many subsequent trips up river, there have been no such incidents and everyone now seems to be sticking to the rules. By half past one we were locking in to St Katharine Dock, thankful that no disaster had occurred, and ready for the excitement of the Tall Ships over the next few days.

A fortnight later, we were on our way downriver again, locking out just after ten and reaching the gateway through the Wallet spitway soon after low water - the lowest depth recorded was two and a half metres, which to an Essex boy is plenty (if your boat draws only five feet - almost a full metre of water under us). Seven and a half hours after leaving St Katharine's, we anchored in the Colne above Brightlingsea (the wind being in the North east), before completing our voyage to the Orwell the next day. During that autumn season, we poked "CORYDALIS" into many of the old haunts last visited in "CELANDINE" - the Butley River, Slaughden Quay and above on the River Ore / Alde before returning to Woodbridge for laying up.

A ROUGH START TO THE YEAR - BATTLES WITH AUTHORITY - AND ANOTHER TALL SHIPS RACE

THE year 1990 started badly in that I managed to get pleurisy; it was not a particularly bad winter, but after a busy day which included a visit to the Boat Show and an RYA reception in the evening, I arrived at Liverpool Street station to find vast crowds and no trains. Nobody knew what was wrong, and the whole station was undergoing a major refit which made things even more chaotic - there was nowhere to sit down or get out of the cold damp wind so by the time I boarded a train I was shivering like an aspen in a breeze. The nett result was to lay me low for some time - not really ill, just going off like a damp squib.

Towards the end of January we endured another near hurricane force wind - perhaps not quite as fierce as that of October '87, but from the West rather than South. The trees were not in leaf, so they did not suffer as much as in the 1987 hurricane, but my nextdoor neighbour came round to say the lead had come off one of my attic dormer windows, and had blown against the wall three doors down the street. After inspecting it, I was able to tell him it was his lead (the properties are a pigeon pair). I then took a pair of binoculars and surveyed my house from the green - the news was worse, as not only had the lead stripped off one of my dormers, but it had gone no further than my own roof, making a sizeable hole where it landed.

The damage to the house was quickly repaired, but it was felt that I needed repairing as well, having developed pleurisy during the winter. I described how one year we drove out to see my sister in Milan, motoring through the Alps, and returning via the Italian and French rivieras; on this retun trip we had stayed at a small family and commercial hotel, the "Brise Marine" at St Jean, Cap Ferrat. Now, over thirty years later, Beryl dug out their card, we telephoned and booked, so in March flew to Nice and stayed there again. M. le patron had died, but it was being run by his daughter and son-in-law; I will swear we had the same bedroom, with an elaborate ornamental ironwork balustrade to the balcony, which overlooked the coast Eastwards towards Monaco. Without a car, we successfully used public transport or taxis to get about, and, of course, there were superb coastal walks.

That repair having been made by the warm balmy Spring climate of the Riviera, then in May Beryl fell down the last part of a temporary staircase at Liverpool Station, still in a chaotic state from all the alterations being made. She arrived home late, flung me the car keys and said "Don't look at me, take this taxi and go and get my car from the station, so still in my slippers (I don't think driving in slippers is an offence, just a bit odd) I did this. When I returned home with the car, she had a black eye, severe bruising and her wrist hurt. In the morning she was due to attend an important British Gas board meeting, but it was my turn to play nurse - with all the authority I could command, I said she should see the doctor first. To my surprise, she did - and as soon as she walked in to Michael Bailey's consulting room, he said "I suppose you realise you've broken it" - there was no meeting for her that day. Plans had been made to sail to the West Country, leaving in a few days' time, but that was promptly all cancelled, to be replaced with a very local programme.

During my time as president of the CA, there were the usual ongoing battles with one or another authority behaving unreasonably as far as the cruising yachtsman was concerned. One, in which we supported the RYA was an ongoing battle with the BBC over shipping forecast timings - they regularly want to change everything - "change must be better" - they would change the shipping forecasts to an ever less convenient time or reduce the information given. On this occasion, the RYA received a letter from the BBC (which I think should have been framed and put on public display) saying that under the terms of its charter, it had no duty to consult with other bodies. This sums up the kind of arrogance one faced at the time, although as I write, there does seem to be a better climate in that they are consulting; their culture is however, that things like shipping forecasts are an interference with their programmes and lack any artistic merit.

The other fight which the CA took on its shoulders concerned the marina berthing fees charged by a certain company whose managing director was reported as having said that they would go on putting up the charges "until the pips squeaked" or words to that effect. Whilst involved in this, I was asked if I would appear on a television feature about high marina charges in a Channel 4 programme. The interviewer made no bones about the name of the company they were taking to task, but I was careful not to mention the name - a large television company can no doubt cope with the odd legal action (for all I know they may have insurance to cover such an eventuality), but I certainly didn't have any such protection. How much effect our output had, I don't know, but it was not long before they came unstuck on some property deals, and this together with a temporary fall in demand for berths, probably not unconnected with falling property prices created a slump. Most of the problems related to the South coast, of which my late lamented friend George Jones had said "Your hand will always be in your pocket".

After a relatively quiet period with "CORYDALIS" berthed in Suffolk Yacht Harbour for occasional short trips out while Beryl's wrist improved, towards the end of July, we sailed from Levington for Fecamp, where we were to act as communications vesel on the finishing line of that year's Tall Ships' race coming up from Bordeaux. With a high barometer and a light wind from the North East, we set off in good form across the Estuary. The sky was cloudy in spite of the high barometer - in the Navy there was a wonderful meteorological instructor, Commander Benstead (yes, I'm afraid we did call him "Bedstead") who, when asked why when under such conditions you still sometimes got dull cloudy weather, he would explain it as "anti-cyclonic gloom". This was one such day. Later, as we neared the South Foreland, the sky cleared - were we moving into better weather, or was it clearing everywhere?

Darkness came as we passed Dungeness, which we rounded and stood into Rye Bay to heave to under a tightly strapped in mains'l, shut down the engine, and enjoy a peaceful supper sheltered from the Northeast wind. Course was resumed before midnight at easy revs - we were putting in at Brighton for a crew change that would bring aboard those prepared to spend some days rolling about off Fecamp, and I preferred to enter after daylight, entering at quarter to six.

Three days later, we were off again, with a crew of seasoned stalwarts - Michael "bald" Rose, Pam Coombs, and the staunch sailor from Cornwall, Richard White. With only a light wind, our sails gave little help, but we had a calm uneventful crossing which brought us to Fecamp in just under ten hours. We berthed in the inner harbour; although there were plenty of "iron rations" aboard to cope with sustenance in bad conditions, in view of the settled weather conditions, decided we might eat well while doing our stint so visited a supermarket and local shops to ensure a Gallic flavour to our meals. The following afternoon saw us making our way to the finishing line, where vessels were expected to call us and report their finishing times. We would make link calls to the temporary race office in Zeebrugge, at which port all the ships were due to gather after the race.

After all the expectations of rolling about off Fecamp, the benign weather continued and life on board was very easy; with four of us, the watch keeping was not difficult. Eventually, the communications vessel coming up Channel with the fleet took over from us, so after a night in port at Fecamp, we set off Northwards for Zeebrugge. Once again, the Normandy coast with its great "falaises" slowly slipped by, to be replaced with the low marshy coast of the Baie de la Somme, which receded further and further from our course. The barometer had dropped a bit, and I wondered if the fine weather was eventually ending - that afternoon, some wag entered in the log "6 drops of rain fell, end of drought". The barometer had started to rise again, so I think we had 6 drops of Commander Benstead's "anti - cyclonic gloom". By six on a fine, calm summer evening we had Cap Gris Nez abeam, and I headed for the Calais approach channel, which runs parallel to the coast.

I suppose the parting of a mooring chain in Calais outer harbour over 40 years previously will never be eradicated from my memory, and when we entered the outer harbour, there on the mooring was a cluster of boats attached to the single mooring, looking rather like the spokes of a wheel. Even in fine weather it looked to me like too many boats, and which one of them had any idea what lay beneath the mooring buoy? I dropped anchor a short distance away and hoisted our anchor ball on the forestay.

The next morning, after an early breakfast, we prepared to leave, but coming on deck found a large number of boats alongside on either side of us. Nobody had asked if they might do so, but they clearly had great confidence in our ground tackle. Most of them had some very neat shining anchors securely lashed on deck, and some had none in view; one suspects it is a piece of nautical equipment not often used aboard these boats. At eight we announced we were weighing and leaving - some of them thought there would be a mooring we would hand over to them - clearly they had either not seen or failed to understand the significance of our anchor signal. As the anchor came up off the muddy bottom, we handed their mooring lines back to the owners and proceeded out of the harbour. Our last sighting as we went round the corner was of two rafts of boats floating about in a state of some confusion.

Our voyage Northwards up the coast started in quite thick fog, which closed in as we left the harbour pierheads. At reduced speed, we successfully buoy hopped, checking our position constantly with the Decca, until the sun finally burnt away the fog - typical of this kind of weather. The banks and channels along this coast are complex, so it was a relief when visibility improved. At six in the evening we entered the outer harbour of Zeebrugge, unrecognisable from the one we had entered 40 years ago in "Campion". The old lock into the canal to Bruges was no longer in use, and a vast new one, capable of taking very large ships, served the canal which now led to a vast new port complex and to Bruges. We entered the lock towing "Gaudeamus", a Polish sail training yacht experiencing trouble with his propeller shaft coupling. We both berthed for the night at a staging above the lock, before towing her to a berth where repairs could be effected the following morning. By way of thanks, he insisted we have a Polish drink with him, and a beautiful set of small pony glasses was produced from a polished hardwood canteen in the lid of which was a set of spaces to hold the glasses securely in place. There was quite a ritual to all this; I don't remember the name of the drink, but I was a bit wary as it looked pretty potent to me.

Later in the morning, we went up to Bruges and secured in a large modern, but under utilised commercial dock, the "Kleine Handelsdok" - such a contrast to the slimy brick wall with its exotic slugs which we used in "Campion" all those years ago. The place was totally changed, but it was a dock intended for somewhat larger ships, and our wheelhouse roof was level with the top of the quay; Richard went off on a foray ashore and came back triumphantly bearing a large plank that just happened to be lying around, so our access ashore was greatly simplified. He had to go back to the UK the next day, but as he had worked in the area at one time, knew a good place to eat somewhere near the main square, and found it navigating with his nose. It was very good, with superb seafood. When Richard wasn't sailing, he was in great demand as a computer expert, and had done quite a lot of work in Europe. He taught me a valuable basic principle - when leaving on an early morning departure, the Decca refused to give a position but constantly said it was "checking position". This small box of tricks which told you where you were, took signals from three transmitting points and by means of a computer inside, instantly worked out your position in lat and long; Richard turned the whole thing off, re-started, and away it went. All sorts of electronic equipment can get into a bad mood, and his trick of turning off, then re-starting nearly always solves the problem.

This reminds me of another of the battles while I was President - the Decca system was under threat because all the transmitters were in need of repair, and in this the CA joined with fishermen's organisations and others to have it retained. The system the Government wanted to replace it was an American system, "Loran". Experts in the CA and elsewhere said it had shortcomings, and in any case, depended on at least one more transmitter being built. How much our protests prevailed, I don't know, but a collapse of the pound against the dollar suddenly made repairing the Decca chain a cheaper option. It lasted another 10 years, by which time GPS had replaced it anyway - and there are still problems with Loran.

From Bruges, we then moved down to Zeebrugge where all the big sailing ships were gathering in the Northern Inlet basin - a vast dock. At night, most of the big sail training vessels were lit overall, but all I could manage was to dress ship overall - an operation I find quite difficult with our ketch rig, but how much more complicated aboard a four master! Zeebrugge did the Tall Ships event well, and laid on a lot of events, including a spectacular firework display.

Finally, it now being early August, we cleared the outer mole of Zeebrugge homeward bound at half past eight in the morning - to do this had meant a pretty early start from the dock, down the canal and through the enormous sea lock. The weather remained fine and calm, with a light Southsouthwest wind blowing, which enabled us to set the sails well strapped in to give us a little extra push. One of the things about motorsailing closehauled is that you actually increase the apparent wind speed. Although we were now a crew of three, there were no watchkeeping problems as Zeebrugge to Harwich is a relatively short crossing, and took eleven and a half hours, compared with thirteen for the trip to Flushing.

AN ADMIRAL AT LAST

COMBINING pleasure with business, early in September we flew out to Atlanta, Georgia, picked up a rental car and drove North to a minute place called Sawtee. Beryl had found the inn we were to stay through Fodor's guide, and it had a reputation for good European food; we made our own reservation by phoning direct - Ham, the proprietor, was thrilled - "gee, you're the first booking I've ever had direct from England". The journey from Atlanta was about a hundred miles, which is nothing as the roads are so empty. The two litre whatever it called itself seemed to have no go in it, but then we turned off the air conditioning and it seemed to go much better. It still did not compare with the two litre Montego we had left behind in the UK, but it really didn't matter.

Ham's place at Sawtee was quite small, and had four letting bedrooms, all furnished with antique furniture. The dining room sat about twenty people, and was full every night - his reputation covered a large area. It made a good touring centre for us; there were some other guests staying at the weekend, otherwise we had it to ourselves. On his day off he asked if we would mind helping ourselves to breakfast from the kitchen - it was all delightfully casual. One night there was a violent thunderstorm, the door of the bedroom burst open and a dog crept in. "Get it out" said Beryl. The dog had gone under the bed, and on investigation turned out to be a very large beagle bitch, who looked at me with soulful eyes and a slight wag of the tail. "It's very large and heavy, and absolutely scared stiff" was my reply. It finished up with four trembling paws showing from under the frilly edge of the bedcover, and we went back to sleep. Early in the morning, as it was getting light and the storm had passed, the dog sauntered out of the room and settled down on the thick Oriental rug in the passage outside the room. By the time we got up. the dog had gone. Ham, who knew the dog, had no idea it could get in - not only did it know how to get in, but also which was the only occupied room to seek human companionship while the storm raged.

Sawtee was a sprawling community set in pleasantly undulating country, with one modest sized general store having two antique petrol pumps on the dirt forecourt. These pumps were modern in that there was an electric pump, but the gallons taken and price were shown on a display of numbers which whizzed round as you served yourself. Before starting, you pulled down a massive lever to set all the numbers to zero, and although I knew petrol was cheap in the US, I could not believe how little it cost to fill the tank - just as well, as I got the impression you almost poured the stuff straight through this car.

There were nearby lakes in which we swam; officially the season was over (it was early September) and the official bathing places closed; people said it would be too cold, but to us Essex folk used to bathing in the North Sea off Frinton beach, it seemed wonderful. Our favourite was a large artificial lake created by the North Georgia Power Company to provide hydro electric power, they had built a great dam trapping the waters of several rivers to form an enormous lake, which had over the years naturalised. There was a convenient quay from which you could dive, dispersing shoals of small fish swimming in the crystal clear water, with steps to get out again. We hired an aluminium dinghy with outboard to make a trip on the lake, whose steep wooded shores were sprinkled with desirable houses built on plots bought from the entrepreneurial company.

Nearby, was a construction workers' camp with the canteen still being run by the original firm contracted to feed the workers; here you paid a flat six dollars to sit at long tables and eat the same food that they ate. There were not too many people there that day, so we were all down one end of a long table and we found ourselves sitting next to a solicitor and his family out from Atlanta. Lavish supplies of simple dishes like stew and dumplings were served with wholesome vegetables. As a serving dish was finished, another was put in its place and you went on helping yourself till you'd had enough. The puds were spotted dick and the like, whilst the whole meal was washed down with either water or cold tea from great jugs - there was no alcohol, as in the construction workers' days.

Returning to Atlanta, we flew to New Orleans to be enchanted by the colonial French architecture of the old quarter, the street cars and the whole atmosphere of good food everywhere at reasonable prices. We liked the gumbo - a sort of New World bouillabasse; unfortunately something upset my tummy and laid me low for the end of this stay. From here we flew to Houston, where Beryl was on gas business; realising I might be at a loose end, a sailing trip in Galveston Bay was organised for me, and a 35 foot bermudian cutter with professional skipper was hired for the day; two company employees keen on sailing nobly gave up their day's work to accompany me. The boat was the kind that I understand, sweet lined, long keeled and reasonable displacement. One or two things took a bit of getting used to - the American buoyage system is the opposite way round from that used in Europe, and I had never come across a 'bimini' before. In Galveston Bay you needed it as the sun was extremely fierce, but I notice they are beginning to appear over here now - I'm not sure why, unless it is to keep the sleet and snow off the occupants of the cockpit.

Finally, having had a good day's sailing in near perfect weather, the professional skipper, with considerable courage, allowed me to take the boat back under power and berth her in the marina. Fortunately, we didn't hit anything, but she was an easy boat to handle and of the type I like best. Soon after returning to the UK, I received my certificate, signed by the Governor and Secretary of State appointing me an Honorary Admiral in the Texan Navy. Texas, the "lone star" state, was the last to join the United States, and prior to doing so, had its own Navy. I am charged with the duty of assisting in the preservation and defense of the State, and am still awaiting the call; if I could do it in a cutter similar to the one we chartered that day their honorary admiral is ready. Promotion comes rather quicker in the Texan Navy than the Royal Navy, where I never got beyond sub-lieutenant; as a souvenir of an unforgettable day out, the impressive framed certificate hangs in my study.

ZIMBABWE

IN February 1991, Beryl and I flew out to see her cousin Jimmy, now turned 80, and whom she had last seen in 1948, the year before we were married, when she stayed with him in Trieste where he was serving with the Allied Military Government in the disputed town. He was now running a business transfer and estate agency in Harare, where he was a very popular character; he had been widowed a year or so earlier, and both of them were very much part of the local scene. The flight is long - well over nine hours through the night - but fortunately there is only a small time difference to cope with, so the body clock is easily adjusted. His garden in the suburb of Greendale was spacious and filled with exotic plants; the architecture of his bungalow, like most of the houses in the vicinity, could be described as "Surrey", with modifications to suit the climate out there. Being over 6000 feet above sea level, the climate is very pleasant - warm and sunny most of the year, whilst there is enough rainfall in most years to support good crops, although most farmers have large dams (reservoirs) to carry them through lean years.

With Jimmy, we drove out to the Nyanga area, close to the border with Mozambique, to stay at a delightful small country hotel, the Pine Tree Inn, set in beautiful, well wooded, undulating country. From here we explored the surrounding area and one of my deepest impressions is of a lonely small church or chapel set quite alone in a country area close to the village of Juliasdale. It was well built, but very simple in style and the East window had no need of stained glass - it looked down a lush valley towards Mozambique and nature did more for that window than could be achieved with stained glass. It was beautifully kept, and we both found it spiritually very inspiring. One day we had lunch at the rather up-market Troutbeck Hotel - a very well run and welcoming establishment, always with a log fire burning in the central lounge area.

After our return to Harare, we left Jimmy for a few days and flew to the Victoria Falls Hotel, surely one of the most romantic destinations in the world. The hotel is luxurious and reminiscent of a bygone colonial era, built by the railway that was intended to run from Capetown to Cairo, but never finished before air travel rendered such a route no longer necessary. In the evenings at dinner, a dance band played dance music of the 1930's - we as children were admonished by our parents - "must you listen to that rubbish?". Many of them are now played as light classics, virtually collector's pieces, but they were the stuff of ballroom dancing such as we were taught in our youth and we were able to step out in style.

There was a swimming pool and patio with light meals available - we were there one evening for a late swim when they closed down the catering facility; before they even closed some monkeys had appeared on top of the surrounding wall, but the moment the staff left, they invaded the area, concentrating particularly on the garbage bins and bags. Monkeys are something of a menace, and have to be kept at bay; it is easier to pinch food this way than get it in the raw, swinging from trees. One morning, a party of French guests were breakfasting at a table close by when a monkey dropped from the tree above, ran off with an orange right in front of the guest, and then sat on a nearby roof top to deftly peel and eat it in her full view, as if to taunt her. There was a children's play area in the grounds, and the monkeys were always there playing with the equipment when there was no one about.

While we were in Harare, there was a heavy round of social engagements with friends of Jimmy's, who were very hospitable and became our friends as a result of subsequent visits over the next few years. Many were retired, but we also visited a large working tobacco farm, run on very business-like lines, with good equipment for drying and curing the leaves. They were enlightened employers, building good housing for their employees as well as a school for their children. In the economy generally, there were shortages - and surpluses caused by the government control over all trade. There was a terrible shortage of cement that year, but the next time we came out there was so much cement no one knew what to do with it all.

The following year we had gone to Madeira for our late winter "tonic", but I think he missed us, and we were very pleased to revisit him and his friends out there, using the Zim sun as our winter "top up". Things were improving; the rigid socialist control over everything was being eased, with a resultant improvement in the economy, and particularly noticeable was the reduction in black smoke from lorries and buses. A rigid import control system had not permitted the import of spares so the vehicles could not be properly maintained, but this had now been changed, and there also seemed to be more press freedom in that an independent newspaper was now being published and was critical of government policies. Even so, if they went too far, there would be a strange shortage of newsprint on which to print their paper, whereas the official Government controlled paper had no such problems; reports in this about political matters always conferred the honour "Cde" (comrade) to the names of prominent politicians; I suppose every country has to have some sort of class distinction.

This time, instead of driving Jimmy's car (which he was very happy for me to do), we hired one. His BMW (past the first flush of youth) was unreliable, and not an easy car to drive, so I was pleased to be driving an ordinary "cooking" car such as I always use at home. As far as I am concerned, you can keep such exotic beasts with their twin carburettors - there were times when Beryl's engineering experience and my more basic knowledge were sore taxed when the brute packed up

This time we set out Southeastwards to the Vumba mountains via Mutare (formerly Umtali) where we stayed at what became one of our favourite destinations, the "Inn on the Vumba". This pleasant small hotel with a good dining room, was perched on the side of a hill overlooking a lush valley down to the Mozambique border; from the hotel you could clearly see freight trains and lorries way down in the valley awaiting customs clearance at the frontier post. Another attraction was the swimming pool, which also looked out on the same view; Beryl and I used it daily, and we had hoped Jimmy might make use of the pools in places we visited during the several years that Zimbabwe became a regular destination for us; Jimmy was crippled by arthritis in spite of the warm benign climate, but this proved to be so bad that he could not really manage steps down into a pool.

For the next five years, visits to Zimbabwe became a regular feature of our lives, visiting Troutbeck in the Nyanga, the Vumba, and "La Rochelle", a house built by Sir Stephen Courtauld who took up residence in Zimbabwe, and became a rich benefactor to many worthwhile initiatives that would improve the quality of life for people out there. It had become a Zimbabwe National Trust property, rented to a hotelier, but it still had the atmosphere of a home. In the snug little bar (which had probably been a study) was a half model of a very finely proportioned yacht hull. It was the "Virginia", a very handsome twin screw yacht, modern in that she was diesel powered, but traditional with a clipper bow and graceful counter. She had belonged to Sir Stephen, and when I returned from that visit, was able to do a potted history for the proprietor, researched from old copies of Lloyd's Register in the Cruising Association library - it should be remembered that although the rare historic books had been sold, there remained an enormous library covering every conceivable nautical subject.

On another visit, we went up to stay at "Bumi Hills", a hotel and safari centre on high ground overlooking lake Kariba - from the terrace, one could watch families of elephants visiting the water's edge to bathe, something they clearly enjoyed a lot, hosing each other down and generally playing about. To get there, we had flown to Kariba and transferred to a very small aircraft; before they can land on the airstrip, a Landrover is sent along the dirt runway to clear off straying wild animals, before taking you up to the hotel. We went on a trip in another four wheel drive vehicle, from which we watched an elephant and her progeny feeding; they are very destructive and to eat grass first dig it up with their hooves; they will happily rub against a tree, usually knocking it over in the process. We also went out with a guide in a launch, who on rounding a small headland on an island, cut the engine to drift quietly into the full view of a hippopotamus family grazing on the bank. The element of surprise did not last long, and they stampeded into the water with a tremendous "splosh" (the Flanders & Swann description in their famous song is accurate!) and then re appeared as humps in the water a little way off.

One year we returned the generous hospitality of so many friends by putting on a large lunch at the Harare club; on other occasions we did the same thing at an Italian restaurant in Harare, Guido's. Jimmy had been born in Italy and brought up there, although educated in England at Westminster choir school - he had a fine singing voice, and was very musical. Jimmy loved going to Guido's, where he was well known and would chattter away in Italian to Guido; each of the latter years we went, the cost of these lunches became less because of the fall in value of their currency, although for the locals there was a high rate of inflation. Whereas to start with, things seemed to get better, then sadly they began to go downhill badly as some of Mugabe's megalomaniac actions began to take hold; this was a real tragedy, because here was a country with every reason to be prosperous, and the people were all regarding themselves as Zimbabwean citizens, black and white doing business happily together. In the last years of our visits, this was breaking down in certain areas because of an outbreak of racism on his part against the white population, and there was a developing breakdown in law and order.

Jimmy was a sick man by the time of our last visit in 1998, but we had hoped to see him again the following year; fate intervened and I developed a hernia which was operated on about the time we should have been out there, but by then his illness was becoming critical and by July he was dead. Whilst for us, it was the end of an enjoyable era in our lives, the situation was deteriorating monthly and we were both glad he was spared the spectacle of his country of adoption being destroyed. Since then there has been almost total economic disaster; we hear little from our friends, but I think they are too frightened by the whole set-up to put anything in writing or to telephone as you never know what may be monitored or intercepted. Zimbabwe is a beautiful country with great potential, which is now being thrown away by the misdeeds of a dictator and his corrupt government.

WRITTLE CHURCH - ANOTHER FIRE AND A NEW WINDOW

ALMOST exactly 17 years after the Parish Church was damaged by fire, there was yet another. In the small hours of April the 3rd 1991, a strong West wind was blowing, and Tom Slator, of Romans House, which lies to the East of the church was awakened by an acrid smell of burning; to his horror he could see flames coming from the chancel roof and immediately raised the alarm. The noise of the crackling flames and disintegrating roof tiles roused other people in the vicinity, and very soon, in spite of the early hour, there was a team of helpers headed by the vicar and Churchwardens salvaging valuables from the blazing building. The route taken by the fire was almost identical to that of the previous one, but the new plaster and steel mesh ceiling confined the flames to the roof, and thus there was far less damage to the furnishings below in both chancel and the Vicar's vestry.

Volunteers appeared from all over the village armed with cleaning materials, a partition was erected to seal off the chancel, and normal services took place the following Sunday. The indomitable spirit shown by a Christian community overcame a disaster that might have disheartened many. I suppose you could at least say that second time round we knew what had to be done. The previous fire had been started by a boy, whereas this was the work of a demented adult, but there was insufficient firm evidence to bring him to trial. As a result, the door through which he gained access has been permanently sealed, and a smoke alarm system installed. Smoke alarms and candle lit services are not a good mix, so that now there has to be an interval between extinguishing the candles and switching on the system. Our grand daughter Rachael, then aged five was staying with us, and could not believe what she had seen, saying to Beryl "How could anyone be so wicked as to set a church on fire?".

Writtle has two claims to fame, one being that it is almost certainly the birthplace of Robert the Bruce - the De Bruis family held the Lordship manor as an old Norman French family, and due to various complicated marriages coupled with the odd case of an ambitious woman poisoning other contenders, he was in line of succession to the Scottish Throne. His persistence in achieving this goal is immortalised in the story of the spider;

however, when he took the Scottish throne, that was the end of the De Bruis family's tenure of Royal lands in Writtle, including the hunting lodge built by King John, known to Writtle's inhabitants as King John's Palace.

Long after this, the Marconi Wireless Telegraph Company, based in Chelmsford, opened a research station in Writtle, in Lawford Lane just outside the village. The work of this establishment was to perfect speech between radio stations, as opposed to morse code signals, particularly with a view to communications between aircraft. The primitive establishment, housed in a large wooden shed, was manned by some very keen young men who pioneered the first public entertainment broadcasts, the first of these being on February the 14th, 1922. The call sign they used was "2 emma-toc, Wrrrittle calling", and I first heard this in my early childhood when my father, who was a radio buff would walk round the house repeating the call sign that made such a significant impression on him in those very early days. Out of this, before long a consortium formed the British Broadcasting Company, later to become a public corporation. The serious research at Writtle continued, but from those pioneers came some famous names - Captain Eckersley, Freddie Grisewood. Many of them lodged in the house that, years later, I found myself restoring. The actual shed used for those inaugural broadcasts is now preserved in Chelmsford's Industrial museum, and the whole story told in "2MT Writtle" - the birth of British Broadcasting by Tim Wander.

Because of this establishment, Writtle was home to many Marconi people - indeed we bought our house in 1952 from George Tyler, a senior radio engineer (and keen yachtsman). Eventually, the establishment, by then housed in up to date buildings, was closed - it now has a complex of apartments built on the site, and Writtle lost its Marconi connection. There were many discussions as to how this could be commemorated, and eventually it was agreed to place a stained glass window in the refurbished South Chapel of Writtle Church, which had a two light Gothic-arched window above the altar. One light was to commemorate the Marconi connection, and the other Beryl's elevation to the peerage - local girl made good! Jane Grey, a leading stained glass artist was chosen to create the window, which was dedicated on June the 15th by the Bishop of Chelmsford; it had been hoped that Marconi's widow would be able to attend, but her daughter, Princess Elettra had suffered a fall which broke a leg; her mother couldn't travel without her, so Marconi's grandson, Prince Guglielmo came to represent the family. At the subsequent reception and exhibition, this charming young man gave a brilliant and well thought out speech - in excellent English.

Perhaps these days we take wireless communication for granted, but it should never be forgotten what this great man introduced to the world, resulting in television, radio direction finding techniques, or that he chose to do this in England. Nor, when we listen to a radio concert or news broadcast, should we forget those pioneers and the technologies they fathered; those radio waves could cross boundaries - and iron curtains, ultimately to bring the truth to those imprisoned behind them.

THE WEST COUNTRY AGAIN - AND COMPASS PROBLEMS

THE postponed West country trip was re-instated for this season, but before setting off, I handed over the Presidential burgee to my successor, Ron Browne. At least, by this time the CA had decided on the building of purpose built premises at Limehouse, and now had the money available to do it. To Ron would fall the responsibility of overseeing the whole project, which at the time he took over, was an untidy desolate site next to Limehouse Basin.

On the 25th of May we set off in benign weather conditions, with my old schoolfriend Philip Andrews, ex naval and Customs Revenue cutter officer, and John and Mary Barrington, with their son Hervey. There was quite an age disparity with Philip and myself at the top end of the sixties, Mary and John in their forties and Hervey aged an adult and responsible 13, and I did wonder how this would work out. In the event I needn't have worried, they melded into an excellent combination. Leaving Levington at seven on the Saturday morning after boarding on the Friday evening - Writtle is an hour's drive away, so for an early start, boarding the night before is important in order to get everything stowed and prepared for sea.

Our cross estuary course took us from Harwich across the Northern tips of the Gunfleet and Sunk sands to gain the Black Deep channel; all these features spread in a Southwest - Northeast pattern and prevent a direct cross estuary course. Towards the Southern end of the Black Deep is a gutway or gat through the Sunk Sand, the Fisherman's Gat, leading you to clear open water all the way to the North Foreland, which in reasonable conditions should be visible by the time you're through the gat. It is a sizeable headland which, being chalk, shows up well and encourages the mariner into thinking he is well across the estuary, although this day was rather misty. By lunch time, we were sweeping past Ramsgate towards my least favourite piece of water at eight knots - the reason for the early start from Levington was to catch the strong tide through the Downs and past Dover. The Straits were in tranquil mood that day, although there is always disturbance from ferries and shipping out in the shipping lanes, and I always have to have something to complain about them - this time it was that the mist had thickened to a fog. Needless to say, it began to thin again the further we got from Dover.

After passing Folkestone, the tides become of less importance as you cross Hythe bay towards Dungeness, where the tides sweep round with some ferocity, but then become weak as you cross Rye bay. Passing Dungeness is another milestone, as it is the last dreary and desolate feature to be passed, after which it all gets better as you approach Fairlight Cliff. The calm conditions enabled a good supper to be served - I always say that the number of Michelin rosettes awarded for cuisine afloat is in inverse ratio to the wind strength on the Beaufort scale.

Darkness was falling as we brought Beachy Head light abeam, and then, at a minute past midnight the log records "Crossed into Western Hemisphere". The same meridian is crossed on the way up to London, of course, but Decca was still a new toy to me, and it is fascinating to see the display on the set wind down on the figures for Easterly longitude till it suddenly flashes a Westerly reading.

I was doing a headland to headland navigation, the quickest and shortest route West if you are under power and do not have to pay consideration to wind and weather, so from Beachy Head we were steering for St Catherine's Point at the Southern tip of the Isle of Wight. After leaving Beachy Head, the coast recedes from your course and the long line of lights that stretches almost continuously from Newhaven to Selsey were soon lost in the mist on this trip - we were very much on our own. By the time daylight came we had the Isle of Wight clearly showing on the starboard bow, and once again the shore came closer to our track.

There is an entry recording St Catherine's light abeam at 0720 (at last!), as we had been suffering an adverse tide, although a light Easterly wind had come along to fill our mains'l and give a little extra push. Later in the morning, the tide turned and we swept along heading for a point well South of Portland Bill - clear of the infamous race. The coast from now on is far more interesting with hills and cliffs replacing the low lying and heavily conurbated areas between Beachy head and the Island, although again it receded from our course deep in to Bournemouth Bay, - Portland Bill forces you a long way out in the Channel, far from the attractive Dorset coast. On the other hand, this route gets you to your objective, the cruising areas of the West Country quickly, and keeping on the move is no problem when you have a capable crew aboard.

At ten past seven on a golden early summer evening we swept into the River Dart , thirtysix hours out from Levington, and then went on up to Dittisham, where the steep tree lined banks create a superb river beauty spot, best viewed from the decks of a boat. There is something very satisfying about the completion of a successful passage - just over 255 nautical miles at a little over seven knots; it was taking me time to adjust to a totally different aspect of making passages under power and we had a celebratory dinner aboard that evening. I enjoy cooking, and that evening inflicted my culinary efforts on the crew - fortunately they all had good appetites, induced by a very healthy dose of sea air.

After a day's leisure at Dittisham, we slipped the visitor's mooring at the gentlemanly hour of nine thirty and headed seawards under a sunny sky with white puffy clouds scudding across, driven by a strong Northeasterly wind. As we headed

downriver past Dartmouth town, a harbour master's launch came out to tell us it was rough outside and a number of boats had turned back; I don't think I've ever had such service before, and of course they were trying to be helpful, so I thanked them, but it is each master's decision whether to sail or not, and we hardly looked like a fragile butterfly. It seemed to me rather like somebody coming out to the QE II as she headed seawards through the Needles Channel and warning them it was a bit rough out there. The wind strength was recorded as force 6 from the Northeast, and with the whole of Lime Bay to windward of this coast, we were breasting in to a lively sea as we made an offing to pass outside the Skerries Bank. We were thrown about a bit at first, but it was not long before we began to turn to a more Southwesterly course, putting the seas astern of us, and as the great bulk of Start Point came abeam, we began to feel its shelter as both wind strength and seas reduced.

Preparing a celebratory dinner at Dittisham; I describe "Corydalis" as a sea- going country cottage, and her galley is as large as you would get in many a small London flat. The hat does not denote any culinary qualifications and is a joke that has gone through all three boats. (Photo by Mary Barrington)

Our next port of call was Newton Ferrers, and being anxious not to cross the bar into the river Yealm to early on the tide, eased our speed which encouraged us to put out spinners, but not with any success. Although Corydalis looks very much like a Scottish fishing boat, I regret that in 14 years not a fish has ever been caught. I need not have worried about the bar - the least depth on the sounder was nearly 4 metres - a veritable feast of water for an Essex boy. After picking up a visitor's mooring, we all went shore for a very splendid tea laid on by Betty Barlow, widow of my former crew member Robert. The next day we slipped round to Plymouth in superb weather, with little sign of the previous day's Northeaster , although even if it was there, a lot of high ground was now giving shelter. Sadly our young crew had to depart, but I hope they had enjoyed the trip as much as I had; Plymouth has an excellent train service to London, whereas from any point further West it becomes tedious and less frequent.

During our trip Westwards, I had began to realise that there was serious deviation on the compass, particularly on Westerly courses, and I had started making allowances of up to twenty degrees, which was a cause for worry. After reaching Plymouth, where we had another day off before completing our voyage, I gave serious thought to the problem. After completion, she had been swung and adjusted by Eric Diggens, who with his customary skill had got the deviation down to miniscule measurements on all headings. Suddenly the penny dropped. I had some welding carried out during the winter, and this can drastically affect the ship's magnetism - I should have remembered this from Naval days, where if we had work carried out on the ship, not only did the compasses need re-adjusting, but in those days the effectiveness of the "de-gaussing" loop round the ship had to be tested by passing over a "DG" range on the seabed, which checked that you were not producing a magnetic field likely to touch off a magnetic mine.

Immediately, I contacted a compass adjuster in Falmouth, based on a recommendation through the CA's Hon. Local Representative, and arranged for her to be "swung". It was fortunate that during this voyage we had the Decca checking our position, and giving the true (as opposed to magnetic) course made good - the variation between true and magnetic North was a little over 5 degrees at that time. It was the Decca that kept us pointing where we should be going and enabled me to calibrate the approximate error on our compass. I was ashamed of my carelessness in not having the compasses checked after the welding had been completed, particularly as the Navy had taught me about this, albeit over forty years previously.

Since leaving the Navy, I had only been concerned with wooden ships, although there still can be shocks with those. There are stories of galvanised buckets and other pieces of ironmongery being stowed away out of sight in a locker, only a few inches from the compass and producing some strange readings in both wooden or fibreglass boats.

My biggest previous compass shock was with "CAMPION" in the year we took her to Dover, Calais and Holland. Before setting out on this trip, I had taken her from Walton to Heybridge Basin, and was lying alongside the concrete quay face just inside the lock gates; looking at the compass I could not believe my eyes. Having known the Basin for many years, I had a pretty accurate idea of where everything lay in relation to compass bearings. Looking East downriver, the compass told me I was looking West, and looking aloft at the burgee, this confirmed that the wind was coming from the West - and the compass said East. This was alarming, and I immediately started a locker search for an offending piece of iron, without any result.

Then I remembered back to earlier days in the fifties when we used the place a lot, and that it was then just a grassy bank. At that time, timber was being imported by Sadd's of Maldon, and Browns of Chelmsford. The ships bringing timber from the Baltic and Scandinavia were old fashioned steamers drawing a lot of water which anchored in deep water near Osea Island, whence the timber was lightered up to Maldon or into Heybridge, where it was transferred again to very shallow beamy barges for towing up to Chelmsford - the horses were eventually replaced by large diesel powered outboard engines. Then more modern motorships came along, drawing less water, and they were able to go alongside Sadd's quay, whereas Browns had to continue the grossly inefficient lightering process. Then they started importing in ships that could go through the lock into the basin - and to create a quay face, steel sheet piling was driven in to contain the grassy bank, and then capped with concrete. One of the ways of changing the magnetism of a piece of steel is to constantly hit it - like with a pile driver. "CAMPION'S" compass was about level with where the tops of the sheet piling would be; I let go her stern rope and let her drift away from the quay; when the stern was probably no more than three feet from the quay, the compass card quietly rotated, and the Blackwater Estuary started flowing down towards the East again. It was a great relief.

The weather for our passage West had been excellent, apart from the mist at the beginning. With Phillip as my sole companion, we sailed for Falmouth at eight on another fine calm day, passing through the Bridge Channel and then rounding Rame Head (a great headland which must give a wonderful view Westward down Channel - one of the observation points signalling the progress of the Armada, the first being the Lizard). The coastline is spectacular, with the Dodman as another great promontory before reaching Falmouth, where we berthed in the new Yacht Haven constructed by Falmouth Harbour Commissioners since our last visit some years earlier, in "CELANDINE". From there Philip was able to get home relatively easily , as he lived in South Modbury, near Newton Ferrers; It would have been easy for him to leave the ship there, but Phillip volunteered to stay with me to the end of the voyage.

Beryl joined the next day, and then we had the compass adjuster, who was extremely professional and competent - it had been a good recommendation - and new

deviation cards were produced, with the compass now being only very slightly out on every heading. We returned to the Yacht Haven, spending a few days there, renewing our acqaintance with Falmouth and replenishing the ship's victuals, depleted from the voyage down. Then followed a fortnight of local pottering, with Mary Dainty once more joining us, with her sister Anne and brother-in-law Peter. The weather, sadly took a turn for the worst and the rains came, interspersed with very few fine breaks. Most of the time it blew, from between Southwest and Northwest. Then we had a visit from Frank and Lorna Chorley; Beryl had met Frank through

Falmouth, 1991 - view looking over the Church tower towards the Carrick Roads. The new visitors pontoons provided by the Harbour Commissioners, and which we found so useful are just beyond the church roofline.

the Engineering Council on which both had served, and Frank was ex MD of Plessey - he was a radio, radar and electronics guru, who also had a boat. One wet evening, we went ashore to dine at the Riverside Restaurant at Helford - a gastronomic oasis. To say the rain cascaded down would be an understatement, and although we were quite smartly dressed underneath, a coating of dripping wet oilies successfully camouflaged this. We dripped on their doormat as we struggled out of this kit.

On another evening, the sky miraculously cleared to give us a sighting of what was described as a "massing of the planets", an event last recorded in 1769. At half past ten, Mars, Venus and Jupiter were in a closely packed triangle, just above the new moon. It will not be seen again for another 286 years (how do they work these things out?) so we were very lucky to have sighted the phenomenon. The next morning we returned to Falmouth for Frank and Lorna to go home, and fortunately the weather was going through one of its brief bright periods; then as if laid on for the occasion, HMY BRITANNIA was turning in the Carrick Roads; an extremely smart harbour launch went out to her, ferrying someone ashore. It was the C-in-C Royal yachts, who lived nearby, and dropped off after a long cruise, before the yacht returned to her base at Portsmouth. As she gathered way towards the sea, we had a superb view of her gleaming dark blue hull, and of the Marines band playing on deck - a stirring sight.

The wet and windy weather continued with little respite, and another CA boat, "PURSUIT", a capable looking 38 foot Moody, with Roy Laver and Jean Goater aboard, came in to await a break in the weather, hoping to make Southern Ireland. One day we all went in our Avon inflatable dinghy up to Bishops Quay in Mawgan Creek; before ever reaching there, we were bailing rainwater from the dinghy, whence we walked about a mile to an excellent hostelry in the village of Mawgan, still in torrential rain, where four sets of wet oilies again produced puddles on the floor. On a wet Sunday, we determined to go to church in Manaccan - the church where we met our friends the Alders - and we encountered white water running down either side of the steep road up from Helford. The distance from the landing place is only just over a mile, but Cornish miles seem longer than Essex miles, because you are always going up or down steep hills, and when we reached the church, we yet again had to do our dripping oilies act. On the other hand, another excursion made with Roy and Jean on one of the rare sunny days was to Porth Navas, where we bought oysters and had lunch en plein air overlooking this delightful, but tidal, creek - such a contrast to our usual wet arrivals everywhere.

"CORYDALIS" was taken into many little creeks up the Fal, including a brief afternoon visit to Truro at high tide - the tides down here are almost exactly six hours different from those in our home waters, so Spring tides occur when high tides are about six in the morning and evening, whereas back home they happen on tides mid-day and midnight. I'm not sure which is the better, but it is the way the Lord has ordained it, so you make the best you can of the arrangement. Crew for the return trip began to filter through; first the intrepid Pam, then a few days later Mike ("bald") and Jean Rose, while Beryl left - all this was done using the new visitor's pontoons and the nearby rail terminus - a rather sad sight, once constructed on a rather grand scale in the days when the Great Western Railway were encouraging passenger ships to call in there whence the passengers would be whisked to London in a fast boat train. It never was a success, any more than the attempts to do the same thing from Plymouth. The line is now a very pathetic affair, with a very infrequent diesel car service as far as Truro, where you change for London.

After a little pottering in the Falmouth area, we sailed from the Helford river in weather that had greatly improved; during the last few days of Beryl's stay down there the barometer had been steadily rising giving a promise of better things to come, but she had a pretty rough deal for her time aboard. The wind was now light and from a Southerly direction as we headed East along the coast, making for Salcombe, where we anchored for the night in a peaceful and secluded spot well above the town, off Saltstone rock. Yachts by now were greatly increased in numbers, compared with earlier years, and particularly as it was already early July. Fortunately they seem to be gregarious and all lie in clusters on visitor's moorings near the town to leave anchorages, such as the one we chose, for loners like us.

The next morning we slipped round to Dartmouth, where after obtaining permission from the harbour master, berthed alongside the Town jetty, with considerable difficulty. There was a great cluster of boats milling around in there, and one is very aware of the damage that a big heavy steel hull could do, even with a gentle unprotected nudge. We managed to get in sufficiently close to take on water and land a shore party to obtain one or two supplies of fresh victuals, before extricating ourselves to go upriver to the more desirable pleasures of Dittisham. The following morning we were off early for a long day's passage to the Solent; the barometer stood high, there was a light Southeast wind to fill the sails, but it was also quite misty and we soon lost sight of the shore. The wind backed into the East in the afternoon, so the sails came down and we ploughed on towards the Island, under auto pilot (another new bit of gadgetry!). The mist lifted in the early evening to reveal the Isle of Wight in outstanding clarity, bathed in the late sunshine. Fourteen hours after leaving Dittisham, we made fast to some vacant piles off Shepards Wharf, Cowes.

Having thought this would be an expensive night's stay, no one had arrived to collect any dues by the time we left at eight the following morning, disproving the story that "your hand will always be in your pocket on the South Coast". The wind had developed into quite a fresh Northeaster, from which we were well sheltered as we took a well trodden route through the Looe Channel off Selsey Bill and worked our way inshore towards Brighton marina - not a particularly long haul, and we were comfortably berthed soon after two in the afternoon. Jean Rose went home by train from here - she had enjoyed a very comfortable ride so far, but with the Northeaster that was gathering in strength, I envisaged a rough ride after leaving the lee of Beachy Head, and the last thing I wanted was for her to have a rough and tumble in the Dover Straits; such an experience might put her off ever coming again.

At eight the following evening we sailed, now three strong, heading to clear Beachy Head, which was sheltering us from the strong Northeast wind for which we had set the mains'l only. As darkness closed in, I was conscious of a dark cloud coming up to the South of us, but once it became totally dark, it was no longer possible to identify it. Suddenly, the storm broke shortly before ten, and we were subjected to a spectacular but rather awesome display of lightning whilst the thunder rolled around almost continuously and torrential rain set in. The wind suddenly dropped, but returned within a minute or so, blowing from the South - a fair wind to help us the rest of the way home! By the time we reached Dover, it was getting light and we seemed to have again struck a good time for paucity of ferry traffic. The day improved for a relatively calm cross Estuary passage, and soon after a hasty lunch we were berthing in Suffolk Yacht Harbour, Levington, six weeks after leaving.

ESCORTING A FERRY

T HE remainder of the season was spent in cruising in our local haunts, including a visit to Heybridge Basin - the first time I had taken "CORYDALIS" there, and my first visit for some years. I could not get over how much it had been smartened up, with well trimmed grass and fresh paint on the lock gear, under the influence of Colin Edmund, a young man with more energy and enthusiasm than had been shown by some of his predecessors.

The highlight that autumn was escorting Beryl out of Harwich Harbour. She was on a House of Lords select committee on marine safety, which was to visit laboratories and test tanks in Holland and Hamburg, crossing from Harwich to the Hook on a day crossing. I then said "I will escort your ship from Harwich to see you safely on your way". Everyone got quite interested in the idea, and the captain of the ferry, the "STENA BRITANNICA", was advised in advance.

So with Mike ("bald") and Jean Rose aboard, we slipped from Suffolk yacht harbour in good time, and then hove to near the Guard buoy, with the ship's radio tuned to the Harwich harbour channel 71 (nicknamed by us the "Harwich Harbour chat show" - a good deal more interesting than most radio chat shows). In due course, "STENA BRITANNICA" called Harwich to say they were ready to sail in five minutes, and believed they would be escorted out by a yacht. Harwich confirmed, and added that there was an MFV type yacht hove to near the Guard buoy, probably waiting for her. As the ferry began to turn after passing the Guard buoy, we took up position alongside her. There, just behind

Honfleur, outside the Vieux Lieutenance.
(Photo by Mike Rose)

the bridge was a minute figure waving - Beryl. On the same channel, some banter passed between the Captain and ourselves, he saying that he had this young lady photographer taking shots of us - I'm not sure that you're really supposed to do this on a serious thing like the Harwich Harbour channel, but nobody seemed to mind as I think it was just a little light relief in the otherwise routine nature of things.

As the ferry proceeded down the harbour, he began to increase speed; by this time I had our throttle lever as far forward as it would go and the revs went up to two thousand - their maximum. It felt like being on a destroyer as the bow wave mounted and our stern squatted; I suppose we may have been just about doing nine knots - half the speed at which the ferry would cross the North Sea. Down by the Cliff Foot buoy, I called them up and said we would be leaving them now, wished them a pleasant voyage and asked them to to take care of my wife - the response was gracious and I was assured they would do just that. The real truth was that the ferry was now leaving us, having increased speed to something like 12 or 14 knots, at which speed they were walking away from us. I was pleased to ease that throttle back and drive the horses at a more normal cruising speed, 7 knots at about 1650 revs.

The photographs Beryl took were fascinating - her viewpoint from the bridge was such that she could see over the roof tops of Harwich, right round the corner to Landguard Point, but the shots she took of us showed a minute pimple surrounded by a lather of wake; unfortunately she had no zoom facility on her camera. The weather was good, and there was plenty of autumn sunshine, so they did have a very good crossing. The technicalities of berthing the ship at the Hook also fascinated her - although she is an aeronautical engineer, all technical affairs interest her, so that she has been on a number of select committees on engineering, scientific and medical matters - indeed they have taken up a lot of her time over the years.

HOLLAND AGAIN - LAKE ONTARIO AND THE CANYON

THIS year, 1992 was a busy year and so we took the easy (for us East Coast folk) option with the boat again - a quick early season visit to Holland. Towards the end of May, with a light Northeasterly wind blowing and the sun shining, we made our 13 hour passage to Flushing - I still cannot get used to the greater predictability of passages under power. As we closed the Schelde Estuary through the shallow Duerloo channel, a squall and thunderstorm came up from the Northeast, but this was of no concern as we were now under the lee of the Walcheren coast.

All the old favourites in South Holland were revisited, and one new - Hellevetsluis, once the port where sailing packets left for Harwich, but now well in from the sea. At Goes, in our favourite little harbour "De Werf", there was a crew change, and our outward crew, John Barrington, Richard White, the young Cornishman, and Geoff

Green (the one who runs a garden centre when he isn't sailing!) left for the UK, while Beryl joined, with Peter Darwent and his brother David, who is professionally involved in supervising the construction of large and expensive yachts.

Zieriksee was revisited on this brief trip, then on the Sunday, we secured at Middleburg, where Beryl took the train to connect with that night's sailing from the Hook. By eight the following morning we were pushing out into the Schelde once more with a pleasant Northeast wind between force 2 and three, but poor visibility as we headed for the tricky Duerloo channel. Just over thirteen hours later, the anchor went down at "Stone Heaps", just upstream from Shotley Spit. It is said to have acquired the name because it was the place where sailing traders dumped their ballast before loading cargoes up at Ipswich. The following morning, suitably refreshed, we berthed in Suffok Yacht Harbour at a gentlemanly hour.

Shortly after the window ceremony, we were both on a flight to Toronto, where Beryl had gas business, and as happened on a previous occasion, while she was involved in her work, I was taken out sailing on Lake Ontario. We left from a small marina on the delightful islands just offshore from Toronto's waterfront; the boat, "RAMBLING ROSE" was a sturdy heavy displacement Bermudian cutter with both heads'ls on rollers. The wind was light as we headed out into the lake, the coast of America just visible in the misty distance, and the hot sun beat down on us. The Canadians have far more of these more traditional heavier displacement boats, and this boat certainly suited me, although we could have done with more wind. It was hot, but my hosts said that your survival time in the icy water was not much more than 15 minutes - Lake Ontario is fed by Niagara Falls, and their winters are pretty harsh, so this deep inland sea never really warms up; it is very large, connects with the sea via the St Lawrence seaway to bring large commercial ships into Toronto docks, and with other upstream lakes via the Welland Canal - a waterway that obviates the tricky navigation problem posed by the Falls.

Flying from Toronto via Los Angeles, we arrived at Grand Canyon. This a National Park, and obviously a very popular tourist destination, so great precautions are taken to preserve its environment; we came by air and bus, but if you came by car you would be directed to a car park well out on the park perimeter and taken to your hotel or lodge by the frequent service of shuttle buses. One day we did the whole tour on a shuttle, but the next we took a picnic lunch and got off the shuttle at a suitable stop to walk along the path below the brow of the cliff. The path was quite narrow and sloped a bit in places; the drop was probably between two or three thousand feet, although that would not be to the very bottom, but to the nearest ledge. Once a little way from the bus stop, the silence was eerie and the air hung still and hot; because few Americans walk far we did not meet another soul. We re-connected with the bus service two stops on from where we left . Before leaving Grand Canyon we visited an I-max screening of the canyon - a historical feature, firstly on the pioneers who took fragile boats through the white waters and rapids, then a helicopter flight between the canyon walls - at the end of this film I felt distinctly queasy, but the whole visit was an unforgettable experience.

Returning to LA, we joined a National Parks coach tour up the Pacific coast, starting with two nights in our old friend San Fransisco, thence to Yosemite National park, with its great redwoods. Some one had already recommended that we must dine at the Awhanee hotel, and our tour guide offered to book us a table before the trip started - I suspect he rather liked the idea of booking for a Baroness, something they don't have in America. I don't know what yarn he spun, but our table was in a bay of the large dining room next to the table at which the Queen dined during a Royal visit. The most extraordinary event of this evening was that the lady pianist tinkling away on the grand moved into *"La Vie en Rose"* (our "signature" tune) as we made our way to the table. This was a most extraordinary coincidence because no one could have been briefed on such a detail; at the end of dinner the pianist may have wondered why such a generous tip was placed in the tumbler standing on the piano for that purpose.

Our tour took us up the West coast of California and on to Oregon; the weather became noticeably cooler as we travelled up the wild and awe-inspiring cliffs and beaches before heading inland to Mount St Helens National Park. The mountain is a volcano which erupted seriously in the Spring of 1980, virtually blowing itself apart. The devastation to natural life in the Park covered a large area, but had been well forecast by a series of earth quakes (it is a seismically active zone) and eruptions so that most of the sparse poulation had been moved out in advance, but 56 people died as a result of the great explosion Finally, our last night with the tour was spent at the Paradise Inn, Mount Rainier National Park, high in the Cascade Mountains. Our latitude was about 471/4 North, compared with our home latitude of 511/4 (240 nautical miles further North) and it was the end of June, but in the morning there was frost and a sprinkling of snow.

We left the tour at Vancouver, having covered over 1400 land miles in a week, which I am glad I did not have to drive. My sister and brother-in-law Dino were there waiting for us, to spend a week with them at Abbotsford, in the foothills of the Rockies. A memorable trip with them was made by boat going up Howe Sound through scenery that had probably not changed since Lieutenant Vancouver first set eyes on it. At Squamish, virtually the head of navigation, we disembarked to board the "Royal Hudson", a steam hauled passenger train - there were glimpses of the train from the boat, as it steamed majestically along the winding cliffside track to meet the boat. Boat and train then did the return trip to North Vancouver; we had opted to go Northbound by boat as it involved a smoked salmon lunch, and salmon is something they are rather good at in that part of the world.

I am a sucker for steam, be it on a boat or rails, even though I know it is a form of propulsion that is totally outmoded by more modern sources of power. The engine hauling our train, the "British Columbia" was the very final development of the Pacific type of engine that was universally used in the latter days of steam; oil fired, with a stainless steel covering to the boiler and maroon livery, she gave an impressive display of great power. Of course, it is only in use as a summer tourist attraction on this relatively short stretch of standard gauge line - a little over 30 land miles. Indian woodcarvers in Squamish sold wooden whistles imitating the sound of the great Pacific steam engine, and we could not resist bringing one home. To blow it off in the middle of a room full of people has a dramatic effect, although I don't think anyone has been fooled into thinking a train was just coming.

A LAST VISIT TO ST KATHARINE'S

TOWARDS the end of September 1992, the country was enjoying a spell of pleasant autumnal weather, and we set off for London, with a bit of meandering on the way. From Levington, we went round to the Colne, anchoring in Pyefleet for the night, within sight of "CELANDINE" whose permanent mooring was there, before continuing up the Blackwater on the tide right up to Fullbridge at Maldon, the effective head of navigation. Our crew consisted of the stalwart Pam (recently returned from one of her Polar adventures - she spends a lot of time in one or another of the Poles, or other places where most people don't go!), staunch friend Michael ("bald") Rose, and Frank Chorley, the great master of radio and electronics. Fullbridge, Maldon, is not somewhere I would want to stay, and if your ship draws five feet, the tide must be watched carefully; berthing alongside the quay, we crossed the road for a drink at the "Welcome Sailor", which we were able to enjoy in the mid-day sunshine on the river bank, watching the end of the flood tide lazily expending itself on the last tidal stretch of the river before Beeleigh Falls - the "Teddington" of the Blackwater. With the ebb tide setting in, we were soon off downriver to once again spend the night in Pyefleet - it was now Saturday, and there were more boats than the previous night, it being a popular weekend anchorage.

The next day, we slipped through the well used Spitway to the Thames; there was a very slight wind from Southeast and the sun shone; in a moment of nostalgia I decided to revisit scenes of my childhood, and the tide being right, took "CORYDALIS" along the shore, past Bell Wharf (no puffing steam cranes there now!) as far as Theobald's (LBS) wharf (now "Mike's Boatyard"), where I deemed it prudent to turn around and proceed stern first, past Billet Wharf where the Sunday crowds were enjoying their pint from "The Crooked Billet" by the waterside. As we reached the first of the cocklesheds, I decided it was time to clear out - again, as at Maldon I had no wish to park. At the "Low way" buoy, off the Ray entrance, we turned her upriver, where we were now punching a foul ebb tide; visibility was good and we repassed the Chalkwell and Leigh shores, taking a more distant view. The anchor went down in a place used many times before - near Shornmead, below Gravesend - there was no point in going any further against a strong tide and anyway, there are not a lot of suitable anchorages upriver from here.

Our voyage was completed the next day, and the log for this trip notes for the first time "1014, passed under QE II bridge, Dartford". You get a superior feeling as you pass under this high bridge, watching the traffic overhead crawling along - they have to pay, we don't! A short stop for lunch was taken by anchoring off Wren's masterpiece at Greenwich, where it was warm enough to eat al fresco. Because of those remains of an old river wall or building on the bottom, I have had difficulty getting an anchor to bite home; this time when we weighed, it came up with a large flint jammed between the flukes. In St Katharines we moored to a berth at the back of the Tower Hotel, and were to stay there for a month, using her as a London flat (the "Seagoing country cottage"). Our crew were all able to disperse from there by train, Michael and I to Chelmsford via Liverpool Street; sadly we were never to welcome Frank aboard for another trip as he died early in the following year.

During our stay, a trip was taken downriver to inspect the site of the new Cruising Association headquarters, and a team consisting of The President, Ron Browne, Bob Parker, Chairman of Council, Tony Brett-Jones, Hon Editor of the Handbook, and in line to be the next President, came. We locked in and out of St Katharine's on the same tide - one of the restrictions there is the limited times of access through the lock; it was a cold grey day, and although the site had been cleared and preparation work begun, it has to be said it was not a very inspiring outlook.

Our return trip at the end of October with Peter Darwent and Michael Rose was less of a cruise and more of a passage back to Woodbridge for winter - we were now on GMT with the evenings drawing in rapidly. Leaving St Katharine's just before high water, we were soon being swept downriver by a powerful Spring ebb tide - speeds over the ground of 9.8 and 10.2 knots were being logged, and five hours after leaving, the anchor went down inshore of West Leigh Middle buoy, by which time it was completely dark and approaching low water; the wind was light and from a point North of West, so we were comfortably sheltered, but cold, and were happy to retreat to the warmth of our well heated quarters below. The next day saw us round to the Stour, the tide not being right for entering the Deben in daylight and we anchored off Erwarton Ness. The passage was completed during the morning, helped by a strengthening of the Westerly wind and using all our sail area to assist the engine in pushing us over a strong adverse tide till the Deben entrance was reached; we still had to wait for the tide to rise before there was enough depth for us to enter the Tidemill, but all was secured and we were on our way home before dark.

INLAND FRANCE REVISITED

*(parts of this account were first published in the CA magazine
"Cruising" Winter 1993 edition)*

LETTING go from Suffolk Yacht Harbour at the very crisp hour of 0500, we shaped our cross estuary course down the Black Deep to the Fisherman's Gat, passing the outer Tongue buoy, once a Lightvessel. That winter Radar had been fitted (Platt was slowly entering the twentieth century!), and we were fascinated by the "Racon" display given by this buoy - activated by your own radar pulses which throw back a broad beam of light on the screen, well before you may have seen the buoy. Our crew for this trip consisted of the ever faithful Mike Rose (yes, the "bald" one- it was now becoming rare for "Thatch" to come as he had been somewhat diverted from sailing by an addiction to work and golf), chubby and cheerful John Barrington and the ever stalwart Peter Darwent.

The wind was coming from near ahead on our cross estuary course, giving us a slightly bumpy ride, but it was not too bad until we approached my much unloved Dover Strait. I think one of the troubles is that wind and tide tend to get funnelled through it - off Dover, we were wrestling with a fresh Southwest wind which was also knocking up a lively sea against the tide, which was intended to help us past here. Suddenly, the parrel line which runs through wood beads and holds the gaff against the mast, broke. Slowing right down, we lowered and stowed the mains'l with considerable difficulty, and then steamed into Hythe bay in order to give ourselves a rest under the lee of Dungeness. Having manoeuvred into relatively shallow and calm water, the anchor cable then refused to run out. The only way to free it was to take off the heavy steel hatch in the watertight collision bulkhead forward, and to do this required each bolt removing with a spanner, while someone was left keeping the boat chugging about in roughly the same position. The chain had been badly stowed so that the part that should have run out was weighed down by chain which should have been at the bottom - although "CORYDALIS" was now beginning her fifth season, we were still learning; I have made sure since that there would be no recurrence, and the hatch is secured now by bolts with lever handles, obviating the need for any other tools. It took nearly three quarters of an hour before the anchor finally went down to hold us, while we had a meal and rested from punching into a sea.

I don't know whether it was because we were now out of the Dover Strait or that there had been a sudden improvement in the weather generally, but when we weighed anchor at seven that evening, the wind had miraculously dropped. The barometer was rising, what little wind there was as we cleared the shore was from the Northwest, and there was just a slight hint of mist, while a slight swell left over from the blow rolled us gently as "CORYDALIS" ploughed her way at 7 knots towards the as yet unseen Normandy coast. By the small hours, the radar screen showed very clearly the cliffs stretching down towards Cap de la Heve and comfortingly confirming our Decca position. Our first port of call was to be Honfleur.

At this time there was a big dredging operation in the Honfleur approach channel, intended to make it accessible at all states of the tide, but this was far from complete, so we would not be able to enter until the tide had risen by a certain amount. Speed was eased as we closed the Seine Estuary on a morning that was rapidly becoming a warm and sunny day with a light Westerly wind, and this enabled us to enjoy a superb cooked breakfast prepared by Peter before reaching port. Our plan was to spend only the night there, but the lock gate to the inner harbour jammed, so we had to spend a further day incarcerated in this delightful place - advantage was taken of the delay to lower the masts instead of waiting till Rouen. By the afternoon tide, the defective gate had been repaired and we slipped across to Le Havre where Beryl was due to arrive by ferry, and from whence one could take full advantage of the flood tide up to Rouen. The flood stream in the Seine is powerful, but of short duration. However, high water in Rouen is about 5 hours later than Le Havre, so you can carry it all the way with reasonable power - certainly our 7 knots got us to Rouen well before high water, and at times we were achieving 10-11 knots over the ground.

In the event, taking the masts down at Honfleur proved a mistake. Apart from a feeling of nakedness without them, the steadying effect of the sails is lost. We left Le Havre with a fresh breeze from the West knocking up a lively chop and sending a bit of spray over the bows from time to time. As we turned to bring the wind abeam, without the dampening effect of weight aloft, "CORYDALIS" was too stiff and had a very lively snappy roll. The butts of the two wooden masts plus spars were lashed to a beam across the rails in the bows, and to a gallows on the wheelhouse roof. Lubricated by the spray, the whole lot started sliding

to and fro on the forward beam and extra emergency lashings had to be applied, but until we turned to run up the channel towards Honfleur and the rolling eased, the spars remained a threatening insecure load. I was concerned about reaching Rouen before dark as yachts are not supposed to navigate later than half an hour after sunset. We had our port, starboard and stern lights which are permanently mounted on the wheelhouse super-structure, but our masthead steaming light was now lying down with the mast. The little motor boat mast rigged in its place was originally used on "CELANDINE" when the masts were out of her, and had a platform on it for a steaming light, but I think that light was probably somewhere in the garage loft at Writtle. This was another snag about not having the masts up, and as darkness set in we were still about 15 km from our nearest refuge at Rouen - a torch was lashed to the motorboat mast as a poor replica of a steaming light. Although we didn't need it for lowering masts, the Bassin St Gervais was our first refuge out of the channel, so we thankfully went in, finally making fast shortly before eleven in total darkness.

At Rouen, we berthed at the

The small lock at Amfreville - Mike Rose using the "central locking" technique which enabled us to secure the boat in the lock with one line only. As you rise, the next bollard upwards must be lassooed.

halte de plaisance, to shop in the parade of small shops close by; the Co-op there sells an extremely good sparkling Saumur which costs about half what you might pay at the cheapest outlet in the UK. All the necessities of life can be found within this small shopping area! We let go from there mid-afternoon to reach the non-tidal part of the Seine that evening; the tidal Seine above Rouen is boring and best dealt with as quickly as possible - there is little point in fussing about tide any more as it is not as strong here, and anyway very dependent on how much river water is coming downstream. Some of the bends are such that it feels as if you have passed a place, and hour later you are still off the same place at the other end of the high street. By seven o'clock, still in bright sunshine, we entered the smaller of the great Amfreville locks and twenty minutes later secured alongside at a great long quay originally provided for waiting commercial traffic, but now little used except for a part near the locks; the far end where we moored is now very rural and peaceful.

The whole character changes for long stretches once you are in the non tidal reaches - the current will only be going one way - downstream - and except in time of flood (usually early Spring) will not be more than about half a knot. There are pretty little towns

The old bridge at Vernonnet - "Corydalis" was moored just beyond, almost at the exact place where the first pontoon bridge across the Seine was sited, giving the Allied armies a much needed crossing point for supplies.

and villages, with many attractive waterside properties in the traditional Norman style - ornamental half timbering and thatched roofs capped at the ridge with a line of iris growing out of the thatch; many of them are weekend and holiday pads for wealthy Parisians. Having started early from Amfreville, and after passing through our first lock on the Seine, we reached Vernonnet, where the local sailing club has a pontoon for use by visiting yachts. This place, which we have used regularly on our visits to the Seine, is attractive, although the same cannot be said of the large town on the opposite bank, Vernon, fortunately largely obscured by a well wooded island. There are the remains of an old ruined bridge close by - like every bridge below Paris, it was destroyed by one side or the other in the second World War, but it was here during that War, after the allies broke out from the Normandy beachhead that they made the first crossing of the Seine at the end of August 1944 - there was a wonderful morale boosting picture in all the British papers of Montgomery crossing the Seine on September the 1st - by means of a "Goliath"pontoon bridge from part ruined Vernon to almost exactly the spot where "CORYDALIS" was moored. Although many beautiful old bridges were destroyed, none of them would have been able to cope with the growth of road traffic in the subsequent years whereas those built to replace them were. Some railway bridges on little used branch lines never have been replaced (the continent did not need Dr Beeching - the War did the job for them).

Realising that we were near Giverny, we got a taxi to take us to Monet's house and garden - some of our crew had to leave before this point, so we were down to three. There had been a shower of rain earlier, but the sun was shining again by the time we reached Monet's house, so went straight into the gardens as there were clouds about, and we were able to tour the gardens, complete with the lily pond, Chinoiserie bridge and green punt on the

Monet's lily pond.

water. The earlier shower of rain had left droplets of water standing on blooms and leaves, which made for some very good photographs. By the time we were ready to leave Vernonnet steady rain had set in - we had been very lucky, and now pressed on through the rain towards Paris, winding our way round the many bends to reach the halte de plaisance at Limay, previously used five years earlier, in an evening of clearing skies. A shaft of evening sun caught the ancient stonework of its ruined bridge a little way upstream from the halte - another casualty of the War, replaced by a modern bridge far more suited to carrying heavy motor traffic.

The following afternoon we entered the Paris Arsenal marina; I was not going to be caught there again, and had made sure there was sufficient currency aboard; at that time, the French banks (in Paris, anyway) were being very sniffy about changing currency even though we had dollar traveller's cheques; the rate of exchange was about 8.50 francs to the pound. However, in that respect the marina had advanced to the point of accepting the "carte bancaire", but the extraordinary electric connections that were going to be standardised at the time of our previous visit five years earlier still had not been replaced. While in Paris we had considerable difficulty over our "vignette" permitting navigation on the Voies Navigables de France; this was the first year of its introduction and early in the year a cheque was sent for the amount due, with a calculation of the "surface" - the square measurement of a rectangle calculated by multiplying length by breadth. This has been simplified since by dividing boats into five categories. I wrote a covering letter in the best commercial French I could muster, in response to which they sent a charming reply, a formal receipt for the money, and a promise to send on the vignette as soon as ready. After several phone calls during which I was assured it was coming, we left the UK without it, and the only place it was requested was Amfreville, where we showed the receipt and the letter - and rather gathered that the new system was in chaos. Finally, after quite a stormy session we obtained the vignette, but I have never done that again, because when things go wrong, the French do not want to know. I subsequently have paid at their offices at Rouen, very near the halte de plaisance.

After a day or so in Paris, we were joined by Tony and Topsy Easteal from Writtle; the only member of the crew that came out from England was Michael Rose who was to leave at our next port of call. Soon after leaving, we passed the confluence with the Marne, through which we had come on our previous visit and I was astonished to see that there was now an enormous hotel on the right bank of the Marne, with Eastern tiled toofs and pagoda like structures - the "Guong Dong" hotel. As we progressed upstream, the bankside scenery improved to a more rural aspect, although still with some serious outbreaks of urbanisation and semi derelict industrial sites. In the afternoon we found a ruined disused commercial quay to break our voyage - old commercial quays are good places for us, because if once they berthed laden peniches drawing two metres or more, then there will be enough depth for us. There was some rather unpleasant broken concrete sticking out, but we managed to protect ourselves from this; handling a stern rope on to a substantial bollard ashore necessitated working gloves as it was completely overgrown with brambles. Once secured it was a pleasant enough spot, with steep wooded banks on the opposite bank, from which the occasional rather grand chateau peeped out across the river. Beryl, Tony and Topsy went ashore on what might be called a "nature walk", to discover wild orchids, including bee orchids, and other natural delights all growing close to the river bank. That evening fell quiet and calm with the closure of locks at seven, enabling us to enjoy aperitifs en plein air before descending below to eat.

The next day saw us enter the Canal du Loing and moor a little way above the first lock at what had been a loading quay, and where a laid-up peniche was taking up a fair amount of the available space. The skipper was aboard, and explained that the engine was "en pannage" (bust!) and the owners had not decided whether to repair or lay her up. The commercial barge traffic has shrunk at such a rate that a lot of the places indicated as temporary moorings are filled with laid up peniches, many of which ultimately are converted into houseboats. The fall in commercial traffic is what prompted VNF to start charging pleasure boats, and develop more facilities to promote the potential of these vast and beautiful waterways for tourism. Unfortunately, the development of the facilities is lagging, but it is an enormous task because of the sheer size of the system. Our berth gave us easy access to the ancient town of Moret immortalised by the impressionist Sisley who died there. The scenic and riverside charms are not matched by facilities; the shops near the river are limited, the nearest supermarket being right the other end of town, near the railway station. The local taxis are unreliable and cannot be guaranteed to arrive when ordered, whilst there are no facilities at all for "plaisanciers" - you could not call the quay we were using a facility, and no water supply was available. In spite of all this, we managed to effect crew changes there with Michael leaving for the UK, and Mary Dainty with sister Anne and brother-in-law Peter joining us for the next stage.

From Moret, we made a leisurely day trip (through seven locks) to Nemours, another fine historic town grouped more compactly close to the canal, and once home of the noble Dupont family which bred the famous scientist who founded the chemical company now based in America. Still no water - we had taken none since Paris, although the canal map indicates water at the lock at the entrance to the town, this is incorrect. Above Nemours,we found another good spot to moor, just above the Pont de Dordives where there once had been a stone quarry. The rock face of the cliff was now much overgrown, and the quay covered in lush grass - the chart indicated it as an "amarrage agreable" which it certainly was and we determined that we would stay the night.

Finally, the next day, we struck water at Vallees ecluse - a delightfully rural spot, where the lock keeper grew and sold fresh vegetables which were irresistible. It took quite some time to fill our parched tank while we were in the lock, but there was no other traffic about, so it didn't matter. "CORYDALIS" does carry a 10 litre plastic can of fresh water (which we use for drinking - Beryl and I were brought up in the old school that says you don't drink water out of ship's tanks). The idea of trying to fill a 200 gallon (just over 900 litres) tank using this, even if you could find a public tap within reasonable walking distance, does not bear thinking about - we had not run out, but must have been very low by the time we eventually re-filled. Later that afternoon we secured alongside at what is rather grandly described on the chart as "Port de Montargis" - a largely derelict area that no doubt had once been bustling with commercial traffic, but now the only part used was that nearest to the main road, where some rusty machinery was used once a year for loading grain at harvest time. The nearest bustling activity was about a hundred yards back from the quay where there was a large builders' merchants and "bricolage" depot. Between us and that was an area of weeds and scrub, with a set of rusty railway lines ending near where we moored.

Montargis has an important station on the main line, and good shops, as well as some delightful old buildings but it is busy and noisy, so another crew left here, leaving

Beryl and I alone for a day or so before being joined by "Polar" Pam. So undisturbed was this "Port de Montargis", that one morning while, shaving, I watched a large rabbit eyeball to eyeball, quite close to the window, virtually doing the same thing. Rabbits do not actually shave (just as well - they have splendid whiskers), but the fastidiousness of this creature in completing his morning toilet fascinated me. A great variety of wildlife is to be seen in the remoter parts of the canals, but this confrontation was so near the boat and in an urban situation.

From Montargis, we were on the Canal de Briare, although we had not yet completely done with the now very small River Loing, which was still supplying make up water to the canal; canals all need a supply of make up water, so rivers are always to be found nearby, but on the summit of a canal this is not always possible, and pumping has to be used. A night stop was made at Chatillon Colligny, where a brand new halte de plaisance had been built, complete with good bollards, two metres depth of water and water and elecricity points. Chatillon was given the name Colligny in belated recognition of one of the most famous French admirals, a Huguenot killed in one of the massacres, which depleted the French Navy as a large proportion of its men from admiral to seaman were protestants, and many of those who escaped joined the British Navy.

From here we went on to Rogny, where the Loing and the canal finally parted company and we started the final climb to the summit reach - the "Bief de Partage" - the reach where the waters parted. The canal de Briare is very old, the construction of which was initiated by Sully, Henri IV's henchman, to link navigation between the lush Loire and the Seine, to help feed the growing population of Paris. The engineer responsible, Hugues Cosnier, is said to have been the inventor of the lock with double gates, one at each end, and under his direction work started in 1604, only to be abandoned on the death of Henri IV and subsequent fall from grace of Sully. For almost 20 years civil troubles and local wars left the incomplete works abandoned with only 12 km unfinished. Cosnier, the engineering genius, died before his work was finally opened to navigation in 1642. The original staircase of seven locks to reach the summit was finally disbanded in 1887 to be replaced by six larger locks curving gently round the hill, and it was these which we used; the original staircase is well preserved as a national historic monument.

The canal in the summit reach (where we were over 540 feet above sea level) is flanked by great artificial "etangs" into which water is pumped from the Loire by a pumping station in Briare - it still has its great chimney, and steam engines are preserved there, but it is now electric pumps which do the

Rogny - les sept ecluses, now a national monument.

Entering the Pont Canal at Briare.

work of topping up these reservoirs. The etangs have naturalised, are lush with reed beds and lakeside vegetation, and teeming with fish and wild fowl. Here we made one of our most peaceful nightstops, and the sun went down over the nearest etang, glimpsed through the foliage of canalside trees - an unforgettable sight in an atmosphere of tranquillity. The next day, we made our descent through 8 locks into Briare, an inland Venice created by the many canals and waterways; the original canal of Henri IV went through the centre of the town and then descended through several locks to the turbulent waters of the Loire, where a perilous passage was made between piles to reach the canal lateral a la Loire - how horse drawn barges were towed upstream against the swift flowing stream, I cannot imagine. At Briare we came to the great engineering work which carries the canal over the treacherous waters and flood plain of the Loire, and one of the objectives of our trip. The old canal winds its way through the town, where a port de plaisance has been constructed, and other parts have been made into attractive lily covered ornamental waterways. Unfortunately, the old canal is too shallow for "CORYDALIS "and we made fast alongside the dusty former commercial quay, within sight of the entrance to the aqueduct, opened in 1896 and linking the two canals independently of the Loire river. The aqueduct ("Pont Canal") still has the magnificent ornamental electric lights installed on its completion, and lit by hydro-electric power utilising the Loire current; consulting engineers from the famous Eiffel company advised on the plans, and monuments to the engineers actually engaged in the construction flank either end - the continentals give far greater honour to their engineers than is the case in our own country.

On a fine Sunday morning, we made our crossing of the Loire, which calls for some concentration in keeping the boat on the straight and narrow for 663 metres; the width is 6.2 metres and our beam 3.9 metres - so there is plenty of room for us, but it does not feel like it when you view the long length ahead (622metres). The depth is just over 2 metres, so there was no risk of our keel punching a hole in the bottom of the metal trough forming the aqueduct; at either side were wide walkways borne on strong brackets, and originally intended for the horses towing the barge traffic, but now being used by the inhabitants and tourists as a pleasant Sunday walk, with the Loire running 11 metres below; our progress at a slow speed enabled us to converse with some of the promenading groups, but the actual time for the crossing was little more than ten minutes.

Once across, we were running along the Loire valley close to the left bank of the river, with the disused stretch of the canal laterale that was by- passed by the Pont Canal running way below us - not only did the new construction enable the crossing of the river in safety, but because of its high level, a whole series of ancient locks were eliminated until it finally reached the present canal at the small village of l'Etang, a good few kilometres South of Briare. What seemed a very pleasant place to stop for lunch was the village of Belleville, within sight of the Loire and alongside a grassy bank where other boats were moored in the strong sunshine. However, it might not seem possible to encounter a bore on the placid non-tidal waters of a canal, but we did and it ruined this pleasant spot. The bore, best described as a Scottish cockney was living on a British motor yacht of unknown vintage nearby, fastened on to us as soon as we berthed, and insisted on telling us how poular he was locally - he wasn't with us, as it forced us to retreat below for lunch to get away from his incessant chatter, instead of eating up on the bridge en plein air, before moving on to moor up at our destination for this trip, in an embranchment off the canal which joined the Loire itself by means of a lock at St Thibault.

From our mooring in this quiet branch we could see the hilltown of Sancerre, the centre for the wine of that name grown in the region. The following day, with Pam, we visited Sancerre by taxi, and drank a glass of the refreshing white wine sitting in the central square; however, when we went to see the prices of the wine, which tends to be overpriced, it did not matter whether we looked at a grotty downmarket vendor in a backstreet or a posh upmarket place in the centre, it was all the same price. There may be European laws about cartels and competition, but it clearly was not affecting these people - I do have a sneaking admiration for the French, who will go on doing what they have always done, quite regardless of what Brussels may decree. Our taxi back to the boat was driven by Mme Annie Frottier, who we found more reliable than some of the other French taxi drivers, so we took her card. Pam left us at St Thibault to go and visit a friend further South, but Beryl and I stayed on for a further day or so before returning home.

We arranged with Mme Frottier to take us to the chateau at Chapelle d'Angillon, where Alan Fournier wrote his classic "Le Grand Meaulne". En route, Mme Frottier, who turned out to be a well informed driver and tour guide, mentioned that Mme at the chateau had died recently, but it was not until we reached there that we realised she had been tragically killed, at the age of about 50, in a motoring accident only a few days before. In the circumstances, we could have understood if they had decided to close it to visitors for a few days, but a guide was on hand to show us round; there were only two other couples, Belgian and German waiting there, and we mutually agreed that a French language tour was acceptable to us all.

Once inside, we first visited the chapel, which was filled with lilies whose heady perfume totally pervaded the atmosphere. Continuing our tour, there was a background of uncontrolled sobbing echoing down the ancient stone corridors; the tragedy had clearly shaken the family, and local community. Another surprise was to come across a large room in which was a "Musee d'Albanie". When Albania was overrun during the Second World War, King Zog and Queen Geraldine were given refuge at this chateau - there was a family connection which brought this about. It seems they were quite safe in this remote rural haven, which must have been largely unaffected by the War. Parts of the establishment were very ancient, in particular the stables, which were being restored under some French heritage organisation - they were very grand with great pillars, but in those days the horses were very often housed in quarters that seemed superior to that of the residents, and certainly that of their servants. There was great antiquity and a mystical quality about this whole place, which looked out on one side over a vast etang - from its regular shape, it did not look like a natural lake.

Finally, before leaving to return to the UK, we were told by a local that the lock keeper in the first lock ro be passed on our return journey sold cases of Sancerre, and would put them aboard for you - thus saving having to return up the great hill by taxi to collect our wine rations. When we did go through the lock, the price was still the standard cartel price, but with the advantage of the wine being delivered straight on board.

The homeward bound trip obviously was a retracing of our route outwards; for the first part of the trip, Garry and Sally Alder, who we first met all those years ago in the Church at Manaccan came with me. We met up in Paris, whence we were taking an express train to Nevers, the first stop, and coming back the short distance to St Thibault by a local train. Unfortunately the booking clerk at the Gare de Lyon misinterpreted what they intended to do. We left on the train, which was very crowded so we could not sit together; the ticket inspector came along, and my ticket which had been bought in the UK was to Nevers, where I intended to buy a ticket for the local train, but the clerk had only booked them to St Thibault. Garry explained the situation and offered to pay whatever supplement was necessary. The inspector asked them to wait while he spoke to his "confrere" (in fact the driver). He arranged to stop the train at Montargis, where a local train which would stop at St Thibault was due to leave very shortly. He radioed Montargis to hold the local train until we arrived - there was even someone to meet us at Montargis and escort us to the right platform - all this was done to save Garry paying the extra fare (I wonder what it cost SNCF to stop that express train!). All this seems almost unbelievable, but when you realise that there was not another train due on the express track for nearly two hours, the whole procedure was not going to disrupt the timetable, and the driver was probably able to make up the time lost due to the unplanned stop.

Garry and Sally are wonderful company to have on any kind of journey - certainly this one was very different from our previous voyages in Brittany and down Channel. There are a number of entries or additional remarks in the log such as "Ouzouer-sur-Trezee (une belle eclusiere ici)". or at the amarrage agreeable at Dordives "Garry abandoned helm and jumped ashore in panic" - I have no recollection of the incident and I am sure this was a wifely exaggeration of whatever happened - Garry is the last person I would expect to panic. Our voyage Northwards was taken at a faster rate than the Southbound passage, and we were careful not to stop at Belleville with its hazard of a dangerous bore; there was time to show them Briare, and to stop again in the peaceful summit reach.

The Alders left at Nemours to be replaced by the entire family, who had flown out with Beryl from Stansted; the railway station at Nemours is very close to the canal. I am not sure how every one was accommodated, and I think there must have been grandchildren sleeping in the wheelhouse; they left at Paris, where we were joined by Mike Rose, Polar Pam and Mike Selby for the passage down the Seine to Le Havre, whence Beryl would take the ferry home. After rerigging the masts at the insalubrious Bassin Gervais, we left mid afternoon to continue downstream, but it was rather late to start the voyage, and with it being almost seven in the evening, I began to think about breaking the journey. At Caudebec, there is a rather fine pontoon berth; there was already a French flagged ketch alongside at one end, so we berthed alongside at a respectable distance to leave plenty of empty pontoon.

Caudebec, a very old Norman town, suffered heavily during the Normandy campaign, but had been very carefully and sensitively rebuilt as a pleasant riverside town, complete with promenade. After dinner, we explored a little, and enjoyed a cognac at one of the numerous cafes, with a view over the river. It had been a long day, and rerigging is always hard work, so we were soon all in our bunks and sound asleep. Just after midnight I was awoken by the sound of a ship's siren, and wondered what was happening out in the river. When it sounded again, I lept out and could see what looked like a miniature QE II ablaze with lights and creeping nearer and nearer to the pontoon; pulling on something warm, I went on deck to be told by a Frenchman on the pier we had to leave immediately. By this time we were all up - navigation lights switched on, engine running in an instant, and we let go to steam off into the dark abyss beyond the blaze of the cruise ship's lights. At this point, a guardian angel appeared in the form of a French pilot boat who had probably just taken the pilot off the cruise boat; after a brief discussion he said follow me, and he led us to a nearby area with a number of vacant mooring buoys - they were yacht sized, and I had no idea what strength they were, but it was something to hitch on to. We hastily rigged a pennant to go through the ring of the buoy, profusely thanked our friends and once again retired to our bunks.

The next morning was sunny and calm; we were a little way downstream from the pier and had a view of some of the older buildings including the Mairie which had obviously survived the War in good condition. Thoughts of inflating the Avon dinghy to go ashore were quickly dispelled by the thought of mooring it to cope with the great rise and fall of tide here - we were getting near the mouth of the Seine with its 40 foot plus rise and fall - and also of having to cope with the flood tide shortly due, which would run past us like a mill race. A lazy morning, resting in the sun, undertaking little jobs about the ship while Michael sketched the nearby shoreside buildings, restored us to normality, and in the afternoon completed our passage to Le Havre.

The following day, after shopping in a not very special supermarket (where we stupidly bought some wine they were almost giving away - it proved virtually undrinkable), Beryl caught the night ferry back to Portsmouth; we left about nine that evening and the ferry left soon after to head Northwards with us following. Having already proved that "CORYDALIS" cannot keep up with ferries, we were content to see the bright lights pulling away from us, but were surprised how long we had them in view - night ferries are usually run slower than daytime crossings so she was probably doing rather less than 18 knots. The night was calm, with a bit of swell left from several days of strong Westerlies, and we made good progress towards our objective - the new Sovereign marina at "Eastbourne", which is really almost in Pevensey, and had only just opened for business.

Soon after nine in the morning, our night passage completed, we were berthing within the large locked basin. Everything was new and worked well, with two impressive parallel locks to lock you in swiftly; needless to say, once we were in there was plenty of room, as few boats had arrived so soon after the opening; our visit was essentially a nose blacking operation. The area in which it is sited is one of the bleakest I have ever come across - a wilderness of low-lying gravel soil with hardly a tree in sight. There was another ambition I had, which was to see Eastbourne, a town I had never visited but of which I always had mental pictures, so we took a taxi into town - it is quite a way from the marina. It was a warm and sunny day with a gentle breeze blowing on shore, and there were well manicured lawns and flowerbeds along the spacious promenade, with rows of deck chairs containing elderly people (many nearly as old as me!) taking the sea air; close by a military band played popular light classics and music from the shows in exactly the kind of bandstand I would have expected. Further along the promenade, there was the famous "Grand Hotel" whose Palm Court orchestra music played every Sunday on the "Home Service" during the War, under the direction of that master of light music, Albert Sandler, with his signature tune *"Roses from the South"*. Now, here it was before me, looking rather faded (I believe part had been damaged by fire). Happily, I believe that since then there has been some major refurbishment to restore it to its former glory.

The following morning (it was now early August) we left early, with the intention of reaching Harwich harbour by nightfall. The barometer was dropping rather ominously, and at half past nine Coastguard were issuing a force 8 Northwesterly gale warning for sea area Thames, so plans were revised to only make Ramsgate that day; the outer Thames is not much fun in a gale, particularly from the Northwest - there would be little shelter until we neared the Essex coast. As far as Ramsgate, we would be protected by the Kent coast; later Coastguard revised their forecast down to force 7, but that still would not be much fun, and we were supposed to be doing this for pleasure. Previous experiences of Ramsgate had not been particularly good, but I radioed on ahead, and they confirmed there would be a berth for us - in fact, they could not have been more helpful, as they actually shifted some boats around to create a berth long enough to accommodate us. By the time we arrived early in the afternoon, the barometer was rising again; it still was blowing hard, although difficult to judge its true strength as we were sheltered by the town which stands on rising ground. There was little we required in the way of victuals so near the end of our voyage, but I was astonished to find a Waitrose supermarket not far from the harbour - this hardly fitted the picture of the Ramsgate I remembered from younger days.

By the time we sailed the following morning at the civilised hour of 1015 (we had not so far to go from here and this also meant more favourable tides) the wind had dropped to between force 4 or five, and backed nearer to West - no longer a dead noser for our Estuary crossing - the sun was shining, the barometer still climbing. At half past five that evening we re-entered Suffolk Yacht Harbour exactly ten weeks after leaving it.

DOWN UNDER

SHORTLY after our return, we had a joint birthday party to celebrate our 70th birthdays, with a marquee in the largest possible space available in our garden without felling any trees; it was a hectic time for social life in Writtle as soon after that, crew member Peter Darwent's daughter Tiffany was married in Writtle Church, followed by another marquee job. Fortunately for all, it was a dry and warm late summer. The next day we were off to New Zealand, where the hundredth anniversary of the enfranchisement of women was being celebrated.

Beryl had been invited as keynote speaker to a vast gathering of women scientists and engineers in Wellington; her economy class fare had been paid for, but some negotiations with QANTAS (Queensland and Northwest Territories Air Services!) enabled both of us to travel business class, in return for a very reasonable extra contribution from us - it was an opportunity not to be missed. Wellington, the administrative capital of New Zealand (known to the locals as "windy Wellington") is a sophisticated modern city, but one of the most remarkable features that impressed me were the open air murals. One, on the rather plain end wall of a building housing an Italian restaurant showed a realistic vista of Venice, another painted on the wall of a rather drab warehouse, showed the view you would have seen had the building not been there - a view of the harbour. Another, on the wall of a public lavatory showed an elaborate war time composition of people in the street, including service personnel and other uniformed services - a complete cross section of the community and an unusual War memorial.

There were various events to which I was invited, and enjoyed, but fond as I am of the opposite sex, the thought of the main conference day with some 400 women present, was just more than I felt able to cope with. I took myself on a day trip across the Cook Strait to the South Island, a trip of just under 40 nautical miles, of which nearly half is in the sheltered waters of a winding sound leading to Picton, on about the 41st parallel of latitude South. The day was bright, but there was a stiff Westerly wind blowing. The ship I travelled in, the "Aratika" was a drive - on car/rail ferry operated by New Zealand Railways; a good looking but ageing ship, built at Nantes nearly twenty years earlier and converted from a commercial ro-ro ferry in Hong Kong. The conversion had been well done, and she was a good looking vessel; such ships I prefer to the latter day ferries, built up like wedding cakes to give more and more saloons and less seaworthiness and stability.

The ferry made good work of the open water of the Cook Strait before reaching the sheltered but intricate waters of the Sound. The coastal scenery was craggy, lush in the valleys and sparsely populated. Every so often you would pass a sheltered North facing cove, at the head of which would be a sun drenched isolated house or minute community - having lived my life in the Northern hemishpere, I found it quite difficult to adjust to the idea that the most desirable sites for such places would be North facing. The trip took just over two and a half hours; I had little more than an hour to look at Picton, a pleasant old fashioned seaside resort which had barely started to stir from its winter slumbers - this was September the 2nd, and early Spring out here.

On the return trip I made my way to the dining saloon as I now had a healthy appetite; suddenly I was in a time warp. This ship belonged to a state run company, and I suspect that really meant they were run by the powerful trade unions, whose interests were more in looking after their members than service to the customer - already the memory of those days back home were receding. The dining saloon was small, clean and relatively low down in the ship - that suited me, as the lower you are in a ship, the less movement you get. The stewards were friendly, but I doubt whether they had ever had any real training in the job; the menu was extremely limited and I chose fish and chips. I was hungry, so I am not complaining - in some ways it was a nostalgic reminder of the standards of service we were used to not so many years previously, The wind was blowing harder on the return trip, but the ship made good work of it and I had thoroughly enjoyed the experience.

The following day, storm force winds raged through the Cook Strait, an area where the Tasman Sea and Pacific Ocean vent their fury through the channel between North and South Islands, and all shipping movements were suspended. These are the "roaring forties" where the Southern oceans and winds rage unimpeded by any major land masses. It was in this stretch of water that New Zealand's worst passenger ferry disaster occurred, in April 1968, when the two year old Clyde built ferry "Wahine" met disaster in the entrance to Wellington harbour, with the loss of 51 lives. I remember reading about it in the UK papers, but it only merited a few words and I found it difficult to understand how a ferry could founder in such a narrow channel, but like so many things in life, once you have seen the place where it happened, it is so much more easily understood. The ship was a handsome and seaworthy design, powered by steam turbo-electric propulsion, built for the Union Shipping Company for ferry service between Lyttelton, Christchurch and Wellington; she was making an overnight passage to arrive in Wellington early in the morning. The forecasters had said a cyclone in the Tasman sea would abate, but it did not and unexpectedly hit Wellington overnight, causing structural damage ashore, and it was into this that the "Wahine" sailed.

Wellington harbour is a big enclosed natural inlet with a narrow and rock strewn entrance into which the doomed ship was sailing, in torrential horizontal rain and hurricane force winds. At that crucial moment, first her radar failed, and then she was caught by a massive sea which effectively caused her to broach to. Thirty minutes of struggle with her powerful engines failed to bring her under control, and she struck rocks, which ripped her engine room open to the sea. She now lost power and drifted slowly up the harbour, filling with water. It was some seven hours later that she finally rolled over on her side, in relatively shallow water, accompanied by a spectacular explosion and escape of steam as the cold salt water hit her boilers. It is an event New Zealanders will not forget easily, and it once again shows the power of the sea in that it overwhelmed a powerful and seaworthy ship, in the worst possible place, close to the shore.

From Wellington, we flew to Christchurch - what a delightful city, with the river Avon flowing gently through parkland in the city centre. From here, where we picked up a hire car, we drove down into the Southern alps, where we encountered a blizzard before reaching Queenstown in brilliant sunshine. It is a lakeside resort, overlooked a snow topped mountain range on the opposite shore, aptly named the Remarkables, and among the attractions here, was a trip on the coal burning twin screw steamer, "EARNSLAW", a ship originally built by the government to maintain a fast post and delivery service to the otherwise inaccessible lakeside farmsteads and settlements, but now run as a tourist attraction. Looking down the open skylight from the upper deck, I could see the two triple expansion reciprocating engines, reminding me of the single, but somewhat larger engine I knew on HMS TUSCARORA, and giving that nostalgic aroma of hot grease, paint and oil that only can be obtained from steam engines.

Given more time, we would have gone to the scenic attractions of Doubtful Sound and other verdant spots on the Southwest coast, but instead our course was directed North, first to Wanaka, where Beryl visited a fighter aircraft museum and found friends of people she had known in her aircraft industry days. Lake Wanaka itself was beautiful and utterly deserted - we were in a country with three and a half million people and sixteen million sheep (does anyone really know?). We made our way to the wild and rugged West Coast of the South Island through the Haast Pass, past Mount Cook, a volcano that blew off its peak in its last eruption, and the Franz Josef glacier - in the carpark here, there was a warning about the Kea parrots, a most destructive bird which would attack anything soft - like a soft top case on the roof rack . We saw one pulling away at the rubber insert round a car's windscreen. The coast itself had a mixture of good beaches and rocky cliffs, and the sea threw up ancient bleached portions of tree on to the shores, reminiscent of those we had seen on the West coast of Oregon, USA. There were small towns and resorts, of which our favourite was Hokitika, a pretty seaside town complete with tearooms, and in the main street an impressive war Memorial unveiled by Edward the VIIth commemorating new Zealanders who lost their lives in the Boer War.

A little further North on the West coast was the rather neglected port of Greymouth, whose harbour had a dangerous entrance and was really no longer suitable for the larger ships in use today. Here there was a railhead, and we turned in the hire car to catch the Transalpine Express back to Christchurch; I can't remember whether the Stationmaster acted as the agent for the returned car, or whether the hire car agent acted as stationmaster, but they seemed to fit happily into either job. The rail journey, crossing the Alps through Arthur Pass, was spectacular, and there was an open platform car from which you could view and photograph - but not for long, it was too cold. From Christchurch, we flew to Rotorua where another hire car was waiting for us.

Rotorua is a centre of volcanic activity in the form of thermal vents which issue forth steam and sulphur fumes everywhere - there is steam issuing from many private gardens, through the drains - everywhere. There is an area of geysers issuing great founts of steaming hot water, interspersed with mud pools in which small mud craters are created as the hot gases bubble up through the mud. A little way outside town we found an open air swimming pool fed by a gushing stream of water so hot that it had to pass through cooling chambers before it was at a temperature safe for swimming. The weather in North Island, as we drove North was more of a Mediterranean climate, except that they receive good rainfall to keep the landscape verdant; the parallel of latitude here was about 381/4 South, equivalent to Valencia in the Northern hemisphere. Pressing on Northwards, we visited Whangarei to see Alan and Mary Poulton - she had been up at Cambridge with Beryl, and with them as our guides, saw some of the most superb cruising areas in the North East of the island, including some harbours and inlets on the famous Bay of Islands and Waitangi, where the Maori treaty was signed. We were now on a latitude South, comparable with Northern Morocco in the Northern hemisphere - but very much more refreshing because of the surrounding cool Southern seas. On our way back to the UK, we made a stop in Australia to visit neighbours from Writtle, who had done a house exchange with some people in Perth, and under their guidance during our brief visit we saw kangaroos and koala bears at close quarters.

On return, we had an autumn cruise which included a nostalgic voyage up the Colne to the Anchor pub at Rowhedge, where we lunched with Ian Brown, and viewed the site of the fomer boatyard, where the buildings had been demolished and there was little to show there had ever been a large boatyard there. Our cruise included a visit to Paglesham, one of my earlier sailing haunts, before retreating up the Deben to Woodbridge for winter moorings, from which we made one or two of our usual frostbiting winter river trips. During that winter, there was a lot of activity in the CA as the new headquarters neared completion, and I was involved in some of the meetings, particularly concerning the management of the marina. I had very clearly said when I relinquished the post of President, that past presidents should "sit down and shut up" - but having said this, I would be happy to work in the background wherever I might contribute.

LIMEHOUSE, THE NEW CA HEADQUARTERS AND HOLLAND - FOR THE LAST TIME

IN mid-April 1994, "CORYDALIS" sailed from Levington, running up the Wallet and round to Brightlingsea with a fresh Northeasterly wind blowing, reminding me of the years we went to Woodbridge from Leigh at Easter, when it was nearly always blowing from that quarter - quite usual at that time of the year; however, this time it was with us, and still blowing from the same quarter when we went round to the Thames, to anchor for the night in the Ray, off Chalkwell - well sheltered in a Northeaster. The following day, starting at a gentlemanly hour just as the flood tide started to make, we set off upriver, and were locking in to Limehouse Basin for the first time. Limehouse basin is a good deal smaller than when in its commercial days, but much of this is due to the fact that it has a road tunnel ("The Limehouse Link") running under what had been water, but the tunnel still goes under part of it, reserved for shallow draft canal boats; I don't think they would take too kindly to Platt grounding his twenty tons of steel boat on the tunnel roof - in fact, there are ample safety margins, and anyway, I have no intention of straying into that part of the basin.

Having arrived on Monday, by Friday, when the new CA headquarters were officially opened, she was not only dressed overall (I do find this more complicated on a ketch than a boat with a single stick), but also by night we had lights overall - this was even more difficult than putting up flags, but they did look splendid and helped to make the occasion more festive. I had bought low wattage bulbs well within the capacity of our generator, but in the event, they had just got the electricity supply to the pontoons completed and were able to use shore supply with a time clock so they came on each night for the whole period. After a week of celebrations, we locked out again late Friday afternoon and were soon being carried along on a strong ebb tide to anchor for the night in the Yantlet small ships anchorage just off the edge of the sands on the Kentish side - what little wind there was came from a Southerly direction. By the end of April the evenings are drawing out well, and the sun was still shining when we anchored at seven that evening - on the Kentish shore we were virtually opposite the West Leigh Middle buoy.

By the next morning there was a light wind blowing from Northwest, which enabled the sails to help us down Swin and through the Spitway into the Wallet, but just after we had gone through this tricky gap in the sandbanks, the wind shifted round rapidly into the Northeast, a dead noser for the rest of the trip, so the sails were handed and we became a pure motor boat. At the same time, it freshened, and there was a sharp drop in temperature; unavoidably, we were also punching the tide until reaching the entrance to Harwich, where the last of the flood tide helped us upriver to reach Levington by four. What a satisfactory episode it had been - I had, along with many others, long wanted to see the CA in headquarters of their own, and now it had really happened with "CORYDALIS" there for the opening.

Early in June, we were off to Holland again, sailing from Levington at quarter to five in the morning, just as the sun was coming up at the start of a fine summer's day, with a promise of good Westerly winds that would enable the sails to give us some extra push. It was thirteen and a half hours later that we were locking in at Flushing - with the fair wind we should not have taken so long, but I believe we had a foul tide coming out of the Schelde Estuary and through the Duerloo channel. I was beginning to accept the predictability of passages made under power and worked on thirteen hours to Flushing from Levington - you might think I was trying to run a scheduled ferry service. Just after eight that evening we were secured alongside at Middleburg.

From here, we went through the Veersemeer and the great Kats lock into tidal waters before locking into the canal up to Goes, where crew changes took place. Mike Rose and Peter Darwent left, to be replaced by Mary Dainty and Beryl. The little yacht harbour "De Werf" was as charming as ever, but sadly, the group of volunteers who helped to keep it all so trim were getting visibly older - I think we had been coming there since 1968 when we first visited in "CELANDINE". It was difficult to find younger people who had the time or inclination to take on such a labour of love, sadly something so many voluntary organisations are finding these days, and they were concerned for the future of this delightful little haven.

Back in tide water, we headed down the Ooster Schelde to Zierikzee, where, after passing under the great Oosterschelde Bridge which we had seen in construction - there was 15 metres air height for our eight and a half metres - it still looks worrying as you approach, but of course, there was ample clearance. It was the weekend, and when we left at half past nine on Sunday morning we had to disentangle ourselves from four boats rafted alongside. I cannot remember the flag, but I think it was German - certainly continental; these are the people who for some time had been subject to regulation and certificates, and you ask yourself what it is all worth when you see an idiot like this handling a boat with immense power. Willemstad was more crowded than I had ever seen it before, as were most places we visited, even though facilities had been extended.

Two days later, we were steaming up the waters of Dordsche Kil, leading to Dordrecht, when a high speed Dutch Police rib came up under our stern and a police officer leapt aboard without any introductory remarks, and immediately lectured me because we were not far enough over to the starboard side of the channel. I pointed out that I was on the starboard side, and that the channel was completely empty - had a large vessel come in to sight from either direction I would have moved further over. He ordered me to leave the helm - I slowed her down and left a somewhat apprehensive pair of females to continue. Fortunately, Beryl and Mary are both very competent, and certainly Beryl knew the waterway pretty well; this young man did not seem to be concerned with the safety of the vessel, but after inspecting the ship's papers, then proceeded to examine everything including my VHF radio operator's licence. His manner was officious to the point of rudeness and arrogance. By this time, although I do not believe in arguing with authority, this did not seem to me to be the way to treat visitors and I pointed out that we were a British registered ship and complied with the requirements of British authorities (not many for yachts of our size - perhaps this is what irked him), but his attitude remained more like that of a Nazi SS officer than a Dutch civil policeman. He finally left in an atmosphere that can best be described as frigid, perhaps diappointed that he could find nothing wrong. This was not the Holland I had long known; whether he was trying to take it out on us because it was even then becoming pretty obvious that disenchantment with a lot of European regulation was growing in England, but his attitude all seemed so uneccessary, and left an unpleasant feeling - were we now sailing in a police state?

Visits were made to Schoonhoven before heading for our old favourite Warmond; on the way we secured for the night in a very downmarket yacht harbour on the edge of an industrial suburb of Gouda; having just missed an opening of a railway bridge, and the weather, which up till now had been fine and warm, broke - the barometer had been falling from a high for a couple of days. We moored in steady rain at an empty berth, but with shore electricity available, and were glad to retreat below - the surroundings hardly would have encouraged one on deck to admire the view, but this didn't matter in the rain. The next morning the harbourmaster came and collected 9 guilders berthing fee, including electricity, which seemed very reasonable; the rain had stopped, and we caught the railway bridge opening, as well as various other opening bridges, rail and road, to arrive at CIECO marina, Warmond. This was about to change hands, as the Lloyd family which had run this immaculate and quiet haven for a great many years, were retiring and retreating to warmer climes. Mary's sister Anne and brother-in-law Peter came out for a short visit - Warmond is quite a good centre for one or two interesting little day trips - before we turned South again, spending a night at anchor in the Brassemer Meer.

Revisiting Willemstad and Zieriksee - still just as crowded, we also went back to "De Werf" at Goes. The former commercial basin in the town centre had by now been turned into a yacht harbour, and most people went in there - indeed, it is quite easy to miss the more attractive alternative with its small rural entrance - or are they looking for something smarter? From here we made our way to Flushing; Mary and Beryl left, whilst Mike Rose and cousin Polar Pam arrived. The weather had improved again, and the wind was now coming from Easterly directions, which boded well for a good smooth crossing; to prepare for an early start we passed through the last opening bridge at Flushing, and secured to an outer berth in the small yacht harbour just beyond it. It was pretty full, but we found a berth on a pontoon just outside the entrance, and although the general surroundings are not exactly salubrious, it was a highly convenient place for a very early departure.

Our clocks were changed back to BST before we turned in, and at 0335 the next morning, Monday July the 4th, we let go in darkness and called the sea lock on the radio - the answer was terse, but simple and adequate - "Kleine sluis", and by the time we presented ourselves at the gates, the lights were changing in our favour - indeed within a quarter of an hour of letting go from our berth, we were heading down the Estuary, hoisting our mains'l and heading for the Duerloo channel. As we approached this tricky channel, it was already getting light; all three of us were on the bridge when we spotted it. A rat was making its way along the narrow metal beading that tops the bulwarks, rather gingerly, and casting glances at the roaring bow wave. It obviously didn't feel very safe up there, and came down on deck. Mike and I left Pam steering and rushed to shut the wheelhouse doors, while at the same time I made a grab for the boat hook with the idea of pushing him overboard. Just as Michael's door was almost closed, the rat dashed over his feet and made its way straight down the steps, turning right into the galley.

A search of the lockers, and banging of pots and pans failed to flush him out, and as we were by now closing the first buoys in the Duerloo, we had to abandon the rat and concentrate on pilotage; the light was by now quite good - not long to sunrise. Finally, after clearing the channel and reaching open water, another rat search was conducted, to no avail. Then a thunderstorm approached - this was my first experience of seeing a storm on the radar screen; there was torrential rain, violent thunder and lightning accompanied by a very vicious squall, which had come up against the wind, and our course, so we sailed through and out the other side. We were soon back outside again, enjoying an extremely pleasant crossing. The wheelhouse doors were wide open again - to the best of our knowledge there were no more rodents waiting to go down there, and we wanted plenty of fresh air.

We had already arranged with John Barrington to meet us at Levington, with an approximate ETA of 1730, to be confirmed by a telephone link call through Orfordness radio when we were within range. Soon after two, we called him to confirm our ETA, and at the same time asked if he could manage to bring a rat trap with him. You would not usually ask a friend to bring a rat trap when meeting you, but John Barrington is different. He has so many contacts, he is the one chap in Essex who could probably locate a rat trap at short notice. We berthed at 1730 when John was waiting to take our lines, accompanied by an enormous metal trap. When shutting the boat down, the trap was set in the galley, where the stowaway had last been seen, and baited with some strong "Ouda Gouda" cheese - slightly reminiscent of Parmesan. Only the best would do for visitors to my boat, and any way it was a Dutch rat, so it seemed appropriate.

There are very strict rules about landing animals from boats, and the official notice includes a very clear picture of a rat among the forbidden creatures. With the boat completely locked up, it was impossible for him to get ashore, but I wondered what damage he might inflict, particularly on electric cables - they are very partial to PVC. All the cartons of cereal and any other dry goods that might be an attraction were carefully put in what we considered to be rat proof containers, which might, of course, make him even more partial to the electric cables. Revisiting a few days later - no attempt on the beautiful cheese bait, which would have brought the most terrifying spring loaded device snapping down on him. On advice received, I also laid a small trail of corn leading in to either end of the metal tunnel, but about a week after berthing, nothing was disturbed, and I took up floorboards - by now I was looking for a dead rat and a smell, but there was none. Finally, Mike Rose and I went down nearly a fortnight after our return to spend a quiet night anchored off Stutton Ness in the river Stour. There was no wind that night, and all was still - if a rat was still aboard and alive, we would have heard it scratching about in the night. No rat, no body, no smell - the only conclusion was that it abandoned ship in the North Sea - perhaps as a result of the thunderstorm, the general vibration or just the movement of the boat at sea, so the experts on rat behaviour advised. By now I had to tell Beryl about it, but until that point the whole thing was a closely guarded secret.

That autumn, we returned to Limehouse Basin, now fully operational and with few empty berths. With a fresh East wind blowing, we left Levington for the Colne, where we anchored for the night on the East side just above Brightlingsea - sheltered, and out of the way of commercial traffic, which sadly was declining. A few years earlier, there would have been several coasters at anchor awaiting the tide, or for a pilot to berth at Wivenhoe, Rowhedge or Colchester Hythe, but this trade had largely come about during the great post war labour troubles in the big ports, and owners were reluctant to send their ships in only to suffer endless delays and inefficient handling. These smaller ships collected the cargoes from bulk carriers berthing at places like Europort at Rotterdam to unload at the smaller ports where there were no such problems; it was nevertheless, not efficient and Britain paid the cost in higher import charges.

Our trip was by way of some slightly nostalgic (for me) cruising to anchor for one night up Stansgate Creek, all part of the stamping ground in my young days; the East wind had moderated, the barometer stood high, so after some exploration up the Medway I went across the Estuary to anchor in the Ray off Westcliff - the log says "off the Grosvenor Hotel", which is where our wedding reception was held - by this time it had become an old people's home. The next morning, there was hardly a breath of wind and both Essex and Kent shores were covered by a thin pearly mist. Our trip upriver was, as always, full of interest, with fresh developments replacing some of the grottier derelict sites, and more shipping - it was beginning to return to the Thames once more. At quarter to four that afternoon, the Narrow Street road bridge was swinging open and we pushed on into the lock.

A few days later, after lunch in the CA Headquarters, we set off mid afternoon to plug an hour or so of foul tide - going downstream you are nearing the point where the tide will soon be with you, because the turn of tide becomes earlier as you make your way downriver. Summer time had finished, and by the time we reached the Lower Hope it was dark, and we anchored off Mucking, sheltered from the light Westerly wind and well out of the busy main channel. During the night, as had been predicted, the Westerly wind freshened to fill our sails the next morning and push us on our way up the Essex coast like an express train. A waggish entry in the log just after half past nine read "Southend Pier abeam to port - fortunately!", bearing in mind that over the years there have been vessels which failed to pass it on the correct side, with disastrous results for both vessel and pier. Our fast passage brought us to West Mersea just after two, where we secured to a substantial looking mooring close to the Cut leading to the town hard; after hastily inflating the Avon dinghy, the cockpit (or bridge) cover was ferried ashore to Gowens for a minor alteration - Gowens had made the sails, and the cockpit cover, as indeed they had for "CELANDINE". Soon, the dinghy was on deck again and drying off before deflating - for this I use the domestic vacuum cleaner suction, with a John Barrington insert to make its hose fit the dinghy valves. It is very effective, totally removing all air, which makes rolling the "pig" up and stowing in its bag relatively easy.

The next morning, we did not slip the mooring till half past eleven - no point, as our destination was Woodbridge, where I did not want to cross the bar before four that afternoon. With a fresh Southwest wind, a swift passage was made and I waited off for the tide to rise further, during which time a vicious obliterating rainsquall developed as the light faded; fortunately an easing in the rain enabled us to identify the leading marks and sweep in over the bar, borne by the flood tide. There was two and a half metres of water over the shallowest part, giving us a metre of clearance, but the force six wind was knocking up a lively sea out there, and in those conditions it is important not to cut things too fine. It was dusk and calm by the time we picked up a mooring off Kirton Creek, ready for a start early the following morning, at first light, to get the tide over the sill into the Tidemill.

BACK TO FRANCE - AND LIMEHOUSE

TOWARDS the end of May 1995, "CORYDALIS" slipped from her berth at Suffolk Yacht Harbour, Levington, and headed off across the Thames Estuary with stalwarts Mike Rose, Polar Pam and Peter Darwent aboard. The trip across the Estuary was made into a Southwest wind of force three to four - the barometer stood high, so the outlook seemed good for a calm sea and prosperous voyage (I'm not sure who was going to get prosperous!). By lunch time we were through the Fisherman's Gat and free of the sandbanks barring our way across to Kent; the wind was easing and the North Foreland lay fine on the starboard bow shining in the mid-day sun. At Dover, we recorded a calm and the barometer was still climbing - perhaps I ought to stop being so beastly about the place, because clearly fine weather is possible; I briefly stopped the engine just South of Dungeness to check oil and water (the engine is cooled by a closed circuit freshwater system, which in turn is cooled by salt water acting through a heat exchanger). It had been so calm that evening, we did not even heave to for supper, but must have taken it in watches; at seven we eased speed for the Great British Breakfast taken off the Falaises just North of the Seine Estuary - how superb is the smell of bacon and eggs after a night passage!

The visibility that morning was outstanding - unusual for the time of year, as mist and fog are very prevalent in the English Channel in early Spring and summer during fine weather. Ahead to starboard we could see across the Seine Estuary to the Calvados coast stretching away Westwards, bright in the morning sun; I reminisced that it was 51years since I first saw that coast in the same morning sunlight, but under rather different circumstances - now all was peaceful.

For the first time, we entered the new lock at Honfleur which we had seen under construction on previous visits - the whole lock chamber was floated into place as if it were a large concrete barge, but its completion was delayed because after location in its final position, the whole structure took a list that was clearly visible to the naked eye. However, it was now operational - we had heard the news through CA sources, and that it gave almost round the tide access to the port, obviating the need for a lock gate on the old inner harbour. Entry was still restricted by the opening times of the narrow road bridge across its entrance, but soon after midday (local time) we were berthing outside the Vieux Lieutenance, the berth we had always used since our first visit in "CELANDINE". The new locking arrangements at Honfleur meant that you could leave there around low water to catch the flood tide up to Rouen, instead of starting from Le Havre. On this trip, Beryl was able to get away in time to join us by ferry at Le havre, so we sailed back to Le Havre to meet her off the ferry early on Sunday morning and almost immediately get underway to catch the flood tide up the Seine; starting from Le Havre instead of Honfleur adds another hour and a half to the length of the passage.

By four in the afternoon we were joining the rats and grot in the Bassin St Gervais to lower our masts - so fast did we complete the operation that we were secured alongside the port de plaisance on the Ile La Croix by eight that evening. The Bassin is very convenient for lowering masts, but not a place in which to spend any time. Before we got underway again, Beryl had expressed a nostalgic desire to call at Les Andelys to have dinner at the "Chaine d'Or" - a hotel we once stayed at on a brief motoring trip, and as I had read somewhere in the yachting press that the silted yacht harbour there had been dredged, we entered and immediately ran aground. With a great deal of ploughing, I managed to berth alongside the outer protective wall of the yacht harbour, in which a few bijou vessels of minimal draught were berthed on the pontoons. Our berth, into which we had more or less dug ourselves like some floating JCB, entailed jumping ashore on to a slightly muddy grass bank; ever resourceful (with the prospect of a good meal to be taken overlooking the Seine), we found some bricks and stones to create a hard landing place. I am sure the French would approve of the effort that was made on behalf of gastronomy - the Chaine d'Or is Michelin listed. The name comes from a chain (not of gold!) across the river by means of which freight charges were levied on the river traffic, the gold from the levy going into the pockets of the proprietors.

However, the feature which dominates the river and surrounding country is the great ruined Chateau Gaillard, built by Richard Lionheart in 1196, and stormed by the French in 1204, when King John was on the English throne. The immensely strong fortification was taken when French sapeurs climbed the latrine chutes to place primitive but massive explosives which blew breaches in the walls and enabled their troops to storm in and overcome the defenders; as ever, all's fair in love and war - not that I have ever done anything so dastardly in the former, but certainly deceipt and dirty tricks played a big part

The ruin of Chateau Gaillard broods over the Seine at Les Andelys.

in the only war (thank God) in which I have been involved. The following morning, our departure from this absurd harbour was described by an entry in the log which described it as a "stirring experience". It probably took some hours for the silt we disturbed to settle. A little further upstream, one passes another ancient fortification, La Roche Guyon, some 200 years older than Chateau Gaillard, and whose "Donjon" stands on a rocky crest overlooking the river - it is a forbidding looking place, but at the foot of the prominence is an attractive domestic chateau dating from the 13th century. Its most recent claim to fame was to serve as headquarters for the great German General Rommel during the battle for Normandy.

That afternoon, we entered the Ecluse de Mericourt, where major engineering works were in progress and consequently all traffic was concentrated in the one working lock. Squeezing into a tight space, making considerable use of the bow thruster, I suddenly lost hydraulic power - the very powerful hydraulic pump driven off the main engine must not be run at excessive speeds for fear of busting a joint in the system by overloading the pressure; in effect the engine should not be allowed to go much over 1000 rpm while the hydraulic system is in operation. In the sudden responses required by a tricky situation, I must have revved the engine well beyond that limit. Reaching the pontoon at Limay, we berthed outside a Danish yacht that was clearly well established there - the pontoons are supposed to be for short stops of not over 24 hours when on passage.

The following morning, our two intrepid women, Beryl and Polar Pam went ashore to see if we could get the hydraulic system repaired, and after braving an alsatian dog, they entered the office of a small boat building establishment a little way down the backwater. It was a shrewd move - with their reasonable French, they did the trick - no Frenchman could ignore two ladies in distress, and after a telephone call, he announced that someone would arrive at 2 pm. Peter Mayle's best seller *"A Year in Provence"* inferred that French artisans could not be relied upon to turn up on time, if ever - it made amusing reading but cast an unfortunate slur on their reputations. It has not been my experience in France, and this was no exception - at two o'clock a "van blanc" drew up. Mike and I had

Chateau La Roche Guyon

already dismantled the panelling to expose the blown joint - fortunately all panelling is removable (even though you may suffer wrist ache from excessive use of the screwdriver!), and the mechanic swiftly removed the length of pipework. The joints have to be factory fitted, and he announced that he would be back within two hours - I was horrified to see, clearly marked on the pipe, 3/4" bore, and asked if this would be a problem - we were in the land where the metric system came from, and had Napoleon's ambitions been rewarded with success it would have been inflicted on us nearly two hundred years earlier - but he reassured me as he left "Pas de problème, m'sieur".

Within the two hours, he was back with the new pipe and joints fitted, plus a supply of hydraulic oil to replace that which had leaked out. I travelled back to his depot in the van to pay the bill, and as we drew in the reason for the ease of fitting became obvious - it was an enormous John Deere agency - this American company is very strong in that part of France, supplying tractors, agricultural and earth moving equipment, all of which rely on hydraulic power. The Americans, who sometimes do use the metric system, normally work in feet and inches; they would become very stroppy if someone told them they must use the metric system. Mike and I soon had the panelling in place again, and the next morning we were off again with our hydraulic system again fully operational. After a stop at a "halte de plaisance" at Bougival, which is not particularly pleasantly sited, the next day we drove on through Paris to the "Port au Cerises", on the right bank opposite Juvisy. At this point, one is emerging from the worst industrial and suburban surroundings of Paris" - the "Port au Cerises" is a large park and recreational area created out of what must originally have been vast gravel pit workings, part of which forms the port de plaisance. It is deep enough once inside, but is entered through a hole in the wooded bank and guarded by a sand bar that could deter all but the enthusiasts (or those with a powerful engine!), and entering this across the flow of the Seine is an interesting experience.

Nobody seemed interested in us, and after watering at a fairly inconveniently placed hose connection, we left in pouring rain the next morning, to find that on Whitsunday the locks on the Seine are closed - but will open on payment. At each lock, we signed a chit so that eventually I received a bill at home, which I paid very promptly as I believe that those who are boating for pleasure should pay towards use of facilities; it was not an enormous bill, and doing so enabled us to keep to our itinerary, bearing in mind the hydraulic breakdown had cost us a day.

Once again, our trip took us through Moret and on into the Canal du Loing; the berth used at Nemours on a previous visit was undergoing major renovations - I can't remember the actual wording on the notice, but Beryl and I have always had a habit of producing absurd translations, so this one came out as "Urban assassination". In fact I am sure it was going to improve the bankside appearance, but it would not be a mooring place again. We found an even better place - an abandoned commercial quay once probably used for building materials, and even nearer the station than the previous berth. One of the bollards set in a great lump of concrete had been uprooted - perhaps by the pull of a heavily laden peniche; I moored "CORYDALIS" to it quite happily, but when a peniche passed us, she strained hard at the ropes and to my horror saw that we also managed to rock that great lump of concrete. At Nemours, Roland and Louise joined us with all three of their children; our berth was so near the station that it was only two minutes' walk to meet them off the train and escort them back on board.

Retracing our route of two years earlier (how much easier it is when you already know the best mooring spots) we stopped at Montargis, but instead of using the rather unattractive berth at the near derelict commercial port, we used a far more attractive berth we had noticed on our previous trip, above the two locks that lay in the old part of the town. This was a good idea, except for the fact that it was not really deep enough and berthing developed into another ploughing match. Roland and family left at this point, and we were joined by Keith and Pat Warren who had driven out. Keith and Pat both had been part of our "gang" sailing 12 ft dinghies from the shore at Leigh, and we had all been to Westcliff High School. It is surprising how many boys managed to marry inmates of the girls school, when you consider the rigid non fraternisation (or should it be non sororization?) policy that existed in those days. For our generation we had to have a war and many upheavals before these marriages took place.

Keith and Pat brought good weather with them, and on this trip we penetrated further South than before, crossing a tributary of the Loire, l'Allier by another "Pont Canal", but quite a minor affair compared with the great engineering masterpiece at Briare. Our visitors left here, at Plagny,where a good train service is available from nearby Nevers. It was at this point that our generator engine gave up the ghost, and a local mechanic was not able to cure it - the problem seemed terminal. Generator engines have given more trouble than any other pieces of equipment; the first, of Swedish origins, was scrapped, and now this one, of German origin had packed up. Those problems have been compounded by numerous elecrical faults, mainly due to sloppy connections on the electric controls, designed to shut the engine down in the event of overheating or lack of oil pressure. Over the years most of these faults have been overcome, but at this point we bought a small Honda portable generator to mount on the bridge deck to charge batteries

On our return trip we sailed for Poole from Le Havre so that Beryl could cross on the night ferry to Portsmouth. She had a speaking engagement in Poole and I thought it might be useful to have the boat there; this trip made me realise how much easier it is for a South coast based boat to reach France - we were making fast in Salterns Marina soon after nine the following morning. None of the long haul down channel or the near 40 mile crossing of the Thames Estuary for them! Nevertheless,I would not swap my base - too far from home, and all much too crowded.

Almost a fortnight later, we sailed for Levington in idyllic weather, with a few days to spend en route. Entering the Solent by the North channel, close to Hurst Castle, we found the tide was with us all the way so we coasted along in the warm sunshine; being a Wednesday there was some space to cruise in a reasonably relaxed way, and we anchored for the night inside East Head, Chichester harbour - I am told it is choc-a-bloc at weekends, but on this Wednesday night there was plenty of room to swing. The next day, still in perfect weather with a light Southeasterly wind, we pushed on Eastwards and sailed closer than ever before to Beachy Head, shining a brilliant white in the afternoon sun. Using Sovereign Harbour for the night, we then set off at an early hour for Levington, making good progress until the wind freshened from the Northeast just as we entered the Thames Estuary, but then in the evening it backed to Northwest and eased. Harwich harbour is an easy harbour to enter in the dark, and I went up the Stour to anchor off Erwarton Ness just before two in the morning. A lazy late start the next morning brought us to our berth at Suffolk Yacht Harbour by mid day at the end of a benign 3 day coastal cruise.

At the end of September, we set off from Levington for Limehouse, calling in to the Colne and anchoring in the Pyefleet for the night. There was a Westerly wind blowing and I put the anchor down, saw that it bit home, knowing that more chain must be put out to allow for the night tide. I forgot - my excuse being that I was very tired, but it was stupid, because early the following morning, we started to heel over - she had quietly lifted her anchor on the top of the tide; there was by then little or no wind, and she very quietly beached herself on the North bank, which formed part of the army firing ranges. Peter Darwent was rudely evicted from his bunk on the port side, so had to be re-established on the cabin floor, whilst the rest of us, being on the starboard side slept resting against the cabin linings. Breakfast was served at an angle; the Army range officer and his assistant came to view us in our embarassment and jokingly said they would have to start charging rent if we outstayed our welcome. We assured them we would be off the moment she floated, but it was not until two in the afternoon before we finally came off and resumed our trip up the Thames Estuary - the tides were now all wrong so we found ourselves punching a foul tide, finally reaching the anchorage near West Leigh Middle buoy just before eight.

The loss of confidence in the skipper's abilities is exemplified by an entry in the log the following morning - "land still where it ought to be". A well deserved lazy start - no point in going too early as we wanted the flood tide under us - the next morning saw us smugly passing under a traffic jam on the Queen Elizabeth bridge by 1225, after having passed the preserved paddle steamer Waverley outward bound for Southend Pier. By two thirty we were entering the lock at Limehouse Basin.

During this visit, we had a party one evening to which all former crew who had sailed in "CELANDINE" were invited. When the bar area was being designed, a space was left which the architect said ought to have a ship model to give nautical interest. My successor as President, Ron Browne, asked if I might be prepared to give such a model, and I could not think of a better way of commemorating "CELANDINE'S" beautiful hull shape, in which every curve was fair; I found a retired foreman shipwright in Brightlingsea (formerly of the ship and boatbuilders James and Stone) who was skilled at reading off a set of lines from a drawing and fashioning them into models. So George Gray lovingly created a full model, completely rigged, using Francis Jones' original drawings and numerous photographs illustrating the deck gear and fittings; a scale was chosen to ensure it would fit the space available, and with a goodly crowd of Old "CELANDINER'S" present, the model was installed.

A few evenings later, the crew assembled at CA Headquarters for dinner, turned in early in order to make an early start the next morning, so that we were heading downstream before nine the next morning; then we reduced speed to allow river police to board us, they having explained that two of them were very interested in the boat - which does look rather different from most. I am sure owners of super glossy gin palaces feel sorry for me having to make do with this old Scottish fishing boat - "probably still smells of fish" - whereas in fact she has never caught a fish in anger. They were most interested and asked all the right questions about her. Twenty minutes later we were off again at full speed, our friends leaving us with much bonhomie and enthusiasm. By early afternoon, with a light Westerly wind, we were rounding the Low-way buoy into the Ray, where we spent a peaceful night - summer time was over, and so it was not long before dusk began to fall. The weather remained fair - the barometer had actually risen, and by lunch time the next day we were securing to the pontoon in Brightlingsea. Finally, with the wind now in the Northwest, but still light, we completed our voyage to Levington, berthing in Suffolk Yacht Harbour soon after midday; a few days later, with Mike Rose, we pushed round round into the Deben to winter at he Tidemill.

The Spring of 1996 saw a new era in the "CORYDALIS" fitting out procedures; up till that year, we had been hauled out on Whisstock's slipway at Woodbridge, even though the company had finally gone bust for the last time, somehow or another somebody was prepared to operate the slipway until this year, when it was no longer available, and was anyway deteriorating badly. Fortunately, Suffolk Yacht Harbour had managed to acquire (I believe as a result of another receivership elsewhere) a sixty ton boat lift of advanced design. Up till then, our twenty ton displacement would have been a problem, but this new piece of equipment was capable of lifting "CORYDALIS" with as little effort as an elephant carrying a Derby jockey; in future this would be my base, where the ever helpful Jonathon Dyke supervises it all. It was far more satisfactory than the somewhat primitive slipway at Woodbridge and the time between being lifted out, pressure washing of the bottom and being deposited on chocks for fitting out was minimal compared with the previous procedure.

The day we were due to leave for France that year was dreadful - it was blowing hard from the South with a heavy drizzle reducing visibility so that the prospect when we rose at half past five in the morning failed to please. I abandoned the idea of sailing that day; we were a strong crew with Mike Rose, Polar Pam and John Barrington aboard, but we are supposed to be doing this for pleasure and deemed it prudent to wait. During the day, the barometer stopped falling and showed it might even start to rise. Twentyfour hours later, we sailed at six in the morning; the barometer was slowly rising, the wind had veered to Northwest (always a good sign) and although the morning was grey, everything was looking better. Using our well trodden cross estuary route through the Fishermans' Gat, Dover Harbour came abeam at two in the afternoon and soon after dark, we had the Royal Sovereign Light in view. This elaborate concrete structure with living accommodation on the top platform was no longer manned; as with nearly all coastal lights they are now fully automated and, thanks to modern technology, monitored and controlled from Harwich.

The barometer continued to rise, and the light wind continued from a point just West of North. It was a good clear night, and by midnight we were crossing the shipping lanes; in addition to keeping a good lookout, we also had the radar running as it is a wonderful way of keeping a bearing on any ship that looks like getting in the way; needless to say, if there is the slightest doubt I will take avoiding action by going round astern of them. By half past ten in the morning we were closing Cap de la Heve, the Northern headland of the Seine estuary and the nearby fort of Sainte Adresse. Hoisting the French courtesy flag and advancing our clocks one hour, I decided that as the tide was right and we had lost a day due to bad weather, so would carry straight on up to Rouen - of course, it had suddenly become after half past eleven. In spite of the rising barometer, the wind had backed into the Southwest earlier that morning, and now we were being greeted by rain - is this the way to welcome visitors? Crossing the main shipping channel into Le Havre, by half past twelve we were passing our old friend the "DUNCAN L CLINCH" buoy, and then heading up the Rouen channel as we took a light lunch in the dry comfort of the wheelhouse. Sadly having to give Honfleur a miss, we called up Rouen port control to advise them we were proceeding upriver to the bassin St Gervais and then let the powerful Seine flood tide sweep us upriver. It is a long and winding river. and 60 nautical miles of scenery that varies between picturesque and rural to incredibly ugly industrial or worse, derelict industrial. Six and a half hours after passing Honfleur we we greeting the rats of the bassin St Gervais; our speed over the ground had been approaching ten knots, illustrating the strength of the tide - our engine revs would have only given just over seven. We had arrived on the Sunday evening as originally planned, having made up the lost time, some thirty eight and a half hours and 250 nautical miles from Levington without stopping.

By Monday morning, the famous bassin looked just as it should, under a dull grey sky while the barometer continued to rise the rain fell. We lowered the dripping masts before proceeding to the halte de plaisance for some shopping and to get a good night's rest, but it could surely only get better. The next morning we left in bright sunshine to complete the rather boring part up to Amfreville, where the non-tidal river starts. A stop was made at Vernonnet, where the welcoming harbourmaster was as ever ready to greet us after we had ploughed our way alongside; he has an information sheet which describes the ancient Norman Vernon family from the town of that name on the opposite side of the river, and the connection with the famous British Admiral "Grog" Vernon - the man who introduced the rum ration into the navy, but also famous for his waterproof cloak made from layers of oiled grosgrain fabric. On retirement he built a great classical mansion overlooking the river Orwell, complete with observatory (he was a keen follower of astro navigation) and known as Orwell Park - the house has long been used as boy's preparatory school, but still appears from the river as it was in Vernon's day with the observatory dome clearly visible. Another stop was made at Limay, where John Barrington left from Mantes-la-Jolie on the other side of the Seine - it has good rail facilities and a great cathedral like church dominating the view from the river. Otherwise, I don't see a lot to commend the place and make it "la jolie".

On this trip up the Seine I was really beginning to gain confidence in calling up the éclusiers on the radio to say we were a "montant" and would arrive in "dix minutes". Of course, with the lowering of the masts, our normal high radio aerial is disconnected, but we use an emergency one which plugs direct into the back of the radio and is clipped to a convenient point in the superstructure. I was beginning to get better at comprehending the thick Norman accent in which they would reply, and the technical terms they tended to use, but still there were occasions when a torrent of speech would pour out of the radio; you knew they were being helpful, and you had advised them to expect you, so I would pour forth effusive thanks and hope for the best. The words I did understand and liked best were "Je prepare l'ecluse" which meant the gates would be opening as we arrived. The people I could understand clearly were the éclusieres, of which there are several controlling these big Seine locks - their accents were not strong, and at Bougival madame's speech was almost pure Parisian so she was easily understood. If there was no other traffic, a record lock transit could be made - entries in the log read "1700 entered ecluse de Notre Dame de la Garenne - 1707 left - world record?". This was broken on the following day by a 5 minute transit of Andresy, usually very busy, but where the great engineering works encountered the previous year were now complete. Bougival, with the well spoken madame, we did in ten minutes, but the lock they use here for yachts is a little slower than some of the others in filling; rarely do you ever see these lock keepers, since the whole operation is controlled from towers not unlike airport control towers. After a night at Bougival where there is an inadequate apology for a halte - on this occasion we were secured to a road crash barrier designed to stop cars driving straight over the edge, as we were forced to moor beyond the official berthing place.

By now we had dispensed with Paris as a stopping place, and we would once again press on through to the slightly leafy suburbs beyond at Port au Cerises. Eurostar was now up and running, so Beryl was to join us there, using a direct RER link from Gare du Nord to Juvisy. The log of our passage through Paris contained some entries of no great navigational significance - "1300 - overtaken by "EDITH PIAF". Don't imagine this was the great chanteuse herself swimming bravely upstream, but a bateau mouche named after her. There are a great many vessels permanently moored along the banks as restaurants - how they all survive, I don't understand. One was a former Isle of Wight paddle steamer, the "PRINCESS MARGARET" which once had been moored at a City wharf in London, but the one that really took our fancy was a good looking classic motor yacht about 120 feet long (probably originally from the slipways of Camper & Nicholson) bearing the name "ACTE III SEINE I". If we only knew from which play (Shakespeare or Moliere?) it might have had some significance for us.

At Port au Cerises, Beryl joined, and we took a taxi to Draveil where she had stayed with a doctor's family - using maps she had made as a teenager, we found the house, by then in other ownership. Pressing on upstream, Pam left at Melun, then we berthed at Valvins - close to Fontainebleau, where a visit was made to the great chateau at which Napoleon rode up the steps on his charger to bid a tearful farewell to his loyal personal guard before being banished to Elba (which did not last long, and it was only when he was finally banished to remote St Helena that he was unable to make another triumphant return and have another bash at us). The "Port Stephane Mallarme" at Valvins is a good stopping place - a long pontoon for visitors, and an Aldi supermarket nearby, where prices are cheap, but the range of merchandise limited. On this trip, instead of entering the canal system at St Mammes, we pressed on upstream to Montereau, at the confluence of the Yonne and Seine - immediately one is impressed by the fact that the Yonne is the bigger river, and the Seine above this point known as "Le Petit Seine".

Most of the locks on the Yonne have sloping walls at either side, or in some case one side. They are a nightmare which would not be so bad but for a rule that you must have lines to the shore - it is possible to hold "CORYDALIS" in the middle, away from those sloping walls, using main engine and bow thruster, but the drag of ropes fore and aft on one side makes the whole thing more difficult. In fact, the practice was to try and keep the ropes slack so that she could be held fairly central. At Port Renard, where the navigable channel parts from the natural course of the river by means of an artificial "derivation", the lock has vertical sides; there is an excellent quay face in the natural river formed by the outer wall of the lock, and the eclusier was happy to let us lie there for the night - it is a totally rural situation, with partially wooded countryside all round, and no facilities. Because the boat is moored in the natural level of the river, when a peniche left the lock at the higher level of the artificial cut, it gave a very odd sensation to watch a boat go by so close but at a higher level.

At Pont sur Yonne, we stopped at one of the strangest attempts met so far in providing facilities to moor boats. A long, flimsy pontoon was ruined by a series of even flimsier fingers occupied by one or two bijou boats, but most were empty (several had no bollards or cleats!). About the only thing they got right was the angle of the fingers, so that boats were not moored at right angles to the stream, and this fortunately left a short length of pontoon which just accommodated us by putting the bow right up in the angle of the last finger, luckily unoccupied. Our bows hung threateningly right over a mini - runabout moored on the opposite side of the finger; the whole affair was decked with an embossed PVC covering glued to the metal beneath - PVC shrinks badly in heat, and the sunlight had played havoc with it, whilst several of the fingers were already buckled and in a dangerous condition. The chart shows it as a halte "en projet", but it was already a halte in decay - to say it was pathetic would be an understatement. However, it did enable us to get ashore in this

Port Renard - traffic going by at a higher level gave a strange sensation.

pleasant old town - the "pont" after which it was named had long since gone, to be replaced by a more modern steel bridge.

Upstream from there lay Sens, a large busy town with an excellent quay face. Here there were all facilities, with excellent shops - we even were able to buy a bottle of Angostura bitters, remedying a serious problem that had arisen with fuel supplies for the crew. The traffic is heavy, and the berth a complete contrast to the idyllic rural berth downstream at Port Renard. After a night in Sens, we pressed on through rural tranquillity to Villeneuf sur Yonne - the lock, just below the town quay, has sloping sides, but does offer water - some deft work with a heaving line by Michael enabled the delightful éclusiere to pass us the hose end - we now were tethered not only by the obligatory ropes, but also a hosepipe, but all went well and we got the hose back to her without the end going in the water. Any town or street that calls itself "new" is bound to be very ancient, and this was no exception. Built by Louis VII as an entity, it was a new town - in 1163. The great church of Notre Dame was built at the same time in the renaissance style, but the feature which we could not fail to photograph was the tree growing high up on one of the flying buttresses - along with other mixed vegetation at various high points in the structure. At that time, Writtle church had a small sapling growing out of the tower wall (since removed) and Mike and I were keen to show our churchwardens just what could be achieved! What the roots of those substantial growths were doing to the stone work of that beautiful 12th century church, I cannot imagine.

Villeneuf has a very fine old bridge, through which we passed bound for our final destination at Joigny, where there are reasonably secure facilities for leaving the boat at "Locaboat Plaisance". I had telephoned earlier in the year from the UK to check on facilities and depths - so often a problem for us seagoing boats on the waterways. Here we left the boat, having hired a Renault Clio to reach the parts that the boat could not. Our main target was Vezelay, one of the most ancient churches in France, set high on a high ridge from which it dominates the surrounding country. Founded in the 9th century, destroyed by a fire in the 12th, damaged by the Huguenots in 1569 (so the French say) and again damaged in the revolution, it was finally brought to its present condition in the 19th century when its great antiquity was finally appreciated by the state. We stayed two nights at a small hotel, formerly a farmhouse, where Madame ran the hotel, and Monsieur ran a wine business - I'm not sure of his correct description in the world of wine, but he collected and blended wines from prime producers for bottling and reselling. It was an excellent burgundy, which we were able to sample in the hotel, so when we left, there was a case in the car boot. En passant, we visited Auxerre, the limit of navigation for most boats - above there, it becomes the canal de Nivernais, beautiful, but open in the summer only and negotiable only by shallow draft hire boats. We had decided not to go on to Auxerre by boat - quite a few more locks, and it is a large and busy town, whereas at Joigny our berth was on the opposite bank of the river from the main town - to reach it was only a short walk to the bridge.

The last member of the outward crew, Michael Rose had left on arrival at Joigny, but now for our return passage we had a series of visitors. First, the Ahlers joined us - they were American visitors to Writtle, renting a house on the Green while he was trying to   broker a merger of European commercial vehicle makers. His patient handling of the situation was beaten by internal rivalries within the companies, but he certainly tried. They came downstream as far as Montereau, where Keith and Pat Warren joined us as far as Valvins, with Fontainebleau station handy, and where more crew- Mike and Jean Rose and sail training guru John Hamilton joined, Beryl leaving to return home by the painless and fast Eurostar route.   Again stopping at the usual places downstream, we made swift progress to Rouen - although during the summer the stream is weak, it still helps to have it with you. At Rouen, Peter Darwent joined and John Hamilton had to leave - a man with a very full diary.

After re-rigging the masts, we set off downstream; going downstream from Rouen it is impossible to carry the tide with you as on the way up, but the duration of flood tide is short, and I had now realised that our Perkins engine and thrusting propeller could carry us quickly through to meet the point where you are once more in a favourable ebb tide. Once again, we lay at the berth outside the Vieux Lieutenance at Honfleur which we had always occupied from that very first visit in "CELANDINE", but the inner basin was getting very crowded - the visitor's pontoon was stacking yachts 3 or 4 deep, and to berth alongside these smart fibreglass vessels with 20 tons of rather rough looking steel hulled MFV would not have gone down very well. To attract the tourists, there was a growing collection of vintage boats (including an old RNLI Watson lifeboat) which were making it more difficult to berth, and this was to be the last time I used this berth. The locals had been saying for some years that the opening of the great "Pont Normande" would flood the place with tourists, and it certainly meant that weekends were something to be avoided if possible; it is an ill wind that blows nobody any good, and early the following morning a taxi took Jean swiftly to Le Havre where she caught the morning ferry home - before the coming of the bridge, we would have been forced to use Le Havre. Our crew was now down to three - Peter Darwent, Michael Rose and myself.

The previous day, coming down the last reach of the Seine below Tancarville, the wind was blowing very fresh from the West, and I had noticed a high speed motor cruiser rapidly gaining on us - only to disappear as we approached the choppy sea in this last reach before Honfleur - it was a wind over tide situation producing a short steep sea just as you might get in the Thames Estuary. It was not too big to worry us, and our fine entrance cleaved into the chop - throwing up some spray, and there had been a retreat (as usual), led by the gallant captain, into the wheelhouse before it started coming over, so we were very comfortable. The motorboat re-appeared, motoring on the strictly "interdit" to yachts side of the channel , but where he did get some shelter. We locked in together, and he came alongside us waiting to go into the Vieux Bassin; the boat was French flagged and built by a famous French firm; perhaps as a Frenchman he could get away with disobeying the very strict navigation rules. He had slowed down drastically when he hit the choppy water which clearly had given them a very bad ride, but the most amazing thing was his fuel situation - it was down to almost nil, having filled up at Rouen before proceeding downstream - it had petrol engine (engines?), which are prodigious users of fuel.   Also aboard were a not very happy wife and a positively miserable dog - a beautifully groomed miniature poodle.

Not too long after Jean had left for Le Havre, we slipped out of the inner basin and locked out into the Seine; the wind was still quite fresh, but had eased from the previous day's bluster. Once we were far enough down the Estuary to alter our course Northwards, we set our sails - all of them (there are only three). Michael was navigating, and as is our custom, making half hourly position checks on the Decca set; if this should fail, you will not have gone very far, and could then start reasonably accurate navigation

Cross-Channel at 10+knots.

by dead reckoning. Our engine revs were set at a speed to produce just over seven knots, to which we could add a little due to the help from the sails in a beam wind. Michael reported what he felt must be a freak - we were making ten knots between positions, sometimes a bit more. This went on hour after hour, and I observed that this hull had not moved as fast as this since it was on a lorry coming up from Plymouth. It was an exhilarating ride, in quite a sea, but the sails kept us pretty steady with about ten degrees of heel; something like an hour and a half earlier than our original predicted ETA we were lowering the sails off Sovereign Marina at Pevensey; no sooner had we berthed than a voice from a nearby boat called out "Writtle forever" - it was Geoff Baker, local photographer, yachtsman and all round sportsman (sadly no longer with us). Going for a shower, I could hardly believe my eyes when I bumped into our old Dutch friend Feico Elhorst; we had no difficulty in recognising each other even though we were virtually in our birthday suits, and later all enjoyed very pleasant pre-dinner drinks aboard their boat.

Just after eight the following morning saw us underway again, with the sun shining and a few pleasant puffy clouds about; the wind was still West, but lighter (confirming my theory that fair winds always die on you). Visibility was outstanding - not always a good sign - and soon after ten, we could clearly see Beachy Head astern and Dungeness ahead. Off Dover at about noon, a score was entered in the log - 5 ferries and two Seacats! As we approached the great chalk mass of the North Foreland, a sharp rainsquall hit us, and we took in our fores'l and mizzen, leaving the main sheeted in hard as the wind had drawn more ahead of us. Platt's theory about fair winds was completely fulfilled, as there was little more of it that day, so we pushed on across the Estuary under power, dropping the mains'l in disgust as we entered Black Deep from Fisherman's Gat. At quarter past ten the rumble of our anchor chain disturbed the still of a calm summer evening as we anchored for the night off Erwarton Ness in the river Stour; it was only minutes before the boat was silent and dark save for the glow of our riding light - it had been a long day passage from Eastbourne to Harwich.

LIMEHOUSE, PRAGUE, BUDAPEST - AND THE YONNE AGAIN

IN what was becoming an annual pilgrimage, our autumn cruise took us upriver to Limehouse again, via Brightlingsea and Sheerness, with staunch crew members Mary Dainty and Michael Rose. Crossing the Estuary to the Medway entrance, the light Sou'sou West wind gradually picked up from a light force three to force four or more as we entered the Medway; the high coast of the Isle of Grain gave protection and we were soon picking up a large visitor's mooring off Queenborough in time for lunch followed by a snooze (a feature of our age group!). The afternoon saw a little drama as the newly commissioned Sheerness lifeboat towed in a casualty - a steel hulled river cruiser about 35 foot length, with very low freeboard, and which had got into difficulties in the chop out there, following the track we had taken a little over an hour previously. I thought she was full of water, but in fact was floating on her designed waterline - what would have looked quite alright on the upper Thames certainly did not look right in the choppy waters of the Estuary.

One of the slightly incongruous features of arriving at Limehouse (or in former days, St Katharine's) is to shut down the boat and then catch a train home, mingling with the commuters. Mary had the easy option as she caught a train direct from Limehouse to Leigh, whereas Mike and I had to make our way to Liverpool Street. Although I only occasionally was caught in the rush hour trains in my working life, after almost eight years of retirement, it seemed a very daunting way of travelling.

A few days later Beryl and I were on a flight to Prague. Beryl was to be the keynote speaker at an International gathering of women engineers in Budapest, but we decided that this was an opportunity to visit the historic city of Prague en route. Our hotel was centrally placed in Wenceclas Square, and together we explored the centre of Prague on foot, and by boat on the river Moldau. The Moldau is navigable for quite large inland waterway vessels, with modern locks controlled by the same light signals as in France - indeed they have become international; the river connects with the Elbe.

From Prague we travelled by "express" train to Budapest - this was to take about six hours instead of under an hour by plane, but we both love travelling on long distance trains. The train was truly international, and we enjoyed an excellent lunch aboard; I don't think the train ever went very fast by today's standards, but it was a comfortable and interesting ride through undulating sylvan scenery. There were several stops, one at Bratislava on the Czech-Hungarian frontier, where a young American woman was thrown off the train because her papers were not in order. She looked a smartly dressed business woman, who I would have expected to make sure that these things were correct; I think she had to go to some office where the correct papers would be issued, but I don't know how long it would have been before she picked up another train. She would probably have been better off flying - at least she would only be delayed at the airport, having reached her destination. As far as we were concerned, it was a delightful and restful trip, and we had no problems at the border - all we had were our British passports.

I liked Budapest - not as historic as Prague, but it had certainly thrown off years of fighting and communist misrule to become a vibrant and zinging city - or more correctly, pair of cities. We stayed in Pest, at the Hotel Gelert, which was old fashioned and comfortable - our kind of place. Its greatest feature however, was the swimming pools. The indoor pool had great marble pillars and a high opening roof, whilst the outdoor pool was large and sheltered from the wind; both pools were fed by thermal springs, so we were able to swim both inside and outside, although now early October. The conference, at which I attended to hear Beryl's address, was a bit daunting, but there was a reception and dinner at which a number of spouses had infiltrated, so there were a sufficient number of the male sex to prevent my feeling overwhelmed by the sheer number of intense women.

One of the delights of Budapest was the gipsy orchestras which always included a cymballum - an instrument shaped like a miniature grand piano, the strings being struck with sticks. Whereas with a piano, you know if you hit a certain ivory, the appropriate note will issue, with this instrument the player (percussionist?) has to hit the right string, very often at high speed - no room for innaccurate aim! They are very special to Hungary, but occasionally can be heard elsewhere.

Soon after returning from Prague and Budapest, we were using the boat and CA House at Limehouse again as entertaining bases, then CORYDALIS was off back to the East Coast - now on GMT with the evenings suddenly drawing in, although the days are not any shorter. Sometimes I ignore the alteration of clocks, but there was no point in this case, as we could not leave too long before the tide turned in our favour, and it was after lunch before we could leave. Then we discovered the Thames Barrier was closed; I should have appreciated the danger because a strong wind was blowing from Northwest, coupled with very high spring tides - flood conditions in the Thames. As a boy I knew that Northwest winds raised the height of a tide, and even more about it as a result of reading Hilda Grieve's *"The Great Tide"*.

Barrier Control promised to call us when they were ready to re-open, at a time dependent on tide levels. The barrier is closed during the flood tide when an alert is received, allowing sufficient capacity for river water to be contained, before re-opening when the tide level falls to that of the water contained behind the barrier. If only I had listened on the radio before locking out from Limehouse, I would have known, and stayed there, but we found a very convenient pier, once used by the defunct riverbus service, adjacent to a large and busy office block - I believe occupied by Reuters. Nobody came to tell us we couldn't lie there - indeed none of the bustling crowds seemed the slightest bit interested in the river. Barrier Control called us as promised to tell us we were free to proceed and within ten minutes we were sweeping through "C" span at ten to five in the gathering gloom. Our passage downstream was made in a darkness slightly alleviated by the moon, just past full, filtering through the clouds. Making ten knots over the ground with this powerful tide behind us, we were anchoring in the Lower Hope off Mucking soon after seven.

The next morning we had the benefit of the strong West wind, now down to about force five which helped us push our way over the flood tide, with just the mains'l set, but it was almost dark by the time we anchored in Copperas Bay, up the river Stour, before completing the return to our winter base at Woodbridge the following morning in a wind that had backed into the Southwest during the night, and whose strength was given by Harwich Harbour as 35 knots.

After a winter of intense activity caused by political and local affairs - how Beryl stands the pace, I don't know, it would have killed me years earlier, but my diary looked pretty crowded that winter all the same - partly from involvement in some of her activities. In early spring the boat was taken from Woodbridge to Suffolk Yacht Harbour, whose new hoist had revolutionised hauling out this heavy lump of steel boat. In another leap forward into the twentieth century (as it was drawing to a close!) a GPS (Global Positioning System) set was fitted - they had been steadily coming down in price for several years. Beryl questioned why we needed another electronic navigation aid, but by then it was obvious that the faithful and trusty Decca system was coming to an end. During my time as President of the CA there was a campaign to stop them closing it down because the beacons all needed overhauling, and it was reprieved for a few more years.

Thus equipped and refitted, we left Levington at 0700 on May 23rd 1997 with Polar Pam, and what was generally referred to as Mike Rose squared - for once we were able to lure Mike "thatch" away from the city and golf to join us on this trip, together with Mike "bald" - you could not wish for a stronger or tougher crew. I had decided on a change in tactics for this trip down channel - partly to break the voyage into shorter legs (a sign of advancing years!), and although originally I had written down Calais as my first port of call, this seemed crazy on reflection. Experiences there had not been happy, going back to that first visit in "CAMPION" 32 years earlier, and although it has greatly improved in what it has to offer the visitor, Dover now beckoned. Dover realised that ferry services were bound to decline, and looked for other ways of producing revenue. Apart from a cruise liner terminal, they also developed extensive marina facilities, some in a tidal basin, but mainly in the Wellington dock where once you were either covered in fine sand or coal dust, depending on wind direction. Instead of providing little in facilities for yachts (if not actually discouraging them as was the case 30 years earlier), they now welcomed yachts and would actually send a harbour launch out to escort you in.

With a Northeast wind behind us, we bowled across the estuary and by half past eleven had one of our milestones abeam, the Outer Tongue buoy. The banks of the Estuary were behind us, and the North Foreland beckoned ahead. The weather was fair, although as we approached to Dover Strait, the Northeast wind increased in strength - there is undoubtedly a funnelling effect through the constriction between France and England. Lunch was served al fresco - another waggish entry in the log reads "Scotch eggs served - not yet devolved" This was a reference to the general election a week or so earlier, and the socialist promise to devolve Scotland. Beryl and I actually had a few days in Scotland - "before we need passports" immediately after the election, travelling by train and hiring a rather nice small Rover car up there.

By the time we reached Dover Western entrance and obtained permission to enter, quite a lively sea was running so that both we and the escorting launch rolled a bit as we brought the seas abeam; we were in radio contact with the launch who asked us to hurry in as a hovercraft was due to leave shortly, so we pushed in at full speed until clear of the danger. Berthing before five in the afternoon, we had time to do a bit of exploration ashore. Dover is smartening its act considerably; the terrace of Regency buildings overlooking the outer harbour contained the inviting looking Churchill Hotel; everywhere was a contrast to the Dover of thirty years earlier, although there are still some grotty parts that no doubt will eventually come up in the world.

The following morning saw us clearing the Western entrance just after half past five on a fine morning, although the fresh East wind was still blowing. Not far South of Dover we made our crossing of the traffic lanes - this must be done at right angles to the lanes for shipping proceeding up and down channel, and is always a slightly nail biting time as it is like a pedestrian crossing a busy road. By the time we were across and shaping our course Southwards to close the French coast South of the great bay of the Somme, the wind was right behind us and a good force six, speeding us along in a fine, but boisterous style. After passing Berneval nuclear power station (nearly all French electricity is generated by nuclear power) which has its own private harbour (entry strictly "interdit"), shortly before four we were entering Dieppe harbour and given a berth on the visitor's pontoon. Early in the season, there is no problem, but when the continent suddenly pours forth on holiday, finding a berth can be difficult.

Renewing acqaintance with Dieppe was a great pleasure - it has style, character and history, and I proposed stopping for a few days (is this old age or commonsense breaking out?), which enabled Beryl to snatch a few days from her busy programme and join us. The new marina "Jehan Ango" is created from the old ferry terminal only recently moved to an outer part of the harbour. The new terminal is very smart whereas that at Newhaven is a disgrace; the route has always been something of a Cinderella with its much longer (and often rougher) sea crossing. Beryl came out on a high speed "LYNX" which cuts the long crossing time, but the trouble with all these lightweight fast vessels is that they cannot run in the rough

Dieppe - the new yacht marina created from the old ferry port.

weather that a conventional ferry can cope with, so must be regarded as less reliable. Fortunately, there was no interruption to the service and Beryl was able to return on time after two days in Dieppe, and early the following morning we crept out of a still sleeping Dieppe heading for the Seine estuary. Once offshore, the Northeast wind that had been blowing on and off for some days freshened to a stiff force six, and the seas mounted up astern of us.

As we followed the coast round after clearing the Pointe d' Ailly and its off lying rocky ledges (that have claimed more than one Newhaven - Dieppe steamer in foggy weather, before the days of Decca and GPS) we brought the wind dead astern, a difficult point of sailing in a fore and aft rigged vessel, and we had a series of accidental gybes culminating in one that broke the parrel line, sending a shower of wooden parrel beads rattling down on the steel decks. The gaff could no longer be relied upon to stay engaged with the mast, which could result in a torn sail if it went wild - the sail had to come down. Rounding her up into the wind at dead slow, we clawed down the sail and made the best possible stow with some difficulty due to the movement - it was a real case of one hand for the ship and one for yourself. Once stowed, we resumed our course before the wind and set the foresail (a big sail) and mizzen which pulled her along well, and we resumed normal engine speed. I should have set this combination in the first place, knowing that running dead before the wind is not easy, and I believe even more difficult under power because the un-natural progress forward makes the sails more restless.

We swept along the Normandy coast, under clear blue skies, passing the spectacular falaises of Etretat where there is a great archway in a sharp point projecting from the main coastline. then past the great headland Cap D'Antifer, just South of which a great artificial harbour has been constructed for super tankers and giant cargo vessels, presumably to keep the tankers away from Le Havre, which is not capable of handling these leviathans. This place, for many reasons, needs to be given a wide berth, but it has an extremely well buoyed approach channel (dredged to over 24 metres!), and these buoys are a comforting position confirmation after which the coast can be closed again to pass close to the Cap de la Heve, ready to cross the busy approach channel to Le Havre itself (depths maintained to 15.5 metres - hence the need for Port Antifer).

As we crossed the Seine estuary, the seas gradually eased to more estuarial proportions, and soon after one we were entering the sea lock into Honfleur before proceeding to our customary berth outside the Vieux Lieutenance; it was like arriving home again. Sadly, late the following morning, we were off to catch the flood tide upriver, having on this occasion lowered the masts in Honfleur. It was before low water, but it was important to reach Rouen in daylight, and it meant that on leaving the lock we did one of our ploughing jobs through thick mud - then suddenly it is almost like going over a cliff edge as the boat surged forward and the echo sounder reading shot up to an impressive figure. It was some two hours after leaving Honfleur that the flood tide began to pick us up and bear us upstream at an ever increasing speed to berth alongside the halte de plaisance at Rouen - no need to berth in the grotty Bassin St Gervais on this occasion.

Michael (thatch) had to leave us at Rouen to go and earn another crust or two in the City - a pity as he would not see some of the spectacular scenery such as at Les Andelys, but it is really the sea voyaging that he enjoys. After buying the canal toll sticker which gives thirty days navigation (not necessarily consecutive days, so it can last a long time) from the nearby VNF offices, we stocked up at the butcher's, greengrocer's and the Co-op - these places are only a few steps from the halte, then we pushed off up the somewhat boring tidal part of the river to Amfreville, eating newly acquired French charcuterie and baguettes en pleine air in the mild and pleasant weather; we had long since lost the boisterous Northeast wind of the English Channel. Our passage up the Seine continued in fine weather, making our usual stops including the annual ploughing match at Vernonnet, through Paris to Port au Cerises, where the bar across the entrance seemed worse and I had to use more power to blast my way over it. There was a marked deterioration in facilities there - the visitor's pontoon was occupied by live-aboards with potted shrubs and welcome (or bienvenue?) mats. Nearby was a long almost empty pontoon, but the handle had come off the security gate door, and we had to open it with mole grips assisted by WD40; I went up to pay my dues, but as the office has no view of the pontoons they would never have known we were there. Close to where we berthed was a boat whose engine had been rebuilt on the pontoon, leaving an artistic collation that would have qualified for the Tate - old pipework, manifolds and open containers of old sump oil. It was sad to see the deterioration in what had been an excellent stopping place.

Beryl joined us there, and we made our way upriver to Melun, where Polar Pam left after a lunch stop before going on to Fontainebleau for a further crew change - Mike (bald) left and Keith and Pat Warren joined for the trip up the Yonne to Joigny. At Pont sur Yonne we berthed at the crazy pontoon, which had lost more fingers since our last visit, but it was still a squeeze as a bijou motor boat was occupying a berth suitable for a sixty footer, chained to the pontoon with a padlock big enough to act as an anchor. Before going on to our final port of call (Joigny), we revisited a new halte de plaisance in the charming backwater at Cezy - actually this is the natural course of the river as Joigny is reached by an artificial cut. The weather was idyllic and we lunched on one of the picnic tables provided close by - this a really pleasant stopping place in well wooded surroundings.

A little further upstream is a small suspension bridge whose wooden decking rattled when a vehicle crossed, and local lads were diving in from this - obviously

someone had found out there was enough depth of water for this. Nearby is an artificial "Plage" for bathing, which we had used on previous visits, using our hired car to drive the short distance from Joigny. There were no facilities - you changed behind a tree, and if we went before the schoolday finished you would usually have it to yourselves. This time, we used it on a number of occasions without encountering another soul - although nearby the boys were always swimming off the suspension bridge. On our last day there, we enjoyed another refreshing swim in water that was a lot

A new halte de plaisance at Cezy, near Joigny. Beryl, Keith and Pat Warren -Pat is sadly no longer with us.

warmer than the beach at Frinton. Whilst walking back to the car, I idly read a small notice which explained that as the water quality was below standard, swimming from the beach was now prohibited!

With no other crew left, Beryl and I went off to the Foret d' Othe for a few days, using a small hotel in Aix en Othe as our base before returning to prepare for the return voyage and to receive our next visitors, John and Diana King. John had been with me on the epic return from Spain in "celandine", but this was to be a much more placid affair as we retraced our steps down the Yonne to Fontainebleau, where John and Diana King left. Unfortunately, the weather had not been kind and we were getting a lot of rain; as our stopover was to last a few days, I hired a car with which to explore the locality, including the great Chateau de Vaux - le Vicomte. This impressive chateau was built by Fouquet, the man in charge of LouisXIV's finances - chancellor of the exchequer, I suppose you might call him. The construction of the chateau and its vast gardens gave employment to 18,000 workmen and necessitated the erasing of three villages which happened to be in the way. Fouquet made the near fatal mistake of inviting the King to a great and lavish fete in 1661; it was on a scale that the King himself could not match, and within a few days Fouquet was in prison facing a death sentence, later reduced to life imprisonment. Never entertain your boss on too ostentatious a scale - it will only lead to trouble.

On a more practical note, the car also enabled us to visit a nearby "Intermarche" supermarket offering a far wider range than the somewhat downmarket Aldi that lay within walking distance of the boat. It was still raining when crew for our return voyage, the ever stalwart Michael Rose and Mary Dainty, arrived at Fontainebleau station and the car enabled us to meet them - in France, as in England, when it is raining, all the taxis disappear. After a brief stop at Melun, where Beryl left to return by Eurostar, we pushed off downstream. The rain persisted, and the day we went through Paris every log entry was accompanied by "rain" until 1600, when there was finally a note - "rain stopped".

The Seine is a very long winding river, and two overnight stops are needed before reaching Rouen; for our first the choice was either the somewhat miserable and inadequate halte at Bougival or the other at Chatou which is sited close to the wilderness of highway intersections and a large housing estate - fellow CA members had experienced an early hours boarding by some youngsters which did nothing to commend the place. Then, shortly before reaching the first of these somewhat undesirable alternatives, we noticed a very smart and totally empty staging at Rueil-Malmaison, adorned by alternatively placed white and blue fenders; we assumed this must be a private pontoon, but were assured it was not so, and had been placed there to attract visitors by the local Chambre de Commerce. This halte, which did not have water or electricity, was paradise compared with the other grotty places nearby - the water or electricity did not matter to us as we just wanted to lie for the night. Coming ashore, you walked through a beautiful water garden through which flowed a running stream. Ashore, we walked uphill through what had obviously been a recent urban renewal of a former derelict industrial site; various water features cascaded down as we walked up, and then, coming to a square with much new architecture, we could not believe our eyes - before us lay a formal circular pond tilted at something like 101/4. We all know that water always finds its own level so we were seeing an impossibility - close examination showed that in fact it was a thin sheet of flowing water which must have taken a lot of design and experiment to achieve such an amazing effect. Louis XIVth started this French passion for spectacular effects with water when he laid out the gardens of Versailles, and the tradition continues.

After stops at Vernonnet and the overcrowded halte de plaisance at Rouen, we were once more in the placid waters of the infamous Bassin St Gervais, re-rigging the masts; this time it seemed like much harder work, and raising the mainmast a bigger struggle than hitherto. The stark truth was that we were all getting older, and we had done it so many times that a certain amount of ennui had set in. The following morning, we were due to make an early start and there was a magnificent misty sunrise which Michael captured on camera as the sun rose above the hills to the East, giving a romantic Monet style image of this unlovely piece of Rouen docks. Leaving in a misty, pearly sunshine at half past six the following morning, we pressed on downstream with all the prospects of a fine summer day. An hour and a half later, a curtain of fog descended on us - a real pea-souper. We could not see either bank, and were totally disorientated; slowing right down, the radar was switched on - but it takes about 90 seconds warming up before it can start operating, and during that time, I suddenly saw rocky boulders on the port bow - we were heading for the bank on the port side of the river, when we should be navigating on the starboard side. Once the radar was receiving signals, Michael went on the helm, keeping us more or less central between the banks, which showed up well. Mary and I stood in the wheelhouse doors on either side, and every now and then a dark shadow looming through the fog revealed the bank. In the main, for well over an hour, we saw nothing and fortunately there were no tell tale blips ahead or astern indicating the presence of a ship.

Suddenly the fog evaporated as quickly as it had descended, and the day became fine and warm as we sped downstream, passing through the contrary flood tide and on to where it was once again in our favour. That afternoon we were safely secured in Honfleur - I had by this time decided that going into the inner basin was undesireable - the berth outside the Vieux Lieutanance was no longer possible as they were filling the place up with a very attractive display of traditional boats; the visitor's pontoon was not for me, rafted up with English yachts, mainly from the South coast - it was now early July. Instead, I moored up to what was, in the days when we first started calling there, the wall of the once tidal outer harbour, where you would dry out at low water. Getting ashore meant scaling an iron ladder, but it was worth it for the relative peace and quiet; the central part of the town was only a few steps away. The great advantage was that when you were ready to lock out, you went straight down to an empty lock basin before the bridge to the inner basin opened, releasing a flotilla of eager beavers racing for the lock.

Having mentioned the advancing years of our crew, but more particularly the Captain, our next day's trip took us to Fecamp, which we reached in fine weather soon after lunch time. Fecamp is friendly and welcoming, but the town lacks the charm of Honfleur or Dieppe. To me, it brings back childhood memories of Radio Normandy, a commercial radio station transmitting from a cliff top station to bring advertising to the UK - "We are the Ovalteenies" or "Horlicks to prevent night starvation", all set to advertising jingles. During the 2nd World War the same high falaises of the Normandy coast carried German radar stations and other high tech equipment - they were behind us in the development of radar, but by the middle of the war they were well equipped. There were some daring commando raids carried out to sabotage the stations and bring back vital pieces of equipment for examination.

Another gentle leg was made the next day, leaving at ten in the morning - this was bordering on geriatric cruising, and we had an easy trip to Dieppe, where we secured just after lunch. Preparations were made for a somewhat more energetic leg the next day, after an afternoon in Dieppe where we stocked up with our last purchases of French provisions, and set our clocks back to BST in the evening. A five o'clock departure saw us heading Northwardsto the point where the high falaises give way to low lying coast, until the headland of Cap d'Alprech, just South of Boulogne looms ahead. Off Cap Gris Nez, North of a buoy numbered ZC2, a dramatic alteration of course was made to cross the shipping lanes at right angles and the tip of the mid-channel Varne bank close to the Varne lightvessel; although you might not take a large ship across it, there were over 15 metres of water at the point where we crossed. Dover had now become the staging post going either way across the Thames estuary; the whole atmosphere had changed from all those years ago, and we again were escorted in by a harbour launch before going into a pontoon in the once infamous Wellington dock. Although we had previously been using the new Sovereign marina at Pevensey, Dover reduced the total distance considerably and gave us a much shorter leg to Harwich Harbour.

So far, our voyage homeward bound had, apart from fog on the Seine, been very easy, but at sea you must always be prepared for change. An early departure was necessary as the lock gate access to Wellington Dock is limited to a brief period around high water, and as we cleared the Western entrance just before half past five on a bright chilly morning, we turned into a fresh Northeast wind - a dead noser, and just as with our outward trip when it had been in our favour. Fortunately, it eased   as we headed North - another example of the funnelling effect in the Dover Straits. By early afternoon we were heading into Harwich Harbour with a gentle East wind and bright sunshine; as we entered the first reach of the River Orwell, the curved wooded bank between Trimley and Levington came into view, and as we secured to our berth in Levington sheltered by the high wooded bank, I suddenly thought "This is really as good as anywhere else we have seen - it takes some beating."

FAMILY RALLIES AFLOAT

IT is no great surprise that our children, by now in their forties and with three children each, had acquired boats of their own. Roland, after a period with a shoal draft boat called a "NEWBRIDGE NAVIGATOR" now had an even more shoal draft vessel of American origins well suited to exploring the plentiful rivers and creeks of the North Essex and Suffolk coasts, but not man enough to cope with conditions further off shore - he had the rudder break on him in a fresh breeze, which taxed his ingenuity and seamanship in bringing the boat home and at the same time told him he should look for a more robust vessel. Fortunately, he was sailing with male friends and not his wife Louise, who would not have been impressed with this episode.

Vicky and Rhodri had bought "ANDANTE", a Halmatic 30 (i.e. 30' long) with a distictive dark green hull, and this was the first time we organised a family rally, at the Tidemill, Woodbridge, with all three boats present and grandchildren rowing to and fro boat visiting - it was to become a regular event in the family calendar. "CORYDALIS" was still wintering on the Deben, berthing in the sheltered Tidemill Yacht Harbour, so after our autumn visit to Limehouse we would have one or two very pleasant weekends afloat during the depths of winter, with the quarters below warm and snug, and often frost on deck in the mornings and perhaps a dusting of snow on the fields; one of these winter trips was usually shortly before our annual visit to Zimbabwe, and it seemed incongruous to be taking malaria pills, which had to be started some days before travelling. The river was empty and there was always room to anchor at places like Waldringfield; the rest of the family boats would return to Walton for laying up, and the good feature of this was that it maintained the family connection with Halls boatyard.

Leaving Woodbridge to be hauled out at Levington proved to be the last time we would winter in this pleasant spot, although as it was just round the corner from Harwich it would certainly not be our last visit. Since there was no longer a suitable slip at Woodbridge on which to haul out this twenty ton lump of steel boat, the whole operation was so easy with the big hoist at Suffolk Yacht Harbour and it seemed better to winter there; at the same time I was offered a very convenient berth on a permanent basis. There were no tidal restrictions to limit the use of the boat during the short winter hours of daylight, and whereas I would not care to navigate the Deben at night because the river was littered with vacant mooring buoys, there were no problems in the Stour or Orwell which were used by commercial shipping whose needs demanded a well lit clear channel.

That summer, we paid the last visit to the French coast ports and much loved Honfleur, described at the beginning of this saga and from then on horizons shrank closer to home. Our autumn visit to Limehouse was enlivened by a visit to the "Anchor" at Rowhedge, close to Ian Brown's yard where "CELANDINE" had been built and "CORYDALIS" fitted out; there was almost no trace of the yard whose buildings had been demolished, but we were able to have lunch with Ian and Pat Brown who no longer lived in Rowhedge but had decamped to nearby Peldon - and not long after, in a move that surprised us all, this man of the East Coast moved to Lymington (to be near family). A visit to the "Anchor's" quay can only be of short duration, so we returned to Brightlingsea for the night, where a little excitement was provided by the arrival of a fishing boat in sinking condition, towed by a tender from the Trinity House "PATRICIA" accompanied by the Clacton inshore lifeboat. These things are interesting to observe, provided you are not the casualty.

On our return from Limehouse, we spent a night at anchor in what I regard as my native waters, in the Hadleigh Ray, where we anchored as dusk was falling over the Leigh shore. The next day, although we could have gone straight in to Levington (whereas on the Deben there was the double problem of crossing the bar at the entrance and the sill at the entrance to the yacht harbour), we chose to visit the Stour and berth alongside Mistley Quay before returning to Levington. Mistley is a favourite port of call which can only be reached on the tide; in places it is a bit shabby, but full of character and history. There is still some commercial shipping to Mistley Quay, but we lie alongside the public quay further upstream, where there is seldom another boat.

THE TWILIGHT YEARS -
AND A BRIGHT GOLDEN RALLY

HAVING chosen to retire to a more gentle form of cruising, we potter about on the coast of my younger days, and take "CORYDALIS" in to the Norfolk Broads for our main cruise, entering through Lowestoft - very different from the place I knew as the wartime base depot for the Patrol Service. In recent years the fishing fleet has declined, although there is still a thriving fish market, and there is some commercial shipping using the port, including oil rig support vessels. Valiant attempts have been made to enhance the environment; the yacht basin which has recently undergone a major refurbishment is not at exactly the best end of town, but is compensated for by the Royal Norfolk and Suffolk Yacht Club, which is extremely hospitable. By going into the Broads during June, we miss the crowds - unfortunately for the hire boat operators, this business is declining anyway, I suppose giving way to the more exotic destinations now affordable to everyone.

The golden family rally was held in Limehouse, when all three boats converged on the basin in preparation for our golden wedding celebration on October 22nd 1999. Rhodri and Vicky now had "JOCARA", a 38 foot dark blue hulled Bermudian cutter by Victoria yachts, and Roland had acquired "LADY OF HAMFORD", a classic wooden yacht designed by Alan Buchanan and built at Great Wakering by E W Sutton in 1962. This boat had long been based in the Walton Backwaters, and I think locals were pleased to know that she would continue there - although her draft of over 6 feet is not the handiest depth to contend with in those waters.

On the morning of the anniversary, Roland and Ann, his oldest daughter, went up early and dressed all three boats overall before continuing upriver (by Dockland Railway and District Line!) to Westminster. Here we had a large gathering of family and friends for a lunch in the Cholmondeley Room, a room at terrace level in the house of Lords used for functions sponsored by members - being October and the weather still benign we were able to use the marquee on the terrace, and have drinks outside overlooking the Thames. To have such a place for a family occasion is a great privilege, but perhaps more than most people, I see how hard people work to earn that privilege. Certainly Beryl had; she has this passionate sense of duty, and works hard and often long hours doing what she believes to be right. She is on scientific committees that have dealt with a wide range of

Beryl at the helm, with cousin Barbara Brown, the only descendant of the seafaring Magub family still living in Southwold

subjects including marine safety, anti-microbial resistance, aircraft cabin environment. Politics are not strong in these affairs where people are dealing with facts and expert evidence; she, as an aeronautical engineer with a sharp and well disciplined mind is a rare bird indeed.

The family spent the weekend at Limehouse, finishing by attending the morning communion service at that magnificent Hawksmoor church, St Annes which is close to the basin and the CA Headquarters. It was built with money provided under Queen Anne, who felt that the spiritual needs of the suburbs growing to the East of London should be cared for. A large family lunch followed in the Cruising Association - somewhat less formal than that in the House of Lords, but very enjoyable nevertheless. It all seemed a bit of an anti-climax when we locked out on Monday at lunch time - Vicky first, then we came a little later, but Roland had some engine trouble and was delayed a day while a local engineer sorted this out. The wind was light and from the South, whereas on our trip upriver we encountered fresh West and Southwest winds - another example of Platt's theory about winds. Vicky was soon sailing downriver, but that meant slow progress so that by the time they joined us on the visitor's buoy at Queenborough it was dark. The next day, after some mutual photography off the Isle of Grain coast, we left Vicky sailing while we motored with our mainsail set to catch the gentle Southerly wind; both boats met up again at Brightlingsea for the night. The following day, after a lazy departure, "CORYDALIS" was heading up the Wallet and by mid afternoon was berthing at Levington, while the other two family boats returned to Walton for their winter sojourn.

Author at the helm. Beryl relaxing in background.
(Photo by John Aldridge)

REFLECTIONS

THE thread running through these memoirs is, of course ships, boats, and the sea which have played such an important part in my life; with a maritime involvement on both sides of the family, there is a considerable hereditary influence - people who dismiss heredity as an influence must imagine that homo sapiens is the only species to which it does not apply. Environment also has a complementary effect, so that growing up close to the sea became the other encouraging influence which caused the instincts to flourish. I have been lucky in that it became possible to continue the maritime pursuits in conjunction with a job, marriage and raising a family, and in this I must pay tribute to Beryl's great support, particularly in the early years when the family were young.

When I first received serious training in sailing and boat management with the 3rd Chalkwell Bay Sea Scouts, it was in a world where boats were all individual characters, except for the one-design racing classes which were the nearest thing to production boats that existed in those days. Those of limited means (and that was most people in the 1930s) could only hope to get afloat in some second hand retired working boat or convert an open boat like a ship's lifeboat by putting a lid on it - never a very satisfactory solution, but it got them afloat. Gradually it began to occur to some enlightened builders that costs could be saved if instead of building to an individual client's designs, a series could be built using the same architect's plans, and the patterns and moulds necessary for each design. Those who were better off could stretch to boats produced by David Hilliard, Blackwater sloops by Dan Webb & Feasey of Maldon, and gradually the idea spread so that many small cruising yachts built to a standard design began to appear. One of the cheapest examples was the 18 foot long deep keel sloop produced by Johnson and Jago in my native Leigh-on-Sea for £100 - auxiliary engine extra. Even this price limited the number of buyers, and the other limiting factor on the numbers of boats to be found in moorings and anchorages was the time it took to build them, even when the preliminary work had been streamlined.

The boat that my father had before the war was built by Parsons of Leigh who built cheap and cheerful, producing boats that would all come out rather the same; many of the fishing boats he produced were too beamy to go through the doorway of his building shed, so the doorframe was removed, bricks knocked out and replaced after launching - it was a rented shed, so it would have to be restored each time to keep the landlord happy. The building is still to be seen in the High Street, now an art and craft gallery - although the facade has been smartly decorated and painted white, careful examination still reveals where those bricks were knocked out. Our boat, "EUONYM" was really like an overgrown sailing dinghy or centre-board one design, and very reminiscent of some of the designs now being marketed in fibreglass - except that the centreboard is now attached permanently and called a keel; with "EUONYM" the centre board was retracted when not in use. Such boats will sail fast and go to windward well in reasonably sheltered waters, but their keels are a weak point and the saucer shaped hulls will give you a very bumpy ride going to windward in a seaway, particularly in the short steep seas of places like the Thames Estuary. It is, of course, much cheaper to produce than a boat with a shaped underwater body that has the keel as a structural feature. If winning pots is what you want, then go for the long thin fin keel configuration, but don't run aground or dry out; if comfortable cruising is what you want then try and get something with a proper keel that would not mind occasional contact with the bottom, and could go to windward without bouncing from wavecrest to wavecrest.

To our generation, the War was a major watershed in our lives; many things would never be the same again. It was the main reason why Beryl became an aeronautical engineer rather than a mathematician; both of us were still in our late teens at the beginning and adults by the end. Every resource the country had was gradually developed into part of the war effort; boatbuilders round the coast, including Johnson and Jago had extensions built on their main building sheds to enable them to build the wooden "B" MLs (112 feet long) or the smaller HD Mls (72 feet long) or the heavier construction MFVs for general supply and other ancilliary uses. Because every sinew was strained in contributing to the fighting of the War, at the end of the War, there were many vessels of all sizes available for conversion into private yachts, but construction of new sailing yachts only resumed slowly, mainly using pre-war designs and moulds.

On the home front we lived in houses with no central heating, as children, and it was not until 1971 that we had full central heating installed in Greenbury House. Writtle had good village shops close at hand which could supply all our daily needs, and the post office was a short walk from our house, but if you needed a bank it meant either going in to Chelmsford, or in my case I used one at Romford as the nearest to my place of work. Now, as I write these shops - Fairhead's the grocer, Guy's, the general stores, Bill Clarke the greengrocer and Hance, the baker, have all gone. They have been replaced by two convenience stores which ensure that it is possible to live without a car, but to get a good variety it is now necessary to jump in a car to undertake a major shoppping excursion. On the other hand, there are two bank branches, an off-licence, an estate agent, any number of ladies' hairdressers, and an Indian Restaurant (in the former baker's premises). The most remarkable shop was Rumsey's, the seedsman. Here you could buy feed for domestic animals, seeds of all sorts, free range eggs - but because most of the stock was in a long line of sheds, David, the amiable and chatty assistant would be forever at the back while long queues developed which were a source of all the village news and gossip. It could not survive, and is now a chemist's shop.

Afloat, I have seen moorings and marinas develop to accommodate the increasing numbers of boats; although I did not start to make use of marinas until later life when I no longer relished the thought of a long dinghy trip out to my mooring, it has made me realise that if you do not provide marina berths there would be nowhere to put all the boats. A swinging mooring uses a lot of space, and there is now little room for any more in most of the sheltered rivers and creeks; many of the places in which I used to anchor are now choked with moorings. The boats have changed, even since the first production fibreglass boats appeared on the scene in the sixties, and many now resemble floating caravans; because the hulls are shallow, the only way to get headroom is to go upwards. Unfortunately, the higher you go above the waterline, the more violent the motion, so decks are less safe and it is a long way back out of the water should you go over the side.

Modern construction methods have brought the cost of boats down in real terms making sailing affordable to a great many more people, whereas circumstances in my younger days ensured that few people were able to participate, even if they had thought about it at all. Large glamorous boat shows, a proliferation of yachting magazines have all helped, and the whole thing snowballs. Principally, however it is the availability of an enormous variety of boats available at prices compatible with average current income standards.

It is no good longing for the good old days, when you knew a boat almost as soon as she appeared over the horizon and would find room to swing to a single anchor in your favourite spot; there were many disadvantages too in that there was a lack of convenient facilities - there were not enough of us doing it to justify the expense of providing them. The whole thing has become more commercial, but with it comes the benefit of facilities, making it easier for a busy person to get afloat.

For the future, my biggest worry is that Governments will start looking at ways of cashing in on it, introducing qualification requirements in the mistaken idea that handing out certificates will make the sea a safer place (and at the same time use it as a means of levying a tax). Voluntary training and awards of certificates are to be encouraged, and there are many facilities for this, which my family and grandchildren have taken advantage of - there were certainly not many opportunities available in my young days. Making it compulsory changes the whole aspect and in countries where this already is a requirement they have more than their fair share of fully certificated idiots afloat; nor is it a guarantee that they will not get into serious trouble. The very occasional rogue cases of people venturing afloat armed with a road map or school atlas, who inevitably feature in the papers when they get into difficulties, are no argument for withdrawing the present freedom for amateur sailors and youngsters to get afloat without the dead hand of bureaucracy inhibiting them. The sea is a great training ground for life, and its sheer size and changing moods make us realise how small we are by comparison.

Evening sunlight at Suffolk Yacht Harbour, Levington.

Index